Unit Roots and Structural Breaks

Special Issue Editor

Pierre Perron

MDPI • Basel • Beijing • Wuhan • Barcelona • Belgrade

Special Issue Editor
Pierre Perron
Boston University
USA

Editorial Office
MDPI
St. Alban-Anlage 66
Basel, Switzerland

This edition is a reprint of the Special Issue published online in the open access journal *Econometrics* (ISSN 2225-1146) from 2016–2017 (available at: http://www.mdpi.com/journal/econometrics/special_issues/unit_roots_structural_breaks).

For citation purposes, cite each article independently as indicated on the article page online and as indicated below:

Lastname, F.M.; Lastname, F.M. Article title. *Journal Name* **Year**, *Article number*, page range.

First Edition 2018

ISBN 978-3-03842-811-4 (Pbk)
ISBN 978-3-03842-812-1 (PDF)

Table of Contents

About the Special Issue Editor

Pierre Perron has been a Professor of Economics at Boston University since 1997. He received his B.A. from McGill University, M.A. from Queens University, and Ph.D. from Yale University (all in Economics). He held other teaching positions at the Université de Montréal and Princeton University and visiting positions in a number of countries, including Brazil, France, and Switzerland. Professor Perron was a co-editor for the Econometrics Journal and served on the editorial board of numerous journals. He is an elected fellow of the Econometric Society and a fellow of the Journal of Econometrics. He has published more than 100 papers in economics, econometrics, statistics, and climate science journals, and contributed several influential book chapters. He also acted as the main Ph.D. supervisor for over 25 students and numerous others as secondary or external advisors. His work is highly cited in economics as well as in a variety of other fields.

econometrics

MDPI

Editorial

Unit Roots and Structural Breaks

Pierre Perron

Department of Economics, Boston University, 270 Bay State Rd., Boston, MA 02215, USA; perron@bu.edu

Academic Editor: Marc S. Paolella
Received: 26 May 2017; Accepted: 27 May 2017; Published: 30 May 2017

This special issue deals with problems related to unit roots and structural change, and the interplay between the two. The research agenda dealing with these topics have proven to be of importance for devising procedures that are reliable for inference and forecasting. Several important contributions have been made. Still, there is scope for improvements and analyses of the properties of existing procedures. This special issue provides contributions that follow up on what has been done and/or offer new perspectives on such issues and related ones. Both theoretical and applied papers are included. I briefly outline the papers, grouping them by themes.

Structural Change—Theory. Cheol-Keun Cho and Timothy J. Vogelsang consider testing for structural change when serial correlation may be present in the errors of the regression, in which case a common practice is to use a heteroscedasticity and autocorrelation robust Wald test. Following important work by Vogelsang and co-authors (e.g., Kiefer and Vogelsang (2015)), a fixed-bandwidth theory is developed to provide better approximations for the test statistics. It is shown to improve upon the standard asymptotic distribution theory, whereby the bandwidth is negligible compared to the sample size; e.g., Andrews (1993), Bai and Perron (1998, 2003). **Jingjing Yang** considers the consistency of trend break point estimators when the number of breaks is underspecified. As shown in Bai (1997) and Bai and Perron (1998), with stationary variables, if a one-break model is estimated when multiple breaks exist, then the estimate of the break fraction converges to one of the true break fractions (the one that minimizes the overall sum of squared residuals). Interestingly, she shows this to not be the case when considering breaks in a linear trend function. This result suggests that the application of the Kejriwal and Perron (2010) extension of the Perron and Yabu (2009) test should be applied with caution. **Aparna Sengupta** considers the problem of testing for a structural break in the spatial lag parameter in a panel model (spatial autoregressive). She proposes a likelihood ratio test and derives its limit distribution when both the number of individual units N and the number of time periods T is large or N is fixed and T is large. A break date estimator is also proposed.

Unit Root and Trend Break—Theory. Ricardo Quineche and Gabriel Rodríguez provide interesting further finite sample simulation results about the tests proposed by Perron and Rodriguez (2003), who extended the work of Perron (1989, 1997), Zivot and Andrews (1992), and Vogelsang and Perron (1998), among others. They show that the M^{GLS} versions suggested by Ng and Perron (2001) suffer from severe size distortions when using the so-called "infimum method" to select the break date (i.e., minimizing the t-statistic of the sum of the autoregressive coefficients) and common methods to select the autoregressive lag order. This occurs whether a break is present or not. On the other hand, when using the "supremum method" (i.e., minimizing the sum of squared residuals from the trend-break regression), this problem only holds when no break is present. These results point to the usefulness of the methods advocated by Kim and Perron (2009) and Carrión-i-Silvestre et al. (2009).

Fractional integration—Theory. Seong Yeon Chang and Pierre Perron consider testing procedures for the null hypothesis of a unit root process against the alternative of a fractional process, called a fractional unit root test. They extend the Lagrange Multiplier (LM) tests of Robinson (1994) and Tanaka (1999) to allow for a slope change in trend with or without a concurrent level shift under both the null and alternative hypotheses. Building on the work of Chang and Perron

(2016) and Perron and Zhu (2005), they show that the limit distribution of the proposed LM tests is standard normal when using the Kim and Perron (2009) method to estimate the break date. However, unlike in that paper, there is no need to perform a pre-test for a change in slope. **Man Wang and Ngai Hang Chan** consider testing for the equality of integration orders amongst a set of variables. This is useful as a prior step to test for fractional cointegration. They extend the work of Hualde (2013) and propose a one-step residual-based test that overcomes computational issues. The test statistic has an asymptotic standard normal distribution under the null hypothesis.

Structural Change—Empirical Studies. María Dolores Gadea, Ana Gómez-Loscos and Antonio Montañés investigate changes in the relationship between oil prices and the US economy from a long-term perspective. First, they show that neither series have structural breaks in mean, though they have different volatility periods. Using a VAR method, a rolling estimation of causality and long-term impacts, and the Qu and Perron (2007) methodology, they find no significant effect between changes in oil prices and GDP growth when considering the full period. However, a significant relationship is present in some subperiods. Using a time-varying VAR model, they show the that the impact of oil price shocks on GDP growth has declined over time and that the negative effect on GDP growth is greater when large oil price increases occur. **Jesús Clemente, María Dolores Gadea, Antonio Montañés, and Marcelo Reyes** reconsider the common unit root/co-integration approach to test for the Fisher effect for the G7 countries. Using Pesaran's (2007) panel unit root test, they argue that nominal interest and inflation rates are better represented as stationary variables. Then, using the Bai–Perron procedure (1998, 2003), they show the existence of structural changes in the Fisher equation. Once the breaks are accounted for, they find very limited evidence for the Fisher effect.

I think these papers offer an interesting and useful array of contributions under the broad topic of unit roots and structural breaks. Thanks are due to the Editor Marc Paolella, the assitant editors Michele Cardani and Lu Liao, as well as the numerous referees who provided useful comments and advice.

Conflicts of Interest: The author declares no conflict of interest.

References

Andrews, Donald W.K. 1993. Tests for Parameter Instability and Structural Change with Unknown Change Point. *Econometrica* 61: 821–56.

Bai, Jushan. 1997. Estimating Multiple Breaks One at a Time. *Econometric Theory 13*: 315–52.

Bai, Jushan, and Pierre Perron. 1998. Estimating and Testing Linear Models with Multiple Structural Changes. *Econometrica* 66: 47–78.

Bai, Jushan, and Pierre Perron. 2003. Computation and Analysis of Multiple Structural Change Models. *Journal of Applied Econometrics* 18: 1–22.

Carrion-i-Silvestre, Josep Lluís, Dukpa Kim, and Pierre Perron. 2009. GLS-Based Unit Root Tests with Multiple Structural Breaks under Both the Null and the Alternative Hypotheses. *Econometric Theory* 25: 1754–92.

Chang, Seong Yeon, and Pierre Perron. 2016. Inference on a Structural Break in Trend with Fractionally Integrated Errors. *Journal of Time Series Analysis* 37: 555–74.

Hualde, Javier. 2013. A Simple Test for the Equality of Integration Orders. *Economics Letters* 119: 233–7.

Kejriwal, Mohitosh, and Pierre Perron. 2010. A sequential procedure to determine the number of breaks in trend with an integrated or stationary noise component. *Journal of Time Series Analysis* 31: 305–28.

Kiefer, Nicholas M., and Timothy J. Vogelsang. 2005. A new asymptotic theory for heteroskedasticity-autocorrelation robust tests. *Econometric Theory* 21: 1130–64.

Kim, Dukpa, and Pierre Perron. 2009. Unit root tests allowing for a break in the trend function at an unknown time under both the null and alternative hypotheses. *Journal of Econometrics* 148: 1–13.

Ng, Serena, and Pierre Perron. 2001. Lag length selection and the construction of unit root tests with good size and power. *Econometrica* 69: 1519–54.

Perron, Pierre. 1989. The great crash, the oil price shock and the unit root hypothesis. *Econometrica* 57: 1361–401.

Perron, Pierre. 1997. Further evidence from breaking trend functions in macroeconomic variables. *Journal of Econometrics* 80: 355–85.

Perron, Pierre, and Gabriel Rodriguez. 2003. GLS detrending, efficient unit root tests and structural change. *Journal of Econometrics* 115: 1–27.

Perron, Pierre, and Tomoyoshi Yabu. 2009. Testing for shifts in trend with an integrated or stationary noise component. *Journal of Business & Economic Statistics* 27: 369–96.

Perron, Pierre, and Xiaokang Zhu. 2005. Structural breaks with deterministic and stochastic trends. *Journal of Econometrics* 129: 65–119.

Pesaran, M. Hashem. 2007. A simple panel unit root test in the presence of cross-section dependence. *Journal of Applied Econometrics* 22: 265–312.

Qu, Zhongjun, and Pierre Perron. 2007. Estimating and testing structural changes in multivariate regressions. *Econometrica* 75: 459–502.

Robinson, Peter M. 1994. Efficient tests of nonstationary hypothesis. *Journal of the American Statistical Association* 89: 1420–37.

Tanaka, Katsuto. 1999. The nonstationary fractional unit root. *Econometric Theory* 15: 549–82.

Vogelsang, Timothy J., and Pierre Perron. 1998. Additional tests for a unit root allowing the possibility of breaks in the trend function. *International Economic Review* 39: 1073–100.

Zivot, Eric, and Donald W. K. Andrews. 1992. Further evidence on the great crash, the oil price shock and the unit root hypothesis. *Journal of Business and Economic Statistics* 10: 251–70.

econometrics

Article

Fixed-b Inference for Testing Structural Change in a Time Series Regression

Cheol-Keun Cho [1,*] and Timothy J. Vogelsang [2]

1 Korea Energy Economics Institute, Ulsan 44543, Korea
2 Michigan State University, East Lansing, MI 48824, USA; tjv@msu.edu
* Correspondence: chkcho@gmail.com; Tel.: +82-52-714-2070

Academic Editor: Pierre Perron
Received: 19 August 2016; Accepted: 14 December 2016; Published: 30 December 2016

Abstract: This paper addresses tests for structural change in a weakly dependent time series regression. The cases of full structural change and partial structural change are considered. Heteroskedasticity-autocorrelation (HAC) robust Wald tests based on nonparametric covariance matrix estimators are explored. Fixed-b theory is developed for the HAC estimators which allows fixed-b approximations for the test statistics. For the case of the break date being known, the fixed-b limits of the statistics depend on the break fraction and the bandwidth tuning parameter as well as on the kernel. When the break date is unknown, supremum, mean and exponential Wald statistics are commonly used for testing the presence of the structural break. Fixed-b limits of these statistics are obtained and critical values are tabulated. A simulation study compares the finite sample properties of existing tests and proposed tests.

Keywords: HAC estimator; kernel; bandwidth; partial structural change; break point

JEL Classification: C10; C22

1. Introduction

This paper focuses on fixed-b inference of heteroskedasticity and autocorrelation (HAC) robust Wald statistics for testing for a structural break in a time series regression. We focus on kernel-based nonparametric HAC estimators which are commonly used to estimate the asymptotic variance. HAC estimators allow for arbitrary structure of the serial correlation and heteroskedasticity of weakly dependent time series and are consistent estimators of the long run variance under the assumption that the bandwidth (M) is growing at a certain rate slower than the sample size (T). Under consistency assumptions, the Wald statistics converge to the usual chi-square distributions. However, because the critical values from the chi-square distribution are based on a consistency approximation for the HAC estimator, the chi-square limit does not reflect the often substantial finite sample randomness of the HAC estimator. Furthermore, the chi-square approximation does not capture the impact of the choice of the kernel or the bandwidth on the Wald statistics. The sensitivity of the statistics to the finite sample bias and variability of the HAC estimator is well known in the literature; Kiefer and Vogelsang (2005) [1] among others have illustrated by simulation that the traditional inference with a HAC estimator can have poor finite sample properties.

Departing from the traditional approach, Kiefer and Vogelsang [1–3] obtain an alternative asymptotic approximation by assuming that the ratio of the bandwidth to the sample size, $b = M/T$, is held constant as the sample size increases. Under this alternative nesting of the bandwidth, they obtain pivotal asymptotic distributions for the test statistics which depend on the choice of kernel and bandwidth tuning parameter. Simulation results indicate that the resulting fixed-b approximation has less size distortions in finite samples than the traditional approach, especially when the bandwidth is not small.

Theoretical explanations for the finite sample properties of the fixed-b approach include the studies by Hashimzade and Vogelsang (2008) [4], Jansson (2004) [5], Sun, Phillips and Jin (2008, hereafter SPJ) [6], Gonçalves and Vogelsang (2011) [7] and Sun (2013) [8]. Hashimzade and Vogelsang (2008) [4] provides an explanation for the better performance of the fixed-b asymptotics by analyzing the bias and variance of the HAC estimator. Gonçalves and Vogelsang (2011) [7] provides a theoretical treatment of the asymptotic equivalence between the naive bootstrap distribution and the fixed-b limit. Higher order theory is used by Jansson (2004) [5], SPJ (2008) [6] and Sun (2013) [8] to show that the error in rejection probability using the fixed-b approximation is more accurate than the traditional approximation. In a Gaussian location model, Jansson (2004) [5] proves that for the Bartlett kernel with bandwidth equal to sample size (i.e., $b = 1$), the error in rejection probability of fixed-b inference is $O(T^{-1}\log T)$ which is smaller than the usual rate of $O(T^{-1/2})$. The results in SPJ (2008) [6] complement Jansson's result by extending the analysis for a larger class of kernels and focusing on smaller values of bandwidth ratio b. In particular, they find that the error in rejection probability of the fixed-b approximation is $O(T^{-1})$ around $b = 0$. They also show that for positively autocorrelated series, which is typical for economic time series, the fixed-b approximation has smaller error than the chi-square or standard normal approximation, even when b is assumed to decrease to zero although the stochastic orders are same.

In this paper, fixed-b asymptotics is applied to testing for structural change in a weakly dependent time series regression. The structural change literature is now enormous and no attempt will be made here to summarize the relevant literature. Some key references include Andrews (1993) [9], Andrews and Ploberger (1994) [10], and Bai and Perron (1998) [11]. Andrews (1993) [9] treats the issue of testing for a structural break in the generalized method of moments framework when the one-time break date is unknown and Andrews and Ploberger (1994) [10] derive asymptotically optimal tests. Bai and Perron (1998) [11] considers multiple structural change occurring at unknown dates and covers the issues of estimation of break dates, testing for the presence of structural change and testing for the number of breaks. For a comprehensive survey of the recent structural break literature see Perron (2006) [12], Banerjee and Urga (2005) [13], and Aue and Horváth (2013) [14]. The fixed-b analysis can be extended to the case of multiple breaks but the simulation of critical values will be computationally intensive. Therefore, we leave the case of multiple breaks for future research and we consider the case of a single break in this paper.

For testing the presence of break, the robust version of the Wald statistic is considered in this paper and a HAC estimator is used to construct the test statistic. The ways of constructing HAC estimators in the context of structural change tests are well described in Bai and Perron (2003) [15] and Bai and Perron (1998) [11]. We focus mainly on the HAC estimator documented in Bai and Perron (2003) (Section 4.1, [15]) in which the usual "Newey-West-Andrews" approach is applied directly to the regression with regime dummies. Under the assumption of a fixed bandwidth ratio (fixed-b assumption), the asymptotic limit of the test statistic is a nonstandard distribution but it is pivotal. As in standard fixed-b theory, the impact of choice of bandwidth on the limiting distribution is substantial. In particular, the bandwidth interplays with the hypothesized break fraction so that the limit of the test statistic depends on both of them. For the unknown break date case, three existing test statistics (Sup-, Mean-, Exp-Wald) are considered and their fixed-b critical values are tabulated. The finite sample performance is examined by simulation experiments with comparisons made to existing tests. For practitioners, we include results using a data-dependent bandwidth rule based on Andrews (1991) [16]. This data-dependent bandwidth is calculated from the regression using the break fraction that yields the minimum sum of squared residuals (Bai and Perron, 1998 [11]). One can calculate a bandwidth ratio $\left(b^* = \frac{M^*}{T}\right)$ with this data-dependent bandwidth (M^*) and proceed to apply the fixed-b critical values corresponding to this specific value of b^*.

The remainder of this paper is organized as follows. In Section 2, the basic setup of the full/partial structural-change model is presented and preliminary results are provided. Section 3 derives the fixed-b limit of the Wald statistic and the fixed-b critical values, for the case of unknown break dates, are tabulated in Section 4. Section 5 compares empirical null rejection probabilities and provides the size-adjusted power for tests based on the b^* data-dependent bandwidth ratio. Section 6 concludes. Proofs and definitions are collected in Appendix A.

2. Setup and Preliminary Results

Consider a weakly dependent time series regression model with a structural break given by

$$\begin{aligned} y_t &= w_t'\beta + u_t, \\ w_t' &= \left(x_{1t}', x_{2t}'\right), \ \beta' = \left(\beta_1', \beta_2'\right), \\ x_{1t} &= x_t \cdot \mathbf{1}(t \leq [\lambda T]), \ x_{2t} = x_t \cdot \mathbf{1}(t \geq [\lambda T]+1), \end{aligned} \tag{1}$$

where x_t is $p \times 1$ regressor vector, $\lambda \in (0,1)$ is a break point, and $\mathbf{1}(\,\cdot\,)$ is the indicator function. Define $\nu_t = x_t u_t$ and $v_t = w_t u_t$. Recalling that $[x]$ denotes the integer part of a real number, x, notice that $x_{2t} = \mathbf{0}$ for $t = 1, 2, ..., [\lambda T]$ and $x_{1t} = \mathbf{0}$ for $t = [\lambda T]+1, ..., T$. For the time being, the potential break point (fraction) λ is assumed to be known in order to develop the asymptotic theory for a test statistic and characterize its asymptotic limit. We will relax this assumption to deal with the empirically relevant case of an unknown break date. The regression model (1) implies that coefficients of all explanatory variables are subject to potential structural change and this model is labeled the 'full' structural change model.

We are interested in testing the presence of a structural change in the regression parameters. Consider the null hypothesis of the form

$$H_0 : \mathbf{R}\beta = \mathbf{0}, \tag{2}$$

where

$$\underset{(l\times 2p)}{\mathbf{R}} = \left(\mathbf{R}_1, \ -\mathbf{R}_1\right),$$

and $\mathbf{R}_1$ is an $l \times p$ matrix with $l \leq p$. Under the null hypothesis, we are testing that one or more linear relationships on the regression parameter(s) do not experience structural change before and after the break point. Tests of the null hypothesis of no structural change about a subset of the slope parameters are special cases. For example, we can test the null hypothesis that the slope parameter on the first regressor did not change by setting $\mathbf{R}_1 = (1, 0, \ldots, 0)$. We can test the null hypothesis that none of the regression parameters have structural change by setting $\mathbf{R}_1 = I_p$. We focus on the OLS estimator of β given by $\widehat{\beta} = \left(\widehat{\beta}_1', \widehat{\beta}_2'\right)' = \left(\sum_{t=1}^T w_t w_t'\right)^{-1}\left(\sum_{t=1}^T w_t y_t\right)$.

In order to establish the asymptotic limits of the HAC estimators and the Wald statistics, two assumptions are sufficient. These assumptions imply that there is no heterogeneity in the regressors across the segments and the covariance structure of the errors is assumed to be the same across segments as well.

Assumption 1. *$T^{-1}\sum_{t=1}^{[rT]} x_t x_t' \xrightarrow{p} rQ$, uniformly in $r \in [0,1]$, and Q^{-1} exists.*

Assumption 2. *$T^{-1/2}\sum_{t=1}^{[rT]} x_t u_t = T^{-1/2}\sum_{t=1}^{[rT]} \nu_t \Rightarrow \Lambda W_p(r), r \in [0,1]$, where $\Lambda\Lambda' = \Sigma$, $W_p(r)$ is a $p \times 1$ standard Wiener process, and $\Rightarrow$ denotes weak convergence.*

For later use, we define a $l \times l$ nonsingular matrix A such that $\mathbf{R}_1 Q^{-1}\Lambda\Lambda' Q^{-1}\mathbf{R}_1' = AA'$ and $\mathbf{R}_1 Q^{-1}\Lambda W_p(r) \overset{d}{=} AW_l(r)$, where $W_l(r)$ is $l \times 1$ standard Wiener process. For a more detailed discussion about the regularity conditions under which Assumptions 1 and 2 hold, refer to Kiefer and Vogelsang (2002) [3] and see Davidson (1994) [17], Phillips and Durlauf (1986) [18], Phillips and Solo (1992) [19], and Wooldridge and White (1988) [20] for more details.

The matrix Q is the second moment matrix of x_t and is typically estimated using the quantity $\widehat{Q} = \frac{1}{T}\sum_{t=1}^{T} x_t x_t'$. The matrix $\Sigma \equiv \Lambda\Lambda'$ is the asymptotic variance of $T^{-1/2}\sum_{t=1}^{T} v_t$, which is, for a covariance stationary series, given by

$$\Sigma = \Gamma_0 + \sum_{j=1}^{\infty}(\Gamma_j + \Gamma_j') \text{ with } \Gamma_j = E(v_t' v_{t-j}).$$

Consider the non-structural change regression equation where $\beta_1 = \beta_2$ and this coefficient parameter is estimated by OLS $(\widehat{\beta})$. In this particular setup, the long run variance, Σ, is commonly estimated by the kernel-based nonparametric HAC estimator given by

$$\widehat{\Sigma} = T^{-1}\sum_{t=1}^{T}\sum_{s=1}^{T} K\left(\frac{|t-s|}{M}\right)\widehat{v}_t\widehat{v}_s' = \widehat{\Gamma}_0 + \sum_{j=1}^{T-1} K\left(\frac{j}{M}\right)\left(\widehat{\Gamma}_j + \widehat{\Gamma}_j'\right),$$

where $\widehat{\Gamma}_j = T^{-1}\sum_{t=j+1}^{T}\widehat{v}_t\widehat{v}_{t-j}'$, $\widehat{v}_t = x_t\widehat{u}_t = x_t\left(y_t - x_t'\widehat{\beta}\right)$, M is a bandwidth, and $K(\cdot)$ is a kernel weighting function.

Under some regularity conditions (see Andrews (1991) [16], DeJong and Davidson (2000) [21], Hansen (1992) [22], Jansson (2002) [23] or Newey and West (1987) [24]), $\widehat{\Sigma}$ is a consistent estimator of Σ, i.e., $\widehat{\Sigma} \overset{p}{\to} \Sigma$. These regularity conditions include the necessary condition that $M/T \to 0$ as $M, T \to \infty$. This asymptotics is called "traditional" asymptotics throughout this paper.

In contrast to the traditional approach, fixed-b asymptotics assumes $M = bT$ where b is held constant as T increases. Assumptions 1 and 2 are the only regularity conditions required to obtain a fixed-b limit for $\widehat{\Sigma}$. Under the fixed-b approach, for $b \in (0,1]$, Kiefer and Vogelsang (2005) [1] show that

$$\widehat{\Sigma} \Rightarrow \Lambda\mathbf{P}(b, \widetilde{W}_p)\Lambda', \tag{3}$$

where $\widetilde{W}_p(r) = W_p(r) - rW_p(1)$ is a p-vector of standard Brownian bridges and the form of the random matrix $\mathbf{P}(b, \widetilde{W}_p)$ depends on the kernel. Following Kiefer and Vogelsang (2005) [1], we consider three classes of kernels which give three forms of $\mathbf{P}$. Let $H_p(r)$ denote a generic vector of stochastic processes. $H_p(r)'$ denotes its transpose. $\mathbf{P}(b, H_p)$ is defined in Appendix A.

Getting back to our structural change regression model, fixed-b results depend on the limiting behavior of the following partial sum process given by

$$\begin{aligned}\widehat{S}_t &= \sum_{j=1}^{t} w_j\widehat{u}_j = \sum_{j=1}^{t} w_j\left(y_j - x_{1j}'\widehat{\beta}_1 - x_{2j}'\widehat{\beta}_2\right) \\ &= \sum_{j=1}^{t} w_j\left(u_j - x_{1j}'\left(\widehat{\beta}_1 - \beta_1\right) - x_{2j}'\left(\widehat{\beta}_2 - \beta_2\right)\right).\end{aligned} \tag{4}$$

Under Assumptions 1 and 2, the limiting behavior of $\widehat{\beta}$ and the partial sum process $\widehat{S}_t$ are given as follows.

Proposition 1. *Let $\lambda \in (0,1)$ be given. Suppose the data generation process is given by (1) and let $[rT]$ denote the integer part of rT where $r \in [0,1]$. Then, under Assumptions 1 and 2 as $T \to \infty$,*

$$\sqrt{T}(\widehat{\beta}-\beta) = \begin{pmatrix} \sqrt{T}\left(\widehat{\beta}_1-\beta_1\right) \\ \sqrt{T}\left(\widehat{\beta}_2-\beta_2\right) \end{pmatrix} \xrightarrow{d} \begin{pmatrix} (\lambda Q)^{-1}\Lambda W_p(\lambda) \\ ((1-\lambda)Q)^{-1}\Lambda\left(W_p(1)-W_p(\lambda)\right) \end{pmatrix},$$

and

$$T^{-1/2}\widehat{S}_{[rT]} \Rightarrow \begin{pmatrix} \Lambda & 0 \\ 0 & \Lambda \end{pmatrix} F_p(r,\lambda) \equiv \begin{pmatrix} \Lambda & 0 \\ 0 & \Lambda \end{pmatrix} \begin{pmatrix} F_p^{(1)}(r,\lambda) \\ F_p^{(2)}(r,\lambda) \end{pmatrix},$$

where

$$F_p^{(1)}(r,\lambda) = \left(W_p(r) - \frac{r}{\lambda}W_p(\lambda)\right)\cdot \mathbf{1}(r \le \lambda),$$

and

$$F_p^{(2)}(r,\lambda) = \left(W_p(r) - W_p(\lambda) - \frac{r-\lambda}{1-\lambda}\left(W_p(1)-W_p(\lambda)\right)\right)\cdot \mathbf{1}(r > \lambda).$$

See Appendix A for the proof.

It is easily seen that the asymptotic distributions of $\widehat{\beta}_1$ and $\widehat{\beta}_2$ are Gaussian and are independent of each other. Hence the asymptotic covariance of $\widehat{\beta}_1$ and $\widehat{\beta}_2$ is zero. The asymptotic variance of $\sqrt{T}(\widehat{\beta}-\beta)$ is given by $\mathbf{Q}_\lambda^{-1}\Omega\mathbf{Q}_\lambda^{-1}$, where

$$\mathbf{Q}_\lambda \equiv \begin{pmatrix} \lambda Q & 0 \\ 0 & (1-\lambda)Q \end{pmatrix} \text{ and } \Omega \equiv \begin{pmatrix} \lambda\Sigma & 0 \\ 0 & (1-\lambda)\Sigma \end{pmatrix}. \tag{5}$$

In order to test the null hypothesis (2), HAC robust Wald statistics are considered. These statistics are robust to heteroskedasticity and autocorrelation in the vector process, $v_t = x_t u_t$. The generic form of the robust Wald statistic is given by

$$Wald = T\left(\mathbf{R}\widehat{\beta}\right)'\left(\mathbf{R}\widehat{\mathbf{Q}}_\lambda^{-1}\widehat{\Omega}\widehat{\mathbf{Q}}_\lambda^{-1}\mathbf{R}'\right)^{-1}\left(\mathbf{R}\widehat{\beta}\right), \tag{6}$$

where

$$\widehat{\mathbf{Q}}_\lambda = \begin{pmatrix} T^{-1}\sum_{t=1}^{[\lambda T]} x_t x_t' & 0 \\ 0 & T^{-1}\sum_{t=[\lambda T]+1}^{T} x_t x_t' \end{pmatrix},$$

and $\widehat{\Omega}$ is a HAC robust estimator of Ω.

We consider a particular way of constructing the HAC estimator. This estimator is the same one as in Bai and Perron (2003) [15]. Denoted by $\widehat{\Omega}^{(F)}$, it is constructed using the residuals directly from the dummy regression (1):

$$\widehat{\Omega}^{(F)} = T^{-1}\sum_{t=1}^{T}\sum_{s=1}^{T} K\left(\frac{|t-s|}{M}\right)\widehat{v}_t\widehat{v}_s', \tag{7}$$

where $\widehat{v}_t = w_t\widehat{u}_t = \left(x_{1t}'\widehat{u}_t,\ x_{2t}'\widehat{u}_t\right)'_{2p\times 1}$. We denote the components of $\widehat{v}_t$ as $\widehat{v}_t^{(1)} = x_{1t}\widehat{u}_t = x_t\widehat{u}_t\mathbf{1}$ $(t \le [\lambda T])$ and $\widehat{v}_t^{(2)} = x_{2t}\widehat{u}_t = x_t\widehat{u}_t\mathbf{1}(t \ge [\lambda T]+1)$. Notice that $\widehat{\Omega}^{(F)}$ is the variance estimator one would be using if the usual "Newey-West-Andrews" approach is applied directly to the dummy regression (1).

Using $\widehat{v}_t' = (\widehat{v}_t^{(1)\prime}, \widehat{v}_t^{(2)\prime})$ we can write $\widehat{\Omega}^{(F)}$ as

$$\widehat{\Omega}^{(F)} = \begin{pmatrix} \widehat{\Omega}_{11}^{(F)} & \widehat{\Omega}_{12}^{(F)} \\ \widehat{\Omega}_{21}^{(F)} & \widehat{\Omega}_{22}^{(F)} \end{pmatrix}$$
$$= \begin{pmatrix} T^{-1}\sum_{t=1}^{T}\sum_{s=1}^{T} K\left(\frac{|t-s|}{M}\right)\widehat{v}_t^{(1)}\widehat{v}_s^{(1)\prime} & T^{-1}\sum_{t=1}^{T}\sum_{s=1}^{T} K\left(\frac{|t-s|}{M}\right)\widehat{v}_t^{(1)}\widehat{v}_s^{(2)\prime} \\ T^{-1}\sum_{t=1}^{T}\sum_{s=1}^{T} K\left(\frac{|t-s|}{M}\right)\widehat{v}_t^{(2)}\widehat{v}_s^{(1)\prime} & T^{-1}\sum_{t=1}^{T}\sum_{s=1}^{T} K\left(\frac{|t-s|}{M}\right)\widehat{v}_t^{(2)}\widehat{v}_s^{(2)\prime} \end{pmatrix}$$
$$= \begin{pmatrix} T^{-1}\sum_{t=1}^{[\lambda T]}\sum_{s=1}^{[\lambda T]} K\left(\frac{|t-s|}{M}\right)\widehat{v}_t^{(1)}\widehat{v}_s^{(1)\prime} & T^{-1}\sum_{t=1}^{[\lambda T]}\sum_{s=[\lambda T]+1}^{T} K\left(\frac{|t-s|}{M}\right)\widehat{v}_t^{(1)}\widehat{v}_s^{(2)\prime} \\ T^{-1}\sum_{t=[\lambda T]+1}^{T}\sum_{s=1}^{[\lambda T]} K\left(\frac{|t-s|}{M}\right)\widehat{v}_t^{(2)}\widehat{v}_s^{(1)\prime} & T^{-1}\sum_{t=[\lambda T]+1}^{T}\sum_{s=[\lambda T]+1}^{T} K\left(\frac{|t-s|}{M}\right)\widehat{v}_t^{(2)}\widehat{v}_s^{(2)\prime} \end{pmatrix} \quad (8)$$
$$= \begin{pmatrix} T^{-1}[\lambda T]\widehat{\Sigma}^{(1)} & T^{-1}\sum_{t=1}^{[\lambda T]}\sum_{s=[\lambda T]+1}^{T} K\left(\frac{|t-s|}{M}\right)\widehat{v}_t^{(1)}\widehat{v}_s^{(2)\prime} \\ T^{-1}\sum_{t=[\lambda T]+1}^{T}\sum_{s=1}^{[\lambda T]} K\left(\frac{|t-s|}{M}\right)\widehat{v}_t^{(2)}\widehat{v}_s^{(1)\prime} & T^{-1}(T-[\lambda T])\widehat{\Sigma}^{(2)} \end{pmatrix}$$

Three important observations are in order. First, the main component of the two diagonal blocks are within regime HAC estimators of Σ , the long run variance of $\{v_t\}$. However, one should see that the "effective" bandwidth ratio being applied to $\widehat{\Sigma}^{(1)}$ is not b $\left(= \frac{M}{T}\right)$ but $\frac{M}{\lambda T} = \frac{bT}{\lambda T} = \frac{b}{\lambda}$, which is bigger than b since $0 < \lambda < 1$. Similarly, the effective bandwidth ratio for $\widehat{\Sigma}^{(2)}$ is $\frac{M}{(1-\lambda)T} = \frac{b}{1-\lambda}$. As documented in fixed-b literature (e.g., Kiefer and Vogelsang (2005) [1]), the bias in HAC estimators not accounted by traditional inference increases as the bandwidth ratio gets bigger. So, when the HAC estimator is constructed as in (8), traditional inference might be often exposed to size distortion—more than expected—due to this mechanism of determining effective bandwidths. The second issue is that the above estimator has non-zero off-diagonal blocks. So, the methodology based on partial samples such as in Andrews (1993) [9] does not exactly cover this case because the off-diagonal blocks in Andrews (1993) [9] are assumed to be zero, matching the zero asymptotic covariance of the OLS estimators of the slope coefficients between pre- and post-regimes. It is presumable that the influence of having non-zero off diagonal terms might be small since the off-diagonal blocks converge to zero under the traditional assumption $\frac{M}{T} \to 0$ as sample size grows (see a proof in Cho (2014) [25] for the Bartlett kernel) but it might still negatively affect the performance of tests in finite samples and we need to develop an alternative asymptotic theory to explicitly reflect the presence of these components. Third, there is another issue when a researcher uses a data-dependent bandwidth as in Andrews (1991) [16]. For a given hypothesized break fraction, a data-dependent bandwidth can be calculated based on the pooled series of $\left\{\widehat{v}_t^{(1)}\right\}_{t=1}^{[\lambda T]}$ and $\left\{\widehat{v}_t^{(2)}\right\}_{t=[\lambda T]+1}^{T}$. This method would result in an optimal bandwidth which minimizes the MSE in estimating Σ but the presence of non-zero off-diagonal terms are not taken into account in this procedure. Moreover, when the break date is treated as unknown, a sequence of data-dependent bandwidth across potential break dates will be generated. In this case, the fixed-b limits are not useful approximations because the sequence of the data-dependent bandwidth is random by nature so the limiting distributions of corresponding test statistics cannot be characterized by a single particular value of b.

Denote by $Wald^{(F)}(T_b)$, the Wald statistic given by (6) using the break date T_b with $\widehat{\Omega}^{(F)}$ used for $\widehat{\Omega}$. Tests for a potential structural break with an unknown break date are well studied in Andrews (1993) [9], Andrews and Ploberger (1994) [10], and Bai and Perron (1998) [11]. Andrews (1993) [9] considers several tests based on the supremum across breakpoints of Wald and Largrange multiplier statistics and shows that they are asymptotically equivalent. Andrews and Ploberger (1994) [10] derives tests that maximize average power across potential breakpoints.

As argued by Andrews (1993) [9] and Andrews and Ploberger (1994) [10], break dates close to the end points of the sample cannot be used and so some trimming is needed. To that end, define $\Xi^* = [\epsilon T, T - \epsilon T]$ with $0 < \epsilon < 1$ to be the set of admissible break dates. The tuning parameter, ϵ, denotes the amount of trimming of potential break dates. We consider the three statistics following Andrews (1993) [9][1] and Andrews and Ploberger (1994) [10][2] defined as

$$SupW^{(F)} \equiv \sup_{T_b \in \Xi^*} Wald^{(F)}(T_b), \tag{9}$$

$$MeanW^{(F)} \equiv \frac{1}{T} \sum_{T_b \in \Xi^*} Wald^{(F)}(T_b), \tag{10}$$

$$ExpW^{(F)} \equiv \log\left(\frac{1}{T} \sum_{T_b \in \Xi^*} \exp\left[\frac{1}{2} Wald^{(F)}(T_b)\right]\right). \tag{11}$$

The next section provides asymptotic results for the robust Wald statistics under the fixed-b asymptotics.

3. Asymptotic Results

3.1. Asymptotic Results under the Fixed-b Approach

We now provide fixed-b limits for the HAC estimators and the test statistics in the full structural change model (1). The fixed-b limits presented in the next Lemma and Corollary approximate the diagonal blocks of $\widehat{\Omega}^{(F)}$ by random matrices. Also, it is shown that the fixed-b approach gives a non-zero limit for the off-diagonal blocks, which further distinguishes fixed-b asymptotics from traditional asymptotics.

Lemma 1. *Let $b \in (0,1]$ be given and suppose $M = bT$. Then under Assumptions 1 and 2, as $T \to \infty$,*

$$\widehat{\Omega}^{(F)} \Rightarrow \begin{pmatrix} \Lambda & \mathbf{0} \\ \mathbf{0} & \Lambda \end{pmatrix} \times \mathbf{P}\left(b, F_p(r,\lambda)\right) \times \begin{pmatrix} \Lambda' & \mathbf{0} \\ \mathbf{0} & \Lambda' \end{pmatrix}, \tag{12}$$

where

$$F_p(r,\lambda) = \begin{pmatrix} F_p^{(1)}(r,\lambda) \\ F_p^{(2)}(r,\lambda) \end{pmatrix}, \tag{13}$$

$$F_p^{(1)}(r,\lambda) = \left(W_p(r) - \frac{r}{\lambda} W_p(\lambda)\right) \mathbf{1}(0 \le r \le \lambda), \tag{14}$$

$$F_p^{(2)}(r,\lambda) = \left(W_p(r) - W_p(\lambda) - \frac{r-\lambda}{1-\lambda}\left(W_p(1) - W_p(\lambda)\right)\right) \mathbf{1}(\lambda < r \le 1), \tag{15}$$

and $\mathbf{P}\left(b, F_p(r,\lambda)\right)$ is defined by (A1)–(A3) with $H_p(r) = F_p(r,\lambda)$.

See Appendix A for the proof.

Next, Corollary presents alternative representations for $\mathbf{P}\left(b, F_p(r,\lambda)\right)$ for three classes of kernels. The definitions of these classes of kernels (Classes 1, 2 and 3) are given in Appendix A. Three popular kernels—the Quadratic Spectral, Bartlett and Parzen kernels—belong to Classes 1, 2 and 3, respectively. See Cho (2014) [25] for the proof of this Corollary.

1 We used the critical values provided in Andrews (2003) [26] for traditional inference.
2 The definitions for the mean and exponential statistics are slightly different in the divisor of the summation. For traditional inference, we adjusted the critical values in Andrews and Ploberger (1994) [10] to our definitions of the statistics.

Corollary 1.

$$\mathbf{P}\left(b, F_p\left(r,\lambda\right)\right) = \begin{pmatrix} \mathbf{P}\left(b, F_p^{(1)}\left(r,\lambda\right)\right) & \mathbf{C}\left(b, F_p^{(1)}\left(r,\lambda\right), F_p^{(2)}\left(r,\lambda\right)\right) \\ \mathbf{C}\left(b, F_p^{(1)}\left(r,\lambda\right), F_p^{(2)}\left(r,\lambda\right)\right)' & \mathbf{P}\left(b, F_p^{(2)}\left(r,\lambda\right)\right) \end{pmatrix}, \tag{16}$$

where

$$\mathbf{C}\left(b, F_p^{(1)}\left(r,\lambda\right), F_p^{(2)}\left(r,\lambda\right)\right)$$

$$= \begin{cases} -\int_0^1 \int_0^1 \frac{1}{b^2} K''\left(\frac{|r-s|}{b}\right) F_p^{(1)}\left(r,\lambda\right) F_p^{(2)}\left(s,\lambda\right)' drds, \\ \frac{1}{b}\int_0^{1-b} F_p^{(1)}\left(r,\lambda\right) F_p^{(2)}\left(r+b,\lambda\right)' dr, \\ -\int\int_{|r-s|<b} \frac{1}{b^2} K''\left(\frac{|r-s|}{b}\right) F_p^{(1)}\left(r,\lambda\right) F_p^{(2)}\left(s,\lambda\right)' drds + \frac{K'_-(1)}{b}\int_0^{1-b} F_p^{(1)}\left(r,\lambda\right) F_p^{(2)}\left(r+b,\lambda\right)' dr, \end{cases}$$

for Classes 1,2 and 3 kernels respectively.

The expression for $\mathbf{P}\left(b, F_p\left(r,\lambda\right)\right)$ in this Corollary makes it easier to compare the fixed-b limit of $\widehat{\Omega}^{(F)}$ with the standard fixed-b limit (see (3)) appearing in a non-structural change setting. Since each diagonal block of $\widehat{\Omega}^{(F)}$ is basically a HAC estimator (up to a scale factor; see (8)) based on one of the pre- or post- break data, its limit should take the same form as (3), which is verified in this Corollary. So, each diagonal component of $\mathbf{P}\left(b, F_p\left(r,\lambda\right)\right)$ serves to reflect the randomness and bandwidth/kernel-dependence of the associated HAC estimator. Second, unlike the traditional approach, the fixed-b limit of the off-diagonal component is non-zero. This implies that the fixed-b approach is able to take account of the covariance between $\widehat{\beta}_1$ and $\widehat{\beta}_2$ which is generally non-zero in finite samples. The limits of the Wald statistics can be derived by using Lemma 1 and the result is presented in the next Theorem.

Theorem 1. *Let $b \in (0,1]$ be given. Suppose $M = bT$. Then under Assumptions 1 and 2, as $T \to \infty$,*

$$Wald^{(F)} \Rightarrow \left(\frac{1}{\lambda}W_l(\lambda) - \frac{1}{1-\lambda}\left(W_l(1) - W_l(\lambda)\right)\right)'$$

$$\times \left(\mathbf{P}\left(b, \frac{1}{\lambda}F_l^{(1)}\left(r,\lambda\right) - \frac{1}{1-\lambda}F_l^{(2)}\left(r,\lambda\right)\right)\right)^{-1} \times \left(\frac{1}{\lambda}W_l(\lambda) - \frac{1}{1-\lambda}\left(W_l(1) - W_l(\lambda)\right)\right) \tag{17}$$

See Appendix A for the proof.

The next Corollary provides an alternative representation for the limit given in (17). The proof for this Corollary is given in Cho (2014) [25].

Corollary 2. *For a given value of $\lambda \in (0,1)$, the fixed-b limit of $Wald^{(F)}$ has the same distribution as*

$$\frac{1}{\lambda(1-\lambda)}W_l(1)'\left(\frac{1}{\lambda}\mathbf{P}\left(\frac{b}{\lambda}, \widetilde{W}_l(r)\right) + \frac{1}{1-\lambda}\mathbf{P}\left(\frac{b}{1-\lambda}, \widetilde{W}_l^*(r)\right) + \mathbf{CP}\left(\lambda,b\right) + \mathbf{CP}\left(\lambda,b\right)'\right)^{-1} W_l(1), \tag{18}$$

where

$$\mathbf{CP}\left(\lambda,b\right) = \begin{cases} \frac{\sqrt{\lambda}\sqrt{1-\lambda}\int_0^1\int_0^1 K''\left(\frac{|\lambda t-(1-\lambda)s-\lambda|}{b}\right)\widetilde{W}_l(t)\widetilde{W}_l^*(s)'dtds}{b^2} \text{ for Class-1 kernels,} \\ \frac{\int_0^{1-b}\widetilde{W}_l(\frac{r}{\lambda})\widetilde{W}_l^*\left(\frac{r+b-\lambda}{1-\lambda}\right)'1(\lambda-b<r\leq\lambda)dr}{b\sqrt{\lambda}\sqrt{1-\lambda}} \text{ for Class-2 kernels,} \\ \frac{\sqrt{\lambda}\sqrt{1-\lambda}\int_0^1\int_0^1 K''\left(\frac{|\lambda t-(1-\lambda)s-\lambda|}{b}\right)\widetilde{W}_l(t)\widetilde{W}_l^*(s)'1(|\lambda t-(1-\lambda)s-\lambda|<b)dtds}{b^2} \\ -\frac{\int_0^{1-b}K'_-(1)\widetilde{W}_l(\frac{r}{\lambda})\widetilde{W}_l^*\left(\frac{r+b-\lambda}{1-\lambda}\right)'1(\lambda-b<r\leq\lambda)dr}{b\sqrt{\lambda}\sqrt{1-\lambda}} \text{ for Class-3 kernels,} \end{cases}$$

and $\widetilde{W}_l(r)$ and $\widetilde{W}_l^*(r)$ are $l \times 1$ Brownian Bridge processes which are independent of each other and of $W_l(1)$.

The limit in (18) shows how the components of $\widehat{\Omega}^{(F)}$ affect the distribution of $Wald^{(F)}$. As mentioned earlier, the random matrix $\mathbf{P}\left(\frac{b}{\lambda}, \widetilde{W}_l(r)\right)$ reflects the random nature of $\widehat{\Omega}_{11}^{(F)}$ which is part of the estimator of the asymptotic variance of $\widehat{\beta}_1$. Notice that the effective bandwidth for $\widehat{\Omega}_{11}^{(F)}$ turns out to be $\frac{b}{\lambda}$ not b. Thus, we implicitly use the bandwidth ratio $\frac{b}{\lambda}$ for $\widehat{\Omega}_{11}^{(F)}$ when we use a full sample bandwidth ratio b for constructing $\widehat{\Omega}^{(F)}$. The second component, $\mathbf{P}\left(\frac{b}{1-\lambda}, \widetilde{W}_l^*(r)\right)$, is related to $\widehat{\Omega}_{22}^{(F)}$ (and $\widehat{\beta}_2$) in exactly the same fashion. Finally, the third component, $\mathbf{CP}(\lambda, b)$, captures the impact of finite sample covariance between $\widehat{\beta}_1$ and $\widehat{\beta}_2$ on structural change inference.

Now consider the unknown break date case and let $Wald_{\infty}^{(F)}(\lambda)$ denote the limit of $Wald^{(F)}(T_b)$, where the form of $Wald_{\infty}^{(F)}(\lambda)$ depends on whether traditional or fixed-b asymptotic theory is being used. In the case of fixed-b theory, $Wald_{\infty}^{(F)}(\lambda)$ is given in (17). Under the traditional assumption that the bandwidth ratio goes to zero as T grows,

$$Wald^{(F)} \Rightarrow \lambda(1-\lambda)\left(\frac{1}{\lambda}W_l(\lambda) - \frac{1}{1-\lambda}\left(W_l(1) - W_l(\lambda)\right)\right)'$$
$$\times\left(\frac{1}{\lambda}W_l(\lambda) - \frac{1}{1-\lambda}\left(W_l(1) - W_l(\lambda)\right)\right)$$

The asymptotic limits of Sup-, Mean-, and Exp-Wald statistics immediately follow from the continuous mapping theorem given by

$$\begin{aligned}
SupW^{(F)} &\xrightarrow{d} \sup_{\lambda\in(\epsilon,1-\epsilon)} Wald_{\infty}^{(F)}(\lambda),\\
MeanW^{(F)} &\xrightarrow{d} \int_{\epsilon}^{1-\epsilon} Wald_{\infty}^{(F)}(\lambda)d\lambda,\\
ExpW^{(F)} &\xrightarrow{d} \log\left(\int_{\epsilon}^{1-\epsilon} \exp\left[\frac{1}{2}Wald_{\infty}^{(F)}(\lambda)\right]d\lambda\right).
\end{aligned}$$

3.2. Extension to the Partial Structural Change Model

This section derives the fixed-b limit of $Wald^{(F)}$ in the partial structural change model. The main result of this section is that the limit is the same as the limit for the full structural change model. The regression model with partial structural change is given by

$$\begin{aligned}
y_t &= z_t'\alpha + x_{1t}'\beta_1 + x_{2t}'\beta_2 + u_t \\
&= z_t'\alpha + X_t'\beta + u_t,
\end{aligned} \tag{19}$$

where x_t is $p \times 1$ and z_t is $q \times 1$ vector and

$$\begin{aligned}
&x_{1t} = x_t 1(t \leq [\lambda T]),\ x_{2t} = x_t 1(t \geq [\lambda T] + 1),\\
&X_t' = (x_{1t}'\ x_{2t}'),\ \text{and}\ \boldsymbol{\beta}' = (\beta_1'\ \beta_2').
\end{aligned}$$

The coefficients on the x_t regressors are unrestricted in terms of a structural change whereas the coefficients on the z_t regressors are assumed to not have structural change. Denote

$$\begin{aligned}
&y = (y_1, y_2, \ldots, y_T)',\ X = (X_1, X_2, \ldots X_T)',\\
&Z = (z_1, z_2, \ldots, z_T)',\ u = (u_1, u_2, \ldots, u_T)'.
\end{aligned}$$

The parameters $(\alpha, \boldsymbol{\beta})$ are estimated by OLS and the OLS residual vector can be written as

$$\widehat{u} = \widetilde{y} - \widetilde{X}\widehat{\boldsymbol{\beta}} = u - \widetilde{X}\left(\widehat{\boldsymbol{\beta}} - \boldsymbol{\beta}\right) - P_Z u,$$

where

$$\widetilde{y} = (I - P_Z)\, y, \; \widetilde{X} = (I - P_Z)\, X, \text{ and } P_Z = Z(Z'Z)^{-1}Z'.$$

The residual for an individual observation is given by

$$\widehat{u}_t = u_t - \widetilde{X}_t' \left(\widehat{\beta} - \beta\right) - z_t' \left(Z'Z\right)^{-1} Z'u. \tag{20}$$

Also, note that

$$\widetilde{X}_t = X_t - X'Z(Z'Z)^{-1}z_t = \begin{pmatrix} \underset{p\times 1}{\widetilde{X}_t^{(1)}} \\ \underset{p\times 1}{\widetilde{X}_t^{(2)}} \end{pmatrix}.$$

The following assumptions replace Assumptions 1 and 2:

Assumption 3. $T^{-1/2}\sum_{t=1}^{[rT]} \begin{pmatrix} x_t u_t \\ z_t u_t \end{pmatrix} \Rightarrow \Lambda W_{p+q}(r) \equiv \begin{pmatrix} \Lambda_1 \\ \Lambda_2 \end{pmatrix} W_{p+q}(r)$, *where* Λ_1 *is a* $p \times (p+q)$ *matrix,* Λ_2 *is a* $q \times (p+q)$ *matrix, and* $W_{p+q}(r)$ *is a* $(p+q) \times 1$ *vector of independent Wiener process.*

Assumption 4. $p\lim \frac{1}{T}\sum_{t=1}^{[rT]} z_t z_t' = rQ_{ZZ}$, $p\lim \frac{1}{T}\sum_{t=1}^{[rT]} x_t x_t' = rQ_{xx}$, *and* $p\lim \frac{1}{T}\sum_{t=1}^{[rT]} x_t z_t' = rQ_{xZ}$ *uniformly in* $r \in [0,1]$, *and* Q_{ZZ}^{-1} *and* Q_{xx}^{-1} *exist.*

We continue to focus on tests of the null hypothesis of no structural change in the x_t slope parameters of the form

$$H_0 : \mathbf{R}\beta = \mathbf{r}$$

with

$$\underset{l\times 2p}{\mathbf{R}} = \begin{pmatrix} \underset{l\times p}{\mathbf{R}_1}, & \underset{l\times p}{-\mathbf{R}_1} \end{pmatrix} \text{ and } \mathbf{r} = 0. \tag{21}$$

Recall that the OLS estimator, $\widehat{\beta} = \left(\widehat{\beta}_1', \widehat{\beta}_2'\right)'$ can be rewritten as

$$\widehat{\beta} = \left(\sum_{t=1}^{T} \widetilde{X}_t \widetilde{X}_t'\right)^{-1} \left(\sum_{t=1}^{T} \widetilde{X}_t \widetilde{y}_t\right). \tag{22}$$

Proposition 2. *Under Assumptions 3 and 4, as* $T \rightarrow \infty$

$$T^{1/2}\left(\widehat{\beta} - \beta\right) \xrightarrow{d} Q_{\widetilde{X}\widetilde{X}}^{-1} \begin{pmatrix} \Lambda_1 W_{p+q}(\lambda) - \lambda Q_{xZ} Q_{ZZ}^{-1} \Lambda_2 W_{p+q}(1) \\ \Lambda_1 \left(W_{p+q}(1) - W_{p+q}(\lambda)\right) - (1-\lambda) Q_{xZ} Q_{ZZ}^{-1} \Lambda_2 W_{p+q}(1) \end{pmatrix},$$

and

$$\sqrt{T}\left(\mathbf{R}\widehat{\beta} - \mathbf{r}\right) \Rightarrow \mathbf{R}_1 Q_{xx}^{-1} \Lambda_1 \left(\frac{1}{\lambda} W_{p+q}(\lambda) - \frac{1}{1-\lambda}\left(W_{p+q}(1) - W_{p+q}(\lambda)\right)\right), \tag{23}$$

where $Q_{\widetilde{X}\widetilde{X}} = p\lim\left(T^{-1}\sum_{t=1}^{T} \widetilde{X}_t \widetilde{X}_t'\right)$.

See Appendix A for the proof.

As seen from the above proposition, $\widehat{\beta}_1$ and $\widehat{\beta}_2$ are not asymptotically independent in the partial structural change regression model. This is true because we are projecting out the variation of explanatory variables z_t so that $\widehat{\beta}_1$ and $\widehat{\beta}_2$ depend on the entire series of x_t and z_t. The dichotomy that $\widehat{\beta}_1$ is dependent only on the pre-break data and that $\widehat{\beta}_2$ depends only on the post-break data no longer holds in the partial structural change model. The dependence manifests in the common term, $Q_{xZ}Q_{ZZ}^{-1}\Lambda_2 W_{p+q}(1)$, in Proposition 2. However, this term cancels out in (23) when the restriction matrix takes the form of (21). As a result, and also as suggested by Equation (23), in principle we need to estimate only $\Lambda_1\Lambda_1'$ for testing for partial structural change. Because $\widehat{\Omega}^{(F)}$, extended for the case of partial structural change, does not impose any restrictions on the asymptotic correlation between $\widehat{\beta}_1$ and $\widehat{\beta}_2$, $Wald^{(F)}$ continues to allow asymptotically pivotal fixed-b tests for partial structural change. While not obvious at first glance, $Wald^{(F)}$ has the same fixed-b limit in the partial structural change case as it does in the full structural change case.

The Wald statistic for testing for partial structural change is given by

$$Wald = T\left(\mathbf{R}\widehat{\beta}\right)'\left(\mathbf{R}\widehat{Q}_{\widetilde{X}\widetilde{X}}^{-1}\widehat{\Omega}\widehat{Q}_{\widetilde{X}\widetilde{X}}^{-1}\mathbf{R}'\right)^{-1}\left(\mathbf{R}\widehat{\beta}\right), \tag{24}$$

where $\widehat{Q}_{\widetilde{X}\widetilde{X}} = T^{-1}\sum_{t=1}^{T}\widetilde{X}_t\widetilde{X}_t'$. For constructing $Wald^{(F)}$, we use the HAC estimator $\widehat{\Omega}^{(F)}$ which is computed using $\left\{\widetilde{X}_t\widehat{u}_t\right\}_{t=1}^{T}$:

$$\widehat{\Omega}^{(F)} = T^{-1}\sum_{t=1}^{T}\sum_{s=1}^{T}K\left(\frac{|t-s|}{M}\right)\widehat{\xi}_t\widehat{\xi}_s', \tag{25}$$

where $\widehat{\xi}_t = \widetilde{X}_t\widehat{u}_t$. By the Frisch-Waugh-Lovell Theorem, this is the straightforward extension of $Wald^{(F)}$ to the case of partial structural change.

The next Lemma provides the limit of the scaled partial sum process of $\widehat{\xi}_t$ premultiplied by an appropriate term.

Lemma 2. *Let $\widehat{S}_t^{\xi} = \sum_{j=1}^{t}\widehat{\xi}_j$. Under Assumptions 3 and 4, as $T\to\infty$,*

$$\mathbf{R}\widehat{Q}_{\widetilde{X}\widetilde{X}}^{-1}T^{-1/2}\widehat{S}_{[rT]}^{\xi} \Rightarrow \mathbf{R}_1 Q_{xx}^{-1}\Lambda_1\left(\frac{1}{\lambda}F_{p+q}^{(1)}(r,\lambda) - \frac{1}{1-\lambda}F_{p+q}^{(2)}(r,\lambda)\right),$$

where

$$F_{p+q}^{(1)}(r,\lambda) = \left(W_{p+q}(r) - \frac{r}{\lambda}W_{p+q}(\lambda)\right)\mathbf{1}(0\le r\le\lambda),$$

$$F_{p+q}^{(2)}(r,\lambda) = \left(W_{p+q}(r) - W_{p+q}(\lambda) - \frac{r-\lambda}{1-\lambda}\left(W_{p+q}(1) - W_{p+q}(\lambda)\right)\right)\mathbf{1}(\lambda<r\le 1).$$

See Appendix A for the proof.

As Lemma 2 shows, the partial sums of the inputs to $\widehat{\Omega}^{(F)}$ are asymptotically proportional to the same nuisance parameters as $\sqrt{T}\left(\mathbf{R}\widehat{\beta} - \mathbf{r}\right)$. This is the key condition for a pivotal fixed-b limit. The next Theorem provides the fixed-b limit of $Wald^{(F)}$.

Theorem 2. *Let $b\in(0,1]$ be given. Suppose $M = bT$. Then, under Assumptions 3 and 4, $Wald^{(F)}$ weakly converges to the same limit in (17), i.e., as $T\to\infty$,*

$$Wald^{(F)} \Rightarrow \left(\frac{1}{\lambda}W_l(\lambda) - \frac{1}{1-\lambda}\left(W_l(1) - W_l(\lambda)\right)\right)'$$
$$\times\left(\mathbf{P}\left(b, \frac{1}{\lambda}F_l^{(1)}(r,\lambda) - \frac{1}{1-\lambda}F_l^{(2)}(r,\lambda)\right)\right)^{-1}\times\left(\frac{1}{\lambda}W_l(\lambda) - \frac{1}{1-\lambda}\left(W_l(1) - W_l(\lambda)\right)\right).$$

See Appendix A for the proof.

According to Theorem 2, the limit of $Wald^{(F)}$ in the partial structural change model is the same as in the full structural change model.

4. Critical Values

While the fixed-b limiting distributions are nonstandard, asymptotic critical values are easily obtained via simulations. We approximate the Wiener processes in the limiting distributions using scaled partial sums of 1000 i.i.d. $N(0,1)$ random variables. Critical values are tabulated based on 50,000 replications[3].

In Table 1, fixed-b critical values for $SupW^{(F)}$, $MeanW^{(F)}$, and $ExpW^{(F)}$ are provided for $l = 2$, $\epsilon = 0.05, 0.1, 0.2$ and for $b \in \{0.02, 0.04, 0.06, 0.08, 0.1, 0.2, 0.3, ..., 0.9, 1\}$. Critical values over the entire grid of 0.02-increment of b are available upon request.

Table 1. (**a**) Fixed-b 95% Critical Values of Sup-/$Mean$-/Exp-$W^{(F)}$, Bartlett kernel, $l = 2$; (**b**) Fixed-b 95% Critical Values of Sup-/$Mean$-/Exp-$W^{(F)}$, QS kernel, l =2.

(**a**)

b	ϵ = 0.05			ϵ = 0.1			ϵ = 0.2		
	$SupW$	$MeanW$	$ExpW$	$SupW$	$MeanW$	$ExpW$	$SupW$	$MeanW$	$ExpW$
0.02	30.293	4.861	9.588	18.230	4.235	5.051	13.542	3.263	3.539
0.04	48.447	5.9489	18.194	26.034	4.974	8.173	16.313	3.688	4.654
0.06	61.976	7.0183	24.816	33.172	5.729	11.483	19.496	4.162	5.967
0.08	73.862	8.001	r30.656	39.957	r6.496	14.695	22.812	4.617	7.364
0.1	84.848	8.973	36.109	46.263	7.278	17.653	26.323	5.146	8.998
0.2	138.92	14.018	63.068	76.971	11.323	32.706	46.122	8.052	18.156
0.3	193.94	19.113	90.408	109.11	15.596	48.657	67.262	11.216	28.446
0.4	254.14	24.443	120.71	142.31	20.009	65.120	89.241	14.464	39.161
0.5	313.06	29.999	149.85	176.51	24.565	82.037	111.18	17.912	49.818
0.6	374.36	35.304	180.46	212.05	29.202	99.596	134.00	21.386	61.205
0.7	433.71	40.902	210.22	245.66	33.625	116.32	153.93	24.666	70.991
0.8	491.83	46.205	239.08	279.65	38.016	133.32	173.96	27.702	81.134
0.9	549.63	51.450	268.05	311.37	42.238	149.22	192.52	30.670	90.145
1	608.99	57.142	297.78	344.26	46.623	165.51	212.76	33.936	100.36

(**b**)

b	ϵ = 0.05			ϵ = 0.1			ϵ = 0.2		
	$SupW$	$MeanW$	$ExpW$	$SupW$	$MeanW$	$ExpW$	$SupW$	$MeanW$	$ExpW$
0.02	64.848	5.678	26.200	24.831	4.641	7.548	15.051	3.458	4.111
0.04	122.00	8.102	54.483	46.350	6.059	17.433	20.670	4.205	6.401
0.06	161.74	10.617	74.329	68.158	7.630	28.148	28.305	5.060	9.666
0.08	207.65	13.202	97.163	91.258	9.461	39.595	38.905	6.143	14.409
0.1	257.31	16.139	122.02	118.67	11.671	53.066	52.759	7.491	20.987
0.2	832.93	40.501	409.56	452.33	30.155	219.29	240.65	19.924	113.55
0.3	3339.8	99.975	1663.0	2055.3	77.012	1020.8	1144.7	51.677	565.45
0.4	13,932	239.82	6959.4	8975.9	185.18	4481.1	4771.4	124.22	2378.8
0.5	47,253	537.89	23,620	31,752	411.53	15,869	16,684	276.98	8334.9
0.6	136211	1115.4	68,099	91,828	850.69	45,907	49,492	580.43	24,740
0.7	328,737	2170.5	164,361	224,463	1674.7	112,225	128,234	1140.0	64,110
0.8	719,812	3982.4	359,899	488,008	3100.4	243,997	283,267	2099.3	141,627
0.9	1,444,833	7015.5	722,409	970,172	5395.5	485,079	565,285	3626.6	282,635
1	2,647,520	11566	1,323,754	1,829,406	9072.3	914,696	1,062,685	5951.4	531,336

3 For the case of a known break date, the 95% critical values for l = 2 are available for selected values of b and λ in Cho and Vogelsang (2014) [27]. The critical values display two main patterns. First, for each given λ the critical values increase as the bandwidth gets bigger. This can be expected given the well known downward bias induced into HAC estimators from estimation error. The fixed-b approximation captures this downward bias and reflects it through larger critical values. Second, for a given value of the bandwidth, the critical values display a V-shaped pattern as a function of λ. As the break point moves closer to zero or one, the critical values increase and the minimum critical values occur at $\lambda = 0.5$.

5. Finite Sample Properties

In this section, we report the results of a finite sample simulation study that illustrates the performance of fixed-b critical values relative to traditional critical values. The data generating process (DGP) is given by (1) with $x_t' = [1, q_t]$ where q_t is a scalar time series, $\beta_1' = [\beta_1^c, \beta_1^s]$, and $\beta_2' = [\beta_2^c, \beta_2^s]$. We use the break point $\lambda = 0.4$. The regressor q_t and the regression error u_t are generated as $q_t = \theta q_{t-1} + \epsilon_t$ and $u_t = \rho u_{t-1} + \eta_t + \varphi \eta_{t-1}$, where ϵ_t and η_t are independent of each other with $\epsilon_t, \eta_t \sim$ i.i.d. $N(0,1)$. We use the parameter values: $\theta \in \{0.5, 0.8, 0.9\}$, and $(\rho, \varphi) \in \{(0,0), (0.5,0.5), (0.9, 0.9)\}$ (see Table 2):

Table 2. Parameter values for simulations

DGP	θ	ρ	φ	q_t	u_t	$v_{1t} = q_t u_t$
A	0.5	0	0	AR(1)	IID	White Noise
B	0.8	0.5	0.5	AR(1)	ARMA(1,1)	Serially Correlated
C	0.9	0.9	0.9	AR(1)	ARMA(1,1)	Serially Correlated

The value of θ measures the persistence of the time varying regressor q_t. The parameters ρ and φ jointly determine the serial correlation structure of the error term u_t. Bigger values of these three parameters lead to higher persistence of the series $v_{1t} \equiv q_t u_t$ except for specification A where bigger values of θ would not increase persistence in v_{1t}. We set $\beta_1^c = 0$, $\beta_1^s = 0$ and $\beta_2^c = \delta$, $\beta_2^s = \delta$. Under the null hypothesis of no structural change, $\delta = 0$, whereas for $\delta \neq 0$ there is structural change in both the intercept and slope parameters. We report results for sample sizes $T = 100, 200, 500$, and 1000 and the number of replications is 2500. The nominal level of all tests is 5%. We compute the $Sup/Mean/Exp\text{-}W^{(F)}$ statistics for testing the joint null hypothesis of no structural change in both the intercept and slope parameters. The frequency of rejections for the case of $\delta = 0$ measures the empirical type-I error.[4]

We report empirical rejection frequencies for traditional inference and for fixed-b inference. In traditional inference, we select the bandwidth following Andrews (1991) [16] for each hypothesized break date using the AR(1) plug-in formula. For fixed-b inference, we report results for different values of b to show how the null rejection probability varies with the choice of b. We also give results for another test in which a single data-dependent bandwidth ratio, denoted by b^*, is used across all hypothetical break dates and a fixed-b critical value is applied. The data-dependent bandwidth ratio, b^*, is computed as follows. We find the break date which minimizes the sum of squared residuals; we use that break date to select Andrews (1991) [16] data-dependent bandwidth (M^*) with the AR(1) plug-in formula and calculate the implied bandwidth ratio ($b^* = M^*/T$); we implement the test using the fixed-b critical values for b^*.

The rationale behind b^* is as follows. If a different bandwidth is used for each potential break point within the trimming range, then the fixed-b limits of the sup/mean/exp statistics will be functions of those bandwidth ratios and tabulation of fixed-b critical values will be computationally prohibitive. To provide practitioners with a data-dependent bandwidth approach that can be implemented with fixed-b critical values, we need a single data-dependent bandwidth to be used for all potential break points in which case the tabulated critical values can be used. Given the nice properties of the least squares estimator of the break point under the alternative of structural change (see Bai and Perron (1998) [11]), it is natural to use the least squares estimator of the break point to generate residuals needed to implement the Andrews (1991) [16] plug-in formula. Under the null of no structural change, any break point, including the least squares break point, will generate useful residuals for the Andrews (1991) [16] plug-in formula. Crainiceanu and Vogelsang (2007) [28] also considered using the least squares estimator of the break point to deal with the nonmonotonic power of the CUSUM test.

4 Cho and Vogelsang (2014) [27] also contains results for the known break date case along with a local power analysis.

Table 3 provides empirical null rejection frequencies for the traditional tests. For each hypothetical break date, the HAC estimator is constructed using the data-dependent bandwidth. For DGP A with zero persistence, all tests using $\epsilon = 0.05$ are subject to severe size distortions when the sample size is 100. Having more data or using more trimming helps reduce the size distortions. The null rejections decrease towards the 5% nominal level for all statistics when T is 500 and $\epsilon = 0.2$. Under the DGP B, as the sample size increases from 100 to 500, the null rejection probabilities drop to 0.194 from 0.594 for the supremum test with $\epsilon = 0.2$ and the QS kernel being used. The T = 500 rejection rate is still far from the nominal level. Size distortions get worse under more persistent data (DGP C). The mean test, which has the least size distortion of the three statistics, only attains a null rejection of 0.368 with the larger trimming value and T = 500. While traditional inference provides tests with reasonable size under DGPs with zero or mild persistence, as the DGP becomes more persistent, over-rejections can be substantial.

Table 3. Empirical Null Rejection Probabilities, traditional $Sup/Mean/Exp\text{-}W^{(F)}$ tests with 5% Nominal Size, H_0: No Structural Change ($\delta = 0$).

		$SupW^{(F)}$				$MeanW^{(F)}$				$ExpW^{(F)}$			
DGP	T	$\epsilon = 0.05$		$\epsilon = 0.2$		$\epsilon = 0.05$		$\epsilon = 0.2$		$\epsilon = 0.05$		$\epsilon = 0.2$	
		Bartlett	QS	Bartlett	QS	Bartlett	QS	Bartlett	QS	Bartlett	QS	Bartlett	QS
	100	0.699	0.742	0.164	0.171	0.278	0.306	0.115	0.121	0.676	0.728	0.176	0.186
A	200	0.368	0.408	0.090	0.095	0.111	0.124	0.069	0.072	0.322	0.356	0.094	0.102
	500	0.165	0.177	0.066	0.068	0.070	0.072	0.060	0.060	0.132	0.146	0.070	0.070
	100	0.967	0.980	0.588	0.594	0.855	0.898	0.440	0.428	0.972	0.981	0.604	0.609
B	200	0.918	0.940	0.392	0.371	0.622	0.653	0.261	0.238	0.906	0.930	0.400	0.371
	500	0.745	0.750	0.218	0.194	0.315	0.297	0.152	0.134	0.688	0.699	0.217	0.196
	100	0.992	0.993	0.910	0.918	0.982	0.984	0.853	0.866	0.995	0.995	0.924	0.930
C	200	0.980	0.984	0.800	0.804	0.946	0.952	0.679	0.672	0.987	0.988	0.819	0.814
	500	0.949	0.955	0.540	0.509	0.784	0.780	0.405	0.368	0.949	0.952	0.548	0.514

Tables 4–6 present simulation results for fixed-b inference. A single bandwidth ratio, b, is applied across all hypothetical break dates in constructing HAC estimators. We report results for $b = 0.02$, 0.1, 0.5, and 1. These tables also contain the null rejection probability when the traditional critical values in Andrews (1993) [9] or Andrews and Ploberger (1994) [10] are used. The traditional critical values are not designed to work well with relatively large bandwidths and this can be clearly seen in the tables. In general, as the bandwidth ratio gets bigger, the tendency to over-reject becomes more and more pronounced because using more lags generates a systematic downward bias in the HAC estimator and pushes up the value of test statistic. The traditional critical values do not take this impact of lag-choice into account. Because the effective bandwidths play important roles for the behavior of the HAC estimator (8), the impact of using large values of b is greater than for HAC estimators in non-structural change settings.

For fixed-b inference, several patterns stand out in Table 4 for the supremum test. Rejections using fixed-b critical values are similar to the rejections in traditional inference when a small bandwidth ratio is used. However, as the bandwidth increases, rejections using fixed-b critical values systematically decrease towards the nominal level of 0.05. Under DGP B, the null rejections decrease as 0.131→0.096→0.083→0.086 over the range of b with T = 500 and the Bartlett kernel and $\epsilon = 0.2$ being used. Even under DGP C, the null rejections approach the nominal level as b increases for all sample sizes when the QS kernel and the trimming value of 0.2 are used.

Table 7 gives null rejection probabilities when using the data-dependent bandwidth ratio b^*. Columns on the left give rejections using fixed-b critical values whereas columns on the right give rejections using traditional critical values. Patterns in Table 7 are similar to patterns in Tables 4–6. Over-rejections are often large when traditional critical values are used. Over-rejections are systematically smaller when fixed-b critical values are used and b^* works reasonably well if the sample size is large enough relative to the strength of the persistence in the data. This is particularly true when the QS kernel is used with 0.2 trimming for the mean statistic and 0.05 trimming for the supremum and exponential statistics.

Table 4. Empirical Null Rejection Probabilities, $SupW^{(F)}$ test with 5% nominal size, $M = bT$, H_0: No Structural Change ($\delta = 0$), $T = 100, 200, 500$.

DGP	ϵ	c.v.	kernel	$b = 0.02$			$b = 0.1$			$b = 0.5$			$b = 1$		
				T = 100	200	500	T = 100	200	500	T = 100	200	500	T = 100	200	500
A	0.05	fixed-b	Bartlett	0.331	0.146	0.093	0.277	0.132	0.084	0.250	0.131	0.083	0.253	0.131	0.081
			QS	0.184	0.094	0.084	0.212	0.118	0.077	0.036	0.028	0.046	0.012	0.016	0.026
		A93	Bartlett	0.721	0.555	0.472	0.954	0.930	0.904	1.00	1.00	1.00	1.00	1.00	1.00
			QS	0.810	0.735	0.696	0.995	0.993	0.992	1.00	1.00	1.00	1.00	1.00	1.00
	0.2	fixed-b	Bartlett	0.104	0.072	0.062	0.094	0.064	0.062	0.081	0.057	0.052	0.080	0.056	0.055
			QS	0.099	0.072	0.062	0.071	0.051	0.056	0.019	0.024	0.042	0.009	0.015	0.028
		A93	Bartlett	0.163	0.124	0.111	0.447	0.397	0.381	0.923	0.912	0.908	0.994	0.990	0.992
			QS	0.201	0.161	0.146	0.649	0.610	0.608	0.999	0.998	0.999	1.00	1.00	1.00
B	0.05	fixed-b	Bartlett	0.665	0.420	0.247	0.351	0.268	0.170	0.302	0.243	0.144	0.309	0.238	0.149
			QS	0.308	0.184	0.109	0.161	0.137	0.089	0.034	0.039	0.037	0.020	0.018	0.032
		A93	Bartlett	0.947	0.855	0.697	0.985	0.975	0.956	1.00	1.00	1.00	1.00	1.00	1.00
			QS	0.947	0.874	0.774	0.994	0.993	0.992	1.00	1.00	1.00	1.00	1.00	1.00
	0.2	fixed-b	Bartlett	0.493	0.274	0.131	0.255	0.160	0.096	0.213	0.132	0.083	0.209	0.131	0.087
			QS	0.376	0.189	0.090	0.128	0.081	0.070	0.034	0.036	0.041	0.018	0.020	0.030
		A93	Bartlett	0.604	0.382	0.216	0.674	0.543	0.447	0.966	0.949	0.926	0.999	0.997	0.994
			QS	0.539	0.333	0.205	0.757	0.686	0.620	0.999	1.00	0.999	1.00	1.00	1.00
C	0.05	fixed-b	Bartlett	0.934	0.824	0.591	0.346	0.257	0.212	0.307	0.216	0.176	0.296	0.209	0.174
			QS	0.586	0.365	0.195	0.092	0.064	0.059	0.036	0.030	0.041	0.026	0.024	0.038
		A93	Bartlett	0.998	0.991	0.945	0.990	0.980	0.971	1.00	1.00	1.00	1.00	1.00	1.00
			QS	0.996	0.986	0.926	0.988	0.987	0.980	1.00	1.00	1.00	1.00	1.00	1.00
	0.2	fixed-b	Bartlett	0.942	0.843	0.512	0.596	0.413	0.204	0.488	0.340	0.180	0.494	0.335	0.174
			QS	0.886	0.731	0.354	0.304	0.176	0.098	0.064	0.050	0.050	0.032	0.036	0.044
		A93	Bartlett	0.967	0.902	0.632	0.900	0.809	0.630	0.994	0.982	0.956	1.00	0.999	0.997
			QS	0.947	0.846	0.532	0.904	0.835	0.698	1.00	1.00	0.998	1.00	1.00	1.00

Note: A93 are critical values from Andrews (2003) [26].

Table 5. Empirical Null Rejection Probabilities, $MeanW^{(F)}$ test with 5% nominal size, $M = bT$, H_0: No Structural Change ($\delta = 0$), $T = 100, 200, 500$.

DGP	ϵ	c.v.	Kernel	$b = 0.02$			$b = 0.1$			$b = 0.5$			$b = 1$		
				T = 100	200	500	T = 100	200	500	T = 100	200	500	T = 100	200	500
A	0.05	fixed-b	Bartlett	0.162	0.077	0.064	0.190	0.090	0.064	0.216	0.100	0.065	0.217	0.100	0.067
			QS	0.148	0.085	0.066	0.226	0.108	0.070	0.120	0.075	0.057	0.097	0.062	0.055
		AP94	Bartlett	0.290	0.174	0.134	0.759	0.623	0.570	0.999	0.998	0.995	1.00	1.00	1.00
			QS	0.376	0.265	0.216	0.952	0.908	0.877	1.00	1.00	1.00	1.00	1.00	1.00
	0.2	fixed-b	Bartlett	0.084	0.057	0.056	0.086	0.055	0.061	0.089	0.059	0.060	0.087	0.060	0.060
			QS	0.082	0.056	0.060	0.081	0.050	0.055	0.065	0.053	0.051	0.055	0.050	0.050
		AP94	Bartlett	0.120	0.087	0.084	0.291	0.248	0.231	0.850	0.828	0.818	0.982	0.974	0.971
			QS	0.132	0.106	0.100	0.449	0.403	0.390	0.998	0.996	0.998	1.00	1.00	1.00
B	0.05	fixed-b	Bartlett	0.664	0.358	0.160	0.445	0.270	0.128	0.462	0.275	0.148	0.455	0.276	0.141
			QS	0.530	0.242	0.110	0.291	0.178	0.103	0.155	0.112	0.078	0.121	0.088	0.073
		AP94	Bartlett	0.806	0.534	0.291	0.926	0.834	0.694	1.00	1.00	0.999	1.00	1.00	1.00
			QS	0.783	0.512	0.318	0.973	0.946	0.908	1.00	1.00	1.00	1.00	1.00	1.00
	0.2	fixed-b	Bartlett	0.420	0.207	0.109	0.216	0.132	0.081	0.224	0.135	0.082	0.229	0.137	0.086
			QS	0.324	0.148	0.085	0.154	0.102	0.070	0.114	0.084	0.065	0.089	0.072	0.065
		AP94	Bartlett	0.488	0.270	0.152	0.521	0.386	0.295	0.938	0.889	0.848	0.996	0.992	0.982
			QS	0.428	0.219	0.137	0.603	0.483	0.417	0.998	0.998	0.998	1.00	1.00	1.00
C	0.05	fixed-b	Bartlett	0.985	0.927	0.653	0.723	0.546	0.324	0.668	0.494	0.316	0.664	0.492	0.304
			QS	0.948	0.827	0.451	0.407	0.247	0.145	0.207	0.137	0.099	0.174	0.127	0.091
		AP94	Bartlett	0.996	0.966	0.788	0.979	0.955	0.868	1.00	1.00	1.00	1.00	1.00	1.00
			QS	0.992	0.949	0.734	0.981	0.968	0.928	1.00	1.00	1.00	1.00	1.00	1.00
	0.2	fixed-b	Bartlett	0.916	0.776	0.429	0.586	0.396	0.206	0.552	0.384	0.204	0.547	0.375	0.204
			QS	0.854	0.661	0.318	0.409	0.257	0.124	0.223	0.144	0.105	0.171	0.114	0.084
		AP94	Bartlett	0.943	0.822	0.502	0.838	0.686	0.469	0.988	0.967	0.918	0.999	0.998	0.992
			QS	0.909	0.753	0.408	0.843	0.705	0.529	1.00	1.00	0.999	1.00	1.00	1.00

Note: AP94 are critical values from Andrews and Ploberger (1994) [10] with an adjustment.

Table 6. Empirical Null Rejection Probabilities, $ExpW^{(F)}$ test with 5% nominal size, $M = bT$, H_0: No Structural Change ($\delta = 0$), $T = 100, 200, 500$.

DGP	ϵ	c.v.	Kernel	$b = 0.02$			$b = 0.1$			$b = 0.5$			$b = 1$		
				T = 100	200	500	T = 100	200	500	T = 100	200	500	T = 100	200	500
A	0.05	fixed-*b*	Bartlett	0.368	0.162	0.094	0.291	0.140	0.086	0.256	0.133	0.083	0.254	0.132	0.082
			QS	0.198	0.100	0.086	0.217	0.120	0.078	0.036	0.028	0.046	0.012	0.016	0.026
		AP94	Bartlett	0.712	0.504	0.404	0.956	0.920	0.888	1.00	1.00	1.00	1.00	1.00	1.00
			QS	0.802	0.693	0.640	0.996	0.992	0.987	1.00	1.00	1.00	1.00	1.00	1.00
	0.2	fixed-*b*	Bartlett	0.108	0.068	0.062	0.104	0.068	0.060	0.086	0.060	0.055	0.082	0.058	0.055
			QS	0.104	0.072	0.064	0.080	0.055	0.055	0.019	0.024	0.042	0.009	0.015	0.028
		AP94	Bartlett	0.179	0.131	0.115	0.454	0.390	0.367	0.929	0.909	0.906	0.996	0.991	0.992
			QS	0.210	0.167	0.142	0.646	0.605	0.591	0.999	0.999	1.00	1.00	1.00	1.00
B	0.05	fixed-*b*	Bartlett	0.708	0.456	0.260	0.372	0.282	0.172	0.309	0.246	0.144	0.313	0.241	0.150
			QS	0.333	0.194	0.113	0.165	0.140	0.090	0.034	0.039	0.037	0.020	0.018	0.032
		AP94	Bartlett	0.954	0.836	0.647	0.986	0.974	0.946	1.00	1.00	1.00	1.00	1.00	1.00
			QS	0.952	0.855	0.734	0.996	0.992	0.993	1.00	1.00	1.00	1.00	1.00	1.00
	0.2	fixed-*b*	Bartlett	0.518	0.281	0.132	0.275	0.169	0.096	0.219	0.136	0.085	0.214	0.133	0.087
			QS	0.398	0.195	0.094	0.139	0.088	0.072	0.034	0.036	0.041	0.018	0.020	0.030
		AP94	Bartlett	0.627	0.384	0.211	0.689	0.554	0.446	0.970	0.956	0.925	1.00	0.998	0.997
			QS	0.564	0.332	0.202	0.763	0.687	0.610	0.999	1.00	0.999	1.00	1.00	1.00
C	0.05	fixed-*b*	Bartlett	0.958	0.870	0.634	0.370	0.277	0.220	0.313	0.219	0.177	0.301	0.210	0.174
			QS	0.624	0.387	0.204	0.095	0.066	0.060	0.036	0.030	0.041	0.026	0.024	0.038
		AP94	Bartlett	0.999	0.992	0.942	0.993	0.988	0.970	1.00	1.00	1.00	1.00	1.00	1.00
			QS	0.998	0.986	0.924	0.993	0.989	0.985	1.00	1.00	1.00	1.00	1.00	1.00
	0.2	fixed-*b*	Bartlett	0.951	0.853	0.517	0.617	0.437	0.218	0.502	0.348	0.183	0.498	0.342	0.177
			QS	0.902	0.751	0.372	0.327	0.190	0.102	0.064	0.050	0.050	0.032	0.036	0.044
		AP94	Bartlett	0.971	0.907	0.641	0.918	0.829	0.637	0.996	0.985	0.961	1.00	1.00	0.998
			QS	0.954	0.854	0.532	0.919	0.845	0.710	1.00	1.00	0.999	1.00	1.00	1.00

Note: AP94 are critical values from Andrews and Ploberger (1994) [10] with an adjustment.

We now examine the power of the tests when using b^*. We report size-adjusted power for T = 200 in Figures 1–6. Recall the break point under the alternative is $\lambda = 0.4$. Odd (even) numbered figures give results with 0.05 (0.2) trimming. Results are given for the three DGPs used for the tables. First note that more trimming leads to higher power in all cases as one would expect. Second, the mean statistic tends to have the highest power regardless of the DGP or kernel. This is not surprising given the power optimality properties of the mean statistic derived by Andrews and Ploberger (1994) [10] using traditional asymptotics. Third, for a given kernel, the supremum and exponential statistics have almost the same power across DGPs and trimming. This is somewhat surprising given that under traditional asymptotics, the exponential statistic is in the class of power optimal tests but the supremum statistic is not. This finding could be driven by values of b^* being far away from zero in which case the traditional asymptotics might not be accurately reflecting finite sample power. Finally, the Bartlett kernel tends to give tests with higher power than the QS kernel; a similar finding was made by Kiefer and Vogelsang (2005) [1] in models without structural change.

The size and power results for the statistics implemented with b^* point to the typical size-power tradeoff when using HAC variance estimators. Configurations that give the least size distortions also tend to have low power. As long as the data is not too persistent relative to the sample size, a reasonable approach for practice that balances size distortions and power is to use the mean statistic with 0.2 trimming implemented with the QS kernel with b^* and fixed-b critical values.

6. Summary and Conclusions

In this paper, fixed-b asymptotics is applied to the problem of testing for the presence of a structural break in a weakly dependent time series regression. The $Wald^{(F)}$ statistic is the Wald statistic that one obtains when structural change is expressed in terms of dummy variables interacted with regressors as in Bai and Perron (1998, 2003) [11,15]. We derived the fixed-b limit of the statistic. In both the full structural change and partial structural change model, the Wald statistic has the same pivotal fixed-b limit. We tabulated fixed-b critical values for $Sup/Mean/Exp\text{-}Wald^{(F)}$ statistics which are commonly used for testing parameter instability when the break point is unknown. In a simulation study, we examined the finite sample properties of traditional and fixed-b inference. With persistent data, traditional inference suffers from substantial size distortions. Using fixed-b critical values markedly improves over-rejection problem. A reasonable approach for practice that balances size distortions and power is to use the mean statistic with 0.2 trimming implemented with the QS kernel, b^* and fixed-b critical values.

Table 7. Empirical Null Rejection Probabilities, $Sup/Mean/Exp\text{-}W^{(F)}$ test using bandwidth ratio b^* with 5% nominal size, H_0 : No Structural Change ($\delta = 0$), $T = 100, 200, 500, 1000$.

$SupW^{(F)}$		Fixed-b c.v.				Andrews (1993) [9] c.v.			
DGP	T	$\epsilon = 0.05$		$\epsilon = 0.2$		$\epsilon = 0.05$		$\epsilon = 0.2$	
		Bartlett	QS	Bartlett	QS	Bartlett	QS	Bartlett	QS
A	100	0.318	0.182	0.103	0.099	0.773	0.830	0.189	0.221
	200	0.147	0.094	0.073	0.072	0.558	0.735	0.126	0.161
	500	0.089	0.081	0.062	0.062	0.479	0.701	0.111	0.146
B	100	0.384	0.164	0.287	0.177	0.972	0.985	0.612	0.627
	200	0.302	0.135	0.187	0.134	0.931	0.962	0.416	0.415
	500	0.206	0.102	0.110	0.088	0.826	0.801	0.249	0.218
C	100	0.328	0.083	0.574	0.289	0.992	0.991	0.915	0.924
	200	0.278	0.070	0.428	0.219	0.982	0.985	0.806	0.814
	500	0.267	0.082	0.250	0.158	0.954	0.965	0.556	0.548
	1000	0.254	0.072	0.188	0.120	0.900	0.928	0.375	0.368
$MeanW^{(F)}$		Fixed-b c.v.				Andrews and Ploberger (1994) [10] c.v.			
DGP	T	$\epsilon = 0.05$		$\epsilon = 0.2$		$\epsilon = 0.05$		$\epsilon = 0.2$	
		Bartlett	QS	Bartlett	QS	Bartlett	QS	Bartlett	QS
A	100	0.172	0.154	0.086	0.082	0.348	0.417	0.132	0.142
	200	0.077	0.085	0.058	0.056	0.176	0.265	0.088	0.106
	500	0.064	0.066	0.056	0.060	0.134	0.216	0.084	0.100
B	100	0.465	0.312	0.237	0.168	0.869	0.912	0.454	0.456
	200	0.278	0.190	0.145	0.110	0.667	0.717	0.277	0.269
	500	0.142	0.108	0.090	0.085	0.408	0.349	0.171	0.143
C	100	0.701	0.382	0.566	0.401	0.982	0.983	0.853	0.875
	200	0.555	0.293	0.408	0.283	0.948	0.956	0.688	0.688
	500	0.374	0.203	0.232	0.171	0.804	0.812	0.415	0.391
	1000	0.258	0.133	0.155	0.104	0.574	0.619	0.257	0.238
$ExpW^{(F)}$		Fixed-b c.v.				Andrews and Ploberger (1994) [10] c.v.			
DGP	T	$\epsilon = 0.05$		$\epsilon = 0.2$		$\epsilon = 0.05$		$\epsilon = 0.2$	
		Bartlett	QS	Bartlett	QS	Bartlett	QS	Bartlett	QS
A	100	0.331	0.196	0.095	0.107	0.761	0.820	0.203	0.230
	200	0.161	0.100	0.068	0.072	0.506	0.593	0.132	0.167
	500	0.093	0.083	0.062	0.064	0.404	0.640	0.115	0.142
B	100	0.402	0.170	0.296	0.195	0.976	0.988	0.626	0.638
	200	0.278	0.143	0.167	0.142	0.923	0.956	0.427	0.423
	500	0.135	0.104	0.068	0.093	0.788	0.762	0.251	0.215
C	100	0.348	0.087	0.601	0.308	0.995	0.994	0.929	0.935
	200	0.298	0.072	0.449	0.241	0.987	0.990	0.826	0.829
	500	0.277	0.083	0.263	0.169	0.955	0.961	0.563	0.556
	1000	0.186	0.072	0.134	0.121	0.881	0.912	0.378	0.369

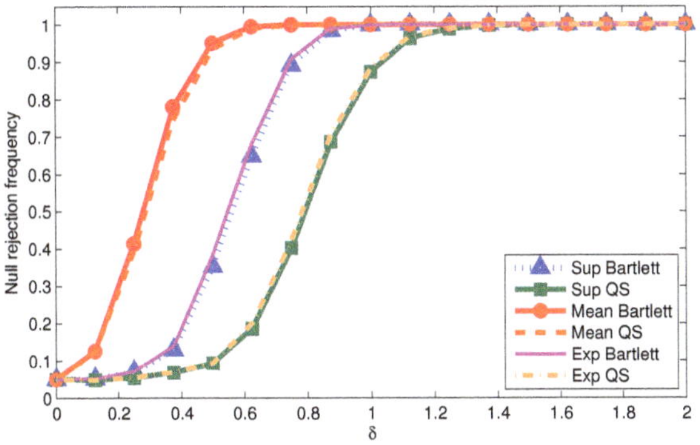

Figure 1. Size adjusted power, DGP A, $\epsilon = 0.05$, T = 200.

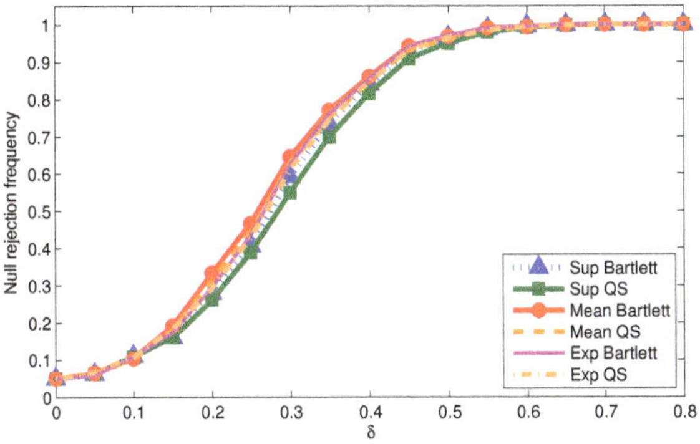

Figure 2. Size adjusted power, DGP A, $\epsilon = 0.2$, T = 200.

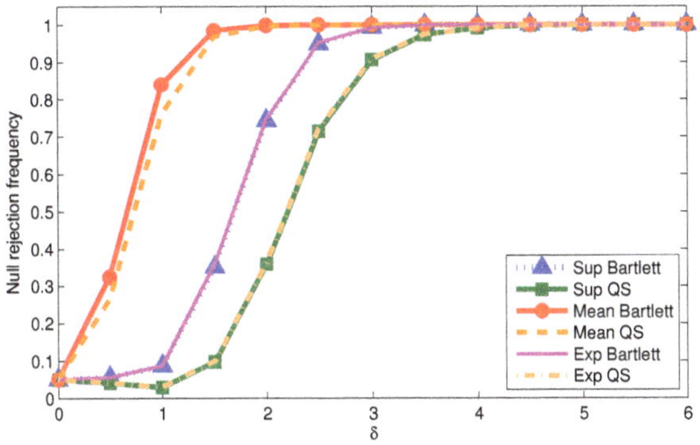

Figure 3. Size adjusted power, DGP B, $\epsilon = 0.05$, T = 200.

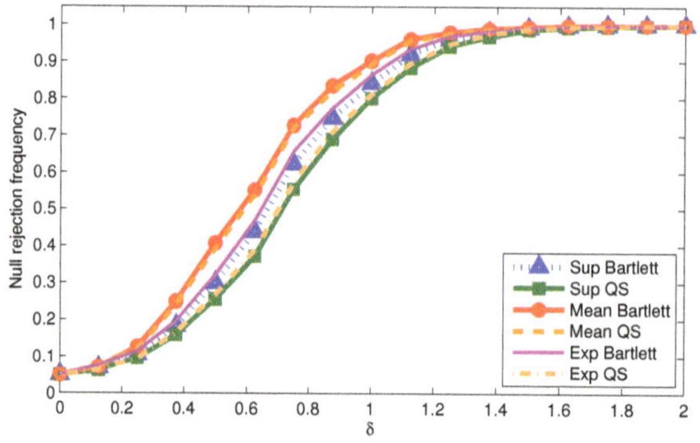

Figure 4. Size adjusted power, DGP B, $\epsilon = 0.2$, T = 200.

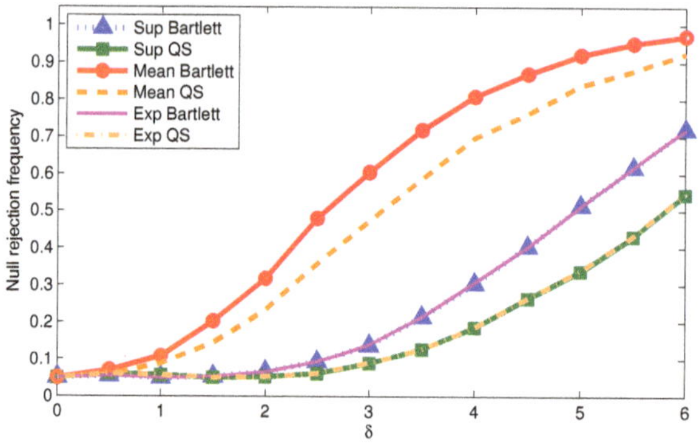

Figure 5. Size adjusted power, DGP C, $\epsilon = 0.05$, T = 200.

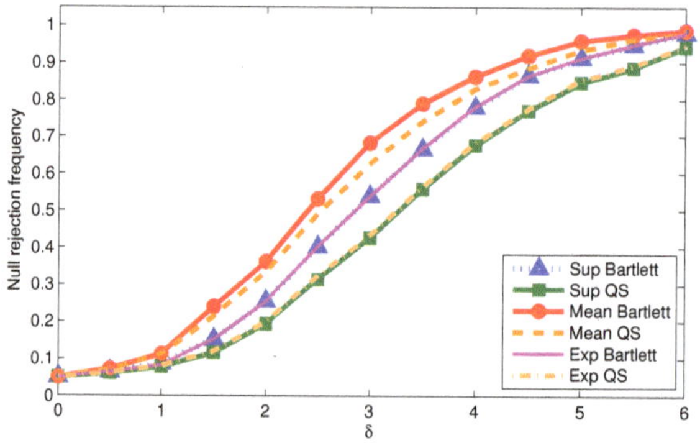

Figure 6. Size adjusted power, DGP C, $\epsilon = 0.2$, T = 200.

Acknowledgments: We thank the editor and three anonymous referees for helpful suggestions and comments.

Author Contributions: Both authors contributed equally to the paper.

Conflicts of Interest: The authors declare no conflicts of interest.

Appendix A. Definitions and Proofs

Definitions

Case 1. *Suppose $K(x)$ is twice continuously differentiable everywhere (Class 1) such as the Quadratic Spectral kernel (QS), then*

$$\mathbf{P}\left(b, H_p\right) \equiv -\int_0^1 \int_0^1 \frac{1}{b^2} K''\left(\frac{r-s}{b}\right) H_p(r) H_p(s)' dr ds, \tag{A1}$$

where $K''(\cdot)$ is the second derivative of the kernel $K(\cdot)$.

Case 2. *Suppose $K(x)$ is the Bartlett kernel (Class 2), then*

$$\mathbf{P}\left(b, H_p\right) \equiv \frac{2}{b} \int_0^1 H_p(r) H_p(r)' dr - \frac{1}{b} \int_0^{1-b} \left(H_p(r) H_p(r+b)' + H_p(r+b) H_p(r)'\right) dr. \tag{A2}$$

Case 3. *Suppose $K(x)$ is continuous, $K(x) = 0$ for $|x| \geq 1$, and $K(x)$ is twice continuously differentiable everywhere except for $|x| = 1$ (Class 3) (e.g., Parzen kernel), then*

$$\begin{aligned} \mathbf{P}\left(b, H_p\right) \equiv & -\int\int_{|r-s|<b} \frac{1}{b^2} K''\left(\frac{|r-s|}{b}\right) H_p(r) H_p(s)' dr ds \\ & + \frac{K'\_(1)}{b} \int_0^{1-b} \left(H_p(r+b) H_p(r)' + H_p(r) H_p(r+b)'\right) dr, \end{aligned} \tag{A3}$$

where $K'\_(1) = \lim_{h \downarrow 0} \left[\left(K(1) - K(1-h)\right)/h\right]$, i.e., $K'\_(1)$ is the derivative of $K(x)$ from the left at $x = 1$.

The following expression is a general representation of the HAC estimators:

$$\widehat{\Omega} = T^{-1} \sum_{t=1}^{T} \sum_{s=1}^{T} K\left(\frac{|t-s|}{M}\right) \widehat{v}_t \widehat{v}_s'.$$

This representation can be rewritten in terms of the partial sum processes $\widehat{S}_t = \sum_{j=1}^{t} \widehat{v}_j$ following Kiefer and Vogelsang (2005) [1] and Hashimzade and Vogelsang (2008) [4] as follows. Let $M = bT$. Then, for the kernels in Class 1, we have

$$\widehat{\Omega} = T^{-2} \sum_{t=1}^{T-1} \sum_{s=1}^{T-1} T^{-1/2} \widehat{S}_t \left(T^2 \Delta_{t,s}^2\right) T^{-1/2} \widehat{S}_s', \tag{A4}$$

where

$$\Delta_{t,s}^2 \equiv \left(K_{t,s} - K_{t,s+1}\right) - \left(K_{t+1,s} - K_{t+1,s+1}\right) \text{ with } K_{t,s} = K\left(\frac{|t-s|}{bT}\right).$$

For the Class 2 kernel (Bartlett), we have

$$\widehat{\Omega} = \frac{2}{bT} \sum_{t=1}^{T-1} \left(T^{-1} \widehat{S}_t \widehat{S}_t'\right) - \frac{1}{bT} \sum_{t=1}^{T-M-1} \left(T^{-1} \widehat{S}_{t+bT} \widehat{S}_t' + T^{-1} \widehat{S}_t \widehat{S}_{t+bT}'\right). \tag{A5}$$

For the kernels in Class 3, we have

$$\begin{aligned} \widehat{\Omega} = & T^{-2} \sum\sum_{|t-s|<bT} T^{-1} \widehat{S}_t \left(T^2 \Delta_{t,s}^2\right) \widehat{S}_s' + \frac{1}{bT} \sum_{s=1}^{T-bT} T^{-1/2} \widehat{S}_s T^{-1/2} \widehat{S}_{s+bT}' \left(\frac{K(1) - K(1 - \frac{1}{bT})}{\frac{1}{bT}}\right) \\ & - \frac{1}{bT} \sum_{s=1}^{T-bT} T^{-1/2} \widehat{S}_s T^{-1/2} \widehat{S}_{s+bT}' \left(\frac{K(-1 + \frac{1}{bT}) - K(-1)}{\frac{1}{bT}}\right). \end{aligned} \tag{A6}$$

Proof of Proposition 1. The limit of the $\widehat{\text{fi}}$ follows immediately under Assumptions 1 and 2. Also, plugging the limits of $\widehat{\beta}_1$ and $\widehat{\beta}_2$ into Equation (4) yields, for $r \leq \lambda$,

$$T^{-1/2}\widehat{S}_{[rT]} \Rightarrow \begin{pmatrix} \Lambda & 0 \\ 0 & \Lambda \end{pmatrix} \begin{pmatrix} (W_p(r) - \frac{r}{\lambda} W_p(\lambda)) \\ 0 \end{pmatrix},$$

and for $r > \lambda$,

$$T^{-1/2}\widehat{S}_{[rT]} \Rightarrow \begin{pmatrix} \Lambda & 0 \\ 0 & \Lambda \end{pmatrix} \begin{pmatrix} 0 \\ \left(W_p(r) - W_p(\lambda) - \frac{r-\lambda}{1-\lambda}\left(W_p(1) - W_p(\lambda)\right)\right) \end{pmatrix}.$$

Thus, we can rewrite this result by using indicator functions as

$$T^{-1/2}\widehat{S}_{[rT]} \Rightarrow \begin{pmatrix} \Lambda & 0 \\ 0 & \Lambda \end{pmatrix} F_p(r,\lambda) \equiv \begin{pmatrix} \Lambda & 0 \\ 0 & \Lambda \end{pmatrix} \begin{pmatrix} F_p^{(1)}(r,\lambda) \\ F_p^{(2)}(r,\lambda) \end{pmatrix},$$

where

$$F_p^{(1)}(r,\lambda) = \left(W_p(r) - \tfrac{r}{\lambda} W_p(\lambda)\right) \cdot \mathbf{1}(r \leq \lambda) \text{ and } F_p^{(2)}(r,\lambda) = \left(W_p(r) - W_p(\lambda) - \tfrac{r-\lambda}{1-\lambda}\left(W_p(1) - W_p(\lambda)\right)\right) \cdot \mathbf{1}(r > \lambda).$$

□

Proof of Lemma 1. Plugging the limit of the partial sum process in Proposition 1 into the HAC estimators in (A4)–(A6), the desired result follows from direct application of the continuous mapping theorem to obtain the desired result in (12). □

Proof of Theorem 1. Recall that

$$Wald^{(F)} = T\left(\mathbf{R}\widehat{\beta}\right)'\left(\mathbf{R}\widehat{\mathbf{Q}}_\lambda^{-1}\widehat{\Omega}^{(F)}\widehat{\mathbf{Q}}_\lambda^{-1}\mathbf{R}'\right)^{-1}\left(\mathbf{R}\widehat{\beta}\right).$$

Using $\mathbf{R} = (\mathbf{R}_1, \ -\mathbf{R}_1)$ it follows that

$$T^{1/2}\left(\mathbf{R}\widehat{\beta}\right) \overset{H_0}{=} \mathbf{R}_1\left(T^{1/2}\left(\widehat{\beta}_1 - \beta_1\right) - T^{1/2}\left(\widehat{\beta}_2 - \beta_2\right)\right) \Rightarrow$$

$$\mathbf{R}_1 Q^{-1}\Lambda\left(\frac{1}{\lambda}W_p(\lambda) - \frac{1}{1-\lambda}\left(W_p(1) - W_p(\lambda)\right)\right).$$

Using Assumption 1 and Lemma 1,

$$\mathbf{R}\widehat{\mathbf{Q}}_\lambda^{-1}\widehat{\Omega}^{(F)}\widehat{\mathbf{Q}}_\lambda^{-1}\mathbf{R}' \Rightarrow \left(\frac{1}{\lambda}\mathbf{R}_1 Q^{-1}\Lambda, \ \frac{-1}{1-\lambda}\mathbf{R}_1 Q^{-1}\Lambda\right) \times \mathbf{P}\left(b, F_p(r,\lambda)\right) \times \left(\frac{1}{\lambda}\mathbf{R}_1 Q^{-1}\Lambda, \ \frac{-1}{1-\lambda}\mathbf{R}_1 Q^{-1}\Lambda\right)'.$$

By writing $\mathbf{P}\left(b, F_p(r,\lambda)\right)$ in the form (A1)–(A3) using $F_p(r,\lambda)' = \left(F_p^{(1)}(r,\lambda)', \ F_p^{(2)}(r,\lambda)'\right)$, we obtain, after some algebra, the following expression for the above limit:

$$\mathbf{R}_1 Q^{-1}\Lambda\mathbf{P}\left(b, \frac{1}{\lambda}F_p^{(1)}(r,\lambda) - \frac{1}{1-\lambda}F_p^{(2)}(r,\lambda)\right)\Lambda' Q^{-1}\mathbf{R}_1'.$$

Now apply the transformation: $\mathbf{R}_1 Q^{-1}\Lambda W_p(r) \overset{d}{=} AW_l(r)$ with $\mathbf{R}_1 Q^{-1}\Lambda\Lambda' Q^{-1}\mathbf{R}_1' = AA'$, and conclude

$$\mathbf{R}\widehat{\mathbf{Q}}_\lambda^{-1}\widehat{\Omega}^{(F)}\widehat{\mathbf{Q}}_\lambda^{-1}\mathbf{R}' \Rightarrow A\mathbf{P}\left(b, \frac{1}{\lambda}F_l^{(1)}(r,\lambda) - \frac{1}{1-\lambda}F_l^{(2)}(r,\lambda)\right)A',$$

yielding the desired result:

$$Wald^{(F)} \Rightarrow \left(\frac{1}{\lambda}W_l(\lambda) - \frac{1}{1-\lambda}\left(W_l(1) - W_l(\lambda)\right)\right)'$$

$$\times \left(\mathbf{P}\left(b, \frac{1}{\lambda}F_l^{(1)}(r,\lambda) - \frac{1}{1-\lambda}F_l^{(2)}(r,\lambda)\right)\right)^{-1} \times \left(\frac{1}{\lambda}W_l(\lambda) - \frac{1}{1-\lambda}\left(W_l(1) - W_l(\lambda)\right)\right).$$

□

Proof of Proposition 2. Standard algebra gives

$$\begin{aligned}\widehat{\beta} &= \left(\textstyle\sum_{t=1}^{T} \widetilde{X}_t\widetilde{X}_t'\right)^{-1}\left(\textstyle\sum_{t=1}^{T} \widetilde{X}_t\widetilde{y}_t\right) \\ &= \left(\textstyle\sum_{t=1}^{T} \widetilde{X}_t\widetilde{X}_t'\right)^{-1}\left(\textstyle\sum_{t=1}^{T} \widetilde{X}_t\widetilde{X}_t'\beta + \textstyle\sum_{t=1}^{T} \widetilde{X}_t u_t - \textstyle\sum_{t=1}^{T} \widetilde{X}_t z_t'(Z'Z)^{-1}Z'u\right) \\ &= \left(\textstyle\sum_{t=1}^{T} \widetilde{X}_t\widetilde{X}_t'\right)^{-1}\left(\textstyle\sum_{t=1}^{T} \widetilde{X}_t\widetilde{X}_t'\beta + \textstyle\sum_{t=1}^{T} \widetilde{X}_t u_t\right),\end{aligned}$$

and it immediately follows that

$$\begin{aligned}T^{1/2}\left(\widehat{\beta} - \beta\right) &= \left(T^{-1}\textstyle\sum_{t=1}^{T} \widetilde{X}_t\widetilde{X}_t'\right)^{-1}\left(T^{-1/2}\textstyle\sum_{t=1}^{T} \widetilde{X}_t u_t\right) \\ &= \left(T^{-1}\textstyle\sum_{t=1}^{T}\left(X_t - X'Z(Z'Z)^{-1}z_t\right)\left(X_t' - z_t'(Z'Z)^{-1}Z'X\right)\right)^{-1} \\ &\quad \times \left(T^{-1/2}\textstyle\sum_{t=1}^{T}\left(X_t - X'Z(Z'Z)^{-1}z_t\right)u_t\right).\end{aligned}$$

Under Assumptions 3 and 4, it follows in a straightforward manner that

$$\sqrt{T}(\widehat{\beta} - \beta) \Rightarrow Q_{\widetilde{X}\widetilde{X}}^{-1}\begin{pmatrix}\Lambda_1 W_{p+q}(\lambda) - \lambda Q_{xZ}Q_{ZZ}^{-1}\Lambda_2 W_{p+q}(1) \\ \Lambda_1\left(W_{p+q}(1) - W_{p+q}(\lambda)\right) - (1-\lambda)Q_{xZ}Q_{ZZ}^{-1}\Lambda_2 W_{p+q}(1)\end{pmatrix} \tag{A7}$$

In order to derive the limit of $\sqrt{T}(\mathbf{R}\widehat{\beta} - \mathbf{r})$, the following standard results are useful:

$$Q_{XZ} \equiv p\lim\left(T^{-1}\sum_{t=1}^{T} X_t z_t'\right) = \begin{pmatrix}\lambda Q_{xZ} \\ (1-\lambda)Q_{xZ}\end{pmatrix}_{2p\times q},$$

$$Q_{XX} \equiv p\lim\left(T^{-1}\sum_{t=1}^{T} X_t X_t'\right) = \begin{pmatrix}\lambda Q_{xx} & \mathbf{0} \\ \mathbf{0} & (1-\lambda)Q_{xx}\end{pmatrix}_{2p\times 2p},$$

$$Q_{\widetilde{X}\widetilde{X}} = p\lim\left(T^{-1}\sum_{t=1}^{T} \widetilde{X}_t\widetilde{X}_t'\right) = Q_{XX} - Q_{XZ}Q_{ZZ}^{-1}Q_{XZ}'.$$

Also, well known matrix algebra properties (see e.g., Schott (1997) [29]), we can write

$$Q_{\widetilde{X}\widetilde{X}}^{-1} = Q_{XX}^{-1} + Q_{XX}^{-1}Q_{XZ}\left(Q_{ZZ} - Q_{XZ}'Q_{XX}^{-1}Q_{XZ}\right)^{-1}Q_{XZ}'Q_{XX}^{-1}, \tag{A8}$$

and using (A8), one can further show that

$$Q_{\widetilde{X}\widetilde{X}}^{-1} = \begin{pmatrix}\frac{1}{\lambda}Q_{xx}^{-1} + P & P \\ P & \frac{1}{1-\lambda}Q_{xx}^{-1} + P\end{pmatrix}, \tag{A9}$$

where

$$P = Q_{xx}^{-1}Q_{xZ}\left(Q_{ZZ} - Q_{xZ}'Q_{xx}^{-1}Q_{xZ}\right)^{-1}Q_{xZ}'Q_{xx}^{-1}.$$

Now plug (A9) into (A7) to conclude that

$$\sqrt{T}(\mathbf{R}\widehat{\beta} - \mathbf{r}) \overset{H_0}{=} \sqrt{T}\mathbf{R}\left(\widehat{\beta} - \beta\right) \Rightarrow \mathbf{R}_1 Q_{xx}^{-1}\Lambda_1\left(\tfrac{1}{\lambda}W_{p+q}(\lambda) + \tfrac{1}{1-\lambda}\left(W_{p+q}(\lambda) - W_{p+q}(1)\right)\right).$$ □

The following lemma is used in the proof of Lemma A1.

Lemma A1. *Let* $K = Q_{xZ}Q_{ZZ}^{-1}Q'_{xZ}$. *Then it holds that* $Q_{xx}^{-1}KP = P - Q_{xx}^{-1}KQ_{xx}^{-1}$.

Proof of Lemma 3. One can easily show

$$Q_{\tilde{X}\tilde{X}} = \begin{pmatrix} \lambda Q_{xx} & 0 \\ 0 & (1-\lambda)Q_{xx} \end{pmatrix} - \begin{pmatrix} \lambda^2 Q_{xZ}Q_{ZZ}^{-1}Q'_{xZ} & \lambda(1-\lambda)Q_{xZ}Q_{ZZ}^{-1}Q'_{xZ} \\ \lambda(1-\lambda)Q_{xZ}Q_{ZZ}^{-1}Q'_{xZ} & (1-\lambda)^2 Q_{xZ}Q_{ZZ}^{-1}Q'_{xZ} \end{pmatrix}.$$

The desired result comes from the identity $Q_{\tilde{X}\tilde{X}}Q_{\tilde{X}\tilde{X}}^{-1} = I$ by substituting Equation (A9) for $Q_{\tilde{X}\tilde{X}}^{-1}$. □

Proof of Lemma 2. First note that implicit in the proof of Proposition 2 is the result that $p\lim \widehat{Q}_{\tilde{X}\tilde{X}}^{-1} = Q_{\tilde{X}\tilde{X}}^{-1}$. For $\mathbf{R} = (\mathbf{R}_1, \ -\mathbf{R}_1)$, it follows that

$$p\lim \mathbf{R}\widehat{Q}_{\tilde{X}\tilde{X}}^{-1} = \mathbf{R}_1 \left(\frac{1}{\lambda} Q_{xx}^{-1}, \ -\frac{1}{1-\lambda} Q_{xx}^{-1} \right) \tag{A10}$$

using (A9). The scaled partial sum process is given by

$$T^{-1/2}\widehat{S}_{[rT]}^{\xi} = T^{-1/2}\sum_{t=1}^{[rT]} \tilde{X}_t \widehat{u}_t$$

$$= T^{-1/2}\sum_{t=1}^{[rT]} \tilde{X}_t u_t - T^{-1}\sum_{t=1}^{[rT]} \tilde{X}_t \tilde{X}_t' \sqrt{T}(\widehat{\beta} - \beta) - T^{-1}\sum_{t=1}^{[rT]} \tilde{X}_t z_t' \left(\frac{Z'Z}{T} \right)^{-1} \left(T^{-1/2}Z'u \right). \tag{A11}$$

For $0 \le r < \lambda$, the first term in (A11) satisfies

$$T^{-1/2}\sum_{t=1}^{[rT]} \tilde{X}_t u_t \Rightarrow \begin{pmatrix} \Lambda_1 W_{p+q}(r) - \lambda Q_{xZ}Q_{ZZ}^{-1}\Lambda_2 W_{p+q}(r) \\ -(1-\lambda)Q_{xZ}Q_{ZZ}^{-1}\Lambda_2 W_{p+q}(r) \end{pmatrix}. \tag{A12}$$

Hence with $\mathbf{R} = (\mathbf{R}_1, \ -\mathbf{R}_1)$, from (A10) and (A12), it follows that

$$\mathbf{R}\widehat{Q}_{\tilde{X}\tilde{X}}^{-1} T^{-1/2}\sum_{t=1}^{[rT]} \tilde{X}_t u_t$$

$$\Rightarrow \mathbf{R}_1 \left(\frac{1}{\lambda} Q_{xx}^{-1}, \ -\frac{1}{1-\lambda} Q_{xx}^{-1} \right) \begin{pmatrix} \Lambda_1 W_{p+q}(r) - \lambda Q_{xZ}Q_{ZZ}^{-1}\Lambda_2 W_{p+q}(r) \\ -(1-\lambda)Q_{xZ}Q_{ZZ}^{-1}\Lambda_2 W_{p+q}(r) \end{pmatrix} = \frac{1}{\lambda}\mathbf{R}_1 Q_{xx}^{-1}\Lambda_1 W_{p+q}(r).$$

For the first part of the second term in (A11), it follows that

$$T^{-1}\sum_{t=1}^{[rT]} \tilde{X}_t \tilde{X}_t' \Rightarrow \begin{pmatrix} rQ_{xx} & \mathbf{0}_{p\times p} \\ \mathbf{0}_{p\times p} & \mathbf{0}_{p\times p} \end{pmatrix} - \begin{pmatrix} r\lambda Q_{xZ}Q_{ZZ}^{-1}Q'_{xZ} & r(1-\lambda)Q_{xZ}Q_{ZZ}^{-1}Q'_{xZ} \\ \mathbf{0}_{p\times p} & \mathbf{0}_{p\times p} \end{pmatrix}$$

$$- \begin{pmatrix} r\lambda Q_{xZ}Q_{ZZ}^{-1}Q'_{xZ} & \mathbf{0}_{p\times p} \\ r(1-\lambda)Q_{xZ}Q_{ZZ}^{-1}Q'_{xZ} & \mathbf{0}_{p\times p} \end{pmatrix} + r \begin{pmatrix} \lambda^2 Q_{xZ}Q_{ZZ}^{-1}Q'_{xZ} & \lambda(1-\lambda)Q_{xZ}Q_{ZZ}^{-1}Q'_{xZ} \\ \lambda(1-\lambda)Q_{xZ}Q_{ZZ}^{-1}Q'_{xZ} & (1-\lambda)^2 Q_{xZ}Q_{ZZ}^{-1}Q'_{xZ} \end{pmatrix}$$

$$= \begin{pmatrix} rQ_{xx} + (r\lambda^2 - 2r\lambda)K & -r(1-\lambda)^2 K \\ -r(1-\lambda)^2 K & r(1-\lambda)^2 K \end{pmatrix},$$

where $K = Q_{xZ}Q_{ZZ}^{-1}Q'_{xZ}$. Hence with $\mathbf{R} = (\mathbf{R}_1, \ -\mathbf{R}_1)$,

$$\mathbf{R}\widehat{Q}_{\tilde{X}\tilde{X}}^{-1} T^{-1}\sum_{t=1}^{[rT]} \tilde{X}_t \tilde{X}_t' \Rightarrow \mathbf{R}_1 \left(\frac{1}{\lambda} Q_{xx}^{-1}, \ -\frac{1}{1-\lambda} Q_{xx}^{-1} \right) \times \begin{pmatrix} rQ_{xx} + (r\lambda^2 - 2r\lambda)K & -r(1-\lambda)^2 K \\ -r(1-\lambda)^2 K & r(1-\lambda)^2 K \end{pmatrix}$$

$$= r\mathbf{R}_1\left(\frac{1}{\lambda}I - Q_{xx}^{-1}K,\ \frac{\lambda-1}{\lambda}Q_{xx}^{-1}K\right),$$

which combined with (A7) and Lemma 3 immediately yields

$$\begin{aligned}
&\mathbf{R}\widehat{Q}_{\widetilde{X}\widetilde{X}}^{-1}\left(T^{-1}\sum_{t=1}^{[rT]}\widetilde{X}_t\widetilde{X}_t'\right)\sqrt{T}(\widehat{\beta}-\beta)\\
&\Rightarrow r\mathbf{R}_1\left(\frac{1}{\lambda}I - Q_{xx}^{-1}K,\ \frac{\lambda-1}{\lambda}Q_{xx}^{-1}K\right)\times\begin{pmatrix}\frac{1}{\lambda}Q_{xx}^{-1}+P & P\\ P & \frac{1}{1-\lambda}Q_{xx}^{-1}+P\end{pmatrix}\\
&\times\begin{pmatrix}\Lambda_1 W_{p+q}(\lambda) - \lambda Q_{xZ}Q_{ZZ}^{-1}\Lambda_2 W_{p+q}(1)\\ \Lambda_1\left(W_{p+q}(1)-W_{p+q}(\lambda)\right) - (1-\lambda)Q_{xZ}Q_{ZZ}^{-1}\Lambda_2 W_{p+q}(1)\end{pmatrix}\\
&= r\mathbf{R}_1\left(\frac{1}{\lambda^2}Q_{xx}^{-1},\ \mathbf{0}_{p\times p}\right)\times\begin{pmatrix}\Lambda_1 W_{p+q}(\lambda) - \lambda Q_{xZ}Q_{ZZ}^{-1}\Lambda_2 W_{p+q}(1)\\ \Lambda_1\left(W_{p+q}(1)-W_{p+q}(\lambda)\right) - (1-\lambda)Q_{xZ}Q_{ZZ}^{-1}\Lambda_2 W_{p+q}(1)\end{pmatrix}\\
&= \frac{r}{\lambda^2}\mathbf{R}_1 Q_{xx}^{-1}\Lambda_1 W_{p+q}(\lambda) - \frac{r}{\lambda}\mathbf{R}_1 Q_{xx}^{-1}Q_{xZ}Q_{ZZ}^{-1}\Lambda_2 W_{p+q}(1).
\end{aligned}$$

Finally, premultiplying the third term in (A11) by $\mathbf{R}\widehat{Q}_{\widetilde{X}\widetilde{X}}^{-1}$ gives

$$\begin{aligned}
&\mathbf{R}\widehat{Q}_{\widetilde{X}\widetilde{X}}^{-1}T^{-1}\sum_{t=1}^{[rT]}\widetilde{X}_t z_t'\left(\frac{Z'Z}{T}\right)^{-1}\left(T^{-1/2}Z'u\right)\\
&= \mathbf{R}\widehat{Q}_{\widetilde{X}\widetilde{X}}^{-1}T^{-1}\sum_{t=1}^{[rT]}\left(X_t - X'Z(Z'Z)^{-1}z_t\right)z_t'\left(\frac{Z'Z}{T}\right)^{-1}\left(T^{-1/2}Z'u\right)\\
&\Rightarrow \mathbf{R}_1\left(\frac{1}{\lambda}Q_{xx}^{-1},\ -\frac{1}{1-\lambda}Q_{xx}^{-1}\right)\times\begin{pmatrix}r(1-\lambda)Q_{xZ}\\ -r(1-\lambda)Q_{xZ}\end{pmatrix}Q_{ZZ}^{-1}\Lambda_2 W_{p+q}(1)\\
&= \frac{r}{\lambda}\mathbf{R}_1 Q_{xx}^{-1}Q_{xZ}Q_{ZZ}^{-1}\Lambda_2 W_{p+q}(1).
\end{aligned}$$

Combining the results for the three terms gives

$$\begin{aligned}
&\mathbf{R}\widehat{Q}_{\widetilde{X}\widetilde{X}}^{-1}T^{-1/2}\widehat{S}_{[rT]}^{\xi} \Rightarrow \mathbf{R}_1 Q_{xx}^{-1}\Lambda_1\tfrac{1}{\lambda}W_{p+q}(r) - \mathbf{R}_1 Q_{xx}^{-1}\Lambda_1\tfrac{r}{\lambda^2}W_{p+q}(\lambda)\\
&+\mathbf{R}_1 Q_{xx}^{-1}Q_{xZ}Q_{ZZ}^{-1}\Lambda_2\tfrac{r}{\lambda}W_{p+q}(1) - \mathbf{R}_1 Q_{xx}^{-1}Q_{xZ}Q_{ZZ}^{-1}\Lambda_2\tfrac{r}{\lambda}W_{p+q}(1) \qquad \text{(A13)}\\
&= \mathbf{R}_1 Q_{xx}^{-1}\Lambda_1\left(\tfrac{1}{\lambda}W_{p+q}(r) - \tfrac{r}{\lambda^2}W_{p+q}(\lambda)\right) = \mathbf{R}_1 Q_{xx}^{-1}\Lambda_1\tfrac{1}{\lambda}F_{p+q}^{(1)}(r,\lambda).
\end{aligned}$$

Similar results can be obtained for $\lambda \le r \le 1$:

$$\mathbf{R}\widehat{Q}_{\widetilde{X}\widetilde{X}}^{-1}T^{-1/2}\sum_{t=1}^{[rT]}\widetilde{X}_t u_t \Rightarrow \mathbf{R}_1 Q_{xx}^{-1}\Lambda_1\left(\frac{1}{\lambda}W_{p+q}(\lambda) - \frac{1}{1-\lambda}\left(W_{p+q}(r)-W_{p+q}(\lambda)\right)\right),$$

$$\begin{aligned}
&\mathbf{R}\widehat{Q}_{\widetilde{X}\widetilde{X}}^{-1}\left(T^{-1}\textstyle\sum_{t=1}^{[rT]}\widetilde{X}_t\widetilde{X}_t'\right)\sqrt{T}(\widehat{\beta}-\beta)\\
&\Rightarrow \mathbf{R}_1 Q_{xx}^{-1}\Lambda_1\left(\tfrac{1}{\lambda}W_{p+q}(\lambda) + \tfrac{r-\lambda}{(1-\lambda)^2}W_{p+q}(\lambda) - \tfrac{r-\lambda}{(1-\lambda)^2}W_{p+q}(1)\right) - \mathbf{R}_1 Q_{xx}^{-1}Q_{xZ}Q_{ZZ}^{-1}\Lambda_2\tfrac{1-r}{1-\lambda}W_{p+q}(1),
\end{aligned}$$

and

$$\mathbf{R}\widehat{Q}_{\widetilde{X}\widetilde{X}}^{-1}T^{-1}\sum_{t=1}^{[rT]}\widetilde{X}_t z_t'\left(\frac{Z'Z}{T}\right)^{-1}\left(T^{-1/2}Z'u\right) \Rightarrow \frac{1-r}{1-\lambda}\mathbf{R}_1 Q_{xx}^{-1}Q_{xZ}Q_{ZZ}^{-1}\Lambda_2 W_{p+q}(1).$$

Now combining the results for the three terms gives $\mathbf{R}\widehat{Q}_{\widetilde{X}\widetilde{X}}^{-1}T^{-1/2}\widehat{S}_{[rT]}^{\xi} \Rightarrow -\mathbf{R}_1 Q_{xx}^{-1}\Lambda_1 \cdot \frac{1}{1-\lambda}F_{p+q}^{(2)}(r,\lambda)$. Thus, we obtain for $r \in [0,1]$,

$$\mathbf{R}\widehat{Q}_{\widetilde{X}\widetilde{X}}^{-1}T^{-1/2}\widehat{S}_{[rT]}^{\xi} \Rightarrow \mathbf{R}_1 Q_{xx}^{-1}\Lambda_1 \left(\frac{1}{\lambda}F_{p+q}^{(1)}(r,\lambda) - \frac{1}{1-\lambda}F_{p+q}^{(2)}(r,\lambda)\right).$$

□

Proof of Theorem 2. To save space, the proof for this Theorem is provided only for the case of the Bartlett kernel with $M = T$ (i.e., $b = 1$). However, the proof given here is applicable to other kernels and different values of b. Note that with $b = 1$, the HAC estimator can be rewritten as (see Kiefer and Vogelsang (2002a) [2]) $\widehat{\Omega}_{b=1}^{(F)} = \frac{2}{T}\sum_{t=1}^{T-1} T^{-1/2}\widehat{S}_t^{\xi} T^{-1/2}\widehat{S}_t^{\xi\prime}$. With this HAC estimator, the term within the inverse in (24) is given by

$$\begin{aligned}
&\frac{2}{T}\sum_{t=1}^{T-1}\left\{\mathbf{R}\left(T^{-1}\sum_{s=1}^{T}\widetilde{X}_s\widetilde{X}_s'\right)^{-1} T^{-1/2}\widehat{S}_t^{\xi}T^{-1/2}\widehat{S}_t^{\xi\prime}\left(T^{-1}\sum_{s=1}^{T}\widetilde{X}_s\widetilde{X}_s'\right)^{-1}\mathbf{R}'\right\} \\
&\Rightarrow \mathbf{P}\left(1, \mathbf{R}_1 Q_{xx}^{-1}\Lambda_1\left(\frac{1}{\lambda}F_{p+q}^{(1)}(r,\lambda) - \frac{1}{1-\lambda}F_{p+q}^{(2)}(r,\lambda)\right)\right)
\end{aligned}$$

where the limit is obtained directly from Lemma A1 and the continuous mapping theorem. The result for (24) can be obtained by using similar arguments as those used in Theorem 1 where we use the transformation: $\mathbf{R}_1 Q_{xx}^{-1}\Lambda_1 W_{p+q}(r) \overset{d}{=} \Xi \cdot W_l(r)$, $0 \le r \le 1$ for a p.d. matrix $\underset{l\times l}{\Xi}$ satisfying $\Xi\Xi' = \mathbf{R}_1 Q_{xx}^{-1}\Lambda_1\Lambda_1' Q_{xx}^{-1}\mathbf{R}_1'$.

References

1. Kiefer, N.M.; Vogelsang, T.J. A New Asymptotic Theory for Heteroskedasticity-Autocorrelation Robust Tests. *Econom. Theory* **2005**, *21*, 1130–1164.
2. Kiefer, N.M.; Vogelsang, T.J. Heteroskedasticity-autocorrelation robust standard errors using the Bartlett kernel without truncation. *Econometrica* **2002**, *70*, 2093–2095.
3. Kiefer, N.M.; Vogelsang, T.J. Heteroskedasticity-Autocorrelation Robust Testing Using Bandwidth Equal to Sample Size. *Econom. Theory* **2002**, *18*, 1350–1366.
4. Hashimzade, N.; Vogelsang, T.J. Fixed-*b* Asymptotic Approximation of the Sampling Behavior of Nonparametric Spectral Density Estimators. *J. Time Ser. Anal.* **2008**, *29*, 142–162.
5. Jansson, M. The Error Rejection Probability of Simple Autocorrelation Robust Tests. *Econometrica* **2004**, *72*, 937–946.
6. Sun, Y.; Phillips, P.C.B.; Jin, S. Optimal Bandwidth Selection in Heteroskedasticity-Autocorrelation Robust Testing. *Econometrica* **2008**, *76*, 175–194.
7. Gonçalves, S.; Vogelsang, T.J. Block Bootstrap HAC Robust Tests: The Sophistication of the Naive Bootstrap. *Econom. Theory* **2011**, *27*, 745–791.
8. Sun, Y. *Fixed-Smoothing Asymptotics in a Two-Step GMM Framework*; Working Paper; Department of Economics, University of California, San Diego: La Jolla, CA, USA, 2013.
9. Andrews, D.W.K. Tests for Parameter Instability and Structural Change with Unknown Change Point. *Econometrica* **1993**, *61*, 821–856.
10. Andrews, D.W.K.; Ploberger, W. Optimal Tests When a Nuisance Parameter is Present Only Under the Alternative. *Econometrica* **1994**, *62*, 1383–1414.
11. Bai, J.S.; Perron, P. Estimating and Testing Linear Models with Multiple Structural Breaks. *Econometrica* **1998**, *66*, 47–78.
12. Perron, P. Dealing with structural breaks. *Palgrave Handb. Econom.* **2006**, *1*, 278–352.
13. Banerjee, A.; Urga, G. Modelling structural breaks, long memory and stock market volatility: An overview. *J. Econom.* **2005**, *129*, 1–34.
14. Aue, A.; Horváth, L. Structural breaks in time series. *J. Time Ser. Anal.* **2013**, *34*, 1–16.

15. Bai, J.; Perron, P. Computation and analysis of multiple structural change models. *J. Appl. Econom.* **2003**, *18*, 1–22.
16. Andrews, D.W.K. Heteroskedasticity and Autocorrelation Consistent Covariance Matrix Estimation. *Econometrica* **1991**, *59*, 817–854.
17. Davidson, J. *Stochastic Limit Theory*; Oxford University Press: New York, NY, USA, 1994.
18. Phillips, P.C.B.; Durlauf, S.N. Multiple Regression with Integrated Processes. *Rev. Econom. Stud.* **1986**, *53*, 473–496.
19. Phillips, P.C.B.; Solo, V. Asymptotics for Linear Processes. *Ann. Stat.* **1992**, *20*, 971–1001.
20. Wooldridge, J.M.; White, H. Some invariance principles and central limit theorems for dependent heterogeneous processes. *Econom. Theory* **1988**, *4*, 210–230.
21. DeJong, R.M.; Davidson, J. Consistency of Kernel Estimators of Heteroskedastic and Autocorrelated Covariance Matrices. *Econometrica* **2000**, *68*, 407–424.
22. Hansen, B.E. Consistent Covariance Matrix Estimation for Dependent Heterogenous Processes. *Econometrica* **1992**, *60*, 967–972.
23. Jansson, M. Consistent Covariance Estimation for Linear Processes. *Econom. Theory* **2002**, *18*, 1449–1459.
24. Newey, W.K.; West, K.D. A Simple, Positive Semi-Definite, Heteroskedasticity and Autocorrelation Consistent Covariance Matrix. *Econometrica* **1987**, *55*, 703–708.
25. Cho, C.K. Essays on Time Series Econometrics. Ph.D. Thesis, Department of Economics, Michigan State University, East Lansing, MI, USA, 2014.
26. Andrews, D.W. Tests for parameter instability and structural change with unknown change point: A corrigendum. *Econometrica* **2003**, *71*, 395–397.
27. Cho, C.K.; Vogelsang, T.J. *Fixed-b Inference for Testing Structural Change in a Time Series Regression*; Working Paper; Department of Economics, Michigan State University: East Lansing, MI, USA, 2014.
28. Crainiceanu, C.; Vogelsang, T.J. Non-monotonic Power for Tests of Mean Shift in a Time Series. *J. Stat. Comput. Simul.* **2007**, *77*, 457–476.
29. Schott, J.R. *Matrix Analysis for Statistics*; Wiley InterScience Publication: New York, NY, USA, 1997.

econometrics

MDPI

Article

Consistency of Trend Break Point Estimator with Underspecified Break Number

Jingjing Yang

Department of Economics, University of Nevada, Reno, 1664 N. Virginia Street, Reno, NV 89557, USA; jingjingy@unr.edu; Tel.: +1-775-784-1112

Academic Editor: Pierre Perron
Received: 31 August 2016; Accepted: 26 December 2016; Published: 5 January 2017

Abstract: This paper discusses the consistency of trend break point estimators when the number of breaks is underspecified. The consistency of break point estimators in a simple location model with level shifts has been well documented by researchers under various settings, including extensions such as allowing a time trend in the model. Despite the consistency of break point estimators of level shifts, there are few papers on the consistency of trend shift break point estimators in the presence of an underspecified break number. The simulation study and asymptotic analysis in this paper show that the trend shift break point estimator does not converge to the true break points when the break number is underspecified. In the case of two trend shifts, the inconsistency problem worsens if the magnitudes of the breaks are similar and the breaks are either both positive or both negative. The limiting distribution for the trend break point estimator is developed and closely approximates the finite sample performance.

Keywords: deterministic trend; linear trend; multiple trend shifts; underspecified break number; Pitman drift; limiting distribution

JEL Classification: C22; C13

---

1. Introduction

A time series can have multiple breaks. For example, U. S. Treasury bill rates can be observed to have multiple level changes over time, while the Grilli and Yang primary commodity price index shows multiple trend shifts. It is common that the number of breaks is unknown and misspecified. Bai (1995, 1997) [1,2] and Chong (1994, 1995) [3,4] study the consequences of underspecifying the number of break points in linear structural break models. They point out that when the number of breaks in a mean shift model is underspecified, the break point estimator is still consistent for a subset of the true break points. Their discussion covers the mean shift model with and without trend. Bai (1997) [2] shows that the mean break point estimator by sequential estimation is not only consistent but also converges at the same rate as with simultaneous estimation. Bai and Perron (1998) [5] extend the estimation of a single unknown break to multiple unknown breaks under both fixed and shrinking shift magnitudes. Based on the consistency property of the mean shift break point estimator, they propose a sequential procedure for multi-break estimates without estimating the multiple breaks simultaneously. Dynamic programming is introduced by Bai and Perron (2003) [6] to deal with the computational burden in multiple break point estimation. Kejriwal and Perron (2010) [7] extend the work of Perron and Yabu (2009) [8,9] to propose a sequential test of the multiple-trend-shift model robust to persistence in noise.

Although trending components are considered by researchers in the mean shift model, there is little discussion of the consistency of multiple trend shift break point estimators when the number of breaks is underspecified. Consistency analysis is important both for break point estimation and for structural breaks in the linear regression model. The main motivation of this paper is to address the gap in the literature concerning the consistency of trend shift break point estimators when the break number is underspecified.

The second motivation of this paper is to explore how to approximate the finite sample distributions of the break point estimator for a multiple break model. Specifically, asymptotics of the break point estimator in a trend shift model are provided for the case of an underspecified break number by employing Pitman drifts. The accuracy of the asymptotic approximation to the finite sample distribution is examined. This work follows Yang (2012) [10] who has shown that the finite sample distribution of the single break point estimator is not normal, but depends on the break dates and magnitudes.

In this paper, finite sample simulations are used to illustrate the potential inconsistency of the break point estimator in the trend shift model with an underspecified break number. Then, the limits of the break point estimator under fixed break magnitudes are provided. Both the simulation results and the expression of the limits show that for the trend shift model, the break point estimator can be inconsistent for any of the true break points, while for the mean shift model, the break point estimator converges to one of the true breaks. Then, extending Yang's (2012) work [10] on the single break point estimator, new asymptotics are provided for the break point estimators under local alternatives.

As will be shown in this paper, the mean shift model leads to a consistent break point estimator while the trend shift model does not. Taking first differences of the trend shift model is shown by Yang (2010) [11] to provide a solution to the inconsistency problem. When the break magnitudes are sufficiently large, the first-difference break point estimator has much higher peaks in the density at the true breaks than the levels break point estimator. When the break magnitudes are small, the densities of the two break point estimators depend on the break magnitudes and locations and the strength of the serial correlation. A detailed analysis of the first-difference estimator is omitted in this paper but can be found in Yang (2010) [11] and Yang (2012) [10].

The paper is organized as follows. Section 2 describes the general settings of the mean shift and trend shift models, assumptions, and break point estimators. Section 3 introduces finite sample simulations to demonstrate the consistency properties of different break point estimators. Section 4 derives the expression of the limits of the single break point estimator when the break sizes are fixed and the data sequences have two breaks under I(0) errors. Both mean shift and trend shift break point estimators are discussed. Section 5 establishes the asymptotic distributions of the break point estimators assuming the breaks are Pitman drifts, which approximate the finite sample distributions accurately. Sections 4 and 5 relate the mean shift results to those of Bai (1997) [2]. The last section concludes the paper. Proofs are provided in the Appendix.

2. The Models, Assumptions, and Break Point Estimators

In this section, I define a mean shift and a trend shift model with multiple breaks. For simplicity, I only include the case where a single break model is estimated while the number of breaks is two. The results can be extended to models with more than two breaks.

Let us start with a mean shift model with two breaks:

$$y_t = \mu + \delta_1 DU_t(\lambda_1^c) + \delta_2 DU_t(\lambda_2^c) + u_t, \tag{1}$$

where

$$DU_t(\lambda_i^c) \doteq \begin{cases} 0, & t \le T_{b,i}^c \\ 1, & t > T_{b,i}^c \end{cases}, \quad i = 1, 2;$$

λ_1^c and λ_2^c are the true break fractions with $T_{b,1}^c = \lambda_1^c T$ and $T_{b,2}^c = \lambda_2^c T$; $T_{b,i}^c$ denotes the time of a break. T is the sample length; δ_1 and δ_2 are the break magnitudes. For convenience of discussion, we define the relative break magnitude ratio $\nu \doteq \delta_2/\delta_1$.

When model (1) is underspecified, the estimated model is given by

$$y_t = \mu + \delta DU_t(\lambda) + u_t, \quad (2)$$

where

$$DU_t(\lambda) \doteq \begin{cases} 0, & t \leq T_b \\ 1, & t > T_b \end{cases};$$

λ is the underspecified single break fraction with $T_b = \lambda T$.

For comparison, the trend shift model with two breaks is

$$y_t = \mu + \beta t + \delta_1 DT_t(\lambda_1^c) + \delta_2 DT_t(\lambda_2^c) + u_t, \quad (3)$$

where $DT_t(\lambda_i^c) \doteq (t - T_{b,i}^c) \cdot DU_t(\lambda_i^c),\ i = 1, 2.$

If model (3) is misspecified with only one break, the estimated model is

$$y_t = \mu + \beta t + \delta DT_t(\lambda) + u_t, \quad (4)$$

where $DT_t(\lambda) \doteq (t - T_b) \cdot DU_t(\lambda)$.

It is assumed that the error u_t is I(0), namely

$$u_t = d(L)e_t, \quad (5)$$

where

$$d(L) = \sum_{i=0}^{\infty} d_i L^i, \quad \sum_{i=0}^{\infty} i|d_i| < \infty, \quad d(1)^2 > 0;$$

L is the lag operator; $\{e_t\}$ is a martingale difference sequence with $\sup_t E(e_t^4) < \infty$, $E(e_t|e_{t-1}, e_{t-2}, \cdots) = 0$, and $E(e_t^2|e_{t-1}, e_{t-2}, \cdots) = \sigma_e^2$.

The break point estimators are obtained by minimizing the sum of squared residuals (SSR) over the trimming set $\Lambda \doteq \{\lambda^*, \cdots, 1 - \lambda^*\}$, namely

$$\hat{\lambda}_{MS} = \arg\min_{\lambda \in \Lambda^*} \{SSR_{MS}(\lambda)\},$$
$$\hat{\lambda}_{TS} = \arg\min_{\lambda \in \Lambda^*} \{SSR_{TS}(\lambda)\},$$

where

$$SSR_{MS}(\lambda) \doteq \sum_{t=1}^{T} [y_t - \hat{\mu}_{MS} - \hat{\delta}_{MS} DU_t(\hat{\lambda})]^2, \quad (6)$$

$$SSR_{TS}(\lambda) \doteq \sum_{t=1}^{T} [y_t - \hat{\mu}_{TS} - \hat{\beta}_{TS} t - \hat{\delta}_{TS} DT_t(\hat{\lambda})]^2, \quad (7)$$

with $\hat{\mu}_{MS}$ and $\hat{\delta}_{MS}$ the OLS estimators from model (2) with no restrictions imposed, whereas $\hat{\mu}_{TS}$, $\hat{\beta}_{TS}$, and $\hat{\delta}_{TS}$ are the OLS estimators from model (4) with no restrictions imposed.

3. Illustration of the Inconsistency Problem of the Trend Shift Break Point Estimator

In this section a simple simulation is used to illustrate the consistency/inconsistency of $\hat{\lambda}_{MS}$ and $\hat{\lambda}_{TS}$ in the presence of an underspecified break number. The data are generated based on models (1) and (3) with two breaks, where $T = 100, 250, 500, 1000$, $\{\lambda_1^c, \lambda_2^c\} = \{1/3, 2/3\}$, $\nu = -2, -1, 1, 2$ (we set $\delta_1 = 1$ without loss of generality), and u_t is an *i.i.d.* $N(0,1)$ process. Equations (6) and (7) are used to estimate $\hat{\lambda}_{MS}$ and $\hat{\lambda}_{TS}$ separately in each replication. While trimming is not necessary, to ensure the invertibility of the regression matrix I use 2% trimming, i.e., $\lambda^* = 0.02$. The replications $N = 20{,}000, 10{,}000, 5000, 2500$ are used for $T = 100, 250, 500, 1000$ respectively.

Figure 1a,b plots the histograms of $\hat{\lambda}_{MS}$ with *i.i.d.* errors. In all cases with the increase of T, the distribution of $\hat{\lambda}_{MS}$ has shorter tails and, when $T = 1000$, concentrates at the two break points or one of them depending on the relative break magnitude ratios. Interestingly, when $|\nu| = 1$ and $T = 100$, the density of $\hat{\lambda}_{MS}$ is bimodal, which can be explained by Yang (2012) [10] through the behavior of the mean shift break point estimator, where the break point estimates concentrate around the end points in the no break model.

Figure 1c,d plots the histograms of $\hat{\lambda}_{TS}$. When $\nu = -2$, the density peaks at a point greater than 2/3. When $\nu = -1$, $\hat{\lambda}_{TS}$ has two equal peaks at $\lambda = 0.2$ and 0.8. When $\nu = 1$, the histogram of $\hat{\lambda}_{TS}$ has only one peak at $\lambda = 0.5$, and with the increase of T the break date estimates are more concentrated. When $\nu = 2$, the histogram of $\hat{\lambda}_{TS}$ peaks at a point between 1/3 and 2/3. This shows that when the number of breaks is underspecified, the trend shift break point estimator does not converge to either of the true break points, and that the limit of the break point estimator $\hat{\lambda}_{TS}$ depends on the break magnitudes and locations.

Empirical data also shows that the break point estimators behave differently when the break number is underspecified in mean shift model and trend shift model. Using the US ex-post real interest rate in Figure 2 as an example of mean shifts (the three-month treasury bill rate between the first quarter of 1961 and the third quarter of 1986 deflated by the CPI inflation rate taken from the Citibase data bank), Bai and Perron (1998) [5] detect three mean shifts in years 1965, 1972, and 1980 while a single mean shift point estimator detects one of the real breaks in 1980. Using the extended Grilli and Yang commodity price index as an example of trend shifts (Copper during 1900–2003), Harvey, Leybourne, and Taylor (2009) [12] identify two breaks in 1945 and 1971, while a single trend shift estimator identifies one in 1930, which is not close to the HLT dates.

Both the finite sample histograms and empirical data suggest an interesting pattern: when the break number is underspecified, the mean shift break point estimator converges to a subset of the true break points, while the trend shift counterpart does not converge to either of the true break points and its limit depends on the break dates and magnitudes.

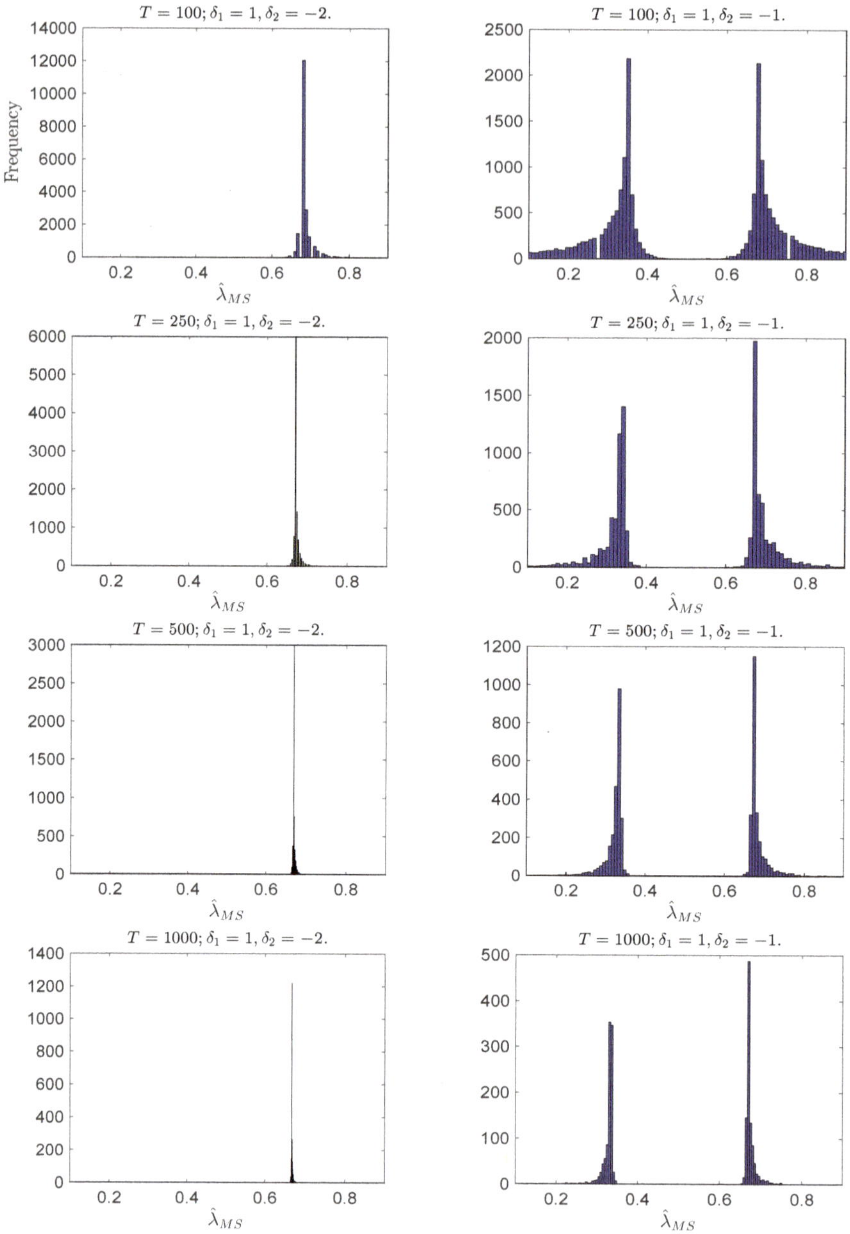

(a)

Figure 1. *Cont.*

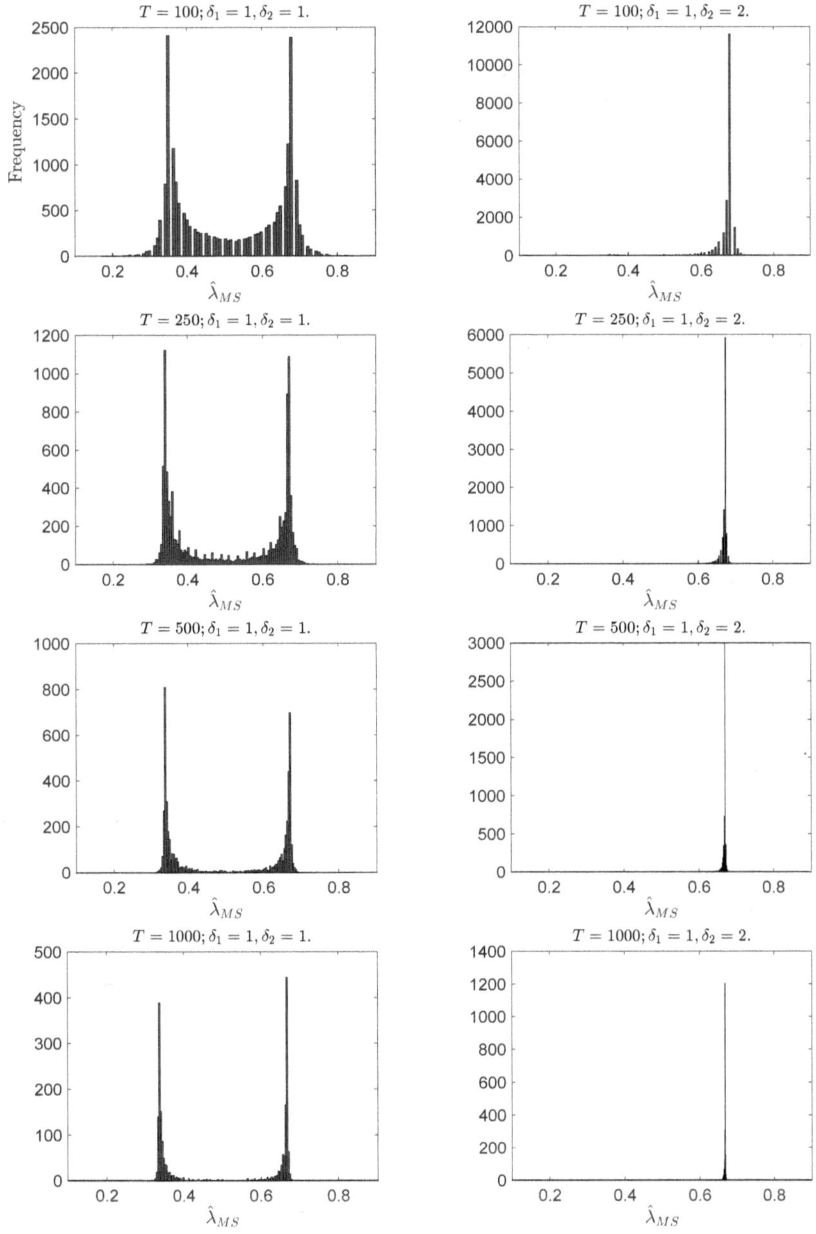

(b)

Figure 1. *Cont.*

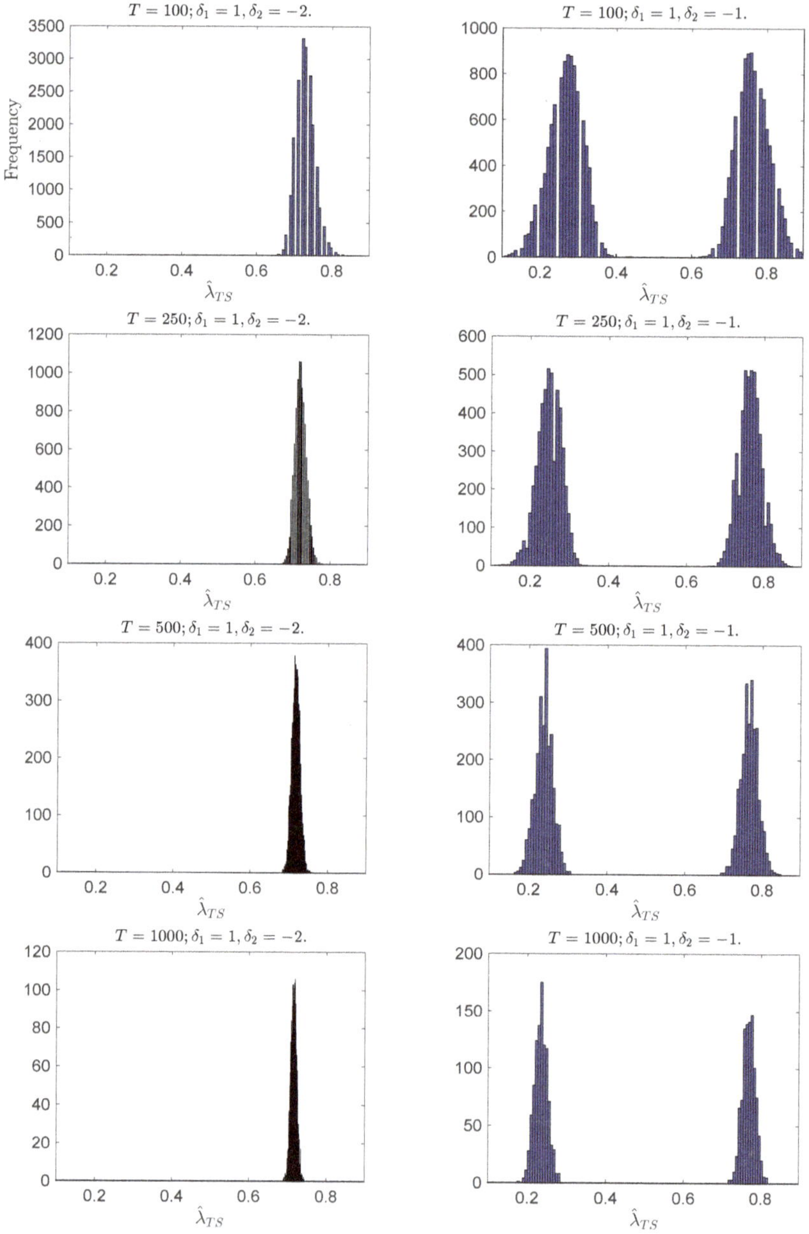

(c)

Figure 1. *Cont.*

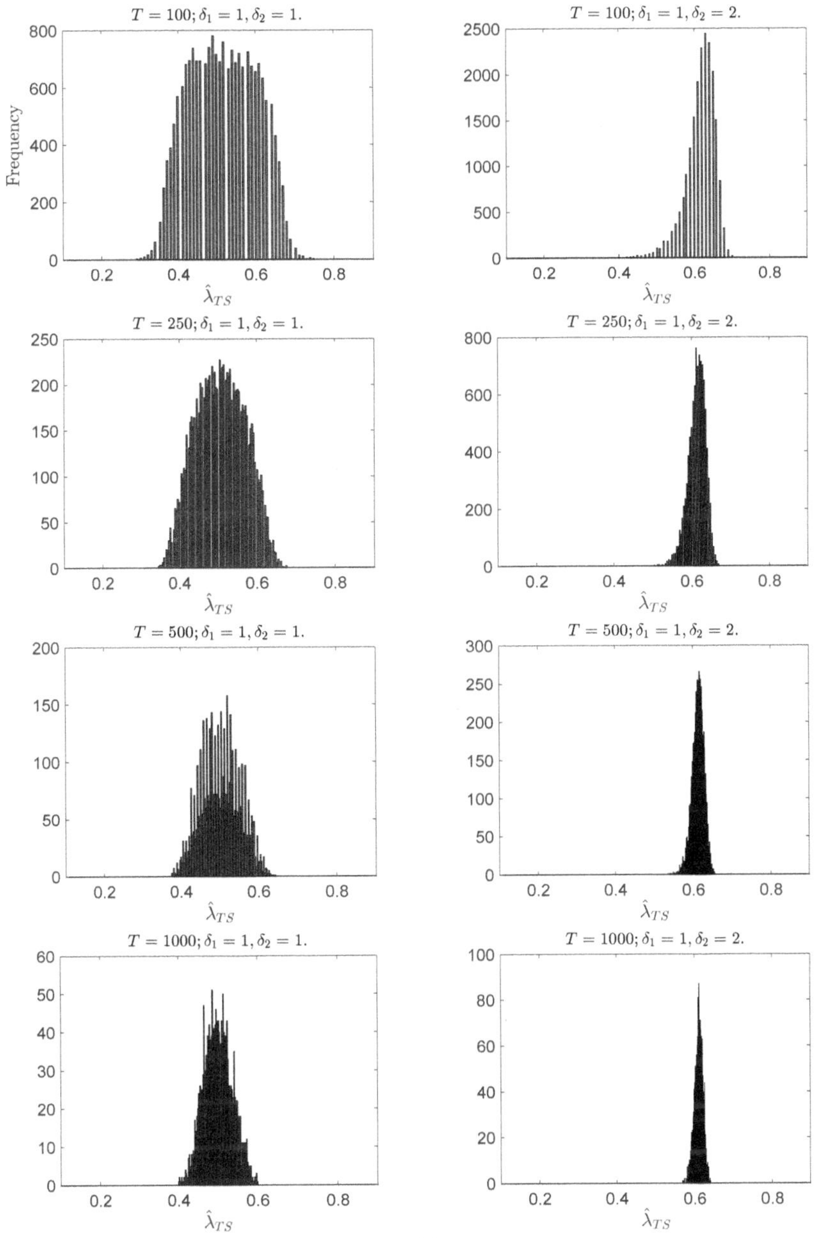

(**d**)

Figure 1. Histograms of the single break point estimator $\hat{\lambda}_{MS}$ or $\hat{\lambda}_{TS}$ when $\{\lambda_1^c, \lambda_2^c\} = \{1/3, 2/3\}$ and $\delta_1 = 1$ always. From top to bottom on each page: T = 100, 250, 500, 1000. (**a**) Histograms of $\hat{\lambda}_{MS}$ when $\nu = -2(\delta_2 = -2), -1(\delta_2 = -1)$; (**b**) Histograms of $\hat{\lambda}_{MS}$ when $\nu = 1(\delta_2 = 1), 2(\delta_2 = 2)$; (**c**) Histograms of $\hat{\lambda}_{TS}$ when $\nu = -2(\delta_2 = -2), -1(\delta_2 = -1)$; (**d**) Histograms of $\hat{\lambda}_{TS}$ when $\nu = 1(\delta_2 = 1), 2(\delta_2 = 2)$.

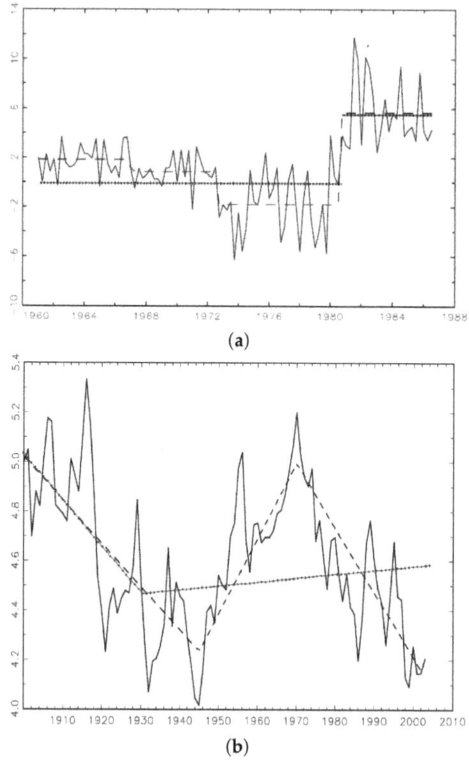

Figure 2. Single break point estimate (dotted line) while multiple mean shifts or trend shifts exist (dashed line). (a) US ex-post real interest rate during Q1 1961–Q3 1986; (b) Primary commodity price index (Copper) relative to the price of manufacture during 1900–2003.

4. Limits of the Break Point Estimators when the Break Magnitudes are Fixed

Similar to the discussion in Bai (1997) [2] for the mean shift results, the limits of the single trend break point estimator $\hat{\lambda}_{TS}$ are derived in this section when the break sizes are fixed and the data sequences have two trend breaks.

Theorem 1. *Assume there are two break fractions λ_1^c and λ_2^c with fixed break magnitudes in models (1) and (3) while the break number is underspecified as one.*

1. *For the mean shift model (1), under assumption (5) with fixed break magnitudes $\delta_1 = \delta_1^*$ and $\delta_2 = \delta_2^*$, the break point estimator $\hat{\lambda}_{MS}$ converges to one of the true breaks:*

$$(\hat{\lambda}_{MS} - \arg\max_{\lambda \in \Lambda} |G2_{MS}(\lambda, \lambda_1^c) + \nu \cdot G2_{MS}(\lambda, \lambda_2^c)|) = O_p(T^{-1/2}), \quad (8)$$

where $\nu = \delta_2^* / \delta_1^*$ and

$$G2_{MS}(\lambda, \lambda^c) \doteq \frac{\Psi(\lambda, \lambda^c)}{\sqrt{\lambda(1-\lambda)}},$$

$$\Psi(\lambda, \lambda^c) \doteq \begin{cases} (1-\lambda^c)\lambda, & \text{if } \lambda \le \lambda^c \\ (1-\lambda)\lambda^c, & \text{if } \lambda > \lambda^c \end{cases}.$$

Essentially

$$(\hat{\lambda}_{MS} - \lambda_1^c) = O_p(T^{-1/2}),\ \ if\ \ \frac{\lambda_1^c}{\lambda_2^c}\delta_1^2 \geq \frac{(1-\lambda_2^c)}{(1-\lambda_1^c)}\delta_2^2;\ (\hat{\lambda}_{MS} - \lambda_2^c) = O_p(T^{-1/2}),\ \ otherwise. \quad (9)$$

2. *For the trend shift model (3), under assumption (5) with fixed break magnitudes $\delta_1 = \delta_1^*$ and $\delta_2 = \delta_2^*$, the break point estimator $\hat{\lambda}_{TS}$ has the following limit:*

$$(\hat{\lambda}_{TS} - \arg\max_{\lambda \in \Lambda} |G2_{TS}(\lambda, \lambda_1^c) + \nu \cdot G2_{TS}(\lambda, \lambda_2^c)|) = O_p(T^{-3/2}), \quad (10)$$

where $\nu = \delta_2^* / \delta_1^*$ and

$$G2_{TS}(\lambda, \lambda^c) \doteq \frac{\int_0^1 F(r,\lambda)F(r,\lambda^c)dr}{\sqrt{\int_0^1 F(r,\lambda)^2 dr}},$$

$$F(r,\lambda) \doteq \begin{cases} \lambda^3 - 2\lambda^2 + \lambda - (2\lambda^3 - 3\lambda^2 + 1)r, & if\ r \leq \lambda \\ \lambda^3 - 2\lambda^2 - (2\lambda^3 - 3\lambda^2)r, & if\ r > \lambda \end{cases}.$$

The limit of $\hat{\lambda}_{MS}$ is either λ_1^c or λ_2^c as shown in Figure 3, which is consistent with the results in Bai (1997) [2] using a different theoretical framework. Not surprisingly, $G2_{MS}(\lambda, \lambda_i^c)$ is maximized at λ_i^c and $\hat{\lambda}_{MS}$ converges to one of the true break points.

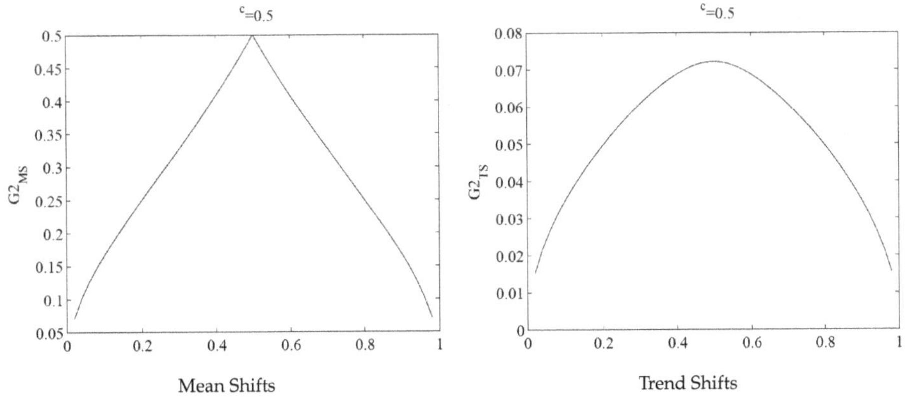

Figure 3. $G2_{MS}(\lambda, \lambda^c)$ and $G2_{TS}(\lambda, \lambda^c)$ with $\lambda^c = 0.5$.

The limit of $\hat{\lambda}_{TS}$ has different patterns. It is still true that $G2_{TS}(\lambda, \lambda_i^c)$ achieves a maximum at $\lambda = \lambda_i^c$ as shown in Figure 3. What makes it different from the mean shift case is when we sum up the two $G2_{TS}$ terms, the function smooths out through the two peaks at each λ_i^c. Hence, when the number of trend breaks is two while assumed to be one, $|G2_{TS}(\lambda, \lambda_1^c) + \nu \cdot G2_{TS}(\lambda, \lambda_2^c)|$ peaks neither at λ_1^c nor at λ_2^c. Figure 4 plots $|G2(\lambda, \lambda_1^c) + \nu \cdot G2(\lambda, \lambda_2^c)|$ with $\nu = \pm 1$ and $\lambda_1^c = 1/4$ and $\lambda_2^c = 3/4$. In both cases $|G2(\lambda, \lambda_1^c) + \nu \cdot G2(\lambda, \lambda_2^c)|$ peaks at neither of the true break points. Certainly, if $|\nu|$ is smaller than 1, $\hat{\lambda}_{TS}$ will be closer to λ_1^c; and if $|\nu|$ is bigger than 1, $\hat{\lambda}_{TS}$ will be closer to λ_2^c. This clearly explains the reason for the inconsistency of the trend shift break point estimator when the break number is underspecified.

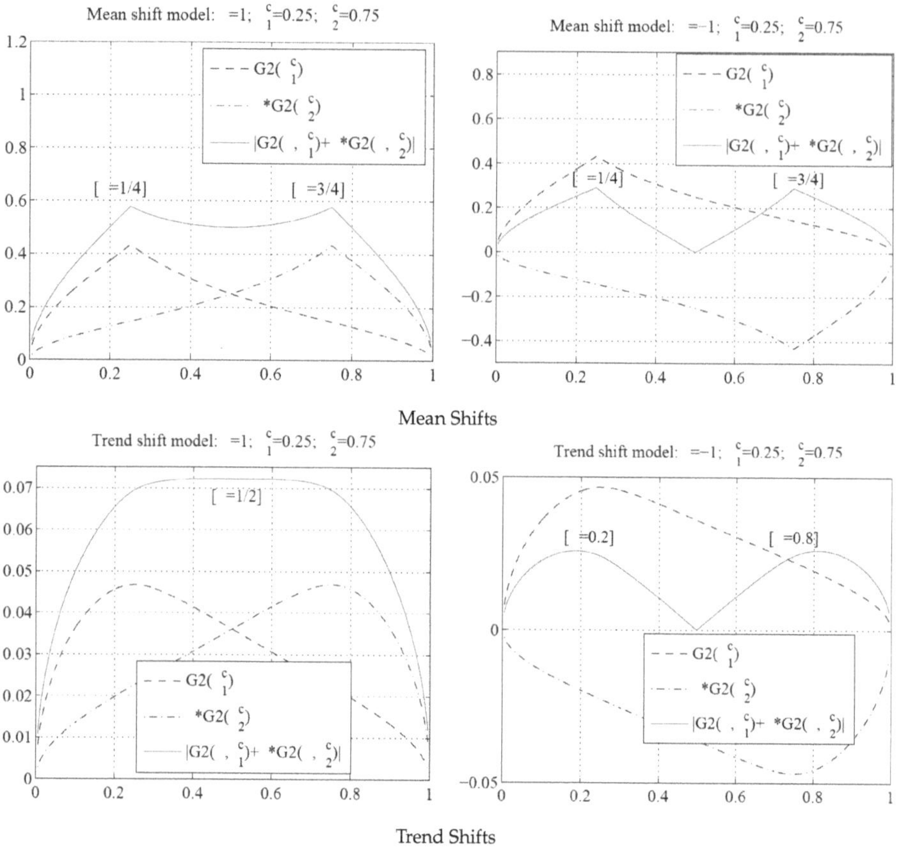

Figure 4. $|G2_{MS}(\lambda, \lambda_1^c) + \nu \cdot G2_{MS}(\lambda, \lambda_2^c)|$ for mean shift model and $|G2_{TS}(\lambda, \lambda_1^c) + \nu \cdot G2_{TS}(\lambda, \lambda_2^c)|$ for trend shift model, where $\nu = 1$ and -1, $\{\lambda_1^c, \lambda_2^c\} = \{1/4, 3/4\}$.

Figure 5 plots the λ's where $|G2_{TS}(\lambda, \lambda_1^c) + \nu \cdot G2_{TS}(\lambda, \lambda_2^c)|$ is maximized along ν when $\{\lambda_1^c, \lambda_2^c\} = \{1/3, 2/3\}$ and $\{1/4, 3/4\}$. When $\nu = 0$, $|G2_{TS}(\lambda, \lambda_1^c) + \nu \cdot G2_{TS}(\lambda, \lambda_2^c)|$ is maximized at λ_1^c. When $|\nu|$ goes to ∞, the limit of the break point estimator will be the true break λ_2^c. Other than these practically uninteresting cases, the limits of $\arg\max\{|G2_{TS}(\lambda, \lambda_1^c) + \nu \cdot G2_{TS}(\lambda, \lambda_2^c)|\}$ will not be the true break points. Take $\{\lambda_1^c, \lambda_2^c\} = \{1/3, 2/3\}$ as an example. When $\nu < -1$, the limiting point is greater than $2/3$. When $-1 < \nu < 0$, the limiting point is less than $1/3$. In both cases, the limiting points are beyond the range of the two true breaks. When $\nu > 0$, the limiting points are between the true breaks. When $\nu = 1$, the limiting point is at $\lambda = 0.5$, the trend shift break point estimator is far away from the true breaks. As ν goes away from 1, the limit of the trend shift break point estimator gets closer to one of the true breaks. The limits tell us the magnitude of the discrepancy between the spurious break and true breaks. Numerically when $|\nu| > 4.3$ or $|\nu| < \frac{1}{4.3}$, the limits of the spurious break point will be between $\pm 2.5\%$ of the true breaks. This threshold can be extended to other cases with different break locations.

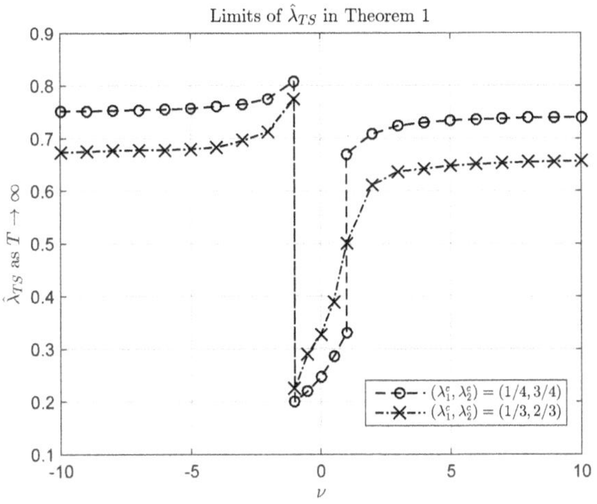

Figure 5. Limits of $\hat{\lambda}_{TS}$ in Theorem 1 when $\{\lambda_1^c, \lambda_2^c\} = \{1/3, 2/3\}$ and $\{1/4, 3/4\}$ along $\nu = -10, \cdots, 10$.

We summarize the findings on the consistency/inconsistency of $\hat{\lambda}_{MS}$ and $\hat{\lambda}_{TS}$ under assumption (5) as follows:

1. For the mean shift model with two breaks, if the break magnitudes are not zero, the single break point estimator $\hat{\lambda}_{MS}$ is consistent for either λ_1 or λ_2:

$$\lim_{T\to\infty} \hat{\lambda}_{MS} \to \lambda_1^c \ \textit{or} \ \lambda_2^c.$$

2. For the trend shift model[1] with two breaks, if the break magnitudes are not zero, the single break point estimator $\hat{\lambda}_{TS}$ is inconsistent for either λ_1 or λ_2:

$$\lim_{T\to\infty} \hat{\lambda}_{TS} \not\to \lambda_1^c \ \textit{and} \ \lim_{T\to\infty} \hat{\lambda}_{TS} \not\to \lambda_2^c.$$

The limit depends on λ_1^c, λ_2^c, and ν:

$$\lim_{T\to\infty} \hat{\lambda}_{TS} = \arg\max_{\lambda\in\Lambda} |G2_{TS}(\lambda, \lambda_1^c) + \nu \cdot G2_{TS}(\lambda, \lambda_2^c)|.$$

5. Limiting Distributions of $\hat{\lambda}_{MS}$ and $\hat{\lambda}_{TS}$ by Employing Pitman Drifts

As shown in the literature, asymptotic results derived under Pitman drifts often closely approximate the finite sample behavior of the test statistics or estimators involved. In the following, the limiting distributions of $\hat{\lambda}_{TS}$ and $\hat{\lambda}_{MS}$ are developed under Pitman drifts.

Theorem 2. *Assume there are two break points λ_1^c and λ_2^c in the linear model while the break number is underspecified as one.*

---

1 If DU_t's are included together with DT_t's in model (3), under the condition of fixed break magnitudes, the trend shifts will dominate the mean shifts in the (in)consistency of the break point estimator, following the results in Theorem 1. If $[t \cdot DU_t]$'s are included in model (3), the slope change will force a large level shift. Under this condition, the consistency property of mean shifts will be dominant and the inconsistency problem in break point estimator will not persist anymore.

1. *For the mean shift model (1), under assumptions (5) and $\delta_1 = T^{-1/2}\delta_1^*$ and $\delta_2 = T^{-1/2}\delta_2^*$, where δ_1^* and δ_2^* are constant scalars, the break point estimator $\hat{\lambda}_{MS}$ has the following limiting distribution:*

$$\hat{\lambda}_{MS} \Rightarrow \arg\max_{\lambda\in\Lambda}\{\frac{[(\lambda W(1) - W(\lambda)) + M_1\Psi(\lambda,\lambda_1^c) + M_2\Psi(\lambda,\lambda_2^c)]^2}{\lambda(1-\lambda)}\}, \tag{11}$$

where $M_1 \doteq \frac{\delta_1^*}{d(1)}$, $M_2 \doteq \frac{\delta_2^*}{d(1)}$, and

$$\Psi(\lambda,\lambda^c) \doteq \begin{cases} (1-\lambda^c)\lambda, & \text{if } \lambda \le \lambda^c \\ (1-\lambda)\lambda^c, & \text{if } \lambda > \lambda^c \end{cases}.$$

2. *For the trend shift model (3), under assumptions (5) and $\delta_1 = T^{-3/2}\delta_1^*$ and $\delta_2 = T^{-3/2}\delta_2^*$, where δ_1^* and δ_2^* are constant scalars, the break point estimator $\hat{\lambda}_{TS}$ has the following limiting distributions:*

$$\begin{aligned}\hat{\lambda}_{TS} \Rightarrow \quad & \arg\max_{\lambda\in\Lambda}\{[\int_0^1 F(r,\lambda)dW(r) + M_1\int_0^1 F(r,\lambda)F(r,\lambda_1^c)dr + \\ & M_2\int_0^1 F(r,\lambda)F(r,\lambda_2^c)dr]^2 \int_0^1 F(r,\lambda)^2 dr\},\end{aligned} \tag{12}$$

where $M_1 \doteq \frac{\delta_1^*}{d(1)} \equiv \frac{\delta_1 T^{3/2}}{d(1)}$, $M_2 \doteq \frac{\delta_2^*}{d(1)} \equiv \frac{\delta_2 T^{3/2}}{d(1)}$, $v = M_2/M_1 \equiv \delta_2/\delta_1$, and $F(r,\lambda)$ is defined in Theorem 1.

The asymptotics in Theorem 2 are an extension of work by Yang (2012) [10] from the single-break case to the multiple-break case. To understand the effect of M_1, λ_1^c, M_2, and λ_2^c on the limiting distributions, I decompose the part inside the arg min in Equations (11) and (12) into three parts, where

$$\begin{aligned}G_{MS}(\lambda,\lambda_1^c,\lambda_2^c) &\doteq G1_{MS}(\lambda) + M_1\cdot G2_{MS}(\lambda,\lambda_1^c) + M_2\cdot G2_{MS}(\lambda,\lambda_2^c) \\ &\doteq \frac{(\lambda W(1)-W(\lambda))}{\sqrt{\lambda(1-\lambda)}} + M_1\cdot\frac{\Psi(\lambda,\lambda_1^c)}{\sqrt{\lambda(1-\lambda)}} + M_2\cdot\frac{\Psi(\lambda,\lambda_2^c)}{\sqrt{\lambda(1-\lambda)}};\end{aligned} \tag{13}$$

$$\begin{aligned}G_{TS}(\lambda,\lambda^c) &\doteq G1_{TS}(\lambda) + M_1\cdot G2_{TS}(\lambda,\lambda_1^c) + M_2\cdot G2_{TS}(\lambda,\lambda_2^c) \\ &\doteq \frac{\int_0^1 F(r,\lambda)dW(r)}{\sqrt{\int_0^1 F(r,\lambda)^2 dr}} + \\ &\quad M_1\cdot\frac{\int_0^1 F(r,\lambda)F(r,\lambda_1^c)dr}{\sqrt{\int_0^1 F(r,\lambda)^2 dr}} + M_2\cdot\frac{\int_0^1 F(r,\lambda)F(r,\lambda_2^c)dr}{\sqrt{\int_0^1 F(r,\lambda)^2 dr}}.\end{aligned} \tag{14}$$

For the asymptotic distribution of $\hat{\lambda}_{MS}$, with the form of $G1_{MS}(\lambda) + M_1\cdot G2_{MS}(\lambda,\lambda_1^c) + M_2\cdot G2_{MS}(\lambda,\lambda_2^c)$ in the limiting distributions, Theorem 2 provides a bridge between the asymptotics under the null of no breaks and the asymptotics under local alternatives of up to two breaks.

The asymptotics are continuous at $\{M_1, M_2\} = \{0,0\}$, i.e., M_1 and M_2 could be as small as possible in the asymptotics. When M_1 and M_2 are small, the random component $G1_{MS}$ dominates G_{MS} and the distribution is close to the case of no breaks. For a small M, $\hat{\lambda}_{TS}$ concentrates more around the middle range exhibiting a bell shape, while $\hat{\lambda}_{MS}$ concentrates more around the boundaries exhibiting a U shape. The detailed explanation is given in Yang (2012) [10]. For a moderate M, the limiting distribution of $\hat{\lambda}_{MS}$ exhibits a shape of W, resulting from the mixed effects of $G1_{MS}$ and $G2_{MS}$ in the asymptotics. If $T \to \infty$, both M_1 and M_2 increase to ∞,

$$\lim_{T\to\infty} \hat{\lambda}_{MS,TS} \quad \to \quad \arg\max_{\lambda\in\Lambda} |G2_{MS,TS}(\lambda, \lambda_1^c) + \nu \cdot G2_{MS,TS}(\lambda, \lambda_2^c)|.$$

The limiting distributions in Theorem 2 are nonstandard. M_1, M_2, λ_1^c and λ_2^c show up in the approximations, and capture the effects of M's and λ^c's on the asymptotics. Besides other deterministic variables in Theorem 2, the main random variables in the asymptotic distributions are functions of a Wiener process. The Wiener process in the asymptotic distributions was approximated by using standard normal *i.i.d.* random deviates. Integrals were approximated by normalized partial sums of 1000 steps using 10,000 replications.

Figure 6 plots the finite sample distributions of $\hat{\lambda}_{MS}$ and $\hat{\lambda}_{TS}$ with $T = 100$ and asymptotic distributions for $\mu = \beta = 0$, $\{\lambda_1^c, \lambda_2^c\} = \{1/3, 2/3\}$. Errors are *i.i.d.* $N(0,1)$. The left panels of Figure 6 are for $\hat{\lambda}_{MS}$ and the right panels are for $\hat{\lambda}_{TS}$. From the top to the bottom are the cases of $\{\delta_1, \delta_2\} = \{1,1\}$, $\{5,5\}$, $\{1,-1\}$, and $\{5,-5\}$. The pdfs of $\hat{\lambda}_{MS}$ and $\hat{\lambda}_{TS}$ are plotted in separated figures with the same scales to show the performance comparison in the presence of an underspecified break number. Kernel smoothing is used to obtain the pdf based on the simulations. Figure 6 compares the asymptotic limits given by Theorem 2 to finite sample distributions. The two lines in each panel are near-identical, which shows that the asymptotics does a good job of approximating finite sample distributions of the break point estimators.

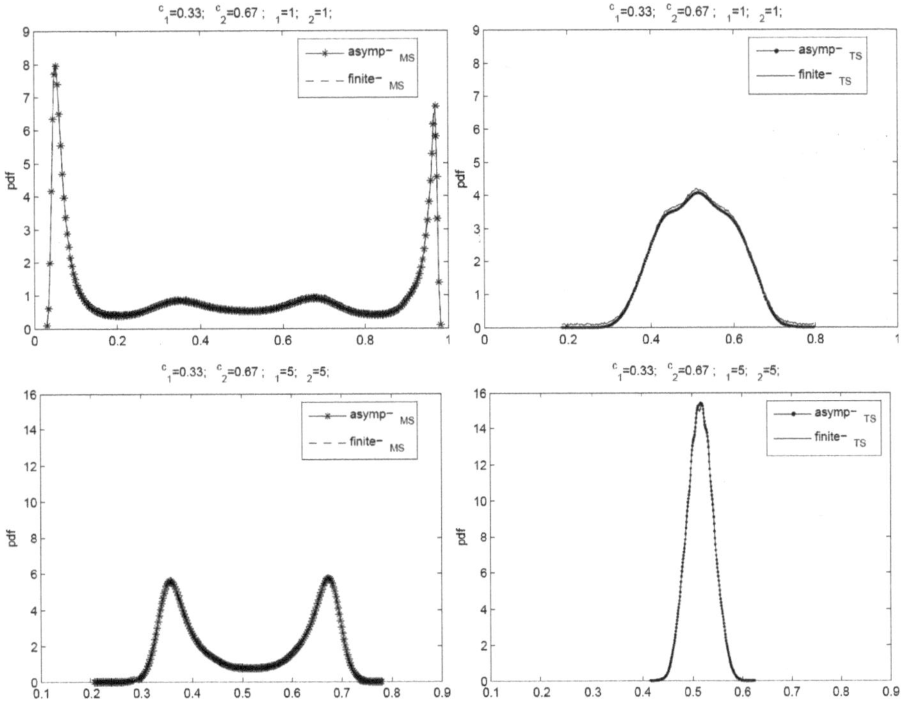

Figure 6. *Cont.*

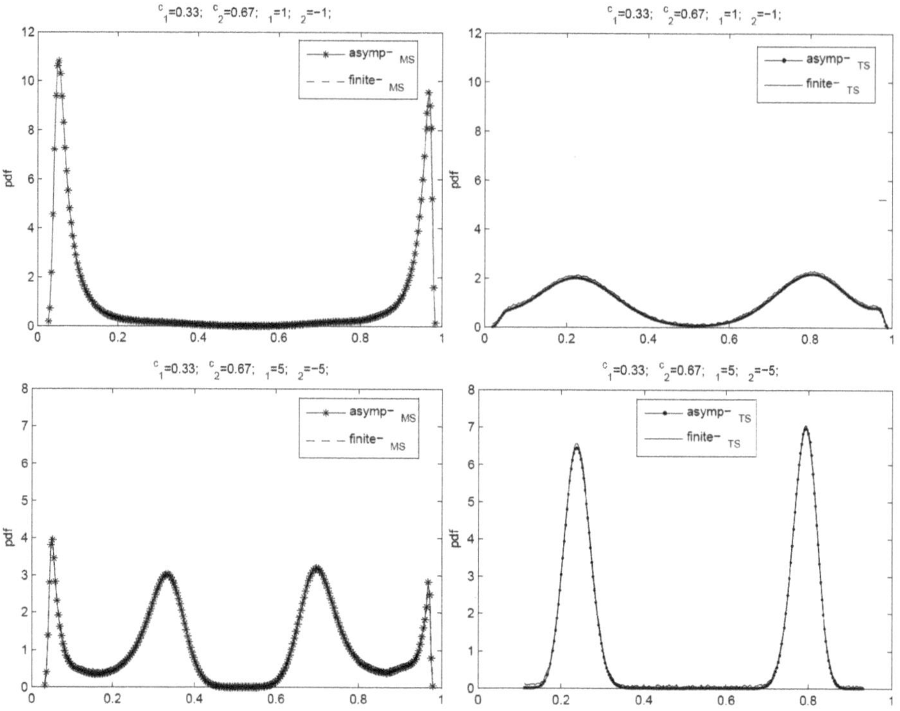

Figure 6. The asymptotic distributions and the finite sample distributions of $\hat{\lambda}_{TS}$ and $\hat{\lambda}_{MS}$ when $T = 100$, $\{\lambda_1^c, \lambda_2^c\} = \{1/3, 2/3\}$, and u_t is an *i.i.d.* $N(0,1)$ process. The left: the distributions of $\hat{\lambda}_{MS}$; the right: the distributions of $\hat{\lambda}_{TS}$. From the top to the bottom: $\{\delta_1, \delta_2\} = \{1,1\}$, $\{5,5\}$, $\{1,-1\}$, and $\{5,-5\}$.

6. Conclusions

This paper analyzes the consistency of trend shift break point estimators when the number of breaks is underspecifed. The limit of the trend shift break point estimator for fixed break sizes is shown to be dependent on the break magnitudes and locations. In general, the trend shift break point estimator does not consistently estimate one of the true break points. Using the Pitman drift assumption, the limiting distribution of the trend shift break point estimator is shown to closely resemble the finite sample distributions.

Acknowledgments: I am very grateful to Tim Vogelsang for his continuous guidance and encouragement, and to Pierre Perron, two anonymous referees for their very helpful and constructive comments. I would also like to thank Mark Nichols and the participants at "The International Symposium on Recent Developments in Econometric Theory with Applications in Honor of Professor Takeshi Amemiya".

Conflicts of Interest: The author declares no conflict of interest.

Appendix A.

Appendix A.1. Proof of Theorem 1

Theorem 1 can be proved simply by following the steps provided in the proof of Theorem 2 below.

Appendix A.2. Proof of Theorem 2

Appendix A.2.1. Asymptotic Distribution of $\hat{\lambda}_{MS}$

Let SSR^0_{MS} be the SSR under the assumption of no breaks. Following Equation (6), we obtain

$$SSR^0_{MS} - SSR_{MS}(\lambda) = [\sum_{t=1}^{T} \tilde{DU}_t(\lambda)^2]\hat{\delta}^2_{MS}.$$

The OLS estimator of δ from (2) is given by

$$\hat{\delta}_{MS} = [\sum_{t=1}^{T} \tilde{DU}_t^2(\lambda)]^{-1} \sum_{t=1}^{T} [\tilde{DU}_t(\lambda)\tilde{y}_t],$$

where $\{\tilde{DU}_t(\lambda)\}$ and $\{\tilde{y}_t\}$ are the residuals from the OLS regressions of $\{DU_t(\lambda)\}$ and $\{y_t\}$ on $[1]'$,

$$\tilde{DU}_t(\lambda) \;=\; DU_t(\lambda) - \sum_{t=1}^{T} DU_t/T = DU_t(\lambda) - \bar{DU}(\lambda).$$

When the DGP is given by (1), simple algebra gives

$$\begin{aligned}
\hat{\delta}_{MS} &= [\sum_{t=1}^{T} \tilde{DU}_t^2(\lambda)]^{-1} \sum_{t=1}^{T} \tilde{DU}_t(\lambda)[\tilde{DU}_t(\lambda_1^c)\delta_1 + \tilde{DU}_t(\lambda_2^c)\delta_2 + u_t] \\
&= [\sum_{t=1}^{T} \tilde{DU}_t^2(\lambda)]^{-1} \sum_{t=1}^{T} \tilde{DU}_t(\lambda)[\tilde{DU}_t(\lambda_1^c)\delta_1 + \tilde{DU}_t(\lambda_2^c)\delta_2] \\
&\quad + [\sum_{t=1}^{T} \tilde{DU}_t^2(\lambda)]^{-1} \sum_{t=1}^{T} \tilde{DU}_t(\lambda)u_t.
\end{aligned}$$

Multiplying both sides of the above equation by $T^{1/2}$, we have

$$\begin{aligned}
T^{1/2}\hat{\delta}_{MS} &= [T^{-1}\sum_{t=1}^{T} \tilde{DU}_t^2(\lambda)]^{-1}[T^{-1}\sum_{t=1}^{T} \tilde{DU}_t(\lambda)(\tilde{DU}_t(\lambda_1^c)\delta_1^* + \tilde{DU}_t(\lambda_2^c)\delta_2^*)] + \\
&\quad [T^{-1}\sum_{t=1}^{T} \tilde{DU}_t^2(\lambda)]^{-1}[T^{-1/2}\sum_{t=1}^{T} \tilde{DU}_t(\lambda)u_t].
\end{aligned}$$

Using

$$[T^{-1}\sum_{t=1}^{T} \tilde{DU}_t^2(\lambda)] \Rightarrow \int_0^1 [I(r > \lambda) - (1-\lambda)]^2 dr = \lambda(1-\lambda),$$

and

$$\begin{aligned}
[T^{-1}\sum_{t=1}^{T} \tilde{DU}_t(\lambda)\tilde{DU}_t(\lambda^c)] &\Rightarrow \int_0^1 [I(r > \lambda) - (1-\lambda)][I(r > \lambda^c) - (1-\lambda^c)]dr \\
&= \begin{cases} (1-\lambda^c)\lambda, & \text{if } \lambda \le \lambda^c \\ (1-\lambda)\lambda^c, & \text{if } \lambda > \lambda^c \end{cases},
\end{aligned}$$

and

$$T^{-1/2}[\sum_{t=1}^{T}\tilde{DU}_t(\lambda)u_t] \Rightarrow d(1)\int_0^1 [I(r>\lambda)-(1-\lambda)]dW(r)$$
$$= d(1)[\lambda W(1)-W(\lambda)],$$

we obtain

$$T^{1/2}\hat{\delta}_{MS} \Rightarrow \frac{\delta_1^*}{\lambda(1-\lambda)}\Psi(\lambda,\lambda_1^c)+\frac{\delta_2^*}{\lambda(1-\lambda)}\Psi(\lambda,\lambda_2^c)+\frac{d(1)}{\lambda(1-\lambda)}[\lambda W(1)-W(\lambda)],$$

where

$$\Psi(\lambda,\lambda^c)=\begin{cases}(1-\lambda^c)\lambda, & \text{if } \lambda\le\lambda^c\\ (1-\lambda)\lambda^c, & \text{if } \lambda>\lambda^c\end{cases}.$$

From this result, it immediately follows that

$$SSR_{MS}^0 - SSR_{MS}(\lambda)$$
$$\Rightarrow \frac{1}{\sqrt{\lambda(1-\lambda)}}[d(1)(\lambda W(1)-W(\lambda))+\delta_1^*\Psi(\lambda,\lambda_1^c)+\delta_2^*\Psi(\lambda,\lambda_2^c)]^2.$$

Applying the CMT theorem gives

$$\hat{\lambda}_{MS} = \arg\max_{\lambda\in\Lambda}\{SSR_{MS}^0-SSR_{MS}(\lambda))$$
$$\Rightarrow \arg\max_{\lambda\in\Lambda}\{\frac{[(\lambda W(1)-W(\lambda))+M_1\Psi(\lambda,\lambda_1^c)+M_2\Psi(\lambda,\lambda_2^c)]^2}{\lambda(1-\lambda)}\},$$

where $M_1=\frac{\delta_1^*}{d(1)}$ and $M_2=\frac{\delta_2^*}{d(1)}$.

It is straightforward to show that $M_1G2(\lambda,\lambda_1^c)+M_2G2(\lambda,\lambda_2^c)$ is maximized at either λ_1^c or λ_2^c. The first derivative of $G2_{MS}$ w.r.t. λ is given by:

$$G2'_{MS}(\lambda,\lambda^c)=\begin{cases}\frac{(1-\lambda^c)\lambda}{2(1-\lambda)\sqrt{\lambda(1-\lambda)}}, & \text{if } \lambda\le\lambda^c\\ \frac{(1-\lambda)\lambda^c}{2(1-\lambda)\sqrt{\lambda(1-\lambda)}}, & \text{if } \lambda>\lambda^c\end{cases}.$$

Assume $\lambda_1^c<\lambda_2^c$, then it follows that

$$[M_1G2(\lambda,\lambda_1^c)+M_2G2(\lambda,\lambda_2^c)]'=M1\frac{(1-\lambda_1^c)\lambda}{2(1-\lambda)\sqrt{\lambda(1-\lambda)}}+M_2\frac{(1-\lambda_2^c)\lambda}{2(1-\lambda)\sqrt{\lambda(1-\lambda)}},$$
$$\text{when } \lambda\le\lambda_1^c;$$

$$[M_1G2(\lambda,\lambda_1^c)+M_2G2(\lambda,\lambda_2^c)]'=M_1\frac{(1-\lambda)\lambda_1^c}{2(1-\lambda)\sqrt{\lambda(1-\lambda)}}+M_2\frac{(1-\lambda_2^c)\lambda}{2(1-\lambda)\sqrt{\lambda(1-\lambda)}},$$
$$\text{when } \lambda_1^c\le\lambda\le\lambda_2^c;$$

and

$$[M_1G2(\lambda,\lambda_1^c)+M_2G2(\lambda,\lambda_2^c)]'=M_1\frac{(1-\lambda)\lambda_1^c}{2(1-\lambda)\sqrt{\lambda(1-\lambda)}}+M_2\frac{(1-\lambda)\lambda_2^c}{2(1-\lambda)\sqrt{\lambda(1-\lambda)}},$$
$$\text{when } \lambda\ge\lambda_2^c.$$

Through simple algebra, one can show that the peak values of $[M_1G2(\lambda,\lambda_1^c)+M_2G2(\lambda,\lambda_2^c)]$ will be obtained at either λ_1^c or λ_2^c.

Appendix A.2.2. Asymptotic Distribution of $\hat{\lambda}_{TS}$

Let SSR_{TS}^0 be the SSR under the assumption of no breaks. From Equation (7), we have the standard result that

$$SSR_{TS}^0 - SSR_{TS}(\lambda) = [\sum_{t=1}^{T}\tilde{DT}_t(\lambda)\tilde{DT}_t(\lambda)]\hat{\delta}_{TS}^2,$$

where

$$\hat{\delta}_{TS} = \sum_{t=1}^{T}\tilde{DT}_t(\lambda)\tilde{DT}_t(\lambda)]^{-1}\sum_{t=1}^{T}\tilde{DT}_t(\lambda)\tilde{y}_t.$$

$\{\tilde{DT}_t(\lambda)\}$ and $\{\tilde{y}_t\}$ are the residuals from the OLS regressions of $\{DT_t(\lambda)\}$ and $\{y_t\}$ on $[1\ \ t]'$.

When the DGP is given by (3), simple algebra gives

$$\begin{aligned}
&T^{3/2}\hat{\delta}_{TS}\\
=&\left[T^{-1}\sum_{t=1}^{T}T^{-1}\tilde{DT}_t(\lambda)\tilde{DT}_t(\lambda)T^{-1}\right]^{-1}\left[T^{-1}\sum_{t=1}^{T}T^{-1}\tilde{DT}_t(\lambda)\tilde{DT}_t(\lambda_1^c)T^{-1}(T^{3/2}\delta_1)+\right.\\
&\left.T^{-1}\sum_{t=1}^{T}T^{-1}\tilde{DT}_t(\lambda)\tilde{DT}_t(\lambda_2^c)T^{-1}(T^{3/2}\delta_2)\right]+\\
&\left[T^{-1}\sum_{t=1}^{T}T^{-1}\tilde{DT}_t(\lambda)\tilde{DT}_t(\lambda)T^{-1}\right]^{-1}\left[T^{-1/2}\sum_{t=1}^{T}T^{-1}\tilde{DT}_t(\lambda)u_t\right].
\end{aligned}$$

Using

$$T^{-1}\tilde{DT}_t(\lambda)\Rightarrow F(r,\lambda)\doteq(r-\lambda)1(r>\lambda)+(\lambda^3-2\lambda^2+\lambda)-(2\lambda^3-3\lambda^2+1)r,$$

and

$$T^{-1}\sum_{t=1}^{T}T^{-1}\tilde{DT}_t(\lambda)\tilde{DT}_t(\lambda^c)T^{-1}\ \Rightarrow\ \int_0^1F(r,\lambda)F(r,\lambda^c)dr,$$

and

$$T^{-1/2}\sum_{t=1}^{T}T^{-1}\tilde{DT}_t(\lambda)u_t\Rightarrow d(1)\int_0^1F(r,\lambda)dW(r),$$

we obtain

$$\begin{aligned}
&T^{3/2}\hat{\delta}_{TS}\\
\Rightarrow&[\int_0^1F(r,\lambda)^2dr]^{-1}[\delta_1^*\int_0^1F(r,\lambda)F(r,\lambda_1^c)dr+\delta_2^*\int_0^1F(r,\lambda)F(r,\lambda_2^c)dr]+\\
&[\int_0^1F(r,\lambda)^2dr]^{-1}[d(1)\int_0^1F(r,\lambda)dW(r)]\\
=&\frac{[\delta_1^*\int_0^1F(r,\lambda)F(r,\lambda_1^c)dr+\delta_2^*\int_0^1F(r,\lambda)F(r,\lambda_2^c)dr]+d(1)\int_0^1F(r,\lambda)dW(r)}{\int_0^1F(r,\lambda)^2dr}.
\end{aligned}$$

From this results, it immediately follows that

$$\begin{aligned} & [SSR^0_{TS} - SSR_{TS}(\lambda)] \\ = & [T^{3/2}\hat{\delta}_{TS}]^2[T^{-1}\sum_{t=1}^{T} T^{-1}\tilde{DT}_t(\lambda)\tilde{DT}_t(\lambda)T^{-1}] \\ \Rightarrow & \frac{\left[d(1)\int_0^1 F(r,\lambda)dW(r) + \delta_1^*\int_0^1 F(r,\lambda)F(r,\lambda_1^c)dr + \delta_2^*\int_0^1 F(r,\lambda)F(r,\lambda_2^c)dr\right]^2}{\int_0^1 F(r,\lambda)^2 dr}. \end{aligned}$$

Furthermore, using the CMT we obtain the limit of the break point estimator as

$$\begin{aligned} & \hat{\lambda}_{TS} \\ = & \arg\max_{\lambda\in\Lambda}\{SSR^0_{TS} - SSR_{TS}(\lambda)\} \\ \Rightarrow & \arg\max_{\lambda\in\Lambda}\{\left[\frac{\int_0^1 F(r,\lambda)dW(r)}{\sqrt{\int_0^1 F(r,\lambda)^2 dr}} + \right. \\ & \left. \frac{M_1\int_0^1 F(r,\lambda)F(r,\lambda_1^c)dr + M_2\int_0^1 F(r,\lambda)F(r,\lambda_2^c)dr}{\sqrt{\int_0^1 F(r,\lambda)^2 dr}}\right]^2\}, \end{aligned}$$

where $M_1 \doteq \frac{\delta_1^*}{d(1)} \equiv \frac{\delta_1 T^{3/2}}{d(1)}$ and $M_2 \doteq \frac{\delta_2^*}{d(1)} \equiv \frac{\delta_2 T^{3/2}}{d(1)}$.

Please refer to Yang (2012) [10] for more details about $\hat{\lambda}_{TS}$ and $\hat{\lambda}_{MS}$.

References

1. Bai, J.S. Least absolute deviation estimation of a shift. *Econom. Theory* **1995**, *11*, 403–436.
2. Bai, J.S. Estimating multiple breaks one at a time. *Econom. Theory* **1997**, *13*, 315–352.
3. Chong, T. *Consistency of Change-Point Estimators When the Number of Change Points in Structural Change Models is Underspecified*; Working Paper; Department of Economics, University of Rochester: Rochester, NY, USA, 1994.
4. Chong, T. Partial parameter consistency in a misspecified structural change model. *Econ. Lett.* **1995**, *49*, 351–357.
5. Bai, J.S.; Perron, P. Estimating and testing linear models with multiple structural breaks. *Econometrica* **1998**, *66*, 47–78.
6. Bai, J.S.; Perron, P. Computation and analysis of multiple structural change models. *J. Appl. Econom.* **2003**, *18*, 1–22.
7. Kejriwal, M.; Perron, P. A sequential procedure to determine the number of breaks in trend with an integrated or stationary noise component. *J. Time Ser. Anal.* **2010**, *31*, 305–328.
8. Perron, P.; Yabu, T. Estimating deterministic trends with an integrated or stationary noise component. *J. Econom.* **2009**, *151*, 56–69.
9. Perron, P.; Yabu, T. Testing for shifts in trend with an integrated or stationary noise component. *J. Bus. Econ. Stat.* **2009**, *27*, 369–396.
10. Yang, J. Break point estimators for a slope shift: levels versus first differences. *Econom. J.* **2012**, *15*, 154–169.

11. Yang, J. Essays on Estimation and Inference in Models with Deterministic Trends with and without Structural Change. Ph.D. Thesis, Department of Economics, Michigan State University, East Lansing, MI, USA, 2010.
12. Harvey, D.I.; Leybourne, S.J.; Taylor, A.M.R. Simple, robust and powerful tests of the breaking trend hypothesis. *Econom. Theory* **2009**, *25*, 995–1029.

econometrics

MDPI

Article

Testing for a Structural Break in a Spatial Panel Model

Aparna Sengupta

Bates White Economic Consulting, 1300 Eye street NW Washington DC 20005, USA; mainaparna@gmail.com; Tel.: +1-857-756-8567

Academic Editor: Pierre Perron
Received: 28 August 2016; Accepted: 24 February 2017; Published: 6 March 2017

Abstract: We consider the problem of testing for a structural break in the spatial lag parameter in a panel model (spatial autoregressive). We propose a likelihood ratio test of the null hypothesis of no break against the alternative hypothesis of a single break. The limiting distribution of the test is derived under the null when both the number of individual units N and the number of time periods T is large or N is fixed and T is large. The asymptotic critical values of the test statistic can be obtained analytically. We also propose a break-date estimator that can be employed to determine the location of the break point following evidence against the null hypothesis. We present Monte Carlo evidence to show that the proposed procedure performs well in finite samples. Finally, we consider an empirical application of the test on budget spillovers and interdependence in fiscal policy within the U.S. states.

Keywords: panel model; structural change; spatial econometrics; spatio-temporal; U.S. state budget

JEL Classification: C01; C22; C23; H72

---

1. Introduction

Spatial dependence represents a situation where values observed at one location or region depend on the values of neighboring observations at nearby locations. One may ask two questions: first, does this dependence stay the same over time; and second, what might cause the dependence to change? This paper answers the first question by proposing a likelihood ratio test of the null hypothesis of no change against the alternative hypothesis of a one-time change. In case there is evidence against the null hypothesis, the paper consequently proposes a break-date estimator. The second question has been reflected upon through an empirical application of budget spillovers in the U.S. states.

In the setup of spatial panel models with N individual units (geographic locations, such as countries and zip codes, or network units, like firms and individuals) observed over T number of periods, where the outcome of each unit depends on its "neighbor's" outcome, there exists a problem of endogeneity. Hence, such models are estimated using maximum likelihood or the generalized method of moments. Similar to the univariate time series case, in this paper a *sup* LR test is proposed, and the asymptotics are derived for large T cases.

In comparison to the vast literature on the change point for univariate series, the corresponding literature for panel data is quite small. One of the most popular and early tests in the univariate literature is the popular F test of Chow (1960) [1], which has been modified for cases of unknown and multiple break dates in Andrews (1993) [2], Andrews and Ploberger (1994) [3], and Bai and Perron (1998) [4], among others. Bai (1997) [5], Bai et al. (1998) [6], and Qu and Perron (2007) [7] have extended the single equation break models to multiple ones. They show that using multiple system improves the estimation precision of the break dates and the power of the tests. Perron (2006) [8] provides a survey of the literature.

In the panel data literature, Bai (2010) [9] establishes the consistency of the estimated common break point, achievable even if there is a single observation in a regime. The paper proposes a new framework for developing the limiting distribution for the estimated break point and lays down steps to construct confidence intervals. The least squares method is used for estimating breaks in means. Feng et al. (2009) [10] study a multiple regression model in a panel setting where a break occurs at an unknown common date. They establish the consistency and rate of convergence both for a fixed time horizon and large panels. In Feng et al. (2009) [10], the limiting distribution is derived without the assumption of shrinking magnitude of break. Liao (2008) [11] uses the Bayesian method for estimation and inference about structural breaks in a panel.

Han and Park (1989) [12] develop a multivariate CUSUM test in order to test for a structural break in panel data, and they apply the test to U.S. manufacturing goods trade data. Kao (2000) [13] proposes two classes of test statistics for detecting a break at an unknown date in panel data models with the time trend. The first is a fluctuation test, while the second is based on the mean and exponential Wald statistics of Andrews and Ploberger (1994) [3] and the maximum Wald statistic of Andrews (1993) [2]. De Wachter and Tzavalis (2012) [14] develop a break detecting testing procedure for the AR(p) linear panel data with exogenous or pre-determined regressors. The method accommodates structural break in the slope parameters, as well as fixed effects, and no assumption is imposed on the homogeneity of cross-sectional fixed effects. Pauwels et al. (2012) [15] provide a structural break test for heterogeneous panel data models, where the break affects some, but not all cross-section units in the panel. The test is robust to auto-correlated errors. The test statistic is based on comparing pre- and post-break sample statistics as in Chow (1960) [1].

A higher availability of geocoded socio-economic datasets has led to a vast expansion of the study of spatial interaction between economics agents. Moreover, the recursive relationship between agents in a network can be modeled using spatial econometric methods. Spatial dependence represents the transmission of developments across "neighboring" agents. Elhorst (2010) [16] provides detailed methodologies for estimating spatial panels and to compare competing models. The above tests in the panel literature do not explicitly consider the endogeneity problem in the model, which arises from the spatial dependence. We consider a spatial autoregressive model and provide a test for a break in the spatial lag parameter. To test for a change in the spatial dependence parameter, we propose a *sup* LR test similar to Bai (1999) [17]. Yu et al. (2008) [18] and Lee and Yu (2010) [19] provide the asymptotic properties of quasi-maximum likelihood estimators for spatial autoregressive panel data models with fixed effects. The results from Yu et al. (2008) [18] are used to derive the limit distribution of the *sup* LR test for large T. An estimator for the break date is proposed that can be employed once evidence against no break in the spatial lag parameter is obtained. The performance of this estimator, as well as the proposed test statistic in small samples is evaluated via a Monte Carlo study. Wied (2013) [20] develops a CUSUM-type test for time-varying parameters in a spatial autoregressive model for stock returns.

Case et al. (1993) [21] show that a state's budget expenditure depends on the spending of similar[1] states. Therefore, a rise in a "neighboring" state's expenditure results in an increase in the state's own expenditure. As an empirical application, we apply the likelihood ratio test to the budget dependence of U.S. states over time. The data consist of annual observations for the continental United States during the period 1960–2011. States that are economically similar are defined as neighbors. The test result shows that the null hypothesis of no break in the spatial dependence parameter is rejected, and the break date is estimated as 1982. The budget spillover is more pronounced post-break. Details of the results and intuitions on why there might be a break are discussed.

---

1 Case et al. (1993) [21] defines similar states in three different ways: (1) similar in location, (2) similar in income and (3) similar in racial composition.

The paper is organized as follows: in Section 2, the spatial lag model is presented and discussed. Section 3 provides motivating examples where the test can be applied. We propose a *sup* LR test, which is described in Section 4. The limiting distribution of the test is stated in Section 5. The outline of the proof is also provided in this section (details are in the Appendix A). In the event of a rejection of the null hypothesis, we propose a break date estimator in Section 6. The finite sample properties of the test and the estimator are discussed in Section 7. Finally, we apply the test to budget spillovers in U.S. states, in Section 8. It shows that there was a change in the budget dependence between similar income states. In Section 9, we provide the conclusion and possible next steps in research.

2. Spatial Lag Model

Let us consider a simple pooled linear regression model

$$y_{it} = x_{it}\beta + \epsilon_{it}, \tag{1}$$

where i is an index of cross-sectional dimension, with $i = 1,..., N$, and t is an index for the time dimension, with $t = 1,..., T$. We discuss all of the results using "time" as the second dimension; however, for a general spatial lag model, the second dimension could very well reflect another cross-sectional characteristic, such as the industry sector or the number of classes or groups. y_{it} is an observation on the dependent variable at i and t, x_{it} a $1 \times K$ vector of observations on the (exogenous) explanatory variables including the intercept, β a matching $K \times 1$ vector of regression coefficients and ϵ_{it} an error term. In stacked form, the simple pooled regression can be written as

$$y = x\beta + \epsilon, \tag{2}$$

with y a $NT \times 1$ vector, X a $NT \times K$ matrix and ϵ a $NT \times 1$ vector. In general, spatial dependence is present whenever the correlation across cross-sectional units is non-zero, and the pattern of non-zero correlations conforms to a specified neighbor relation. When the spatial correlation pertains to the dependent variable, it is known as a spatial lag model. The neighbor relation is expressed by means of a spatial weight matrix.

A spatial weights matrix W is a $N \times N$ positive matrix in which the rows and columns correspond to the cross-sectional observations. An element w_{ij} of the matrix expresses the prior strength of the interaction between location i (in the row of the matrix) and location j (column). This can be interpreted as the presence and strength of a link between nodes (the observations) in a network representation that matches the spatial weights' structure. In the simplest case, the weights matrix is binary, with $w_{ij} = 1$ when i and j are neighbors and $w_{ij} = 0$ when they are not. The choice of the weights is typically driven by geographic criteria, such as contiguity (sharing a common border) or distance. However, generalizations that incorporate notions of "economic" distance are increasingly being used, as well. By convention, the diagonal elements $w_{ii} = 0$. For computational simplicity and to aid the interpretation of the spatial variables, the weights are almost always standardized, such that the elements in each row sum to one, or $w^s_{ij} = w_{ij} / \sum_j w_{ij}$. Using the subscript to designate the matrix dimension, with W_N as the weights for the cross-sectional dimension and the observations stacked, the full $NT \times NT$ weights matrix becomes: $W_{NT} = I_T \otimes W_N$, with I_T an identity matrix of dimension T.

Unlike the time series case, where "neighboring" observations are directly incorporated into a model specification through a shift operator (example $t - 1$), in the spatial literature, the neighboring observations are included in the model specification by applying a spatial lag operator (W) to the dependent variable. A spatial lag operator constructs a new variable, which consists of the weighted average of the neighboring observations, with the weights as specified in W. The spatial lag model or mixed regressive spatial autoregressive model includes a spatially-lagged dependent variable as an explanatory variable in the regression specification. The word "spatial lag" is used to specify the inclusion of the neighboring observations. Similar to the time series "lag operator", Wy emphasizes the first-order location lag in the dependent variable. The spatial lag model can be written as

$$y = \rho(I_T \otimes W_N)y + X\beta + \epsilon \tag{3}$$

where ρ is the spatial autoregressive parameter and the parameter of interest in this paper.

2.1. Endogeneity Problem

The problem in the estimation of the model (3) is that, unlike the time series case, the spatial lag term is endogenous. This is the result of the two-directionality of the neighbor relation in space ("I am my neighbor's neighbor"), in contrast to the one-directionality in time dependence. Rewriting equation (3) in a reduced form:

$$y = [I_T \otimes (I_N - \rho W_N)^{-1}]X\beta + [I_T \otimes (I_N - \rho W_N)^{-1}]\epsilon \tag{4}$$

indicating that the joint determination of the values of the dependent variable in the spatial system is a function of the explanatory variables and error terms at all locations in the system. The presence of the spatially lagged errors in the reduced form illustrates the joint dependence of $W_N y_t$ and ϵ_t in each cross-section. In model estimation, the simultaneity is usually accounted for through instrumentation (IV and GMM estimation) or by specifying a complete distributional model (maximum likelihood estimation). In this paper, we use maximum likelihood estimation.

2.2. Maximum Likelihood Estimation

Assuming a Gaussian distribution for the error term, with $\epsilon \sim N(0, \sigma_\epsilon^2 I_{NT})$, the log-likelihood can be written as:

$$lnL = -\frac{NT}{2} ln2\pi\sigma_\epsilon^2 + Tln|I_N - \rho W_N| - \frac{1}{2\sigma_\epsilon^2}\epsilon'\epsilon \tag{5}$$

where $\epsilon = y - \rho(I_T \otimes W_N)y - X\beta$ and $|I_T \otimes (I_N - \rho W_N)| = Tln|I_N - \rho W_N|$ is the Jacobian of the spatial transformation. To avoid singularity or explosive processes, the parameter space P for the true spatial autoregressive parameter ρ is compact, and ρ_0 is in the interior of P.

Lee (2004) [22] discusses the asymptotic properties of the maximum likelihood estimators for the cross-section case. Yu et al. (2008) [18] and Lee and Yu (2010) [19] derive the properties for the spatial panel model with fixed effects. We use the properties of the maximum likelihood estimators to derive the asymptotic distribution of the test statistic.

3. Motivation

We consider the following model in a spatial lag model:

$$y_{it} = \begin{cases} x_{it}\beta + \rho_1 \sum\limits_{j=1}^{N} w_{ij}y_{jt} + \epsilon_{it} & \text{for } t = 1, ..., k_o, \\ x_{it}\beta + \rho_2 \sum\limits_{j=1}^{N} w_{ij}y_{jt} + \epsilon_{it} & \text{for } t = k_o + 1, ..., T \end{cases} \tag{6}$$

$\rho_1 \neq \rho_2$ means there is a change at an unknown date k_0. We propose a *sup* LR test of the null hypothesis of $\rho_1 = \rho_2$ against the alternative hypothesis of a change: $\rho_1 \neq \rho_2$. The test detects a structural break in the spatial dependence parameter. Following are some empirical models where the test can be applied, providing motivation for the test.

3.1. Sectoral Output

Acemoglu et al. (2012) [23] look into the intersectoral input-output linkages in the U.S. and shows how microeconomic idiosyncratic fluctuations lead to aggregate fluctuations. Defining the sectoral production function as,

$$x_i = z_i l_i^\alpha \prod_{j=1}^{n} x_{ij}^{\beta w_{ij}} \tag{7}$$

where x_i is the output of sector i, l_i is the amount of labor hired by the sector, $\alpha \in (0,1)$ is the share of labor, x_{ij} is the amount of commodity j used in the production of good i and z_i is the idiosyncratic productivity shock to sector i. The exponent $w_{ij} \geq 0$ designates the share of good j in the total intermediate input use of firms in sector i. In particular, $w_{ij} = 0$ if sector i does not use good j as input for production.

Acemoglu et al. (2012) [23] assume that the input shares of all sectors add up to one, so $\sum_j w_{ij} = 1$. With the assumption of market clearing, equation (7) can be rewritten (taking the log on both sides) as equation (3). In this case, labor will be an exogenous variable, and $\beta_1 \neq \beta_2$ would mean changes in the Cobb-Douglas parameter over time.

3.2. Cigarette Sales

Baltagi and Li (2004) [24] estimate a demand model for cigarettes based on a panel from 46 U.S. states and defining W based on the neighboring states:

$$log(C_{it}) = \beta_1 log(P_{it}) + \beta_2 log(Y_{it}) + \rho \sum_{j=1}^{N} w_{ij} log(C_{jt}) + \epsilon_{it} \tag{8}$$

where C_{it} is real per capita sales of cigarettes by persons of smoking age (14 years and older). This is measured in packs of cigarettes per capita. P_{it} is the average retail price of a pack of cigarettes measured in real terms. Y_{it} is real per capita disposable income. The spatial autocorrelation parameter shows the dependence of cigarette sales in the neighboring states. The tax policy on per packet cigarette differs by states, and this leads to substantial cross-state sales. However, over time, tax per packet has become more homogeneous, and hence, one could expect the parameter ρ to change over time. By testing the hypothesis that $\rho_1 = \rho_2$ against the alternative hypothesis of $\rho_1 \neq \rho_2$, we can check if the dependence on neighboring states has changed over time.

3.3. Budget Spillovers

Case et al. (1993) [21] showed that the U.S. states' budget expenditure depends on the spending of similar states:

$$G_{it} = X_{it}\beta + \rho \sum_{j=1}^{N} w_{ij} G_{jt} + \epsilon_{it} \tag{9}$$

where G_{it} is the per capita real government expenditure of state i in year t, X_{it} includes relevant control variables, income and demographic and $w_{ij} > 0$ if a state is the "neighbor" of another state. Case et al. (1993) [21] define "neighbor" in three different ways in the paper: (1) neighbors in location; (2) states having similar income and (3) states having similar racial composition. They found that if the neighboring state increases its budget spending by a dollar, then the state increases its budget expenditure by 70 cents. Policies have changed over the years, and one might be interested in testing if the spillover effect remains the same.

3.4. Other Network Motivations

In many of the network studies, the impact of the network is usually estimated by including Wy in the model, where W is the weighting matrix defining the network and y is the variable of concern. For example, a weighted average of the math test scores of students sitting beside student i determines student i's test score.

With increasing network data availability, we could have repeated samples from such network experiments and then be curious to know how the impact of the network changes over time. Our structural break test could be used in this respect.

4. Test

In this section, we describe the test statistic. The spatial lag model is given by:

$$y_{it} = x_{it}\beta_t + \rho_t \sum_{j=1}^{N} w_{ij}y_{jt} + \epsilon_{it} \tag{10}$$

where $\epsilon_{it} \sim N(0, \sigma^2_{\epsilon it})$. We want to test the null hypothesis:
$H_0 : \rho_1 = ... = \rho_T$ and $\beta_1 = ... = \beta_T$ and $\sigma^2_{\epsilon i1} = ... = \sigma^2_{\epsilon iT}$
against the alternative
$H_1 : \beta_1 = ... = \beta_T$ and $\sigma^2_{\epsilon i1} = ... = \sigma^2_{\epsilon iT}$, but there is an integer k_0, $1 < k_0 < T$,
such that $\rho_1 = ... = \rho_{k_0} \neq \rho_{k_0+1} = ... = \rho_T$.

Rewriting the panel model with a change point at k_0 in the parameter ρ,

$$y_{it} = \begin{cases} x_{it}\beta + \rho_1 \sum\limits_{j=1}^{N} w_{ij}y_{jt} + \epsilon_{it} & \text{for } t = 1, ..., k_o, \\ x_{it}\beta + \rho_2 \sum\limits_{j=1}^{N} w_{ij}y_{jt} + \epsilon_{it} & \text{for } t = k_o + 1, ..., T \end{cases} \tag{11}$$

where $\rho_1 \neq \rho_2$ means there is a change at an unknown date k_0. The problem can be described as testing $\rho_1 = \rho_2$ against $\rho_1 \neq \rho_2$.

Let us write twice the likelihood ratio as

$$2\Lambda_k = 2(lnL_k(\hat{\rho}_k, \hat{\beta}_k, \hat{\sigma}^2_k) + lnL^*_k(\hat{\rho}^*_k, \hat{\beta}_k, \hat{\sigma}^2_k) - lnL_T(\hat{\rho}_T, \hat{\beta}_T, \hat{\sigma}^2_T)), \tag{12}$$

where

- $lnL_k(\hat{\rho}_k, \hat{\beta}_k, \hat{\sigma}^2_k)$ is the log-likelihood defined for the sample that includes the observations $t = 1, .., k$
- $lnL^*_k(\hat{\rho}^*_k, \hat{\beta}_k, \hat{\sigma}^2_k)$ is the log-likelihood defined for the sample that includes the observations $t = k + 1, ..., T$
- $lnL_T(\hat{\rho}_T, \hat{\beta}_T, \hat{\sigma}^2_T)$ is the log-likelihood defined for the sample that includes the observations $t = 1, ..., T$

As k_0 is unknown, we use a maximally selected likelihood ratio and reject H_0 if

$$Z_t = \max_{[Tu] \leq k \leq [T(1-u)]} 2\Lambda_k \tag{13}$$

is large, where $0 < u < 1/2$, typically a small number is the trimming and [.] denotes the largest integer that is less than or equal to the argument. Therefore, the suggested test is to calculate the difference between the log-likelihood under an alternative hypothesis and the log-likelihood under null for every $[Tu] < k < [T(1-u)]$, and then, the test statistic is the maximum difference between them.

5. Limiting Distribution

In this section, we derive the asymptotic distribution of the test statistic. However, before that we specify the assumptions.

5.1. Assumptions

Assumptions on W_N:

Assumption 1. *$w_{ij} \geq 0$, $i \neq j$ for the off-diagonal elements of the spatial weight matrix W_N and its diagonal elements satisfy $w_{n,ii} = 0$ for i = 1,..,N.*

Assumption 2. *W_N is uniformly bounded in both row and column sums.*

Assumption 3. *$|I_T \otimes (I_N - \rho W_N)|$ is invertible for all $\rho \in$ P; moreover, P is compact, and ρ_0 is in the interior of P.*

Assumptions on X and ϵ:

Assumption 4. *ϵ_{it} are iid across i and t with $\epsilon \sim N(0, \sigma_\epsilon^2 I_{NT})$ and $E|\epsilon_{it}|^{4+\eta} < \infty$ for some $\eta > 0$.*

Assumption 5. *The matrices $\frac{1}{Nj}\sum_{i=1}^{N}\sum_{t=1}^{j} X_{it}X_{it}'$ and $\frac{1}{Nj}\sum_{i=1}^{N}\sum_{t=j+1}^{T} X_{it}X_{it}'$ have minimum eigenvalues bounded away from zero in probability for large j. Furthermore, it is assumed that $E||X_{it}^4|| < \infty$.*

Assumption on N and T:

Assumption 6. *N is a non-decreasing function of T and $T \to \infty$*

The following assumption is made to establish the theoretical result of the paper.

Assumption 7. *Let $G_N = W_N[I_N - \rho_N W_N]^{-1}$ and $\frac{1}{\sqrt{N}}(G_N X_{Nt}\beta_0)' = H_{Nt}$ then $H_{Nt} \Rightarrow H^*$ and $\frac{1}{NT}(G_N X_{Nt}\beta_0)'(G_N X_{Nt}\beta_0) \Rightarrow H^{*'}H^*$.*

Assumption 1 is a standard normalization assumption in spatial econometrics, while Assumption 2 is also used in Lee (2004) [22] and Yu et al. (2008) [18]. Assumption 3 guarantees that Model (4) is valid. Furthermore, compactness is a condition for the theoretical analysis. In empirical applications, where W_N is row-normalized, one just searches over (−1,1). Assumption 4 provides regularity assumptions for ϵ_{it}. The normality assumption on errors is used to construct the likelihood function. However, the limit result does not depend on it. The result only needs quasi-maximum likelihood estimation (QMLE). Assumption 5 makes sure that the regressors are asymptotically stationary. Assumption 6 allows two cases: (i) $N \to \infty$ as $T \to \infty$, such that $\frac{N}{T} \to k < \infty$, for $k \geq 0$, and (ii) N is fixed as $T \to \infty$.

Theorem 1. *Let $\Longrightarrow$ denote weak convergence in the distribution under the Skorokhod topology. Under Assumptions 1–6 and H_0, the limiting distribution of Z_t is:*

$$Z_t \Longrightarrow \sup_{s \in (u, 1-u)} \frac{B_1^2(s)}{s(1-s)} \tag{14}$$

where $B_1(s)$, is a standard Brownian bridge and u, the trimming parameter, is a small positive number. For a known break k_0:

$$Z_t \xrightarrow{D} \chi^2(1) \tag{15}$$

Proof of Theorem 1. To prove the result, we first take a Taylor approximation of $2\Lambda_k$ around the true parameter ρ_0. It is found that the approximations involve partial sums of Gaussian random vectors that are independently and identically distributed. Using results from the maximum likelihood estimation of the spatial panel model, we obtain uniform convergence to Wiener processes. As a next step, the partials sums are manipulated to obtain a Brownian bridge distribution. For a fixed k, it is then easy to show that the asymptotic distribution is chi-square. The detailed proof is provided in the Appendix A. □

The intuition as to why the asymptotic distribution from the univariate time series test (Cörgö and Horváth (1997) [25]) is still valid in this case is because the spatial dependence is contained in time; the dependent variable of unit i only depends on the contemporaneous dependent variable of the neighboring units. Therefore, the endogeneity does not spread over time, and hence, the distribution is similar to the one found in the univariate time series case.

There is an explicit form of the distribution function of the limit random variable. The critical values are provided in Kiefer (1959) [26] (p. 438). Some of the relevant critical values are for size = 10%, 1.4978; for size = 5%, 1.8444 and for size = 1%, it is 2.649 for a 5% trimming.

6. Estimation

Following evidence against the null hypothesis, it is important to determine the location of the break date. The proposed estimator of the break date is the one that maximizes the likelihood under the alternative hypothesis,

$$\hat{k} = arg\max_{k}\ lnL_A \tag{16}$$

where lnL_A is the log likelihood under the alternative defined as: $lnL_A = lnL_k + lnL_k^*$ where

$$lnL_k = -\frac{Nk}{2} ln2\pi\sigma_\epsilon^2 + kln|I_N - \rho W_N| - \frac{1}{2\sigma_\epsilon^2}\sum_{i=1}^{N}\sum_{t=1}^{k}\epsilon_{it}\epsilon_{it}$$

$$lnL_k^* = -\frac{N(T-k)}{2} ln2\pi\sigma_\epsilon^2 + (T-k)ln|I_N - \rho W_N| - \frac{1}{2\sigma_\epsilon^2}\sum_{i=1}^{N}\sum_{t=k+1}^{T}\epsilon_{it}\epsilon_{it}$$

where lnL_k is the log-likelihood defined for $t = 1, \cdots, k$ and lnL_k^* is the log-likelihood for the sample that includes the observations $t = k+1, \cdots, T$.

The asymptotic properties of the estimator, including the consistency, rate of convergence and limit distribution, are currently under investigation. Simulation evidence, presented is Section 7, shows that the estimator performs very well in small samples in terms of bias and root mean squared error. The root mean squared error is shown to decrease as the sample size increases, thereby suggesting that the estimator is indeed consistent.

7. Monte Carlo Results

To evaluate the finite sample performance of the LR test and the performance of the estimator, this section reports the results of a limited set of sampling experiments. All results reported are for 1000 simulations. We consider the data generating process:

$$y_{it} = \begin{cases} 1 + x_{it} + 0.6\sum_{j=1}^{N} w_{ij}y_{jt} + \epsilon_{it} & \text{pre-break} \\ 1 + x_{it} + \rho_2\sum_{j=1}^{N} w_{ij}y_{jt} + \epsilon_{it} & \text{post-break} \end{cases} \tag{17}$$

where x_{it} from $N(0,1)$ and ϵ_{it} from $N(0,1.3)$.

We first look into the power of the proposed test. Let $\rho_1 = 0.6$, and the actual break date is $k_0 = T/2$ in each of the cases. We find that the test has high power even with N and T = 50, as seen in Table 1. The power increases with increases in N and/or T (see Table 2).

Table 1. Power of the test: I.

N	T	Rho2	Frequency of Rejection
50	50	0.7	0.957
50	50	0.65	0.337
50	50	0.55	0.263
50	50	0.5	0.807
50	50	−0.6	1

Table 2. Power of the test: II.

N	T	Rho2	Frequency of Rejection
50	100	0.65	0.657
50	100	0.55	0.551
50	200	0.65	0.932
50	200	0.55	0.881
100	50	0.65	0.515
100	50	0.55	0.401
100	100	0.65	0.852
100	100	0.55	0.741
100	200	0.65	0.989
100	200	0.55	0.971

Next, we look into graphical comparisons between empirical and asymptotic distributions of the test presented in Figure 1. The continuous lines are the asymptotic distributions, and the dotted lines are the empirical CDF. It is found that even with a small T, there is no size distortion, and the empirical distribution matches closely the asymptotic distribution. As T increases, the two distributions overlap.

For a known break date, the asymptotic distribution is chi-square with one degree of freedom. The graphical comparison presented in Figure 2 shows that even with N = 50, T = 50, with a known break date, the empirical distribution is very close to the asymptotic chi-square distribution.

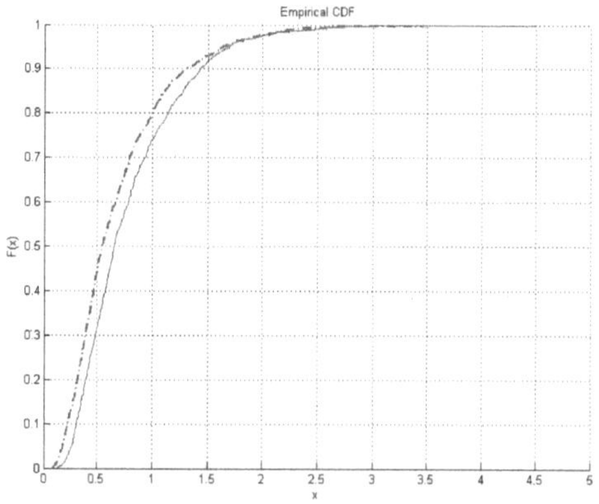

(a) N = 50, T = 50

Figure 1. *Cont.*

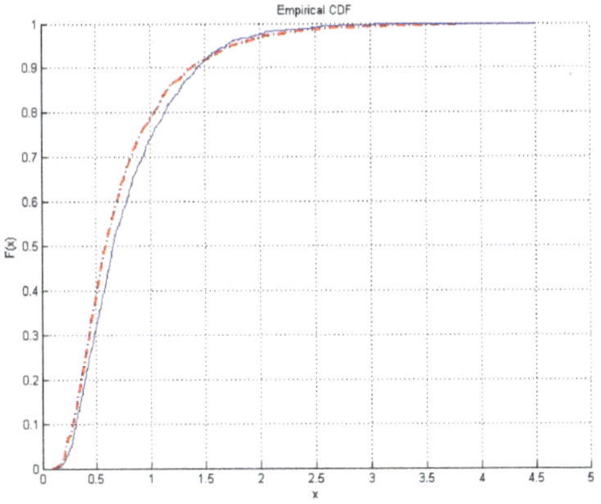

(b) N = 200, T = 200

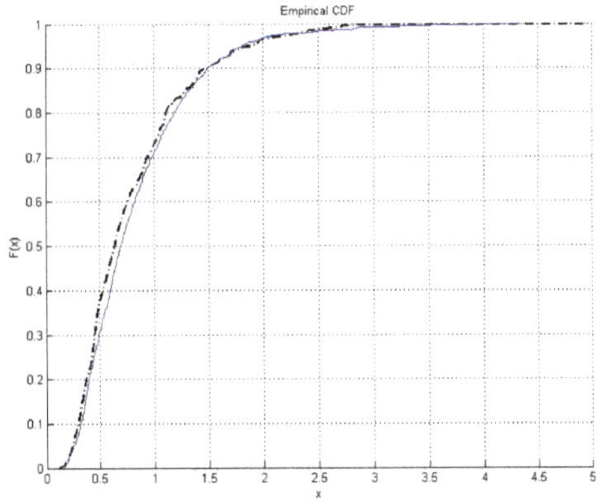

(c) N = 50, T = 500

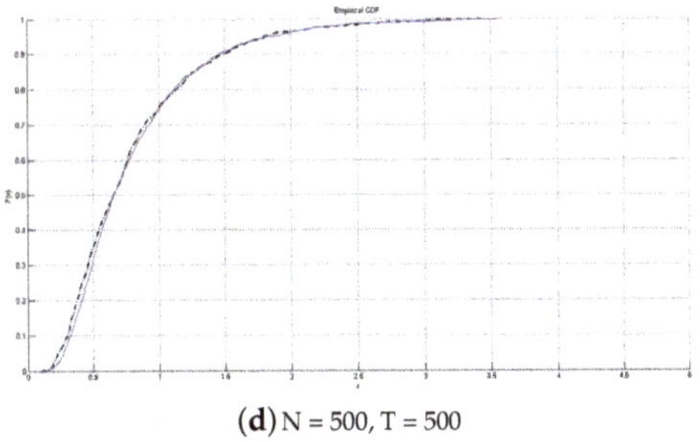

(d) N = 500, T = 500

Figure 1. Emprical versus Asymptotic Distribution of the test.

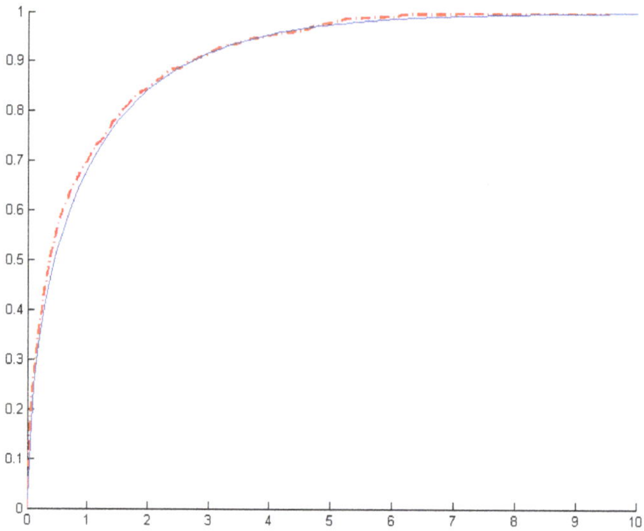

Figure 2. CDF plot for empirical distribution with a known break.

Next, we compare the performance of the break-date estimator (see Table 3). The bias is almost negligible. The root mean square decreases with increases in N. With increases in T, the standard deviation does not go down. This is a well-known result in the univariate time series literature: only the break fraction can be consistently estimated, not the break date.

Furthermore, we make a quick comparison with the ordinary least squares residuals-based method (see Table 4), with the estimator defined by

$$\hat{k} = arg \min_{1 \leq k \leq T} SSR(k) \tag{18}$$

Here, $SSR(k)$ is the sum of squared residuals of the model under the alternative assuming a break at date k. The bias is comparable in the two cases, but the standard deviation and root mean square are higher for the OLS residual-based estimate of break date.

Table 3. Estimator performance: likelihood method.

Rho1	Rho2	N	T	Break Date	Bias	SD	RMSE
0.6	0.7	50	50	25	0.1	1.01	1.01
0.6	0.7	50	100	50	0.08	1.16	1.16
0.6	0.7	50	200	100	0.11	1.1	1.1
0.6	0.7	50	50	25	0.1	1.01	1.01
0.6	0.7	100	50	25	0.04	0.67	0.67
0.6	0.7	200	50	25	0.01	0.23	0.23
0.6	0.7	50	50	25	0.1	1.01	1.01
0.6	0.7	100	100	50	0.06	0.52	0.53
0.6	0.65	50	50	25	0.35	5.77	5.78
0.6	0.55	50	50	25	0.16	6.99	6.99
0.6	−0.6	50	50	25	0	0	0

Looking at the tables closely, an interesting pattern is observed: there is an asymmetry in the behavior of the estimator and the power of the test. When $\rho_2 = 0.55$, the power of the test is lower compared to that when $\rho_2 = 0.65$. Similarly, the break date estimator has a lower standard deviation and root mean square when the post-break parameter is increasing ($\rho_2 = 0.65$) as compared to a comparable reduction in the post-break parameter ($\rho_2 = 0.55$). An explanation for such behavior could be that, when the post-break parameter is increasing ($\rho_2 = 0.65$), there is a higher signal of spatial dependence. This leads to reduction in the variance and makes it easier to assess whether a break is present and locate it. However, when the post-break parameter is comparably lower ($\rho_2 = 0.55$), the signal is lower, giving rise to more variation and making it more difficult to assess whether a break is present and to locate it.

Table 4. Estimator performance: OLS residuals.

Rho1	Rho2	N	T	Break Date	Bias	SD	RMSE
0.6	0.7	50	50	25	−0.2	2.53	2.54
0.6	0.7	50	100	50	−0.31	2.01	2.03
0.6	0.7	50	200	100	−0.36	1.85	1.88
0.6	0.7	50	50	25	−0.2	2.53	2.54
0.6	0.7	100	50	25	-0.14	1.17	1.18
0.6	0.7	200	50	25	−0.09	0.49	0.5
0.6	0.7	50	50	25	−0.2	2.53	2.54
0.6	0.7	100	100	50	−0.22	1.09	1.11
0.6	0.65	50	50	25	−0.51	8.95	8.96
0.6	0.55	50	50	25	−0.03	9.8	9.8
0.6	−0.6	50	50	25	0	0	0

The proposed likelihood-based estimator performs well in a finite sample. As N increases, the root mean square error decreases, suggesting that the estimator is consistent.

8. Budget Spillovers

Case et al. (1993) [21] showed how a U.S. state's budget expenditure depends on the spending of similar states. Quoting Arkansas state Senator Doug Brandon (1989) [2] describing his state's budgetary policy as

> "We do everything everyone else does."

The proposed *sup* LR test is used to check the hypothesis that a state's dependence on another's budget remained the same in the U.S. or has changed over time. The data consists of an annual panel of U.S. states from 1960–2011. All dollar figures are calculated on a per capita basis and deflated using the GDP deflator (the base year being 2009). The dependent variable is the government expenditure of state i in the year t (G_{it}). The budget expenditure is the sum of the direct spending of state and local governments. The variables included in X_{it} other than the intercept are: the real per-capita personal income (Y), income squared (Y^2), real per capita total intergovernmental federal revenue to state and local governments (F), population density ($Popden$), proportion of the population at least 65 years old ($Pop65$), proportion of the population between five and 14 years old ($Pop5to14$) and proportion of the population that is black ($Popblack$). The income and revenue are the resources the state government can use. The square of the income picks up possible non-linear effects of changing resources. The population density captures the possibility that there are potential congestion effects and scale economies in the provision of state and local government services. States with different age and racial structures may have different demands for publicly-provided goods. Hence, demographic variables are included.

[2] Applebome, P. (1989), "Governors in the South Seek to Lift Their States", New York Times, 12 Feb, L26.

The model can be written as:

$$G_{it} = X_{it}\beta + \rho \sum_{j=1}^{N} w_{ij}G_{jt} + \epsilon_{it} \tag{19}$$

where X includes all of the control variables. We consider T = 52 from 1960–2011 and N = 49 states in the U.S. Case et al. (1993) [21] use three different ways to define the weight matrix. We define the elements of the weight matrix as $w_{ij} = (1/|Y_i - Y_j|)/S_i$, where Y_k is the mean income over the sample period and S_i is the sum $\sum_j 1/|Y_i - Y_j|$. According to this definition of the weight matrix, rich states are neighbors to rich states, and poor states are neighbors to poor states. The full model (1960–2011) estimation results are presented in Table 5.

Table 5. Full model estimate.

	Coefficient	Asymptotic t-Stat	p-Value
Intercept	0.6974	0.2143	0.8303
Pop65	−0.4042	-4.8989	0
Pop5to14	−0.0589	−0.5739	0.566
Popblack	−0.0562	−4.3041	0
Popden	−0.0003	−2.2139	0.0268
F	1.7352	58.2555	0
Y	0.1301	14.289	0
Y^2	0	1.622	0.1048
$W \times G$	0.122	7.3024	0

All of the test results are based on tests with size 5%. We reject the null hypothesis of no break, implying evidence for a break. The break date is estimated at 1982. The pre-break budget spillover coefficient is estimated as 0.0229, while the post-break budget spillover coefficient is estimated as 0.1056. As to why there might be a break, there could be two reasons: (1) in 1981, Ronald Reagan became the president of the United States and advocated many different policies across the U.S. states (also known as Reagonomics); (2) the number of Democratic governors in the U.S. started decreasing post-1983, suggesting synchronized Republican economic policies in different states.

To differentiate between trend behaviors and fluctuations, a Hodrick-Prescott filter is applied on all of the dollar value variables to closely look into idiosyncratic budget spillovers in the U.S. states. We reject the null hypothesis of no break. The break date is then estimated to be in 1977. The pre-break ρ coefficient is 0.5718, and the post-break ρ coefficient is 0.3746. Firstly, this suggests that the idiosyncrasy in budget expenditure for a state depends on "similarly"-situated states. Secondly, the dependence goes down post-break. This can be attributed to more power given to the governors in the 1980s. For the federal government (central planner), the budget policies for each state will be similar; compared to individual governors in each state who will adjust the budget expenditures for their states based on individual needs. Therefore, overall, even though the spillovers increase (capturing overall trend in the economy), the budget spillovers in the case of idiosyncracies reduce over time.

9. Conclusions

We consider the problem of structural break in the spatial dependence parameter in a panel model and provide a likelihood ratio test.

We first describe the spatial panel model and the interpretation of the spatial lag or spatial autoregressive parameter. Next we motivate the problem of structural break in such parameter. The *sup* LR test statistic is proposed, and under large T, the limiting distribution is derived. The test is easy to implement, and the critical values can be analytically obtained.

In case there is evidence to reject the null hypothesis, we propose a break date estimator based on the argument that maximizes the likelihood ratio. The finite sample properties of the test and the break-date estimator are provided. The Monte Carlo simulations show that the test has good power even in small samples. The estimator of the break date shows negligible bias, and the root mean square decreases with increases in N, suggesting a consistent break-date estimator for a panel model.

We then consider the problem of budget spillovers across the U.S. states and the change in the spatial dependence over time. The test rejects the null hypothesis of no break in budget spillovers for (1) the spillover in the overall budget expenditure of the U.S. states and (2) the spillover in the fluctuations of budget expenditure. The overall trend of spatial dependence in budget expenditure is found to have increased post-break, but the idiosyncrasies in budget expenditure are less spatially dependent post-break.

The following extensions to the paper are being considered: (1) the asymptotic limit distribution of the test statistic for large N; (2) proving the consistency of the break date estimator and deriving the limiting distribution; and (3) extending the test to multiple structural breaks.

Acknowledgments: I am grateful to my advisors Pierre Perron, Zhongjun Qu, and Hiroaki Kaido for their guidance, support and encouragement. I would also like to thank Iván Fernández-Val, Jushan Bai, Laurent Pauwels, Qu Feng, Hide Ichimura, Fan Zhuo, Anindya Chakrabarti and seminar participants at Boston University for useful conversations and feedback. I am also grateful to the two anonymous reviewers and the editor for their feedback and suggestions. I am thankful to Satadru Sengupta for introducing me to Spatial Econometrics. All errors are my own.

Conflicts of Interest: The author declares no conflict of interest.

Abbreviations

The following abbreviations are used in this manuscript:

CDF	Cumulative distribution function
FCLT	Functional central limit theorem
GMM	Generalized method of moments
IV	Instrumental variable
LR	Likelihood ratio
MLE	Maximum likelihood estimation
OLS	Ordinary least squares
QMLE	Quasi-maximum likelihood estimation
RMSE	Root mean square error

Appendix A. Proof of Theorem

Let $\theta = (\rho, \beta, \sigma_\epsilon^2)$. Then,

$$lnL_T(\theta) = -\frac{NT}{2} ln2\pi\sigma_\epsilon^2 + Tln|I_N - \rho W_N| - \frac{1}{2\sigma_\epsilon^2}\sum_{i=1}^{N}\sum_{t=1}^{T}\epsilon_{it}'\epsilon_{it}$$

$$lnL_k(\theta) = -\frac{Nk}{2} ln2\pi\sigma_\epsilon^2 + kln|I_N - \rho W_N| - \frac{1}{2\sigma_\epsilon^2}\sum_{i=1}^{N}\sum_{t=1}^{k}\epsilon_{it}'\epsilon_{it}$$

$$lnL_k^*(\theta) = -\frac{N(T-k)}{2} ln2\pi\sigma_\epsilon^2 + (T-k)ln|I_N - \rho W_N| - \frac{1}{2\sigma_\epsilon^2}\sum_{i=1}^{N}\sum_{t=k+1}^{T}\epsilon_{it}'\epsilon_{it}$$

Denoting $lnL_T(\theta) = L_c$, $lnL_k(\theta) = L_1$ and $lnL_k^*(\theta) = L_2$; furthermore, defining $\hat{\rho}_k$ as the MLE estimate for the pre-break regime under the alternative, $\hat{\rho}_k^*$ as the MLE estimate for the post-break regime under the alternative and $\hat{\rho}_T$ as the MLE estimate under the null. Taking a Taylor expansion of $2[L_1 + L_2 - L_c]$ around the true value ρ_0 and denoting that by R_k

$$
\begin{aligned}
R_k = 2[&L_1(\rho_0) + L_2(\rho_0) - L_c(\rho_0)\\
&+ L_1'(\rho_0)(\hat{\rho}_k - \rho_0) + \frac{L_1''(\rho_0)}{2}(\hat{\rho}_k - \rho_0)^2\\
&+ L_2'(\rho_0)(\hat{\rho}_k^* - \rho_0) + \frac{L_2''(\rho_0)}{2}(\hat{\rho}_k^* - \rho_0)^2\\
&- L_c'(\rho_0)(\hat{\rho}_T - \rho_0) + \frac{L_c''(\rho_0)}{2}(\hat{\rho}_T - \rho_0)^2] + o_p(1)
\end{aligned}
$$

Now, $L_1(\rho_0) + L_2(\rho_0) = L_c(\rho_0)$. Therefore, R_k can be rewritten as:

$$
\begin{aligned}
R_k = [&2L_1'(\rho_0)(\hat{\rho}_k - \rho_0) + L_1''(\rho_0)(\hat{\rho}_k - \rho_0)^2\\
&+ 2L_2'(\rho_0)(\hat{\rho}_k^* - \rho_0) + L_2''(\rho_0)(\hat{\rho}_k^* - \rho_0)^2\\
&- 2L_c'(\rho_0)(\hat{\rho}_T - \rho_0) + L_c''(\rho_0)(\hat{\rho}_T - \rho_0)^2] + o_p(1)
\end{aligned}
$$

From Lee (2004) [22] and Yu et al. (2008) [18] under Assumptions 1–6

$$
\begin{aligned}
\sqrt{NT}(\hat{\rho}_T - \rho_0) &= [-\frac{1}{NT}L_c''(\rho_0)]^{-1}\frac{1}{\sqrt{NT}}L_c'(\rho_0) + o_p(1)\\
\sqrt{Nk}(\hat{\rho}_k - \rho_0) &= [-\frac{1}{Nk}L_1''(\rho_0)]^{-1}\frac{1}{\sqrt{Nk}}L_1'(\rho_0) + o_p(1)\\
\sqrt{N(T-k)}(\hat{\rho}_k^* - \rho_0) &= [-\frac{1}{N(T-k)}L_2''(\rho_0)]^{-1}\frac{1}{\sqrt{N(T-k)}}L_2'(\rho_0) + o_p(1)
\end{aligned}
$$

Using these relationships and rearranging the terms, R_k can be rewritten as:

$$
\begin{aligned}
R_k = &\frac{1}{\sqrt{Nk}}L_1'(\rho_0)[-\frac{1}{Nk}L_1''(\rho_0)]^{-1}\frac{1}{\sqrt{Nk}}L_1'(\rho_0)\\
&+ \frac{1}{\sqrt{N(T-k)}}L_2'(\rho_0)[-\frac{1}{N(T-k)}L_2''(\rho_0)]^{-1}\frac{1}{\sqrt{N(T-k)}}L_2'(\rho_0)\\
&- \frac{1}{\sqrt{NT}}L_c'(\rho_0)[-\frac{1}{NT}L_c''(\rho_0)]^{-1}\frac{1}{\sqrt{NT}}L_c'(\rho_0) + o_p(1)
\end{aligned}
$$

Let $G_N = W_N[I_N - \rho_N W_N]^{-1}$, then

$$
-\frac{1}{NT}L_c''(\rho_0) = \frac{1}{\sigma_{\epsilon 0}^2}\sum_{t=1}^{T}((W_N Y_{Nt})W_N Y_{Nt} + tr(G_N^2)) + o_p(1)
$$

where $W_N Y_{Nt} = G_N X_{Nt}\beta_0 + G_N\epsilon_{Nt}$.

Let, $\frac{1}{\sqrt{N}}(G_N X_{Nt}\beta_0)' = H_{Nt}$. Then, by Assumption 7, $H_{Nt} \Rightarrow H^*$ and $-\frac{1}{NT}L_c''(\rho_0) = \frac{1}{NT}(G_N X_{Nt}\beta_0)'(G_N X_{Nt}\beta_0) \Rightarrow H^{*'}H^*$.

Furthermore,

$$
\frac{1}{\sqrt{NT}}L_c'(\rho_0) = \frac{1}{\sigma_{\epsilon_0}^2\sqrt{NT}}\sum_{t=1}^{T}[(G_N X_{Nt}\beta_0)'\epsilon_{Nt}] + \frac{1}{\sigma_{\epsilon_0}^2\sqrt{NT}}\sum_{t=1}^{T}[\epsilon_{Nt}'G_N'\epsilon_{Nt} - \sigma_{\epsilon_0}^2 trG_N] + o_p(1)
$$

$$\frac{1}{\sqrt{NT}}\sum_{t=1}^{T}\left[\epsilon_{Nt}'G_N'\epsilon_{Nt}-\sigma_{\epsilon_0}^2 trG_N\right]=o_p(1)$$
$$\frac{1}{\sqrt{NT}}\sum_{t=1}^{T}\left[(G_N X_{Nt}\beta_0)'\epsilon_{Nt}\right]=O_p(1)$$

Now, $\frac{1}{\sqrt{T}}\sum_{t=1}^{T}\left[\frac{1}{\sqrt{N}}(G_N X_{Nt}\beta_0)'\epsilon_{Nt}\right]=T^{-1/2}\sum_{t=1}^{T}H_{Nt}\epsilon_{Nt}$. As $T\to\infty$, by the FCLT, we get:

$$\frac{1}{\sqrt{T}}\sum_{t=1}^{T}H_{Nt}\epsilon_{Nt}\Rightarrow H^*W(1)$$

where $W(t)$ is a standard Wiener process. Thus, if we let $\lim_{T\to\infty}\frac{k}{T}=\lambda$, then by the FCLT,

$$\frac{1}{\sqrt{k}}\sum_{t=1}^{k}H_{Nt}\epsilon_{Nt}\Rightarrow\frac{H^*W(\lambda)}{\sqrt{\lambda}}$$
$$\frac{1}{\sqrt{T-k}}\sum_{t=k+1}^{T}H_{Nt}\epsilon_{Nt}\Rightarrow\frac{H^*(W(1)-W(\lambda))}{\sqrt{1-\lambda}}$$

Hence, we get:

$$\begin{aligned}R_k\Rightarrow&\frac{H^*W(\lambda)(H^*)^{-1}}{\sqrt{\lambda}}\frac{H^*W(\lambda)(H^*)^{-1}}{\sqrt{\lambda}}\\&+\frac{H^*(W(1)-W(\lambda))(H^*)^{-1}}{\sqrt{1-\lambda}}\frac{H^*(W(1)-W(\lambda))(H^*)^{-1}}{\sqrt{1-\lambda}}\\&-H^*W(1)(H^*)^{-1}H^*W(1)(H^*)^{-1}\end{aligned}$$

Let

$$R(\lambda)\equiv\frac{1}{\lambda}[W(\lambda)]^2+\frac{1}{1-\lambda}[W(1)-W(\lambda)]^2-[W(1)]^2=\frac{[\lambda W(1)-W(\lambda)]^2}{\lambda(1-\lambda)}$$

Rearranging the terms, we get:

$$\sup_{\lambda\in(u,1-u)}R_k\Rightarrow\sup_{\lambda\in(u,1-u)}R(\lambda)$$
$$\text{or}\quad\sup_{\lambda\in(u,1-u)}R_k\Rightarrow\sup_{\lambda\in(u,1-u)}\frac{B_1^2(\lambda)}{\lambda(1-\lambda)}$$

where $B_1(\lambda)=[\lambda W(1)-W(\lambda)]$ is a Brownian bridge.

For known k_0, $\lambda_0=\frac{k_0}{T}$, the limit distribution of $R(\lambda_0)$ is χ_1^2.

References

1. Chow, G.C. Test of equality between sets of coefficients in two linear regressions. *Econometrica* **1960**, *28*, 591–605.
2. Andrews, D.W.K. Tests for parameter instability and structural change with unknown change point. *Econometrica* **1993**, *61*, 821–856.
3. Andrews, D.W.K.; Ploberger, W. Optimal tests when a nuisance parameter is present only under the alternative. *Econometrica* **1994**, *62*, 1383–1414.

4. Bai, J.; Perron, P. Estimating and testing linear models with multiple structural changes. *Econometrica* **1998**, *66*, 47–78.
5. Bai, J. Estimation of a change point in multiple regressions models. *Rev. Econ. Stat.* **1997**, *79*, 551–563.
6. Bai, J.; Lumsdaine, R.; Stock, J. Testing and dating common breaks in multivariate time series. *Rev. Econ. Stud.* **1998**, *65*, 395–432.
7. Qu, Z.; Perron, P. Estimating and testing structural changes in multivariate regressions. *Econometrica* **2007**, *75*, 459–502.
8. Perron, P. Dealing with structural breaks. In *Palgrave Handbook of Econometrics*; Hassani, H., Mills, T.C., Patterson, K., Eds.; Palgrave Macmillan: Basingstoke, UK, 2006; Volume 1, pp. 278–352.
9. Bai, J. Common breaks in means and variances for panel data. *J. Econom.* **2010**, *157*, 78–92.
10. Feng, Q.; Kao, C.; Lazarova, S. *Estimation of Change Points in Panel Models*; Mimeo, Center for Policy Research: New York, NY, USA, 2009.
11. Liao, W. Structural Breaks in Panel Data Models: A New Approach. Ph.D. Thesis, New York University, New York, NY, USA, 2008.
12. Han, A.K.; Park, D. Testing for structural change in panel data: Application to a study of U.S. foreign trade in manufacturing goods. *Rev. Econ. Stat.* **1989**, *71*, 135–142.
13. Emerson, J.; Kao, C. *Testing for Structural Change of a Time Trend Regression in Panel Data*; Working Paper 15; Center for Policy Research: New York, NY, USA, 2000.
14. De Wachter, S.; Tzavalis, E. Detection of structural breaks in linear dynamic panel data models. *Comput. Stat. Data Anal.* **2012**, *56*, 3020–3034.
15. Pauwels, L.L.; Chan, F.; Griffoli, T.M. Testing for structural change in heterogeneous panels with an application to the euro's trade effect. *J. Time Ser. Econom.* **2012**, *4*, doi:10.1515/1941-1928.1141.
16. Elhorst, J. Spatial panel data models. In *Handbook of Applied Spatial Analysis*; Fischer, M.M., Getis, A., Eds.; Springer: Berlin/Heidelberg, Germany, 2010; pp. 377–407.
17. Bai, J. Likelihood ratio tests for multiple structural changes. *J. Econom.* **1999**, *91*, 299–323.
18. Yu, J.; Jong, R.; Lee, L. Quasi-maximum likelihood estimators for spatial dynamic panel data with fixed effects when both n and T are large. *J. Econom.* **2008**, *146*, 118–134.
19. Lee, L.; Yu, J. Estimation of spatial autoregressive panel data models with fixed effects. *J. Econom.* **2010**, *154*, 165–185.
20. Wied, D. Cusum-type testing for changing parameters in a spatial autoregressive model for stock returns. *J. Time Ser. Anal.* **2013**, *34*, 221–229.
21. Case, A.C.; Rosen, H.S. Budget spillovers and fiscal policy interdependence: Evidence from the states. *J. Public Econ.* **1993**, *52*, 285–307.
22. Lee, L. Asymptotic distributions of quasi-maximum likelihood estimators for spatial autoregressive models. *Econometrica* **2004**, *72*, 1899–1925.
23. Acemoglu, D.; Carvalho, V.M.; Ozdaglar, A.; Tahbaz-Salehi, A. The network origins of aggregate fluctuations. *Econometrica* **2012**, *80*, 1977–2016.
24. Baltagi, B.H.; Li, D. Prediction in the panel data model with spatial correlation. In *Advances in Spatial Econometrics*; Anselin, L., Florax, R., Rey, S., Eds.; Springer: Berlin/Heidelberg, Germany, 2004; pp. 283–295.
25. Csörgö, M.; Horváth, L. *Limit Theorems in Change-Point Analysis*; Wiley: New York, NY, USA, 1997.
26. Kiefer, J. K-Sample Analogues of the Kolmogorov-Smirnov and Cramer-V. Mises tests. *Ann. Math. Stat.* **1959**, *30*, 420–447.

econometrics

MDPI

Article

Selecting the Lag Length for the M^{GLS} Unit Root Tests with Structural Change: A Warning Note for Practitioners Based on Simulations[†]

Ricardo Quineche [1,2] and Gabriel Rodríguez [2,*]

1 Central Reserve Bank of Peru, 441–445 Antonio Miró Quesada Street, Lima 1, Lima, Peru; rquinecheu@pucp.pe

2 Department of Economics, Pontificia Universidad Católica del Perú, Av. Universitaria 1801, Lima 32, Lima, Peru

* Correspondence: gabriel.rodriguez@pucp.edu.pe; Tel.: +511-626-2000 (ext. 4998)

† This Note is drawn from the Thesis of Ricardo Quineche at the Department of Economics, Pontificia Universidad Católica del Perú (PUCP). This is a substantial revised version of an earlier version circulated under the title *Data-Dependent Methods for the Lag Length Selection in Unit Root Tests with Structural Change* which appear as Working Paper 404 of the Department of Economics, PUCP. The current version has been improved thanks to the relevant comments received from the Guest Editor of the Review (Professor Pierre Perron) and three anonymous Referees. Further, we thank comments of Luis García, José Tavera and Jorge Rojas (PUCP). Any remaining errors are our responsibility.

Academic Editor: Pierre Perron

Received: 31 August 2016; Accepted: 4 April 2017; Published: 16 April 2017

Abstract: This is a simulation-based warning note for practitioners who use the M^{GLS} unit root tests in the context of structural change using different selection lag length criteria. With $T = 100$, we find severe oversize problems when using some criteria, while other criteria produce an undersizing behavior. In view of this dilemma, we do not recommend using these tests. While such behavior tends to disappear when $T = 250$, it is important to note that most empirical applications use smaller sample sizes such as $T = 100$ or $T = 150$. The ADF^{GLS} test does not present an oversizing or undersizing problem. The only disadvantage of the ADF^{GLS} test arises in the presence of $MA(1)$ negative correlation, in which case the M^{GLS} tests are preferable, but in all other cases they are very undersized. When there is a break in the series, selecting the breakpoint using the Supremum method greatly improves the results relative to the Infimum method.

Keywords: unit root tests; structural change; truncation lag; GLS detrending; information criteria; sequential general to specific t-sig method

JEL Classification: C22; C52

1. Introduction

Testing for the presence of a unit root in a time series (i.e., whether or not a structural change can be identified) is now a common starting point in advanced models frequently used in macroeconomics and finance. Recent efficient unit root tests are the ADF^{GLS} and the P_T^{GLS} tests proposed by Elliott et al. (1996), and the M^{GLS} tests proposed by Ng and Perron (2001).[1] All these (GLS-based) tests have been extended to the unit root with one unknown structural change as suggested by Perron

1 For excellent surveys, see Stock (1994), Maddala and Kim (1998), Phillips and Xiao (1998), Haldrup and Jansson (2006), Perron (2006), and Choi (2015).

and Rodríguez (2003), who show that these tests enjoy the same efficiency characteristics. M^{GLS} tests have become increasingly popular in the literature. For example, Haldrup and Jansson (2006) argue that practitioners should abandon the use of ADF tests altogether in favor of M^{GLS} tests because of their excellent size properties and nearly optimal power properties. However, this note arrives at the opposite conclusion, suggesting that the choice of the most suitable testing method should be carefully assessed.

Currently, it is widely accepted that the selection of the lag length (denoted by k) has important implications for the (size and power) behavior of the different unit root tests. See, for instance, Schwert (1989), Ng and Perron (1995), Agiakloglou and Newbold (1992), Agiakloglou and Newbold (1996), Elliott et al. (1996), Ng and Perron (2001), Del Barrio Castro et al. (2011), and Fossati (2012). The consensus is to use data-dependent methods. These rules include *AIC* (Akaike Information Criterion), *BIC* (Bayesian Information Criterion), Modified *AIC* (*MAIC*), Modified *BIC* (*MBIC*), and the t-sig method, which are briefly explained below.

Recently, we performed a routine empirical application of the M^{GLS} tests and obtained strange results. For example, applying the $MZ_{\widehat{\alpha}}^{GLS}$ and the *AIC* method to the labor market of the Spanish region of Cantabria,[2] we obtained an unemployment rate of $-3'140{,}463$, a huge (explosive) negative value with $k = 9$. Using the t-sig procedure , we obtained $-50'078{,}041$ with $k = 10$, which is even more impressive. A straightforward interpretation implies an overwhelming rejection of the null hypothesis, given any of the asymptotic or finite critical values tabulated in Perron and Rodríguez (2003). However, it is clear that the magnitude of this value is counter-intuitive and inadmissible, because its magnitude is very far from standard values. In contrast, other rules yield opposite results (very small values in absolute value). When applied to other three time series (unemployment rates in the Spanish regions of Galicia and Murcia, and to Peru's monetary policy rate), similar results are obtained.[3] In consequence, we consider that it is worth analyzing the source of the poor behavior of the M^{GLS} tests in the cases mentioned above. Hence, we perform extensive finite sample simulations for the M^{GLS} tests using different lag-length criteria, where the size performance is our primary interest.

This note (to our best knowledge) represents the first simulation-based attempt to study the size and the eccentric behavior of the M^{GLS} unit root tests in the context of structural change. We do not pretend to perform an exhaustive analysis of each rule. Rather, this document is only a simulation-based note of caution for users of these unit root tests.[4]

This note is structured as follows. In Section 2, the GLS approach with structural break, the test statistics, the rules used to select k, and the two methods to select the break date are briefly reviewed. In Section 3 we present simulation evidence about the size of the $MZ_{\widehat{\alpha}}^{GLS}$ test linking the results with an explosive behavior of the test. Section 4 provides some conclusions.

2. DGP, GLS Detrending, M^{GLS} Tests with Structural Change, Rules for Selecting the Lag Length, and Methods for Selecting the Breakpoint

2.1. The DGP

Following Perron and Rodríguez (2003), the data generating process (DGP) is:

$$\begin{aligned} y_t &= d_t + u_t, \\ u_t &= \alpha u_{t-1} + v_t, \end{aligned} \tag{1}$$

[2] Quartely data covering the period Q3 1976–Q2 2012 ($T = 144$ observations).

[3] The sample size for Galicia and Murcia are the same as for Cantabria. For Peru's monetary policy rate, the data are monthly for February 2002–August 2010 ($T = 92$ observations).

[4] We recognize the limitations of this note, which is only based on simulations. We agree with a Referee that formal proofs are needed in the spirit of Del Barrio Castro et al. (2013). Hence, further work in the direction of a formal treatment will be addressed in a future research project.

for $t = 0, 1, 2, ..., T$, where $v_t = \sum_{j=0}^{\infty} \gamma_j e_{t-j}$, $\gamma(L) = \sum_{j=0}^{\infty} \gamma_j L^j$, that is, v_t is an unobserved stationary zero-mean process, where $\sum_{j=0}^{\infty} j|\gamma_j| < \infty$ and e_t is a martingale difference sequence. We assume that $u_0 = 0$ throughout, although the results generally hold for the weaker requirement that $E(u_0^2) < \infty$ (even as $T \to \infty$). The process e_t has a non-normalized spectral density at frequency zero given by $\sigma^2 = \sigma_\epsilon^2 \gamma(1)^2$, where $\sigma^2 = \lim_{T\to\infty} T^{-1} \sum_{i=0}^{\infty} E(e_t^2)$.

In the first equation of (1), $d_t = \psi' z_t$, where z_t is a set of deterministic components. Perron and Rodríguez (2003) consider two models in the context of an unknown structural break: (i) Model I, where there is a single structural change in the slope, that is, $z_t = \{1, t, \mathbf{1}(t > T_B)(t - T_B)\}$ where $\mathbf{1}(.)$ is the indicator function and T_B is the time of change and can be expressed as a fraction of the whole sample as $T_B = \delta T$ for some $\delta \in (0, 1)$; and (ii) Model II, which includes a single structural change in intercept and slope, that is, $z_t = \{1, \mathbf{1}(t > T_B), t, \mathbf{1}(t > T_B)(t - T_B)\}$.[5]

2.2. GLS Detrending and M^{GLS} Statistics

The class of M^{OLS} tests are due to Stock (1999) and further analyzed by Perron and Ng (1996). These tests are shown to have far less size distortions in the presence of important negative serial correlation. The M^{GLS} tests are constructed using $\widetilde{y}_t = y_t - \widehat{\psi}^{GLS\prime} z_t$, where $\widehat{\psi}_{GLS} = (z_t^{\bar{\alpha}\prime} z_t^{\bar{\alpha}})^{-1}(z_t^{\bar{\alpha}\prime} y_t^{\bar{\alpha}})$, with $y_t^{\bar{\alpha}} \equiv [y_1, (1 - \bar{\alpha}L)y_t]$, and $z_t^{\bar{\alpha}} \equiv [z_1, (1 - \bar{\alpha}L)z_t]$, for $t = 2, 3, 4....., T$, and for a chosen $\bar{\alpha} = 1 + \bar{c}/T$ and where z_t has been defined in Section 2.1. We also use the P_T^{GLS} test, as defined in Perron and Rodríguez (2003). Hence, defining $S(\rho, \delta) = \sum_{t=1}^{T} (y_t^\rho - \widehat{\psi}^{GLS\prime} z_t^\rho)^2$ for $\rho = \bar{\alpha}, 1$, the M^{GLS} and the P_T^{GLS} are:

$$
\begin{aligned}
MZ_{\bar{\alpha}}^{GLS}(\delta) &= \frac{T^{-1}\widetilde{y}_T^2 - s^2}{2T^{-2}\sum_{t=1}^{T}\widetilde{y}_{t-1}^2}, \quad MSB^{GLS}(\delta) = \left[\frac{T^{-2}\sum_{t=1}^{T}\widetilde{y}_t^2}{s^2}\right]^{1/2}, \\
MZ_{t_{\bar{\alpha}}}^{GLS}(\delta) &= \frac{T^{-1}\widetilde{y}_T^2 - s^2}{[4s^2 T^{-2}\sum_{t=1}^{T}\widetilde{y}_{t-1}^2]^{1/2}}, \quad MP_{T,\mu}^{GLS}(\delta) = \frac{\bar{c}^2 T^{-2}\sum_{t=1}^{T}\widetilde{y}_{t-1}^2 - \bar{c}T^{-1}\widetilde{y}_T^2}{s^2}, \\
MP_{T,\tau}^{GLS}(\delta) &= \frac{\bar{c}^2 T^{-2}\sum_{t=1}^{T}\widetilde{y}_{t-1}^2 + (1-\bar{c})T^{-1}\widetilde{y}_T^2}{s^2}, \quad P_T^{GLS}(\delta) = \frac{S(\bar{\alpha},\delta) - \bar{\alpha}S(1,\delta)}{s^2}.
\end{aligned}
$$

Following Perron and Rodríguez (2003), we use $\bar{c} = -22.5$.[6] The statistics are modified versions of the $Z_{\widehat{\alpha}}$ test of Phillips and Perron (1988), Bhargava (1986)'s R_1 statistic, and the $Z_{t_{\widehat{\alpha}}}$ test proposed by Phillips and Perron (1988), respectively. The term s^2 is an autoregressive estimate of (2π times) the spectral density at frequency zero of u_t, suggested by Perron and Ng (1998), and defined by $s^2 = s_{ek}^2/[1 - \hat{b}(1)]^2$, where $s_{ek}^2 = (T - k_{\max})^{-1} \sum_{t=k+1}^{T} \hat{e}_{tk}^2$, $\hat{b}(1) = \sum_{j=1}^{k} \hat{b}_j$, with $\hat{b}_j$ and $\{\hat{e}_{tk}\}$ obtained from the autoregression:

$$\Delta\widetilde{y}_t = \alpha_0 \widetilde{y}_{t-1} + \sum_{j=1}^{k} b_j \Delta\widetilde{y}_{t-j} + e_{tk}. \tag{2}$$

Another test is the so-called $ADF^{GLS}(\delta)$ test, which is the t-statistic for testing the null hypothesis that $\alpha_0 = 0$ in (2).

2.3. Rules for Selecting the Lag Length (k)

In the derivation of the asymptotic distributions of the different unit root tests, the theoretical conditions provide little practical guidance for choosing k. The literature suggests to use data-dependent rules like the AIC and the BIC where k is chosen by minimizing: $IC_k = \ln \hat{\sigma}_k^2 + \frac{kC_T}{T - k_{\max}}$, where $\hat{\sigma}_k^2 = (T - k_{\max})^{-1} \sum_{t=k+1}^{T} \hat{e}_{tk}^2$, $\frac{C_T}{T - k_{\max}}$ is the penalty attached to an additional regressor, and

---

5 See Rodríguez (2007) for the *crash* model proposed by Perron (1989).

6 Following Elliott et al. (1996) and Ng and Perron (2001), the parameter $\bar{c}$ is selected in such a way that 50% of the Gaussian power envelope is attained.

$T - k_{\max}$ is the number of observations effectively available.[7] The AIC and the BIC are obtained when $C_T = 2$ and $C_T = \ln(T - k_{\max})$, respectively. Another procedure is the sequential t-sig procedure described in Campbell and Perron (1991).[8] Selecting a value for $k_{\max}$, the lag k is selected in a general to specific recursive procedure based on a two-tailed t-statistic on the coefficient associated with the last lag in (2). This approach is denoted by t-sig(10). In a more recent contribution, Ng and Perron (2001) proposed a class of Modified Information Criteria (MIC) that selects k satisfying: $\arg\min MIC_k = \ln\hat{\sigma}_k^2 + \frac{C_T[\hat{\tau}_T(k)+k]}{T-k_{\max}}$, with $\hat{\tau}_T(k) = (\hat{\sigma}_k^2)^{-1}\hat{\alpha}_0^2\sum_{t=k_{max}+1}^{T}\tilde{y}_{t-1}^2$. The modified Akaike ($MAIC$) is obtained when $C_T = 2$, and the modified BIC ($MBIC$) is obtained when $C_T = \ln(T - k_{\max})$. Recently, in order to improve finite (size and power) sample performance, Perron and Qu (2007) have proposed a hybrid approach consisting of two steps: (i) OLS detrended data are used to select k using AIC, BIC, $MAIC$ or $MBIC$; and (ii) estimating (2) using GLS detrended data to construct s^2. In the simulations, we consider this hybrid approach and the methods used are classified as AIC^{OLS}, BIC^{OLS}, $MAIC^{OLS}$ and $MBIC^{OLS}$, respectively.

2.4. Selecting the Breakpoint

Given that the break date (δ) is considered to be unknown, we follow Perron and Rodríguez (2003) using two methods for selecting the break date. The first is to define the break date as the point that minimizes the statistic $t_{\hat{\alpha}_0}$ in (2). This procedure is known as the Infimum method; see Zivot and Andrews (1992) and Perron and Rodríguez (2003) for further details. The second method is based on the maximum absolute value of the t-statistic associated with the dummy variable of the break in the slope. This procedure is known as the Supremum method, which is equivalent to minimizing the SSR; see Perron (1997) and Perron and Rodríguez (2003) for further details.

3. Finite Sample Simulations

3.1. Setup

The DGP is $y_t = \alpha y_{t-1} + u_t$ with three scenarios for the autocorrelation of u_t: (i) the *i.i.d.* case: $u_t = e_t$; (ii) the AR(1) case: $u_t = \phi u_{t-1} + e_t$; and (iii) the MA(1) case: $u_t = e_t + \theta e_{t-1}$. For all cases, $e_t \sim$ *i.i.d.* $N(0,1)$, 1000 replications, $T = 100$ and 250, $\phi = -0.8, -0.4, 0.4, 0.8$ and $\theta = -0.8, -0.5, 0.3, 0.8$ and $\alpha = 1$ (null hypothesis). We performed extensive simulations for all M^{GLS} tests, using both models and both ways to select the break point. We present a selected set of results. We have selected the $MZ_{\hat{\alpha}}^{GLS}$ test as the representative test for the entire family of the M^{GLS} tests. Furthermore, the Infimum method is used to select the break date and results are only reported for Model I. All other results or Tables are available upon request.[9]

3.2. The Problem of Size

Table 1 shows the size of the $MZ_{\hat{\alpha}}^{GLS}$ test for $T = 100$ and for the different criteria for selecting k. The $k_{max} = int[10 \times (\frac{T}{100})^{1/4}]$, that is, $k_{max} = 10$. For the *i.i.d.* case, the results indicate that the test constructed using BIC and BIC^{OLS} have a size around 3.0%, suggesting an undersized test. Testing based on all $MAIC$ (OLS and GLS versions) seems to be extremely conservative (with an exact size of 0.0%). On the other side, testing constructed with AIC, AIC^{OLS} and the t-sig(10) present values implying an extremely oversized test (22%, 27% and 63%, respectively). This same result

---

7 Note that in all experiments we use $T - k_{\max}$ as the available number of observations, which is fixed, as suggested by Ng and Perron (2005).

8 See also Hall (1994) and Ng and Perron (1995).

9 We are agree with the Editor that our scenario is the worst possible scenario because we are using the Infimum method jointly (in some cases) with the t-sig(10) rule. However, this worst scenario is widely used in typical empirical applications. Furthermore, it is a regular or natural option in many statistical packages used by practitioners. Minimizing SSR (or Supremum) is better, as we mention later.

appears when we use some fixed values of k ($k = 5, 6, ..., 10$), where sizes go from 43% to 82%. Indeed, the size is greater when the selected k is higher. For the $AR(1)$ case, very similar results are found. In the $MA(1)$ case, we observe the standard result that the test is oversized. In fact, when $\theta = -0.80$, all selection criteria yield an oversized test. Even when using $MAIC$ and $MBIC$, the sizes are 23% and 24%, respectively.

Table 1. Size of the $MZ_{\widehat{\alpha}}^{GLS}$ Test, Model I, $T = 100$.

	i.i.d.	AR(1) Case				MA(1) Case			
		$\phi = -0.8$	$\phi = -0.4$	$\phi = 0.4$	$\phi = 0.8$	$\theta = -0.8$	$\theta = -0.5$	$\theta = 0.3$	$\theta = 0.8$
AIC	0.22	0.17	0.23	0.30	0.49	0.73	0.30	0.30	0.66
BIC	0.03	0.01	0.07	0.09	0.19	0.90	0.41	0.09	0.40
$MAIC$	0.00	0.00	0.00	0.01	0.10	0.23	0.04	0.01	0.06
$MBIC$	0.00	0.00	0.00	0.00	0.10	0.24	0.04	0.00	0.00
AIC^{OLS}	0.27	0.21	0.27	0.33	0.53	0.80	0.36	0.33	0.70
BIC^{OLS}	0.03	0.01	0.09	0.09	0.20	0.93	0.45	0.10	0.42
$MAIC^{OLS}$	0.00	0.00	0.00	0.01	0.11	0.32	0.04	0.00	0.05
$MBIC^{OLS}$	0.00	0.00	0.00	0.00	0.09	0.33	0.04	0.00	0.00
$t - sig(10)$	0.63	0.54	0.60	0.67	0.82	0.64	0.57	0.66	0.76
$k = 5$	0.43	0.23	0.36	0.46	0.64	0.42	0.30	0.45	0.58
$k = 6$	0.53	0.36	0.48	0.57	0.71	0.44	0.40	0.55	0.46
$k = 7$	0.64	0.48	0.60	0.67	0.79	0.49	0.51	0.65	0.71
$k = 8$	0.70	0.57	0.65	0.73	0.84	0.51	0.58	0.71	0.68
$k = 9$	0.77	0.66	0.75	0.80	0.89	0.55	0.67	0.79	0.81
$k = 10$	0.82	0.73	0.81	0.82	0.91	0.62	0.73	0.83	0.80

In Table 2, the results are presented for $T = 250$, where $k_{max} = 13$. The values of the distortions decrease, meaning that the explosiveness (oversizing) problem decreases. For the *i.i.d.* case, the tests constructed with BIC and BIC^{OLS} yield 2.6% and 2.7%, respectively which are very similar when $T = 100$. With MIC and MIC^{OLS}, the test has sizes of 1.7% and 1.6%, respectively which are better than for $T = 100$, but are still very undersized. Tests using the AIC, AIC^{OLS} and t-sig(10) have sizes of 9%, 11.2%, and 37.9%, respectively, which are smaller than the values for $T = 100$, but they still indicate an oversized test, in particular the t-sig(10) criterion. With a fixed k ($k = 5, 6, ..., 13$), sizes are greater when k is higher, although smaller compared with $T = 100$.

Table 2. Size of the $MZ_{\widehat{\alpha}}^{GLS}$ Test, Model I, $T = 250$.

	i.i.d.	AR(1) Case				MA(1) Case			
		$\phi = -0.8$	$\phi = -0.4$	$\phi = 0.4$	$\phi = 0.8$	$\theta = -0.8$	$\theta = -0.5$	$\theta = 0.3$	$\theta = 0.8$
AIC	0.091	0.054	0.102	0.129	0.197	0.345	0.154	0.155	0.373
BIC	0.026	0.002	0.024	0.053	0.077	0.697	0.246	0.087	0.203
$MAIC$	0.017	0.000	0.008	0.033	0.056	0.038	0.025	0.040	0.089
$MBIC$	0.015	0.000	0.012	0.008	0.058	0.046	0.029	0.003	0.007
AIC^{OLS}	0.112	0.074	0.124	0.155	0.217	0.445	0.173	0.173	0.390
BIC^{OLS}	0.027	0.001	0.026	0.053	0.078	0.802	0.259	0.088	0.211
$MAIC^{OLS}$	0.016	0.000	0.010	0.035	0.057	0.057	0.028	0.041	0.077
$MBIC^{OLS}$	0.015	0.000	0.013	0.006	0.060	0.059	0.029	0.001	0.005
$t - sig(10)$	0.379	0.266	0.345	0.395	0.514	0.233	0.312	0.392	0.467
$k = 5$	0.161	0.051	0.122	0.188	0.229	0.229	0.075	0.173	0.259
$k = 6$	0.204	0.081	0.173	0.223	0.261	0.143	0.110	0.202	0.136
$k = 7$	0.244	0.126	0.216	0.251	0.320	0.152	0.159	0.244	0.315
$k = 8$	0.283	0.168	0.265	0.293	0.359	0.152	0.202	0.278	0.221
$k = 9$	0.304	0.204	0.284	0.333	0.421	0.140	0.219	0.317	0.371
$k = 10$	0.357	0.243	0.329	0.381	0.461	0.162	0.258	0.363	0.335
$k = 11$	0.407	0.287	0.378	0.424	0.507	0.157	0.302	0.419	0.459
$k = 12$	0.459	0.343	0.431	0.479	0.540	0.173	0.354	0.452	0.447
$k = 13$	0.496	0.406	0.462	0.533	0.602	0.191	0.416	0.517	0.537

If we increase k_{max}, the size of the test for higher k values increases considerably. We may emphasize this issue comparing with the same class of test, but without a structural change, that is, with some of the results obtained by Ng and Perron (2001). If we observe Table II.B of Ng and Perron (2001), the $MZ_{\widehat{\alpha}}^{GLS}$ for $\theta = -0.80$ using $k = 10$ yields a size of 18% with $T = 100$. In our case, for the same values, we have a size of 62%. With $T = 250$, Ng and Perron (2001) obtain 3.6%, a size close to the nominal size (5%). However, in our case, for this sample we have a size of 19% (Table 2, $k = 13$). In fact, our simulations suggest that we need $T = 350$ in order to obtain a size close to 5% when $\theta = -0.80$. The results are surely due to the higher number of deterministic components in our models compared with Ng and Perron (2001). However, our conclusion is that practitioners interested in applying the $MZ_{\widehat{\alpha}}^{GLS}$ need a non-trivial number of observations.

A further comparison with Ng and Perron (2001) is possible if we select k using different criteria. Again, in the $MA(1)$ case, where $\theta = -0.80$ and $T = 100$, the test constructed with $MAIC$ and $MBIC$ yields sizes of 23% and 24%, respectively. The OLS versions of these criteria yield 32% and 33%, respectively (see Table 1). However, in the case shown in Table VI.A of Ng and Perron (2001), sizes of 5.9% are obtained using MIC and 12.3% using MIC^{OLS} ($T = 100$). In Table 2, for $T = 250$, the tests constructed with $MAIC$ and $MBIC$ yield sizes of 3.8% and 4.6%, respectively. In the case of Ng and Perron (2001), MIC and MIC^{OLS} yield 1.2% and 1.6%, respectively.

3.3. *Some Additional Results*[10]

Two values are used in the construction of s^2: s_{ek}^2 and $\widehat{b}(1)$. Available simulations show that the reason why $s^2 \rightarrow \infty$ is $\widehat{b}(1) \rightarrow 1$. That is, when a higher k is selected, it is possible to incur in overparameterization in (2) and $\widehat{b}(1) \rightarrow 1$. If s^2 tends to $+\infty$, then the $MZ_{\widehat{\alpha}}^{GLS}$ and $MZ_{t_{\widehat{\alpha}}}^{GLS}$ statistics tend to $-\infty$ and MSB^{GLS} and P_T^{GLS} converge in probability to zero.

Additional simulations show a link between the excessive size of the test and a high probability of selecting higher values of k. Following Ng and Perron (1995), we examine the number of times that $k = i$ is selected by each rule for $i = 0, 1, 2, ..., 10$ and $T = 100$. In the *i.i.d.* case, the results show that AIC, BIC, $MAIC$ and $MBIC$ have probabilities to select $k = 1$ of 56.2%, 93.2%, 74.4%, and 81.6%, respectively. The t-sig(10) criterion has probabilities of selecting lag lengths that are equally distributed for all values of k. For instance, the recursive t-sig(10) has a probability of around 53% of selecting $k \geq 7$. Until now, a basic conclusion is that the AIC, AIC^{OLS}, and t-sig(10) methods are not recommended, as they have high probabilities of selecting higher values of k, which are associated with the size distortions observed in Tables 1 and 2.

When we calculate the mean value for MZ_{α}^{GLS} (in the *i.i.d.* case), explosive negative values are obtained for $k \geq 5$ in AIC, AIC^{OLS}, BIC^{OLS} and t-sig(10). In contrast, reduced values of the test (in absolute value) are given by $MAIC$, $MBIC$, $MAIC^{OLS}$ and $MBIC^{OLS}$. We also examine the number of times that the $MZ_{\widehat{\alpha}}^{GLS}$ test is smaller than a threshold. We consider six possible values: $-500, -1000, -5000, -10,000, -50,000, -100,000$, and the *i.i.d.* case. For all thresholds considered, we find that the number of explosive values of $MZ_{\widehat{\alpha}}^{GLS}$ increases as the value of k is larger. For example, for $k = 7$, the probability of getting a value of $MZ_{\widehat{\alpha}}^{GLS} \prec -1000$ is 13.4%; and the probabilities for $k = 9$ and $k = 10$ are 31% and 40.2%, respectively. Furthermore, the probabilities of finding values of $MZ_{\widehat{\alpha}}^{GLS} \prec -100,000$ are 18% and 22.7% for $k = 9$ and $k = 10$, respectively.

All previous results are less severe when $T = 250$. Among other things, the probabilities of finding elevated k values are lower. In this regard, the oversizing problem is attenuated (see Table 2). Moreover, when a break is included in the simulations, the improvement is greater when $T = 250$. However, explosive negative values are still observed when the lag is selected with AIC, AIC^{OLS}, and t-sig (10).

---

[10] We present a summary of the Tables from the Working Paper version of this Note (see Quineche and Rodríguez (2015)). All other tables are available upon request.

3.4. The ADF^{GLS} Statistic

While the $MZ_{\widehat{\alpha}}^{GLS}$ test (and the entire family of the M^{GLS} tests) shows either oversizing or undersizing problems, depending on the criteria used to choose k, the ADF^{GLS} statistic works well. In the available Tables, we find that the mean value for ADF^{GLS} is not explosive irrespective of the selection criterion used. There are some slightly large negative values when $\theta = -0.8$, but it is a standard result in the literature.

Table 3 shows the exact size of the ADF^{GLS} statistic when $T = 100$. For the *i.i.d.* case, the tests constructed with $MAIC$ and $MAIC^{OLS}$ yield sizes of 3.1% and 3.4%, respectively; that is, they are slightly undersized, but closer to 5%. A similar observation is valid for $MBIC$ and $MBIC^{OLS}$. Other information criteria, like AIC, AIC^{OLS} and t-sig(10), generate oversized tests; but the values are much smaller compared with Table 1 for the $MZ_{\widehat{\alpha}}^{GLS}$ test. For example, for the t-sig (10) procedure, Table 1 (*i.i.d.* case) shows that the statistic $MZ_{\widehat{\alpha}}^{GLS}$ has a size of 63%, which is poor. However, this value is reduced to 14.6% in the case of the ADF^{GLS} test (Table 3). In general, the values in all scenarios are smaller compared with Table 1 for $MZ_{\widehat{\alpha}}^{GLS}$. The only difference (as expected) arises when $\theta = -0.80$. In this case, the $MZ_{\widehat{\alpha}}^{GLS}$ test has sizes of 23% and 24% for the $MAIC$ and $MBIC$, respectively, while for the ADF^{GLS} test the values are 31.5% and 32.6%, respectively.

Table 3. Size (5%) of ADF Test, Model I, $T = 100$.

	i.i.d.	AR(1) Case				MA(1) Case			
		$\phi = -0.8$	$\phi = -0.4$	$\phi = 0.4$	$\phi = 0.8$	$\theta = -0.8$	$\theta = -0.5$	$\theta = 0.3$	$\theta = 0.8$
AIC	0.136	0.117	0.149	0.128	0.167	0.826	0.362	0.145	0.147
BIC	0.072	0.069	0.173	0.069	0.089	0.976	0.568	0.095	0.151
$MAIC$	0.031	0.024	0.039	0.008	0.042	0.315	0.106	0.005	0.004
$MBIC$	0.034	0.025	0.040	0.000	0.034	0.326	0.109	0.004	0.000
AIC^{OLS}	0.145	0.130	0.163	0.132	0.177	0.881	0.402	0.152	0.152
BIC^{OLS}	0.076	0.070	0.196	0.070	0.092	0.985	0.633	0.097	0.155
$MAIC^{OLS}$	0.033	0.030	0.042	0.008	0.042	0.435	0.123	0.006	0.003
$MBIC^{OLS}$	0.038	0.030	0.043	0.000	0.031	0.444	0.127	0.004	0.000
$t-sig(10)$	0.146	0.129	0.154	0.141	0.193	0.516	0.256	0.148	0.136
$k = 5$	0.058	0.056	0.052	0.061	0.058	0.243	0.063	0.056	0.094
$k = 6$	0.054	0.052	0.053	0.054	0.068	0.148	0.054	0.055	0.029
$k = 7$	0.053	0.055	0.061	0.047	0.059	0.122	0.057	0.052	0.060
$k = 8$	0.041	0.037	0.036	0.039	0.063	0.097	0.039	0.037	0.035
$k = 9$	0.049	0.031	0.037	0.049	0.071	0.075	0.034	0.045	0.060
$k = 10$	0.047	0.038	0.047	0.054	0.069	0.059	0.043	0.050	0.036

Table 4 shows the exact size of the ADF^{GLS} test when $T = 250$. Again, the size distortions are clearly smaller compared to those of the $MZ_{\widehat{\alpha}}^{GLS}$ test (Table 2). As in Table 3, the results using the $MZ_{\widehat{\alpha}}^{GLS}$ test are better when $\theta = -0.80$. In Table 4, the ADF^{GLS} test yields 11.5% and 12.8% when $MAIC$ and $MBIC$ are used, respectively. In the case of the $MZ_{\widehat{\alpha}}^{GLS}$ test, the values are 3.8% and 4.6%, respectively. Furthermore, our calculations show that the ADF^{GLS} test will have a size closer to 5% for $\theta = -0.80$ when $T = 350$. This sample size is even more prohibitive for most empirical applications.

A comparison of Tables 1 and 2 against Tables 3 and 4 suggests that it is recommendable to use the ADF^{GLS} test, except when practitioners are sure that they face a strong $MA(1)$ negative correlation. In this case, practitioners should use $T = 350$ or $T = 250$ for ADF^{GLS} or $MZ_{\widehat{\alpha}}^{GLS}$, respectively.

Table 4. Size (5%) of ADF Test, Model I, $T = 250$.

	i.i.d.	AR(1) Case				MA(1) Case			
		$\phi = -0.8$	$\phi = -0.4$	$\phi = 0.4$	$\phi = 0.8$	$\theta = -0.8$	$\theta = -0.5$	$\theta = 0.3$	$\theta = 0.8$
AIC	0.088	0.078	0.075	0.089	0.098	0.527	0.190	0.102	0.102
BIC	0.054	0.049	0.052	0.061	0.059	0.831	0.351	0.092	0.095
$MAIC$	0.032	0.028	0.027	0.033	0.041	0.115	0.054	0.036	0.011
$MBIC$	0.036	0.030	0.031	0.007	0.044	0.128	0.062	0.003	0.004
AIC^{OLS}	0.097	0.085	0.084	0.096	0.107	0.612	0.205	0.106	0.111
BIC^{OLS}	0.054	0.050	0.053	0.061	0.059	0.900	0.373	0.093	0.099
$MAIC^{OLS}$	0.034	0.029	0.029	0.035	0.041	0.156	0.064	0.037	0.011
$MBIC^{OLS}$	0.039	0.033	0.033	0.006	0.047	0.162	0.069	0.003	0.004
$t-sig(10)$	0.092	0.091	0.095	0.100	0.107	0.309	0.153	0.104	0.104
$k = 5$	0.054	0.054	0.052	0.059	0.068	0.501	0.059	0.061	0.099
$k = 6$	0.052	0.054	0.055	0.052	0.058	0.361	0.050	0.057	0.036
$k = 7$	0.058	0.052	0.055	0.056	0.056	0.275	0.056	0.055	0.083
$k = 8$	0.059	0.056	0.055	0.058	0.054	0.214	0.063	0.057	0.042
$k = 9$	0.056	0.055	0.054	0.053	0.058	0.171	0.051	0.049	0.064
$k = 10$	0.046	0.056	0.052	0.046	0.066	0.136	0.053	0.048	0.036
$k = 11$	0.044	0.050	0.050	0.050	0.061	0.117	0.049	0.043	0.061
$k = 12$	0.044	0.047	0.052	0.058	0.064	0.117	0.049	0.043	0.061
$k = 13$	0.053	0.053	0.050	0.056	0.054	0.089	0.055	0.054	0.052

3.5. The Supremum Method and a Single Breakpoint

The results change favorably when the Supremum method is used to select the breakpoint. Several simulations have been performed under the setup of Section 3.1 for Model I: $z_t = \beta_1 + \beta_2 t + \beta_3 \mathbf{1}(t > T_B)(t - T_B)$ with two scenarios: (i) $\beta_3 = 0$, that is, no break; and (ii) $\beta_3 = 0.5, 1.0, 1.5$ with $\delta = 0.50 \times T$. Similar experiments have been performed for Model II. In the first case, the $MZ_{\widehat{\alpha}}^{GLS}$ test still has explosive values, although less frequently; and the values are negative but of a smaller magnitude (in absolute value) than when using the Infimum method. In the second case, the results show considerable improvement, especially when $T = 250$. The explosive values of the $MZ_{\widehat{\alpha}}^{GLS}$ test practically disappear for the MIC and MIC^{OLS} rules, although the cost is to have small values (in absolute value), which produce a conservative test. On the other hand, the rules AIC, AIC^{OLS}, and t-sig(10) continue to present an $MZ_{\widehat{\alpha}}^{GLS}$ test with explosive values which, however, are very small compared to the previous cases, and occur only when a higher k is selected.

The best results with the Supremum method are important, since this method is recommended in the literature to select the break date. For instance, Vogelsang and Perron (1998) argue that this method is to be preferred, since it allows a consistent estimate of the breaking point, a matter that the Infimum method cannot do.

The evidence suggests that, in the empirical applications, the Supremum method should be used to select the breakpoint along with the MIC and MIC^{OLS} rules, although the potential cost is to have a conservative test. The evidence suggests avoiding the use of rules such as AIC, AIC^{OLS}, and t-sig(10) to select k, as well as the use of the Infimum method to select the breakpoint.

4. Conclusions

This note aims to examine the performance of the size of the M^{GLS} statistics to test for the presence of a unit root using different lag length selection criteria in the context of an unknown structural change. In particular, we have focused on the size performance of the $MZ_{\widehat{\alpha}}^{GLS}$ test. Overall, the results show that there is a strong relationship between the explosive negative values of the $MZ_{\widehat{\alpha}}^{GLS}$ test and the values of the selected k. Using the Infimum method to select the break point jointly with some rule, such as AIC, AIC^{OLS} or t-sig(10), produces the worst scenario, in the sense that the test yields explosive negative values, which generates severe oversizing problems. On the opposite side, using other criteria for k implies conservative tests. These issues seem to improve when $T = 250$ (relative to $T = 100$) or more, which creates sample size difficulties for most macroeconomic applications, especially in Latin American countries.

The results indicate that ADF^{GLS} should be used, because it does does not result in explosiveness. Although for other reasons, this recommendation is in the same vein as Harvey et al. (2013). The advantage of the $MZ_{\bar{\alpha}}^{GLS}$ test is that it is intrinsically conservative. So, if we obtain a good size when $\theta = -0.80$, this is achieved at the cost of having an undersized test in the other cases, including the *i.i.d.* case. Our results are in line with those obtained in Del Barrio Castro et al. (2011), Del Barrio Castro et al. (2013), and Del Barrio Castro et al. (2015)[11].

The results change for the better when using the Supremum method (minimizing the SSR) to select the breakpoint. However, this result only occurs when there is a break in the series. With this method, the test values are reduced (in absolute value) and no explosiveness is observed. Furthermore, the advantage is that the method offers a consistent breakpoint estimator which is currently suggested in the literature. Although a possible undersizing problem is addressed, then a possible best scenario is to use the Supremum method together with rules for selecting k such as *MIC*. This potential need to perform a pre-testing to see the existence of a break is similar to what is proposed by Kim and Perron (2009) when there is only one break and the proposal of Carrión-i-Silvestre et al. (2009) when there are multiple breaks.

Author Contributions: Both authors contributed eaully to the paper.

Conflicts of Interest: The authors declare no conflict of interest.

References

Agiakloglou, Christos, and Paul Newbold. 1992. Empirical Evidence on Dickey-Fuller-Type Tests. *Journal of Time Series Analysis* 13: 471–83.

Agiakloglou, Christos, and Paul Newbold. 1996. The balance between size and power in Dickey-Fuller tests with data-dependent rules for the choice of truncation lag. *Economics Letters* 52: 229–34.

Bhargava, Alok. 1986. On the theory of testing for unit root in observed time series. *Review of Economic Studies* 53: 369–84.

Campbell, John Y., and Pierre Perron. 1991. Pitfalls and Opportunities: What Macroeconomists Should Know about Unit Roots. In *NBER Macroeconomics Annual*. Edited by Olivier J. Blanchard and Stanley Fischer. New York: MIT Press, Volume 6, pp. 141–201.

Carrión-i-Silvestre, Josep Lluís, Dukpa Kim, and Pierre Perron. 2009. GLS-based Unit Root Tests with Multiple Structural Breaks both Under the Null and Alternative Hypotheses. *Econometric Theory* 25: 1754–92.

Choi, In. 2015. *Almost All about Unit Roots*. Series: Themes in Modern Econometrics. New York: Cambridge University Press.

Del Barrio Castro, Tomás, Paulo M. M. Rodrigues, and A. M. Robert Taylor. 2011. The Impact of Persistent Cycles on Zero Frequency Unit Root Tests. Working Paper 24. Banco de Portugal, Lisbon, Portugal.

Del Barrio Castro, Tomás, Paulo M. M. Rodrigues, and A. M. Robert Taylor. 2013. The Impact of Persistent Cycles on Zero Frequency Unit Root Tests. *Econometric Theory* 29: 1289–313.

Del Barrio Castro, Tomás, Paulo M. M. Rodrigues, and A. M. Robert Taylor. 2015. On the Behaviour of Phillips-Perron Tests in the Presence of Persistent Cycles. *Oxford Bulletin of Economics and Statistics* 77: 495–511.

Elliott, Graham, Thomas J. Rothenberg, and James H. Stock. 1996. Efficient tests for an autoregressive unit root. *Econometrica* 64: 813–39.

Fossati, Sebastian. 2012. Covariate unit root tests with good size and power. *Computational Statistics and Data Analysis* 56: 3070–79.

[11] They explain both issues (in particular the undersizing feature) in the context of time series admitting for (near-) unit roots at cyclical frequencies. They suggest that the degree of undersizing is worst when $MAIC$ is used. The problem is aggravated if GLS detrended data are used. See these references for further details.

Haldrup, Niels, and Michael Jansson. 2006. Improving Size and Power in Unit Root Testing. In *Palgrave Handbook of Econometrics, Volume 1: Econometric Theory*. Edited by Terence C. Mills, and Kerry Patterson. Basingstoke: Palgrave Macmillan, pp. 252–77.

Hall, Alastair R. 1994. Testing for a Unit Root in Time Series with Pretest Data-Based Model Selection. *Journal of Business & Economic Statistics* 12: 461–70.

Harvey, David I., Stephen J. Leybourne, and A. M. Robert Taylor. 2013. Testing for unit roots in the possible presence of multiple trend breaks using minimum Dickey-Fuller statistics. *Journal of Econometrics* 177: 265–84.

Kim, Dukpa, and Pierre Perron. 2009. Unit root tests allowing for a break in the trend function at an unknown time under both the null and alternative hypotheses. *Journal of Econometrics* 148: 1–13.

Maddala, Gangadharrao S., and In-Moo Kim. 1998. *Unit Roots Cointegration, and Structural Change*. Cambridge: Cambridge University Press.

Ng, Serena, and Pierre Perron. 1995. Unit root tests in ARMA models with data dependent methods for the selection of the truncation lag. *Journal of the American Statistical Association* 90: 268–81.

Ng, Serena, and Pierre Perron. 2001. Lag length selection and the construction of unit root tests with good size and power. *Econometrica* 69: 1519–54.

Ng, Serena, and Pierre Perron. 2005. A note on the selection of time series models. *Oxford Bulletin of Economics and Statistics* 67: 115–34.

Perron, Pierre. 1989. The great crash, the oil price shock and the unit root hypothesis. *Econometrica* 57: 1361–401.

Perron, Pierre. 1997. Further evidence of breaking trend functions in macroeconomic variables. *Journal of Econometrics* 80: 355–85.

Perron, P. 2006. Dealing with Structural Breaks. In *Palgrave Handbook of Econometrics, Volume 1: Econometric Theory*. Edited by Terence C. Mills, and Kerry Patterson. Basingstoke: Palgrave Macmillan, pp. 278–352.

Perron, Pierre, and Serena Ng. 1996. Useful Modifications to Unit Root Tests with Dependent Errors and their Local Asymptotic Properties. *Review of Economic Studies* 63: 435–65.

Perron, Pierre, and Serena Ng. 1998. An Autoregressive Spectral Density Estimator at Frequency Zero for Nonstationarity Tests. *Econometric Theory* 14: 560–603.

Perron, Pierre, and Zhongjun Qu. 2007. A simple modification to improve the infinite sample properties of Ng and Perron's unit root tests. *Economics Letters* 94: 12–19.

Perron, Pierre, and Gabriel Rodríguez. 2003. GLS Detrending, Efficient Unit Root Tests and Structural Change. *Journal of Econometrics* 115: 1–27.

Phillips, Peter C. B., and Pierre Perron. 1988. Testing for a unit root in time series regression. *Biometrika* **75**, 335–46.

Phillips, Peter C. B., and Zhijie Xiao. 1998. A primer on unit root testing. *Journal of Economic Surveys* 12: 423–70.

Quineche, Ricardo, and Gabriel Rodríguez. 2015. Data-Dependent Methods for the Lag Length Selection in Unit Root Tests with Structural Change. Working Paper 404, Department of Economics, Pontificia Universidad Católica del Perú, Lima, Peru.

Rodríguez, Gabriel. 2007. Finite Sample Behaviour of the Level Shift Model using Quasi-Differenced Data. *Journal of Statistical Computation and Simulation* 77: 889–905.

Schwert, G. William. 1989. Tests for unit roots: A Monte Carlo Investigation. *Journal of Business and Economics Statistics* 7: 147–59.

Stock, James H. 1994. Unit Roots, Structural Breaks and Trends. In *Handbook of Econometrics*. Edited by Daniel L. McFaden and Robert F. Engle. Amsterdam: Elsevier, vol. IV, pp. 2740–841.

Stock, James H. 1999. A Class of Tests for Integration and Cointegration. In *Cointegration, Causality and Forecasting. A Festschrift in Honour of Clive W. J. Granger*. Edited by Engle, Robert F. and Halbert White. Oxford: Oxford University Press, pp. 137–67.

Vogelsang, Timothy J., and Pierre Perron. 1998. Additional Tests for a Unit Root Allowing the Possibility of Breaks in the Trend Function at an Unknown Time. *International Economic Review* 39: 1073–100.

Zivot, Eric, and Donald W. K. Andrews. 1992. Further evidence on the great crash, the oil-price shock and the unit root hypothesis. *Journal of Business and Economics Statistics* 10: 251–70.

econometrics

MDPI

Article

Fractional Unit Root Tests Allowing for a Structural Change in Trend under Both the Null and Alternative Hypotheses

Seong Yeon Chang [1,*] **and Pierre Perron** [2]

1 Wang Yanan Institute for Studies in Economics, Deartment of Statistics, MOE Key Laboratory of Econometrics and Fujian Key Laboratory of Statistical Science, Xiamen University, Xiamen 361005, China
2 Department of Economics, Boston University, Boston, MA 02215, USA; perron@bu.edu
* Correspondence: sychang@xmu.edu.cn; Tel.: +86-156-5928-1231

Academic Editor: Steve Cook
Received: 17 November 2016; Accepted: 3 January 2017; Published: 8 January 2017

Abstract: This paper considers testing procedures for the null hypothesis of a unit root process against the alternative of a fractional process, called a fractional unit root test. We extend the Lagrange Multiplier (LM) tests of Robinson (1994) and Tanaka (1999), which are locally best invariant and uniformly most powerful, to allow for a slope change in trend with or without a concurrent level shift under both the null and alternative hypotheses. We show that the limit distribution of the proposed LM tests is standard normal. Finite sample simulation experiments show that the tests have good size and power. As an empirical analysis, we apply the tests to the Consumer Price Indices of the G7 countries.

Keywords: hypothesis testing; LM test; slope change; spurious break; trend function

JEL Classification: C22

---

1. Introduction

Non-stationarity in economic time series is a pervasive feature. In order to carry proper inference, it is important to find the exact features that lead to this non-stationarity. A unit root process is a well-known example of non-stationary processes, and testing for a unit root against stationarity has been a topic of substantial interest from both theoretical and empirical perspectives. Perron (1989) [1], however, showed that the Dickey and Fuller (1979) [2] type unit root test is biased in favor of a non-rejection of the unit root null hypothesis when the process is trend stationary with a structural change in slope. Perron (1989, 1990) [1,3] proposed testing procedures in which a structural break is allowed under both the null and alternative hypotheses. Later, Christiano (1992) [4] and Zivot and Andrews (1992) [5] criticized the assumption that the date of the structural break is known a priori. In succeeding research, Zivot and Andrews (1992) [5], Perron (1997) [6], and Vogelsang and Perron (1998) [7] treated the break date as unknown and proposed testing procedures for a unit root. In much work, especially that of Zivot and Andrews (1992) [5], it was common to allow for a structural break only under the alternative hypothesis, not under the null hypothesis of a unit root. This is very restrictive, and can lead to misleading results. Recent advances in testing for and estimating a structural break in a trend function have made possible the development of unit root tests that allow for a change in trend under both the null and alternative hypotheses. Perron and Zhu (2005) [8] established the consistency, rate of convergence, and limiting distribution of the parameter estimates when there is a break in a trend function with or without a concurrent level shift. Perron and Yabu (2009) [9] suggested a testing procedure for structural changes in the trend function of a time series without any prior knowledge of whether the noise component is stationary or has an autoregressive unit root. Building on this work, Kim and Perron (2009) [10] proposed unit root testing procedures which allow for a structural change under both the null and alternative hypotheses; see also Carrion-i-Silvestre et al. (2009) [11] for an extension to the case with multiple changes.

Fractional processes with the order of integration $d \geq 0.5$ are also non-stationary. Standard unit root tests often reject the null hypothesis when the true process is fractionally integrated with $d \in (0.5, 1)$. This can lead to the misleading conclusion that the process of interest is stationary. This motivated researchers to introduce unit root tests which are powerful against the alternative hypothesis of a fractional process. Robinson (1991) [12] derived a Lagrange Multiplier (LM) test for fractional white noise disturbances in a linear regression, while Robinson (1994) [13] proposed tests for unit root, and actually any real values of d in both the frequency and the time domain. Tanaka (1999) [14] suggested an LM test in the time domain, and showed that it is locally best invariant and uniformly most powerful. Dolado et al. (2002) [15] introduced a Wald-type unit root test against the alternative of fractional integration. This test is based on the Dickey and Fuller (1979) [2] type test using an auxiliary regression with a consistent estimate of the integration order. Lobato and Velasco (2007) [16] established a Wald-type test which is more efficient and is asymptotically equivalent to the LM test. Recently, Cho et al. (2015) [17] suggested combining the test of Kwiatkowski et al. (1992) [18] and a unit root test to test the null of integer integration, i.e., $I(0)$ or $I(1)$ against the alternative of fractional integration, i.e., $I(d)$, $d \in (0, 1)$. In this line of work, the process of interest has been limited to either a random walk or a purely fractional process. Lobato and Velasco (2007) [16] considered short-run dynamics in the process. Dolado et al. (2008) [19] extended the work of Dolado et al. (2002) [15] and Lobato and Velasco (2007) [16] to incorporate some deterministic components; for instance, a constant and a linear trend function.

Our main contribution is to extend the LM test for a fractional unit root to allow for a structural change in a trend function under both the null and alternative hypotheses. This extension has some advantages, as follows: (i) it imposes a symmetric treatment of the nature of the deterministic trend under both the null and alternative hypotheses; (ii) it does not require long memory to be distinguished from structural change;[1] (iii) the power of fractional unit root tests can be substantially improved when a break is actually present. We consider linear trend models in which a structural change in slope occurs with or without a concurrent level shift.

The rest of this paper is organized as follows. In Section 2, we first introduce fractional processes and the Lagrange Multiplier test of Tanaka (1999) [14] along with preliminary results to be used subsequently. In Section 3, the LM tests are generalized to allow for a structural break in trend under both the null and alternative hypotheses. Extensions to processes with short-run dynamics are discussed in Section 4. The results of simulation experiments about the size and power of the tests are presented in Section 5. As an empirical application, we test for a fractional unit root in the Consumer Price Indices (CPIs) of the G7 countries in Section 6. Concluding remarks are provided in Section 7. All mathematical proofs are relegated to the Appendix A.

2. Lagrange Multiplier Test

For an integer $d = 1, 2, \ldots$, the operator $\Delta^d = (1 - L)^d$ denotes the differencing operator with the usual lag operator L; i.e., $LX_t \equiv X_{t-1}$, $\Delta X_t = X_t - X_{t-1}$, $\Delta^2 X_t = (1 - 2L + L^2)X_t = X_t - 2X_{t-1} + X_{t-2}$,

[1] Given that unit root and long memory processes share similar features, distinguishing between long memory processes and short memory processes with structural changes has been an important topic in econometrics and financial economics. Along the lines of Perron (1989) [1], it is well known that short memory processes with level shifts exhibit properties that lead standard tools to conclude that long memory is present (e.g., Diebold and Inoue (2001) [20], Granger and Hyung (2004) [21], Lu and Perron (2010) [22], Perron and Qu (2010) [23], Qu and Perron (2013) [24], Xu and Perron (2014) [25], and Varneskov and Perron (2016) [26], among many others). On the other hand, it has been also documented that long memory processes induce a rejection of the null hypothesis of no structural change when using conventional structural change tests (see Wright (1998) [27] and Krämer and Sibbertsen (2002) [28]).

and so on. For a non-integer real number $d > -1$, the difference operator $\Delta^d = (1-L)^d$ is defined by means of the binomial expansion

$$\Delta^d = \sum_{k=0}^{\infty} \binom{d}{k} (-L)^k = \sum_{k=0}^{\infty} \pi_k(d) L^k,$$

where

$$\binom{d}{k} \equiv \frac{d!}{k!(d-k)!} = \frac{d \times (d-1) \times \cdots \times (d-k+1)}{k \times (k-1) \times \cdots \times 2 \times 1},$$

$$\pi_k(d) \equiv (-1)^k \binom{d}{k} = \prod_{s=1}^{k} \frac{s-1-d}{s} = \frac{\Gamma(k-d)}{\Gamma(k+1)\Gamma(-d)},$$

with $\Gamma(\cdot)$ the gamma function, so that $\pi_k(d) = \binom{k-d-1}{k}$ and $\pi_0(d) = 1$. Recall that $x! \equiv \Gamma(x+1)$, $x = 0, 1, \ldots$, and for $k = 1, 2, \cdots$, $0 < x < 1$, $\Gamma(x-k)$ is defined as $\Gamma(x) = (x-1)\Gamma(x-1) = \cdots = (x-1)\cdots(x-k)\Gamma(x-k)$. To define a fractional process, we use the notation of Robinson (2005) [29]. Let $\{\eta_t, t = 0, \pm 1, \ldots\}$ be a short-memory zero-mean covariance stationary process, with spectral density that is bounded and bounded away from zero. For $d \in (-0.5, 0.5)$,

$$\zeta_t = \Delta^{-d} \eta_t, \quad t = 0, \pm 1, \ldots, \tag{1}$$

is covariance stationary and invertible. The truncated version of ζ_t is defined as

$$\zeta_t^{\#} = \zeta_t \mathbf{1}_{t \geq 1}, \quad t = 0, \pm 1, \ldots, \tag{2}$$

where $\mathbf{1}_A$ is the indicator function for the event A. For an integer $m \geq 0$,

$$u_t = \Delta^{-m} \zeta_t^{\#}, \quad t = 0, \pm 1, \ldots \tag{3}$$

is called a type I $I(m+d)$ process. Let $\mathcal{D}[0,1]$ be the space of functions on $[0,1]$ which are right continuous and have left limits, equipped with the Skorohod topology. Let $\xrightarrow{p}$ denote convergence in probability and $\xrightarrow{d}$ convergence in distribution. Denote by $[a]$ the integer part of $a \in \mathbb{R}$. The order of integration is $d_0 = d + m$, with $d \in (-0.5, 0.5)$ and $m \in \{0, 1\}$.[2]

Remark 1. *Marinucci and Robinson (1999) [30] defined type I and type II fractional Brownian motions with $d \in (-0.5, 0.5)$ on $\mathcal{D}[0,1]$, respectively, as follows:*

$$B_I(t) = \frac{1}{\Gamma(d+1)} \left\{ \int_{-\infty}^{0} [(t-s)^d - (-s)^d] dB(s) + \int_0^t (t-s) dB(s) \right\},$$

$$B_{II}(t) = \frac{1}{\Gamma(d+1)} \left\{ \int_0^t (t-s) dB(s) \right\},$$

where $B(\cdot)$ denotes the standard Brownian motion. Furthermore, Robinson (2005) [29] and Davidson and Hashimzade (2009) [31] pointed out that asymptotic results vary depending on the definition of fractional Brownian motions considered, which requires one to design simulation experiments in accordance with the particular type used.

Now we consider a fractional unit root test. Under the null hypothesis, $\{u_t\}$ is a unit root process; that is, $H_0 : d_0 = 1$ (i.e., $d = 0$ and $m = 1$). The alternative hypothesis can be either one-sided

[2] The restriction that $d_0 \neq 0.5$ is standard in the long memory literature. Tanaka (1999) [14] showed that the case with $d_0 = 0.5$ needs to be treated separately from the case with $d_0 \neq 0.5$.

($H_1 : d_0 > 1$ or $H_1 : d_0 < 1$) or two-sided ($H_1 : d_0 \neq 1$). Robinson (1994) [13] and Tanaka (1999) [14] considered the Lagrange Multiplier test in the frequency and time domain. It is well known that the LM test is locally best invariant. Further, Tanaka (1999) [14] showed that the LM test is locally uniformly most powerful invariant because it achieves the power envelope of all the invariant tests against local alternatives. The test statistic suggested in Tanaka (1999) [14] is

$$\mathcal{LM} = \sqrt{T}\sqrt{\frac{6}{\pi^2}}\sum_{k=1}^{T-1}\frac{1}{k}\rho_k,$$

where $\rho_k = (\sum_{j=k+1}^{T}\Delta u_{j-k}\Delta u_j)/\sum_{j=1}^{T}(\Delta u_j)^2$ is the kth order autocorrelation of the residuals Δu_t. Local alternatives to the null hypothesis are often considered in the literature, with the integration order defined as $d_0 = 1 + \delta T^{-1/2}$ with δ fixed, often referred to as Pitman drifts. We state the limiting distribution of the LM test under local alternatives, as it will be relevant for subsequent derivations.

Lemma 1 (Theorem 3.1 in Tanaka (1999) [14]). *Under the assumption that u_t is generated by (3) with $d_0 = 1 + \delta T^{-1/2}$ and δ fixed, it holds that, as $T \to \infty$, $\mathcal{LM} \xrightarrow{d} \mathcal{N}(\delta\sqrt{\pi^2/6}, 1)$.*

3. Deterministic Components Allowing for a Structural Change

In this section, we extend the LM test for a fractional unit root to allow for a structural change in trend with or without a concurrent level shift. We consider the time series of interest y_t as consisting of a deterministic component (f_t) and fractionally integrated errors. The data-generating process (DGP) is specified as

$$y_t = f_t + u_t.$$

For u_t, we impose $\mathbf{E}(u_t) = 0$ and the following assumption.

Assumption 1. *u_t is a type I $I(m + d)$ process which is defined in (1)–(3). Moreover, the short-memory zero-mean covariance stationary process η_t is assumed to be independent and identically distributed (i.i.d.) with zero mean and finite variance.*

The *i.i.d.* assumption on the short-memory process η_t will be relaxed later to allow for short-run dynamics. The unit root null hypothesis corresponds to the case with $m = 1$ and $d = 0$, which implies that u_t is a weighted sum of η_t.

3.1. Change in Mean

We first consider the case where y_t experiences a level shift at an unknown time T_b. The DGP is specified as

$$y_t = \mu_1 + \mu_b C_t + u_t, \quad \mu_b \neq 0, \tag{4}$$

where C_t is a dummy variable for a level shift defined by:

$$C_t = \begin{cases} 0 & \text{if } t \leq T_b, \\ 1 & \text{if } t > T_b, \end{cases}$$

where $T_b = [T\lambda_b]$ is the true break date with the corresponding true break fraction $\lambda_b \in (0, 1)$.

Theorem 1 (Change in Mean). *Under Assumption 1, suppose that the process $\{y_t\}$ is generated under the null hypothesis of (4). Consider the Lagrange Multiplier test $\mathcal{LM}_M$ defined by:*

$$\mathcal{LM}_M = \sqrt{T}\sqrt{\frac{6}{\pi^2}}\frac{\sum_{t=1}^{T}(-\log\Delta\Delta y_t)\,\Delta y_t}{\sum_{t=1}^{T}(\Delta y_t)^2}.$$

Under the null hypothesis $H_0 : d_0 = 1$*, it holds that as* $T \to \infty$, $\mathcal{LM}_M \xrightarrow{d} \mathcal{N}(0,1)$.

Theorem 1 implies that Tanaka's (1999) [14] LM test is robust to the presence of a level shift. In the following subsection, we consider the LM test in the context of trending series.

3.2. Slope and Intercept Change in Trending Series

We now introduce a deterministic time trend in the models. We follow the notation in Kim and Perron (2009) [10] (henceforth KP) from which we will use some relevant results. The DGPs are specified as

1. Model A0: (Deterministic time trend without a structural change)

$$y_t = \mu_1 + \beta_1 t + u_t, \tag{5}$$

2. Model A1: (Level shift)

$$y_t = \mu_1 + \mu_b C_t + \beta_1 t + u_t, \tag{6}$$

3. Model A2: (Joint broken trend)

$$y_t = \mu_1 + \beta_1 t + \beta_b B_t + u_t, \tag{7}$$

where B_t is a dummy variable for a slope change in trend given by

$$B_t = \begin{cases} 0 & \text{if } t \le T_b, \\ t - T_b & \text{if } t > T_b, \end{cases}$$

4. Model A3: (Locally disjoint broken trend)

$$y_t = \mu_1 + \mu_b C_t + \beta_1 t + \beta_b B_t + u_t.$$

Following KP, we can rewrite Models A1–A3 as follows:

$$y_t = z(T_b)_t' \phi + u_t = z_{t,1}' \phi_1 + z(T_b)_{t,2}' \phi_2 + u_t,$$

where $z_{t,1} = (1, t)'$, $\phi_1 = (\mu_1, \beta_1)'$,

$$z(T_b)_{t,2} = \begin{cases} C_t \\ B_t \\ (C_t, B_t)' \end{cases}, \quad \phi_2 = \begin{cases} \mu_b & \text{for Model A1} \\ \beta_b & \text{for Model A2} \\ (\mu_b, \beta_b)' & \text{for Model A3.} \end{cases}$$

In matrix notation, the models defined previously can be specified as $Y = Z_{T_b}\phi + U$, where $Y = [y_1, \ldots, y_T]'$, $Z_{T_b} = [z(T_b)_1, \ldots, z(T_b)_T]'$, $\phi = (\phi_1', \phi_2')'$, and $U = [u_1, \ldots, u_T]'$.

Consider first Model A0, where no structural change is allowed. By taking first differences, we can rewrite (5) as follows:

$$\Delta y_t = \beta_1 + \Delta u_t = \beta_1 + \Delta^{1-d_0} \eta_t \mathbf{1}_{t \ge 1}. \tag{8}$$

The ordinary least squares (OLS) estimate of β_1 is $\hat{\beta}_1 = T^{-1} \sum_{t=1}^{T} \Delta y_t$, which is consistent under both H_0 and H_1.[3] We define $\widetilde{\Delta y_t} = \Delta y_t - \hat{\beta}_1$, the OLS residuals from the regression model (8).

---

[3] Under H_0, $\hat{\beta}_1$ is a $T^{1/2}$-consistent estimator of the slope coefficient β_1. Hosking (1996) [32] considered a stationary ARFIMA (p, d, q) process $\{y_t\}$ and showed the weak convergence of the sample mean for $d \in (-0.5, 0.5)$. It is not difficult to generalize the result to the case where $d \in (0.5, 1)$, for which $\hat{\beta}_1$ is a $T^{3/2-d}$-consistent estimator.

Theorem 2 (Linear Trend). *Under Assumption 1, suppose that the process $\{y_t\}$ is generated under the null hypothesis of (5). Consider the Lagrange Multiplier test $\mathcal{LM}_T$ defined by:*

$$\mathcal{LM}_T = \sqrt{T}\sqrt{\frac{6}{\pi^2}}\frac{\sum_{t=1}^{T}\left(-\log\Delta\widetilde{\Delta y_t}\right)\widetilde{\Delta y_t}}{\sum_{t=1}^{T}\left(\widetilde{\Delta y_t}\right)^2}.$$

Under the null hypothesis $H_0 : d_0 = 1$, it holds that as $T \to \infty$, $\mathcal{LM}_T \xrightarrow{d} \mathcal{N}(0,1)$.

In what follows, the aim is to devise Lagrange Multiplier tests allowing for a slope change in trend with or without a concurrent level shift. The following assumption is essential to that effect.

Assumption 2. *$\beta_b \neq 0$ and $\lambda_b \in (\pi, 1-\pi)$ for some $\pi \in (0, 1/2)$.*

Assumption 2 ensures that there is a single slope change in trend, and that the pre- and post-break samples are not asymptotically negligible, which is a standard assumption needed to derive useful asymptotic results. Model A1 (level shift only) will be revisited later.

The break date can be estimated by using a global least-squares criterion:

$$\hat{T}_b = \arg\min_{T_1 \in \Lambda} Y'(I - P_{T_1})Y,$$

where P_{T_1} is the matrix that projects on the range space of Z_{T_1}; i.e., $P_{T_1} = Z_{T_1}(Z'_{T_1}Z_{T_1})^{-1}Z'_{T_1}$ and $\Lambda = [\pi T, (1-\pi)T]$, $0 < \pi < 1/2$. Note that Z_{T_1} is the same as Z_{T_b}, except T_b is replaced with a generic break date T_1. Perron and Zhu (2005) [8] (henceforth, PZ) established the consistency, rate of convergence, and limiting distribution of parameter estimates when the error is an $I(1)$ process. With $Z_{\hat{T}_b}$ constructed using the estimate $\hat{T}_b$, the OLS estimate of ϕ is $\hat{\phi} = (Z'_{\hat{T}_b}Z_{\hat{T}_b})^{-1}Z'_{\hat{T}_b}Y$, and the resulting sum of squared residuals is, for an estimated break fraction $\hat{\lambda}_s = \hat{T}_b/T$ (the subscript s refers to the fact that we consider a static regression; a dynamic regression with lagged dependent variables will be considered later):

$$S(\hat{\lambda}_s) = \sum_{t=1}^{T}\hat{u}_t^2 = \sum_{t=1}^{T}\left(y_t - z(\hat{T}_b)'_t\hat{\phi}\right)^2 = Y'(I - P_{\hat{T}_b})Y,$$

where $P_{\hat{T}_b}$ is the projection matrix associated with $X_{\hat{T}_b}$. The rate of convergence of $\hat{\lambda}_s$ for Models A2 and A3 is $\hat{\lambda}_s - \lambda_b = O_p(T^{-1/2})$ with $I(1)$ errors (see Theorem 3 in PZ). Chang and Perron (2016) [33] derived the consistency and rate of convergence of $\hat{\lambda}_s$ when the noise component is a fractional process with the differencing parameter $d_0 \in (-0.5, 0.5) \cup (0.5, 1.5)$. Specifically, for Models A2 and A3, $\hat{\lambda}_s - \lambda_b = O_p(T^{-1/2+d})$ if $m = 1$ and $d \in (-0.5, 0.5)$. With the consistent estimates $(\hat{\lambda}_s, \hat{\mu}_1, \hat{\mu}_b, \hat{\beta}_1, \hat{\beta}_b)$, we can construct the detrended process $\{\tilde{y}_t\}$, and the Lagrange Multiplier test statistic $\mathcal{LM}_{T,\hat{\lambda}_s}$ is given by

$$\mathcal{LM}_{T,\hat{\lambda}_s} = \sqrt{T}\sqrt{\frac{6}{\pi^2}}\frac{\sum_{t=1}^{T}(-\log\Delta\Delta\tilde{y}_t)\Delta\tilde{y}_t}{\sum_{t=1}^{T}(\Delta\tilde{y}_t)^2}.$$

The convergence rate of the estimate $\hat{\lambda}_s$ is not fast enough to guarantee that $\mathcal{LM}_{T,\hat{\lambda}_s}$ has the standard normal limit under H_0. KP faced a similar issue in dealing with unit root tests. They introduced a heuristic explanation of the issue involved, which we briefly review. Let $\hat{\lambda} = \hat{T}_b/T$ denote an estimate of the break fraction such that $\hat{\lambda} - \lambda_b = O_p(T^{-\varkappa})$ for some $\varkappa \geq 0$. The detrended series $\{\tilde{y}_t\}$ is given by

$$\tilde{Y} = \hat{M}_z Y = \hat{M}_z Z(T_b)\phi + \hat{M}_z U = \hat{M}_z Z(T_b)_2\phi_2 + \hat{M}_z U, \tag{9}$$

where $Z(T_b)$ and $Z(T_b)_2$ are matrices stacking $\{z(T_b)'_t\}$ and $\{z(T_b)'_{t,2}\}$, respectively, and the idempotent matrix $\hat{M}_z = I - \hat{P}_z = I - Z(\hat{T}_b)[Z(\hat{T}_b)'Z(\hat{T}_b)]^{-}Z(\hat{T}_b)'$. It is obvious that $\hat{M}_z Z(T_b)_2\phi_2 = 0$ only if the true break date is used in $\hat{M}_z$. In finite samples, $\hat{\lambda} \neq \lambda_b$ in general; thereby, $\hat{M}_z Z(T_b)_2\phi_2$ will not be zero. It turns out that a fast rate of convergence for the estimate of the break date is needed for the effect of $\hat{M}_z Z(T_b)_2\phi_2$ on the Lagrange Multiplier test to become negligible asymptotically. The following proposition provides a sufficient condition under which $\mathcal{LM}_{T,\hat{\lambda}} \xrightarrow{d} \mathcal{N}(0,1)$ under H_0.

Proposition 1. *Suppose that the process $\{y_t\}$ is generated under the null hypothesis of Model A2 or A3, and that Assumptions 1 and 2 hold. Then, it holds that, as $T \to \infty$, $\mathcal{LM}_{T,\hat{\lambda}} \xrightarrow{d} \mathcal{N}(0,1)$ if $\hat{\lambda} - \lambda_b = o_p(T^{-1/2})$.*

Proposition 1 implies that the estimate of the break fraction should converge at a rate faster than $T^{1/2}$. As shown above, $\hat{\lambda}_s$ does not satisfy this condition. Hence, we need to consider alternative ways to accelerate the rate of convergence of the estimate of the break fraction. KP suggested two possible approaches. The first is based on minimizing the sum of squared residuals (SSR) of a dynamic regression model. This method is similar to that in Hatanaka and Yamada (1999) [34]. The relevant dynamic regressions are specified as follows:

$$\begin{aligned} y_t &= \alpha y_{t-1} + \nu_1 D(T_b)_t + \nu_2 \mathbf{1}_{t \geq T_b} + z(T_b)'_t\phi + u_t, \quad &\text{(Model A2)} \\ y_t &= \alpha y_{t-1} + \nu D(T_b)_t + z(T_b)'_t\phi + u_t, \quad &\text{(Models A1 and A3)} \end{aligned} \tag{10}$$

where $D(T_b)_t = 1$ for $t = T_b + 1$ and 0 otherwise. Under the null hypothesis, we obtain an estimate of the break fraction $\hat{\lambda}_d$ which has a faster rate of convergence, such that $\hat{\lambda}_d - \lambda_b = O_p(T^{-1})$ for Models A2 and A3 (see Proposition 1 in KP). Let $\mathcal{LM}_{T,\hat{\lambda}_d}$ denote the Lagrange Multiplier test statistic with $\hat{\lambda}_d$ replacing $\hat{\lambda}_s$. It is worth noting that, as discussed by Hatanaka and Yamada (1999) [34] and KP, the estimate $\hat{\lambda}_d$ has a negative bias in finite samples, especially for Model A3. As we shall see, this will affect the finite sample properties of the tests.

The second approach is to use a trimmed data set using a window whose length depends on the sample size and which contains the estimated break date. The trimmed series then consists of the original one with the data points in the window excluded. KP showed that the rate of convergence of $\hat{\lambda}_s$ can be increased with the trimmed data set. Suppose that the estimate of the break fraction satisfies $\hat{\lambda} - \lambda_b = O_p(T^{-a})$ for some $0 < a < 1$, and the trimming window has length $2w(T)$ with $w(T) \equiv c_1 T^{\delta}$, $c_1 > 0$, and $-1 < -a < \delta < 0$. With this specification, the length of the window is negligible in the limit compared to the sample size T, but is still large enough to include the true break date asymptotically. Following KP's suggestion, one proceeds as follows:

- Estimate the break fraction $\hat{\lambda}_s$ from the original data set and form a window that ranges from $T_l \equiv T(\hat{\lambda}_s - w(T))$ to $T_h \equiv T(\hat{\lambda}_s + w(T))$.
- A trimmed data set is constructed by removing the original data from $T_l + 1$ to T_h and then shifting down the data after the window by $D(T) = y_{T_h} - y_{T_l}$. After the trimming and connecting procedures, we now have a new series $\{y_t^*\}$, for $t = 1, \ldots, T^*(\equiv T - 2w(T)T)$, defined by:

$$y_t^* = \begin{cases} y_t & \text{if } t \leq T_l, \\ y_{t+T_h-T_l} - D(T) & \text{if } t > T_l. \end{cases}$$

- Test the null hypothesis $H_0 : d_0 = 1$ using T_l as the break date (i.e., $\hat{\lambda}_{tr} = T_l/T^*$). The Lagrange Multiplier test statistic is then given by

$$\mathcal{LM}_{T,\hat{\lambda}_{tr}} = \sqrt{T}\sqrt{\frac{6}{\pi^2}} \frac{\sum_{t=1}^{T} (-\log \Delta\Delta\tilde{y}_t^*)\, \Delta\tilde{y}_t^*}{\sum_{t=1}^{T} (\Delta\tilde{y}_t^*)^2},$$

where $\tilde{y}_t^*$ is the detrended version of y_t^* using the estimate of the break date T_l (or break fraction $\hat{\lambda}_{tr}$).

Remark 2. *If the window contains either end of the data, then the process $\{y_t^*\}$ turns out to be Model A0 (no structural break), and the statistic in Theorem 2 should be applied to the trimmed data $\{y_t^*\}$.*

The trimmed process $\{y_t^*\}$ will satisfy the properties of Model A2 regardless of the specification of the original data $\{y_t\}$, which implies that we can use a common limit distribution. The following proposition states the limiting distribution of the Lagrange Multiplier test based on the trimmed data, which is the same as would be obtained if the break date was known in Model A2.

Proposition 2. *Suppose that the process $\{y_t\}$ is generated under the null hypothesis of Model A2 or A3, and that Assumptions 1 and 2 hold. Then, it holds that as $T \to \infty$, $\mathcal{LM}_{T,\hat{\lambda}_{tr}} \xrightarrow{d} \mathcal{N}(0,1)$.*

As shown in KP, under the null hypothesis of a unit root, the estimate of the break fraction $\hat{\lambda}_{tr} = T_l/T^*$ converges in probability to the true break fraction at some rate greater than T. Hence, the sufficient condition in Proposition 1 is satisfied, so that the proof of Proposition 2 is trivial and omitted.

In concluding this section, we consider the case where there is a change in mean; that is, $\mu_b \neq 0$, as in Models A1 and A3. In Model A1, we assume that there is a level shift only; that is, $\mu_b \neq 0$ and $\beta_b = 0$. Under the null hypothesis, a stochastic trend generated by the $I(1)$ error process tends to dominate a level shift. Hence, we cannot estimate the break fraction λ_b consistently, because the magnitude of the level shift is asymptotically negligible. In finite samples, we can ignore the level shift if the magnitude of the break is small. Then, Model A1 can be treated as Model A0, and we can follow the testing procedure pertaining to Theorem 2. However, a loss of power is inevitable if a large change in mean is ignored.

On the other hand, the level shift can be specified as an increasing function of the sample size; i.e., $\mu_b = c_2 T^{1/2+\alpha}$ for some $c_2 > 0$ and $\alpha > 0$. As addressed in Harvey et al. (2001) [35], PZ, and KP, this specification provides better approximations of the properties of the tests in finite samples when the level shifts are not very small. The models with $\mu_b = c_2 T^{1/2+\alpha}$ are labeled as Models A1b and A3b, respectively.

Proposition 3. *Suppose that the process $\{y_t\}$ is generated under the null hypothesis of Model A1b or A3b. Then, $\mathcal{LM}_{T,\hat{\lambda}}$ diverges as $T \to \infty$.*

Although the rate of convergence of the estimate of the break fraction is faster than in the case of a change in slope (see Proposition 7 in KP), Proposition 3 states that the LM tests cannot obtain the standard normal limiting distribution. Hence, the LM test $\mathcal{LM}_{T,\hat{\lambda}}$, using the critical values from the standard normal distribution, suffers from some liberal size distortions, even when $|\mu_b|$ is large.[4]

3.3. Using a Pre-Test for a Break in Slope

The results of Theorem 2 and Proposition 2 show that the limit distribution of the test is the same whether there is a break in slope introduced as a regressor or not, even when the DGP specifies that no break is present. Hence, unlike the case of testing for a unit root as in KP, theoretically there is no need to carry a pre-test to improve the power of the test. However, Chang and Perron (2016) [33] considered Models A2 and A3 with fractionally integrated errors and showed that the so-called spurious break issue occurs with the order of fractional integration $d_0 \in (0, 0.5) \cup (0.5, 1.5)$. This extended the results on Nunes et al. (1995) [36], who considered the unit root case. This means that under both the null

[4] Simulation results related to this issue are available upon request.

and alternative hypotheses, if a break in slope is not present and one is allowed in the regression, the fitted model will with large probability suggests the presence of a break. This could have an effect on both the size and power of the test. On one hand, the slope change regressor may induce added liberal size distortions in finite samples because of the overfit. On the other hand, since when no break exists in the DGP it is a superfluous regressor, power maybe be reduced. Hence, it may be the case that in finite samples it is beneficial to use a pre-test for a change in slope and try to choose between models (5) and (7). Since a test for a change in mean will be inconsistent, there is no point in trying to distinguish between models (5) and (6) or between model (4) and the corresponding one without the change in mean.

Iacone et al. (2013) [37] suggested a sup-Wald type test ($\mathcal{SW}$) for Model A2. In particular, it is robust to any order of fractional integration d_0 located in an interval $[0, 1.5)$ excluding the boundary case 0.5. More precisely, given their recommended choice for the bandwidth when constructing the local Whittle estimate of d_0, their test is consistent for values of d_0 in the interval $[0, 1.32]$, though we believe the proof can be modified to allow the interval $[0, 1.5)$. It follows the generalized least squares approach to construct the test statistic for a structural change in trend by taking d_0-differences from the data. To make the test feasible, the fully extended local whittle (FELW) estimator $\hat{d}_{FELW}$ of Abadir (2007) [38] is considered. While the FELW estimator is constructed under the null hypothesis of no structural change, Iacone et al. (2013) [37] showed that it also satisfies the necessary condition for consistency, even with a local break in trend. Since the true break date is unknown a priori, the final statistic $\mathcal{SW}$ uses the *sup* functional of Andrews (1993) [39] across all admissible break dates. This test is asymptotically size controlled for all d_0's in the prescribed range. Using this pre-test, we can then define the alternative estimate of the break fraction $\tilde{\lambda} = \hat{\lambda} \cdot \mathbf{1}_{\mathcal{SW} > \tau}$, where τ is the critical value for the $\mathcal{SW}$ test with a nominal size $p\%$. Given that $\mathcal{SW}$ is a consistent test, $\text{plim}_{T \to \infty} \tilde{\lambda} = \lambda_b$ if $\hat{\lambda}$ is a consistent estimate of λ_b. If there is no break in the DGP, we can expect that $p\%$ of the estimates $\tilde{\lambda}$'s are nonzero. In order to obtain a consistent estimate of λ_b under the null of no structural break, we assume that the critical value τ is a function of the sample size T. Since $\mathcal{SW} = O_p(T^{\varrho})$, $\varrho > 0$ with a local break, let $\tau = cT^{\varrho - \epsilon}$ for $0 < \epsilon < \varrho$. This specification introduced in KP is useful because it does not have any effect on the consistency of the test $\mathcal{SW}$ and does guarantee that $\text{plim}_{T \to \infty} \tilde{\lambda} = 0$ when no break is present. Hence, based on the consistency of $\tilde{\lambda}$, it is recommended to use $\mathcal{LM}_T$ if $\tilde{\lambda} = 0$ and $\mathcal{LM}_{T,\hat{\lambda}}$ if $\tilde{\lambda} \neq 0$. The LM test statistics with the pre-test are denoted by $\mathcal{LM}^p_{T,\hat{\lambda}_s}$, $\mathcal{LM}^p_{T,\hat{\lambda}_d}$, and $\mathcal{LM}^p_{T,\hat{\lambda}_{tr}}$. Whether using a pre-test is beneficial will be assessed later via simulation experiments about the size and power of the tests.

4. Short-Run Dynamics

We now relax Assumption 1 to introduce short-run dynamics in the noise component. A zero-mean short-memory covariance stationary process η_t can be represented as a one-sided moving average: $\eta_t = \sum_{j=0}^{\infty} \psi_j \epsilon_{t-j}$, $\quad t = 0, \pm 1, \ldots$, where $\psi_0 = 1$, $\sum_{j=0}^{\infty} \psi_j^2 < \infty$, $\psi(1) \equiv \sum_{j=0}^{\infty} \psi_j$, and $\{\epsilon_t, t = 0, \pm 1, \ldots\}$ are *i.i.d.* random variables with mean zero. A special case of interest is an autoregressive moving average (ARMA(p,q)) process given by $\phi(L)\eta_t = \theta(L)\epsilon_t$. In order to implement the Lagrange Multiplier test, we first estimate the parameters $\Psi = (\phi_1, \ldots, \phi_p, \theta_1, \ldots, \theta_q)$ consistently. Then, under the null hypothesis, we can construct $\hat{\epsilon}_t = \hat{\phi}(L)\hat{\theta}(L)^{-1}(1-L)^{d_0}\hat{u}_t$, where $\hat{u}_t$ is the OLS residuals from the model considered, whereas $\hat{\phi}(L)$ and $\hat{\theta}(L)$ are estimated from $\phi(L)(1-L)^{d_0}\hat{u}_t = \theta(L)\epsilon_t$, using $d_0 = 1$. With short-run dynamics in the noise component, we consider the following test statistic:

$$\mathcal{LM} = \sqrt{T} \sum_{k=1}^{T-1} \frac{1}{k} \hat{\rho}_k,$$

where $\hat{\rho}_k$ is the kth order autocorrelation of residuals $\hat{e}_1, \ldots, \hat{e}_T$. Tanaka (1999) [14] derived an important result related to this statistic when no break is present.

Lemma 2 (Theorem 3.3 in Tanaka (1999) [14]). *Under local alternatives—that is, $d_0 = 1 + \delta T^{-1/2}$ with δ fixed—it holds that as $T \to \infty$, $\mathcal{LM} \xrightarrow{d} \mathcal{N}(\delta\omega^2, \omega^2)$, where*

$$\omega^2 = \frac{\pi^2}{6} - (\kappa_1, \ldots, \kappa_p, \xi_1, \ldots, \xi_q)\Phi^{-1}(\kappa_1, \ldots, \kappa_p, \xi_1, \ldots, \xi_q)',$$

$$\kappa_i = \sum_{j=1}^{\infty} \frac{1}{j} g_{j-i}, \qquad \xi_i = -\sum_{j=i}^{\infty} \frac{1}{j} h_{j-i},$$

with g_j and h_j the coefficients of L^j in the expansion of $1/\phi(L)$ and $1/\theta(L)$, respectively, and Φ the Fisher information matrix for ϕ and θ.

Remark 3. *Note that $\omega^2 < \pi^2/6$; hence comparing Lemmas 1 and 2, the LM test has lower local asymptotic power in the presence of short-run dynamics of any kind. As will be shown via simulations, the loss in power can be substantial. It remains, nevertheless, inevitable.*

With the maximum likelihood estimate $\hat{\omega}$, we show that $\mathcal{LM}/\hat{\omega} \xrightarrow{d} \mathcal{N}(0,1)$ as $T \to \infty$ under the null hypothesis. In particular, when $p = 1$ or $q = 1$, it is easy to compute $\hat{\omega}$. Since $v_j = \varsigma v_{j-1} + \epsilon_j$ in both cases, $g_j = \varsigma^j$,

$$\kappa_1 = \sum_{j=1}^{\infty} \frac{1}{j} \varsigma^{j-1} = -\frac{1}{\varsigma} \log(1-\varsigma), \quad \text{and} \quad \Phi^{-1} = 1 - \varsigma^2.$$

Hence, we have

$$\omega^2 = \frac{\pi^2}{6} - \frac{1-\varsigma^2}{\varsigma^2}(\log(1-\varsigma))^2,$$

and $\hat{\omega}$ can be computed using $\hat{\varsigma}$. All these results remain valid for all trending models with a break considered. The relevant correction needed is a simple scaling by $\hat{\omega}$ so that the test becomes $\mathcal{LM}^*_{T,\hat{\lambda}} \equiv \mathcal{LM}_{T,\hat{\lambda}}/\hat{\omega}$.

Proposition 4. *Suppose that the process $\{y_t\}$ is generated under the null hypothesis of Model A2 or A3, and that Assumptions 1 and 2 hold with η_t being an ARMA(p,q) process. Then, it holds that as $T \to \infty$, $\mathcal{LM}^*_{T,\hat{\lambda}} \xrightarrow{d} \mathcal{N}(0,1)$ if $\hat{\lambda} - \lambda_b = o_p(T^{-1/2})$ and $\hat{\omega} - \omega = o_p(1)$.*

The sufficient conditions in Proposition 4 follow from Lemma 2 and Proposition 1, hence the proof is omitted. The finite sample performance of $\mathcal{LM}^*_{T,\hat{\lambda}}$ with $\hat{\lambda} \in \{\hat{\lambda}_s, \hat{\lambda}_d, \hat{\lambda}_{tr}\}$ allowing for a structural break under both the null and alternative hypotheses will be examined in the next section.

5. Simulation Experiments

In this section, we present results from simulation experiments to illustrate the various theoretical results. Throughout the simulations, the true break fraction is set to $\lambda_b = 0.5$.[5] The DGP is specified as $y_t = f_t + u_t$ where

$$f_t = \begin{cases} \mu_1 + \beta_1 t & \text{for Model A0,} \\ \mu_b C_t & \text{for Model A1,} \\ \beta_b B_t & \text{for Model A2,} \\ \mu_b C_t + \beta_b B_t & \text{for Model A3,} \end{cases}$$

[5] Unreported simulation results with $\lambda_b = \{0.3, 0.7\}$ are qualitatively similar to those with $\lambda_b = 0.5$.

and $u_t = \Delta^{-1}\zeta_t^{\#} = \Delta^{-1}\eta_t \mathbf{1}_{t\geq 1}$, $t = 0, \pm 1, \pm 2, \ldots$, where η_t is a short-memory zero-mean covariance stationary process that will be specified below. We set some parameters as follows: $\mu_1 = 1.72$, $\beta_1 = 0.03$, $\mu_b = 1$, and $\beta_b = 1$. The configurations are the same as those in PZ, chosen to obtain distributions that easily reveal the main features of interest. In all cases, the results are obtained via 10,000 replications. Additionally, 5% nominal size tests are considered.

First, to illustrate the effect of a structural break on the power of the fractional unit root test, we consider two different models when a structural change in slope is allowed in the DGP: (i) Model A0 (which ignores a relevant slope change); and (ii) Model A2 (which is well specified). The results are provided in Table 1. It is clear that the power of $\mathcal{LM}_T$ is much lower than that of $\mathcal{LM}_{T,\hat{\lambda}_d}$, which supports the fact that a structural break in the DGP should be allowed when testing for a fractional unit root.

Table 1. The effect of a structural break in trend on the Lagrange multiplier (LM) tests.

	T = 150										
d_0	0.5	0.55	0.6	0.65	0.7	0.75	0.8	0.85	0.9	0.95	1
$\mathcal{LM}_T$	0.767	0.617	0.458	0.290	0.187	0.117	0.070	0.044	0.029	0.020	0.004
$\mathcal{LM}_{T,\hat{\lambda}_d}$	1	1	0.997	0.986	0.949	0.858	0.703	0.485	0.303	0.169	0.036

Note: 5% nominal size tests are used. The data-generating process (DGP) is specified by $y_t = \beta_b B_t + u_t$ and $u_t = \Delta^{-m}(\Delta^{-d}\eta_t)\mathbf{1}_{t\geq 1}$ with $\eta_t \sim i.i.d.\mathcal{N}(0,1)$ where $d_0 = m + d$, $d \in [-0.5, 0)$, and $m = 1$. The values of model parameters are set to $\lambda_0 = 0.5, \beta_b = 0.5$. The test $\mathcal{LM}_T$, designed for Model A1, ignores a structural break in the DGP, while the test $\mathcal{LM}_{T,\hat{\lambda}_d}$, designed for Model A2, is well specified with the estimate of the break date obtained from the dynamic regression (10).

Tables 2–5 present the rejection probabilities of the tests $\mathcal{LM}_T$ and $\mathcal{LM}_{T,\hat{\lambda}}$ at the 5% significance level when $\eta_t \sim i.i.d.\mathcal{N}(0,1)$. In Table 2, no structural change is allowed in the DGP (Model A0); i.e., $y_t = \mu_1 + \beta_1 t + u_t$. The size of $\mathcal{LM}_T$ is well controlled, which is 0.05 and 0.06 with sample sizes $T = 150, 500$, respectively. Table 3 reports the results for Model A1. The break fraction is not estimated consistently, because the level shift is negligible compared to the stochastic trend induced by the $I(1)$ errors. Hence, $\mathcal{LM}_{T,\hat{\lambda}_s}$ and $\mathcal{LM}_{T,\hat{\lambda}_d}$ suffer from severe size distortion, while $\mathcal{LM}_T$ maintains size close to the nominal level 5%. Table 4 presents the results pertaining to Model A2. We also consider the test based on trimmed data, $\mathcal{LM}_{T,\hat{\lambda}_{tr}}$. The test $\mathcal{LM}_{T,\hat{\lambda}_d}$ is size-controlled, while the others show minor size distortion. However, the power of $\mathcal{LM}_{T,\hat{\lambda}_d}$ is always lower than that of the other two tests. Table 5 presents the results pertaining to Model A3. Here, we set $\mu_b = 0$ to consider the effect of an irrelevant level shift. Notice that $\mathcal{LM}_{T,\hat{\lambda}_s}$ exhibits liberal size distortion and $\mathcal{LM}_{T,\hat{\lambda}_d}$ also shows considerable size distortion. As noted by Chang and Perron (2016) [33], the estimate of the break date shows a pattern of bi-modality when an irrelevant level shift is introduced. This phenomenon is referred to the "contamination" effect, because the irrelevant level shift can make the estimate of the true break date less precise. By construction, the contamination effect is marginal on $\mathcal{LM}_{T,\hat{\lambda}_{tr}}$, whose exact size is 6.7% when $T = 500$.

Table 2. Rejection probabilities of the $\mathcal{LM}_T$ test for Model A0.

d_0	0.5	0.55	0.6	0.65	0.7	0.75	0.8	0.85	0.9	0.95	1
						T = 150					
	1	1	1	0.997	0.983	0.924	0.778	0.544	0.307	0.154	0.051
						T = 500					
	1	1	1	1	1	1	0.997	0.920	0.608	0.260	0.056

Note: 5% nominal size tests are used. The DGP is defined by $y_t = \mu_1 + \beta_1 t + u_t$, and $u_t = \Delta^{-m}(\Delta^{-d}\eta_t)\mathbf{1}_{t\geq 1}$ with $\eta_t \sim i.i.d.\mathcal{N}(0,1)$ where $d_0 = m + d$, $d \in [-0.5, 0]$, and $m = 1$. The values of model parameters are set to $\mu_1 = 1.72, \beta_1 = 0.03$.

Table 3. Rejection probabilities of the $\mathcal{LM}_{T,\hat{\lambda}}$ and $\mathcal{LM}_T$ tests for Model A1.

d_0	0.5	0.55	0.6	0.65	0.7	0.75	0.8	0.85	0.9	0.95	1
						T = 150					
$\mathcal{LM}_{T,\hat{\lambda}_s}$	1	1	1	0.989	0.990	0.969	0.897	0.765	0.589	0.410	0.255
$\mathcal{LM}_{T,\hat{\lambda}_d}$	1	1	1	0.997	0.988	0.946	0.839	0.655	0.445	0.263	0.134
$\mathcal{LM}_T$	1	1	1	0.997	0.981	0.927	0.772	0.541	0.309	0.151	0.052
						T = 500					
$\mathcal{LM}_{T,\hat{\lambda}_s}$	1	1	1	1	1	1	0.999	0.970	0.802	0.494	0.252
$\mathcal{LM}_{T,\hat{\lambda}_d}$	1	1	1	1	1	1	0.996	0.932	0.674	0.330	0.118
$\mathcal{LM}_T$	1	1	1	1	1	1	0.997	0.925	0.616	0.250	0.055

Note: 5% nominal size tests are used. The DGP is defined by $y_t = \mu_b C_t + u_t$, and $u_t = \Delta^{-m}(\Delta^{-d}\eta_t)\mathbf{1}_{t\geq 1}$ with $\eta_t \sim i.i.d.\mathcal{N}(0,1)$, where $d_0 = m + d$, $d \in [-0.5, 0]$, and $m = 1$. The values of model parameters are set to $\lambda_0 = 0.5, \mu_b = 1$.

Table 4. Rejection probabilities of the $\mathcal{LM}_{T,\hat{\lambda}}$ tests for Model A2.

d_0	0.5	0.55	0.6	0.65	0.7	0.75	0.8	0.85	0.9	0.95	1
						T = 150					
$\mathcal{LM}_{T,\hat{\lambda}_s}$	1	1	1	0.998	0.987	0.936	0.820	0.610	0.387	0.211	0.077
$\mathcal{LM}_{T,\hat{\lambda}_d}$	0.998	0.994	0.982	0.951	0.882	0.765	0.606	0.409	0.246	0.130	0.039
$\mathcal{LM}_{T,\hat{\lambda}_{tr}}$	1	0.999	0.999	0.997	0.981	0.922	0.794	0.587	0.369	0.205	0.072
						T = 500					
$\mathcal{LM}_{T,\hat{\lambda}_s}$	1	1	1	1	1	1	0.995	0.904	0.567	0.229	0.063
$\mathcal{LM}_{T,\hat{\lambda}_d}$	1	1	1	1	0.997	0.974	0.893	0.717	0.426	0.165	0.048
$\mathcal{LM}_{T,\hat{\lambda}_{tr}}$	1	1	1	1	1	1	0.997	0.917	0.591	0.244	0.071

Note: 5% nominal size tests are used. The DGP is defined by $y_t = \beta_b B_t + u_t$, and $u_t = \Delta^{-m}(\Delta^{-d}\eta_t)\mathbf{1}_{t\geq 1}$ with $\eta_t \sim i.i.d.\mathcal{N}(0,1)$, where $d_0 = m + d$, $d \in [-0.5, 0]$, and $m = 1$. The values of model parameters are set to $\lambda_0 = 0.5, \beta_b = 1$.

Table 5. Rejection probabilities of the $\mathcal{LM}_{T,\hat{\lambda}}$ tests for Model A3.

d_0	0.5	0.55	0.6	0.65	0.7	0.75	0.8	0.85	0.9	0.95	1
						T = 150					
$\mathcal{LM}_{T,\hat{\lambda}_s}$	1	1	1	0.998	0.990	0.953	0.857	0.679	0.480	0.305	0.175
$\mathcal{LM}_{T,\hat{\lambda}_d}$	1	1	0.999	0.995	0.977	0.921	0.806	0.616	0.419	0.258	0.128
$\mathcal{LM}_{T,\hat{\lambda}_{tr}}$	1	1	1	0.996	0.981	0.926	0.798	0.587	0.380	0.218	0.083
						T = 500					
$\mathcal{LM}_{T,\hat{\lambda}_s}$	1	1	1	1	1	1	0.995	0.924	0.659	0.350	0.156
$\mathcal{LM}_{T,\hat{\lambda}_d}$	1	1	1	1	0.999	0.996	0.974	0.851	0.561	0.259	0.101
$\mathcal{LM}_{T,\hat{\lambda}_{tr}}$	1	1	1	1	1	0.999	0.993	0.899	0.571	0.233	0.067

Note: 5% nominal size tests are used. The DGP is defined by $y_t = \beta_b B_t + u_t$, and $u_t = \Delta^{-m}(\Delta^{-d}\eta_t)\mathbf{1}_{t\geq 1}$ with $\eta_t \sim i.i.d.\mathcal{N}(0,1)$, where $d_0 = m + d$, $d \in [-0.5, 0]$, and $m = 1$. The values of model parameters are set to $\lambda_0 = 0.5, \beta_b = 1$.

In Tables 6–8, we provide simulation results when the errors have short-run dynamics; i.e., $(1 - \rho L)\eta_t = \epsilon_t$, $\epsilon_t \sim i.i.d.\mathcal{N}(0,1)$. We set the value of the autoregressive (AR) parameter at $\rho \in \{-0.5, 0, 0.3, 0.6, 0.8\}$. When $\rho = 0$, we can compare the loss of power caused by allowing for dynamics when none is present. The other parameters remain unchanged. Table 6 reports the size and power of the Lagrange multiplier tests pertaining to Model A1, $\mathcal{LM}_T$. It is well size-controlled with less persistent AR parameters $\rho \in \{0, 0.3\}$, but it is very conservative with a higher AR coefficient $\rho \in \{0.6, 0.8\}$, while it shows liberal size distortions with $\rho = -0.5$. We find some interesting features in terms of power. First, power is higher when the AR parameter ρ is negative (in part due to the liberal size distortions). Second, as ρ becomes positive and large, power shrinks considerably. In particular, the loss of power is substantial when the AR parameter ρ increases from 0.6 to 0.8. This implies that a sufficiently large time span is needed to distinguish fractional integration from weak dependence. Comparing Table 3 with Table 6, for the $\rho = 0$ case, it is obvious that power is substantially lower when an irrelevant AR parameter is introduced. This result suggests that selecting the number of lags in the noise component is crucial to obtain good power. Lastly, with a persistent AR parameter $\rho = 0.8$, the LM tests have non-monotonic power; that is, power does not increase when the order of integration d_0 moves away from the null of a unit root. As also discussed in Lobato and Velasco (2007) [16], it is difficult to distinguish fractional integration from a highly persistent stationary short-memory process. Table 7 reports the results pertaining to Model A2. They show similar patterns as for Model A1. It is noticeable that $\mathcal{LM}^*_{T,\hat{\lambda}_d}$ performs well in terms of size across all cases, while its power is always lower than that of the other tests. Table 8 presents the results for Model A3. $\mathcal{LM}^*_{T,\hat{\lambda}_d}$ has size distortion, even with negative and less persistent AR parameters. This happens because when using the dynamic regression to estimate the break fraction, the estimate $\hat{\lambda}_d$ is negatively biased for Model A3. Among the three LM statistics, $\mathcal{LM}^*_{T,\hat{\lambda}_{tr}}$ based on the trimmed data performs well in finite samples. The size of $\mathcal{LM}^*_{T,\hat{\lambda}_{tr}}$ is well controlled across various values of ρ, while $\mathcal{LM}^*_{T,\hat{\lambda}_s}$ and $\mathcal{LM}^*_{T,\hat{\lambda}_d}$ show liberal size distortions. Moreover, the power loss of $\mathcal{LM}^*_{T,\hat{\lambda}_{tr}}$ is minor relative to the other tests. Hence, $\mathcal{LM}_{T,\hat{\lambda}_{tr}}$ and $\mathcal{LM}^*_{T,\hat{\lambda}_{tr}}$ are the recommended tests in practice.

Table 6. Rejection probabilities of $\mathcal{LM}^*_{T,\hat{\lambda}}$ and $\mathcal{LM}_T$ for Model A1 with short-run dynamics.

		d_0										
ρ		0.5	0.55	0.6	0.65	0.7	0.75	0.8	0.85	0.9	0.95	1
		T = 150										
	$\mathcal{LM}^*_{T,\hat{\lambda}_s}$	1	0.999	0.997	0.987	0.965	0.894	0.776	0.618	0.449	0.305	0.187
−0.5	$\mathcal{LM}^*_{T,\hat{\lambda}_d}$	1	0.999	0.997	0.986	0.962	0.891	0.769	0.598	0.429	0.277	0.168
	$\mathcal{LM}_T$	1	0.999	0.994	0.974	0.928	0.813	0.639	0.442	0.259	0.137	0.059
	$\mathcal{LM}^*_{T,\hat{\lambda}_s}$	0.993	0.986	0.967	0.927	0.862	0.774	0.656	0.528	0.424	0.329	0.244
0	$\mathcal{LM}^*_{T,\hat{\lambda}_d}$	0.991	0.981	0.955	0.904	0.824	0.711	0.582	0.435	0.321	0.224	0.143
	$\mathcal{LM}_T$	0.986	0.969	0.930	0.851	0.728	0.572	0.411	0.267	0.163	0.102	0.046
	$\mathcal{LM}^*_{T,\hat{\lambda}_s}$	0.946	0.899	0.839	0.767	0.671	0.553	0.450	0.365	0.272	0.215	0.158
0.3	$\mathcal{LM}^*_{T,\hat{\lambda}_d}$	0.922	0.863	0.788	0.683	0.573	0.441	0.337	0.245	0.168	0.115	0.069
	$\mathcal{LM}_T$	0.894	0.811	0.707	0.576	0.445	0.303	0.209	0.133	0.077	0.054	0.026
	$\mathcal{LM}^*_{T,\hat{\lambda}_s}$	0.558	0.484	0.385	0.296	0.234	0.163	0.127	0.091	0.061	0.048	0.029
0.6	$\mathcal{LM}^*_{T,\hat{\lambda}_d}$	0.456	0.370	0.274	0.197	0.144	0.086	0.060	0.039	0.024	0.020	0.010
	$\mathcal{LM}_T$	0.361	0.277	0.184	0.121	0.079	0.042	0.029	0.018	0.013	0.013	0.007
	$\mathcal{LM}^*_{T,\hat{\lambda}_s}$	0.096	0.074	0.049	0.035	0.025	0.017	0.014	0.010	0.012	0.011	0.008
0.8	$\mathcal{LM}^*_{T,\hat{\lambda}_d}$	0.044	0.033	0.019	0.013	0.014	0.012	0.015	0.022	0.024	0.027	0.036
	$\mathcal{LM}_T$	0.019	0.016	0.011	0.012	0.018	0.026	0.033	0.041	0.042	0.038	0.026
		T = 500										
	$\mathcal{LM}^*_{T,\hat{\lambda}_s}$	1	1	1	1	1	0.999	0.979	0.856	0.581	0.305	0.129
−0.5	$\mathcal{LM}^*_{T,\hat{\lambda}_d}$	1	1	1	1	1	0.999	0.974	0.829	0.537	0.262	0.100
	$\mathcal{LM}_T$	1	1	1	1	1	1	0.980	0.830	0.502	0.215	0.066
	$\mathcal{LM}^*_{T,\hat{\lambda}_s}$	1	1	1	1	0.999	0.992	0.936	0.781	0.576	0.403	0.263
0	$\mathcal{LM}^*_{T,\hat{\lambda}_d}$	1	1	1	1	0.999	0.985	0.894	0.695	0.451	0.273	0.143
	$\mathcal{LM}_T$	1	1	1	1	0.999	0.979	0.858	0.595	0.330	0.168	0.058
	$\mathcal{LM}^*_{T,\hat{\lambda}_s}$	1	1	1	0.998	0.979	0.920	0.777	0.575	0.394	0.257	0.155
0.3	$\mathcal{LM}^*_{T,\hat{\lambda}_d}$	1	1	1	0.996	0.967	0.869	0.684	0.447	0.261	0.162	0.074
	$\mathcal{LM}_T$	1	1	1	0.995	0.957	0.837	0.611	0.376	0.205	0.124	0.051
	$\mathcal{LM}^*_{T,\hat{\lambda}_s}$	0.984	0.956	0.880	0.736	0.559	0.348	0.195	0.114	0.056	0.033	0.016
0.6	$\mathcal{LM}^*_{T,\hat{\lambda}_d}$	0.977	0.935	0.844	0.673	0.487	0.297	0.171	0.105	0.065	0.045	0.023
	$\mathcal{LM}_T$	0.974	0.927	0.833	0.670	0.497	0.316	0.199	0.135	0.083	0.058	0.028
	$\mathcal{LM}^*_{T,\hat{\lambda}_s}$	0.249	0.148	0.075	0.040	0.024	0.015	0.008	0.007	0.005	0.006	0.004
0.8	$\mathcal{LM}^*_{T,\hat{\lambda}_d}$	0.202	0.133	0.084	0.067	0.066	0.069	0.084	0.091	0.101	0.107	0.103
	$\mathcal{LM}_T$	0.217	0.159	0.126	0.120	0.142	0.157	0.171	0.163	0.134	0.102	0.043

Note: 5% nominal size tests are used. The DGP is defined by $y_t = \mu_b C_t + u_t$ and $u_t = \Delta^{-m}(\Delta^{-d}\eta_t)\mathbf{1}_{t\geq 1}$ with $(1-\rho L)\eta_t = \epsilon_t$ and $\epsilon_t \sim i.i.d.\mathcal{N}(0,1)$, where $d_0 = m + d$, $d \in [-0.5, 0]$. We set $\mu_b = 1$.

Table 7. Rejection probabilities of $\mathcal{LM}^*_{T,\hat{\lambda}}$ for Model A2 with short-run dynamics.

		d_0										
ρ		**0.5**	**0.55**	**0.6**	**0.65**	**0.7**	**0.75**	**0.8**	**0.85**	**0.9**	**0.95**	**1**
						T = 150						
−0.5	$\mathcal{LM}^*_{T,\hat{\lambda}_s}$	1	0.999	0.996	0.985	0.949	0.861	0.713	0.515	0.354	0.215	0.100
	$\mathcal{LM}^*_{T,\hat{\lambda}_d}$	0.993	0.982	0.955	0.908	0.816	0.680	0.521	0.350	0.233	0.136	0.054
	$\mathcal{LM}^*_{T,\hat{\lambda}_{tr}}$	1	0.996	0.990	0.969	0.926	0.822	0.671	0.478	0.335	0.203	0.098
0	$\mathcal{LM}^*_{T,\hat{\lambda}_s}$	0.991	0.978	0.943	0.885	0.795	0.652	0.507	0.364	0.268	0.189	0.097
	$\mathcal{LM}^*_{T,\hat{\lambda}_d}$	0.912	0.851	0.779	0.668	0.562	0.425	0.311	0.205	0.153	0.104	0.046
	$\mathcal{LM}^*_{T,\hat{\lambda}_{tr}}$	0.988	0.965	0.931	0.868	0.774	0.645	0.496	0.373	0.280	0.205	0.113
0.3	$\mathcal{LM}^*_{T,\hat{\lambda}_s}$	0.907	0.848	0.761	0.662	0.533	0.429	0.319	0.239	0.170	0.129	0.071
	$\mathcal{LM}^*_{T,\hat{\lambda}_d}$	0.691	0.602	0.502	0.409	0.311	0.230	0.163	0.115	0.076	0.056	0.027
	$\mathcal{LM}^*_{T,\hat{\lambda}_{tr}}$	0.868	0.792	0.696	0.594	0.467	0.369	0.271	0.198	0.141	0.109	0.055
0.6	$\mathcal{LM}^*_{T,\hat{\lambda}_s}$	0.436	0.360	0.282	0.215	0.157	0.119	0.083	0.061	0.050	0.038	0.027
	$\mathcal{LM}^*_{T,\hat{\lambda}_d}$	0.230	0.176	0.130	0.092	0.058	0.044	0.028	0.020	0.019	0.016	0.012
	$\mathcal{LM}^*_{T,\hat{\lambda}_{tr}}$	0.421	0.344	0.269	0.211	0.156	0.118	0.082	0.062	0.054	0.043	0.030
0.8	$\mathcal{LM}^*_{T,\hat{\lambda}_s}$	0.057	0.040	0.038	0.038	0.044	0.053	0.061	0.063	0.058	0.044	0.028
	$\mathcal{LM}^*_{T,\hat{\lambda}_d}$	0.022	0.012	0.013	0.017	0.025	0.032	0.044	0.047	0.044	0.034	0.023
	$\mathcal{LM}^*_{T,\hat{\lambda}_{tr}}$	0.040	0.026	0.024	0.025	0.034	0.039	0.049	0.053	0.051	0.038	0.024
						T = 500						
−0.5	$\mathcal{LM}^*_{T,\hat{\lambda}_s}$	1	1	1	1	1	0.999	0.963	0.785	0.445	0.197	0.068
	$\mathcal{LM}^*_{T,\hat{\lambda}_d}$	1	1	1	1	0.993	0.952	0.824	0.594	0.311	0.129	0.039
	$\mathcal{LM}^*_{T,\hat{\lambda}_{tr}}$	1	1	1	1	1	1	0.975	0.825	0.490	0.221	0.081
0	$\mathcal{LM}^*_{T,\hat{\lambda}_s}$	1	1	1	1	0.998	0.969	0.831	0.575	0.329	0.169	0.076
	$\mathcal{LM}^*_{T,\hat{\lambda}_d}$	1	1	0.993	0.968	0.907	0.793	0.617	0.408	0.225	0.108	0.050
	$\mathcal{LM}^*_{T,\hat{\lambda}_{tr}}$	1	1	1	1	0.998	0.978	0.865	0.617	0.362	0.190	0.099
0.3	$\mathcal{LM}^*_{T,\hat{\lambda}_s}$	1	1	0.999	0.994	0.950	0.826	0.614	0.382	0.233	0.145	0.081
	$\mathcal{LM}^*_{T,\hat{\lambda}_d}$	0.993	0.974	0.929	0.846	0.746	0.613	0.427	0.255	0.149	0.081	0.049
	$\mathcal{LM}^*_{T,\hat{\lambda}_{tr}}$	1	1	0.999	0.994	0.957	0.836	0.625	0.391	0.236	0.145	0.079
0.6	$\mathcal{LM}^*_{T,\hat{\lambda}_s}$	0.975	0.930	0.828	0.687	0.521	0.366	0.257	0.178	0.125	0.099	0.065
	$\mathcal{LM}^*_{T,\hat{\lambda}_d}$	0.788	0.709	0.596	0.475	0.340	0.222	0.144	0.091	0.060	0.040	0.030
	$\mathcal{LM}^*_{T,\hat{\lambda}_{tr}}$	0.976	0.933	0.834	0.690	0.514	0.353	0.240	0.161	0.113	0.090	0.067
0.8	$\mathcal{LM}^*_{T,\hat{\lambda}_s}$	0.245	0.187	0.161	0.169	0.191	0.218	0.238	0.226	0.176	0.122	0.067
	$\mathcal{LM}^*_{T,\hat{\lambda}_d}$	0.143	0.104	0.087	0.085	0.084	0.092	0.101	0.117	0.103	0.082	0.048
	$\mathcal{LM}^*_{T,\hat{\lambda}_{tr}}$	0.235	0.165	0.130	0.124	0.127	0.142	0.161	0.190	0.191	0.199	0.226

Note: 5% nominal size tests are used. The DGP is defined by $y_t = \beta_b B_t + u_t$ and $u_t = \Delta^{-m}(\Delta^{-d}\eta_t)\mathbf{1}_{t\geq 1}$ with $(1-\rho L)\eta_t = \epsilon_t$ and $\epsilon_t \sim i.i.d.\mathcal{N}(0,1)$, where $d_0 = m + d$, $d \in [-0.5, 0]$. We set $\beta_b = 1$.

Table 8. Rejection probabilities of $\mathcal{LM}^*_{T,\hat{\lambda}}$ for Model A3 with short-run dynamics.

							d_0					
ρ		**0.5**	**0.55**	**0.6**	**0.65**	**0.7**	**0.75**	**0.8**	**0.85**	**0.9**	**0.95**	**1**
							***T* = 150**					
	$\mathcal{LM}^*_{T,\hat{\lambda}_s}$	1	0.999	0.996	0.986	0.952	0.880	0.749	0.561	0.403	0.272	0.149
−0.5	$\mathcal{LM}^*_{T,\hat{\lambda}_d}$	1	0.999	0.996	0.983	0.946	0.871	0.738	0.549	0.390	0.258	0.139
	$\mathcal{LM}^*_{T,\hat{\lambda}_{tr}}$	1	0.996	0.989	0.970	0.925	0.832	0.686	0.491	0.339	0.219	0.096
	$\mathcal{LM}^*_{T,\hat{\lambda}_s}$	0.992	0.980	0.946	0.897	0.813	0.697	0.569	0.441	0.344	0.262	0.183
0	$\mathcal{LM}^*_{T,\hat{\lambda}_d}$	0.991	0.973	0.939	0.881	0.786	0.670	0.537	0.401	0.303	0.229	0.149
	$\mathcal{LM}^*_{T,\hat{\lambda}_{tr}}$	0.983	0.963	0.919	0.848	0.740	0.609	0.473	0.343	0.250	0.184	0.095
	$\mathcal{LM}^*_{T,\hat{\lambda}_s}$	0.919	0.868	0.785	0.695	0.587	0.488	0.377	0.302	0.230	0.183	0.137
0.3	$\mathcal{LM}^*_{T,\hat{\lambda}_d}$	0.899	0.835	0.747	0.646	0.518	0.425	0.307	0.236	0.167	0.121	0.083
	$\mathcal{LM}^*_{T,\hat{\lambda}_{tr}}$	0.877	0.809	0.710	0.607	0.483	0.381	0.274	0.208	0.158	0.119	0.069
	$\mathcal{LM}^*_{T,\hat{\lambda}_s}$	0.481	0.396	0.318	0.251	0.191	0.150	0.115	0.086	0.072	0.055	0.039
0.6	$\mathcal{LM}^*_{T,\hat{\lambda}_d}$	0.407	0.317	0.241	0.173	0.125	0.088	0.063	0.046	0.032	0.026	0.016
	$\mathcal{LM}^*_{T,\hat{\lambda}_{tr}}$	0.385	0.298	0.242	0.175	0.127	0.092	0.071	0.051	0.042	0.032	0.021
	$\mathcal{LM}^*_{T,\hat{\lambda}_s}$	0.082	0.059	0.052	0.039	0.036	0.033	0.032	0.033	0.027	0.024	0.019
0.8	$\mathcal{LM}^*_{T,\hat{\lambda}_d}$	0.045	0.028	0.023	0.015	0.014	0.014	0.016	0.019	0.024	0.026	0.030
	$\mathcal{LM}^*_{T,\hat{\lambda}_{tr}}$	0.040	0.030	0.030	0.026	0.031	0.042	0.044	0.050	0.044	0.039	0.026
							***T* = 500**					
	$\mathcal{LM}^*_{T,\hat{\lambda}_s}$	1	1	1	1	1	0.999	0.970	0.807	0.501	0.243	0.103
−0.5	$\mathcal{LM}^*_{T,\hat{\lambda}_d}$	1	1	1	1	1	0.993	0.936	0.741	0.434	0.199	0.079
	$\mathcal{LM}^*_{T,\hat{\lambda}_{tr}}$	1	1	1	1	1	0.999	0.972	0.801	0.476	0.212	0.073
	$\mathcal{LM}^*_{T,\hat{\lambda}_s}$	1	1	1	1	0.999	0.979	0.876	0.674	0.439	0.286	0.164
0	$\mathcal{LM}^*_{T,\hat{\lambda}_d}$	1	1	1	1	0.991	0.953	0.829	0.622	0.379	0.226	0.124
	$\mathcal{LM}^*_{T,\hat{\lambda}_{tr}}$	1	1	1	1	0.998	0.970	0.835	0.591	0.326	0.177	0.077
	$\mathcal{LM}^*_{T,\hat{\lambda}_s}$	1	1	0.999	0.995	0.962	0.859	0.673	0.468	0.307	0.192	0.123
0.3	$\mathcal{LM}^*_{T,\hat{\lambda}_d}$	1	1	0.997	0.978	0.925	0.792	0.580	0.372	0.215	0.124	0.076
	$\mathcal{LM}^*_{T,\hat{\lambda}_{tr}}$	1	1	0.999	0.992	0.945	0.812	0.590	0.371	0.222	0.131	0.078
	$\mathcal{LM}^*_{T,\hat{\lambda}_s}$	0.978	0.935	0.843	0.697	0.521	0.348	0.220	0.140	0.091	0.070	0.050
0.6	$\mathcal{LM}^*_{T,\hat{\lambda}_d}$	0.942	0.864	0.739	0.572	0.393	0.240	0.138	0.080	0.050	0.035	0.025
	$\mathcal{LM}^*_{T,\hat{\lambda}_{tr}}$	0.971	0.917	0.818	0.667	0.493	0.343	0.231	0.162	0.108	0.087	0.063
	$\mathcal{LM}^*_{T,\hat{\lambda}_s}$	0.232	0.153	0.114	0.097	0.095	0.099	0.105	0.093	0.071	0.052	0.052
0.8	$\mathcal{LM}^*_{T,\hat{\lambda}_d}$	0.162	0.101	0.067	0.049	0.041	0.039	0.039	0.047	0.057	0.071	0.067
	$\mathcal{LM}^*_{T,\hat{\lambda}_{tr}}$	0.225	0.173	0.144	0.145	0.154	0.176	0.203	0.190	0.155	0.105	0.055

Note: 5% nominal size tests are used. The DGP is defined by $y_t = \beta_b B_t + u_t$ and $u_t = \Delta^{-m}(\Delta^{-d}\eta_t)\mathbf{1}_{t\geq 1}$ with $(1-\rho L)\eta_t = \epsilon_t$ and $\epsilon_t \sim i.i.d.\mathcal{N}(0,1)$, where $d_0 = m + d$, $d \in [-0.5, 0]$. We set $\beta_b = 1$.

The Size and Power When a Pre-Test Is Used

In Figures 1–4, we present the size and power of the LM tests as the slope change parameter (β_b) changes in Models A2 and A3 with and without the use of a pre-test. As a pre-test, we use the $\mathcal{SW}$ test of Iacone et al. (2013) [37] at the nominal 5% level. We only consider the version of the LM statistics based on the trimmed estimate of the break fraction, denoted $\mathcal{LM}_{T,\hat{\lambda}_{tr}}$ and $\mathcal{LM}^p_{T,\hat{\lambda}_{tr}}$ when no short-run dynamics is allowed, and by $\mathcal{LM}^*_{T,\hat{\lambda}_{tr}}$ and $\mathcal{LM}^{*p}_{T,\hat{\lambda}_{tr}}$ when an AR(1) structure is allowed. To assess the extent of the differences in the size distortion and power, we also report the infeasible LM test based on the true value of break fraction, denoted $\mathcal{LM}_{T,\lambda_b}$ and $\mathcal{LM}^*_{T,\lambda_b}$. The results are presented in Figure 1 for Model A2 (no short-run dynamics), Figure 2 for Model A2, and in Figures 3 and 4 for Models A2 and A3 with short-run dynamics of the form $(1-0.3L)\eta_t = \epsilon_t$, $\epsilon_t \sim i.i.d.\mathcal{N}(0,1)$. For $\mathcal{LM}^p_{T,\hat{\lambda}_{tr}}$ and $\mathcal{LM}^{*p}_{T,\hat{\lambda}_{tr}}$, the trimming window contains six observations (the simulation results are not sensitive to the length of the window). The magnitude of break in the slope of the trend β_b varies from -4 to 4 in increments of 0.2. We set $\mu_b = 0$ for Model A3. The sample sizes are $T = 150, 300$, and the number of replications is 10,000 for each value of the parameters. One-sided tests against the alternative hypothesis $H_1 : d_0 < 1$ are constructed at the nominal 5% level. For power, d_0 is set to 0.8.

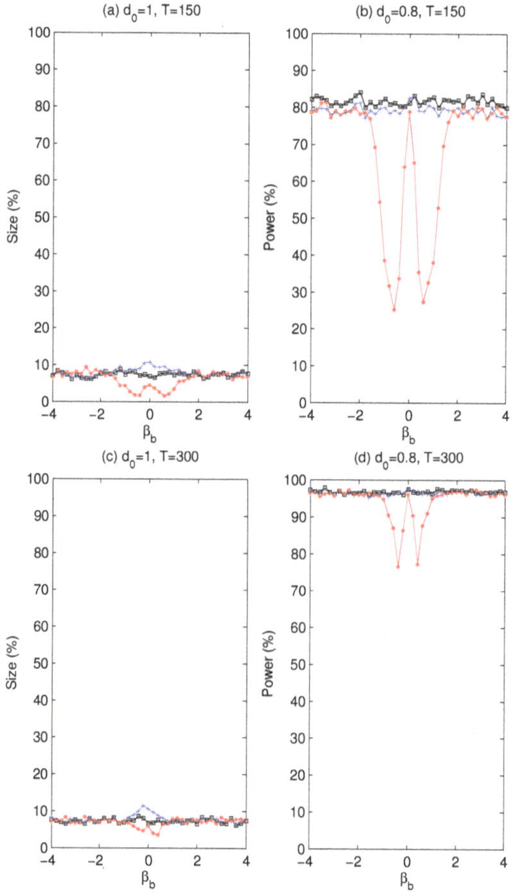

Figure 1. Null rejection probabilities in Model A2, $\lambda_b = 0.5$ [$-+-$: $\mathcal{LM}_{T,\hat{\lambda}_{tr}}$, $-*-$: $\mathcal{LM}^{p}_{T,\hat{\lambda}_{tr}}$, $-\Box-$: $\mathcal{LM}_{T,\lambda_b}$]

The results for Model A2 (presented in Figure 1) show first that the version without the pre-test exhibits some liberal size distortions when β_b is near 0, which reduce when T increases, though remain noticeable even with $T = 300$. On the other hand, the version with the pre-test exhibits conservative size-distortions when β_b is near but not equal to 0, which again reduce but remain noticeable when $T = 300$. The most drastic differences occur when considering the power of the tests. The power of the version without the pre-test is slightly below but near to the power of the version with the true break fraction when $T = 150$ for all values of β_b. When $T = 300$, the power functions are nearly the same. Things are very different when the version with the pre-test is used. When β_b is near but not equal to zero, the power reduces drastically, creating pronounced power valleys. This reduction in power alleviates somewhat when $T = 300$, but remains important. This is due to the fact that for low values of β_b, the $\mathcal{SW}$ test of Iacone et al. (2013) [37] is not powerful enough, so a change in slope regressor is not included. Yet, the magnitude of the change in slope is large enough to induce a considerable loss in power. This is akin to the problem faced by the Kim and Perron (2009) [10] test in the context of testing for a unit root.

The results for Model A3 (presented in Figure 2) show a similar picture. This is also the case when considering the tests $\mathcal{LM}^*_{T,\hat{\lambda}_{tr}}$ and $\mathcal{LM}^{*p}_{T,\hat{\lambda}_{tr}}$ with serial correlation in the DGP (Figures 3 and 4), though here the size distortions of both tests are somewhat higher, liberal for $\mathcal{LM}^*_{T,\hat{\lambda}_{tr}}$, and conservative for $\mathcal{LM}^{*p}_{T,\hat{\lambda}_{tr}}$. The power losses of $\mathcal{LM}^{*p}_{T,\hat{\lambda}_{tr}}$ is severe, especially when $T = 150$.

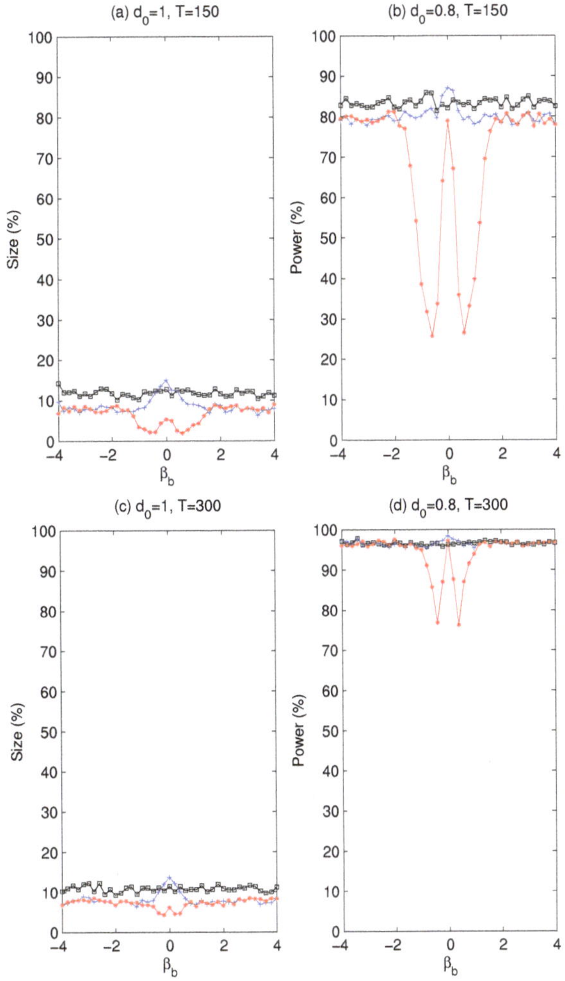

Figure 2. Null rejection probabilities in Model A3, $\lambda_b = 0.5$ [$-+-$: $\mathcal{LM}_{T,\hat{\lambda}_{tr}}$, $-*-$: $\mathcal{LM}^p_{T,\hat{\lambda}_{tr}}$, $-\square-$: $\mathcal{LM}_{T,\lambda_b}$]

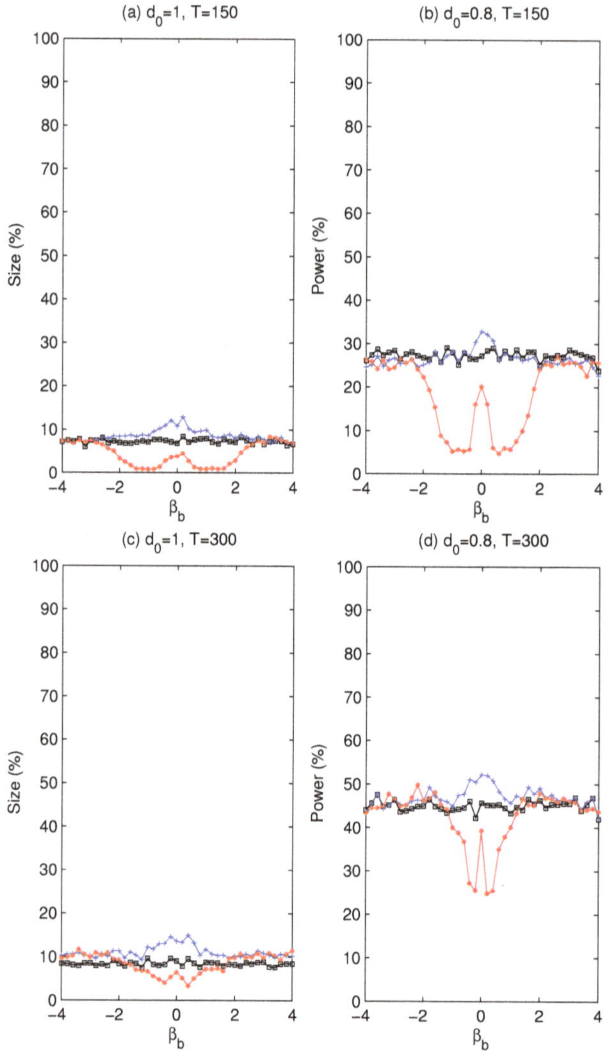

Figure 3. Null rejection probabilities in Model A2, where $(1-0.3L)\eta_t = \epsilon_t$, $\lambda_b = 0.5$ [$-+-$: $\mathcal{LM}_{T,\hat{\lambda}_{tr}}$, $-*-$: $\mathcal{LM}^{*p}_{T,\hat{\lambda}_{tr}}$, $-\square-$: $\mathcal{LM}_{T,\lambda_b}$].

Based on the simulation results, it is recommended to use the $\mathcal{LM}_{T,\hat{\lambda}_{tr}}$ or $\mathcal{LM}^{*}_{T,\hat{\lambda}_{tr}}$ tests without the pre-test. In our view, the reduction in power when using a pre-test considerably outweighs the differences in size distortions. The $\mathcal{SW}$ test of Iacone et al. (2013) [37] is nevertheless still useful to assess the presence of large breaks.

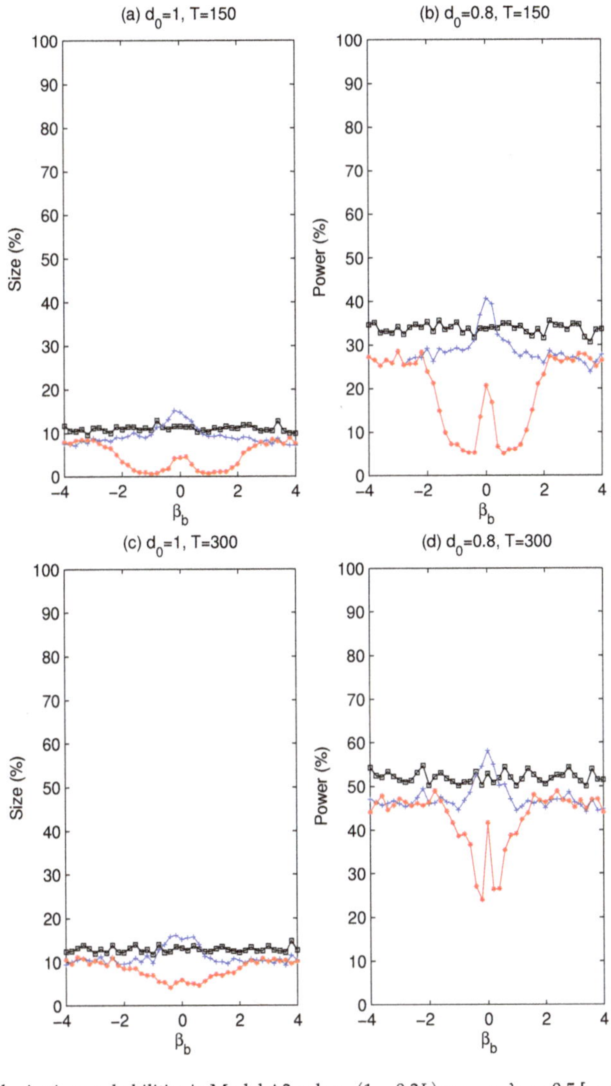

Figure 4. Null rejection probabilities in Model A3, where $(1 - 0.3L)\eta_t = \epsilon_t$, $\lambda_b = 0.5$ [$- + -$: $\mathcal{LM}_{T,\hat{\lambda}_{tr}}$, $- * -$: $\mathcal{LM}^{*p}_{T,\hat{\lambda}_{tr}}$, $-\square-$: $\mathcal{LM}_{T,\lambda_b}$].

6. An Empirical Application

We analyze the aggregate price indices of the G7 countries. Monthly seasonally-adjusted CPI series were obtained from the OECD Main Economic Indicators. All series are analyzed with a logarithm transformation and are plotted in Figure 5, where the vertical line is the break date estimated by minimizing the sum of squared residuals from Model A2.

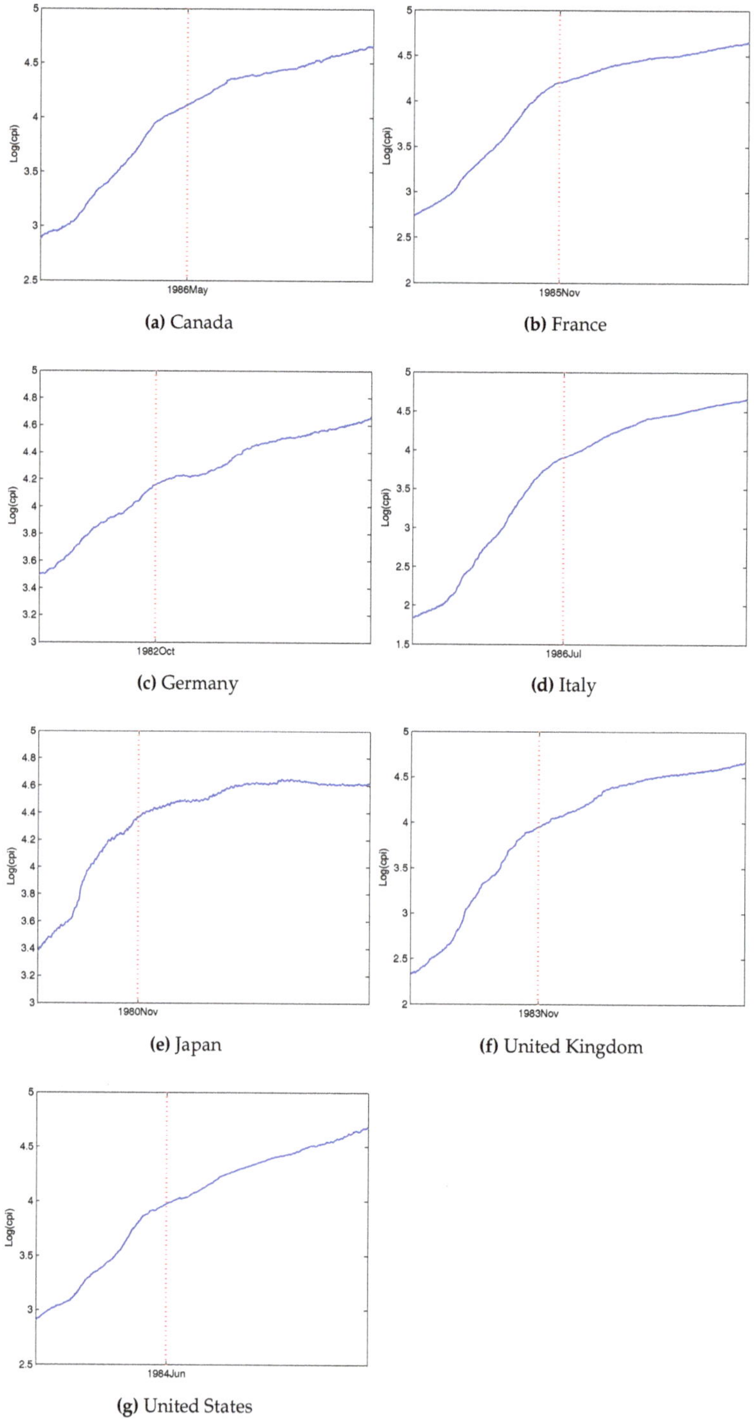

(a) Canada
(b) France
(c) Germany
(d) Italy
(e) Japan
(f) United Kingdom
(g) United States

Figure 5. (log) CPI for the G7 Countries.

The results are presented in Table 9. We only consider Model A2, and use the test for a slope change of Iacone et al. (2013) [37]. Based on the simulation results, we recommend using the LM tests with $\hat{\lambda}_{tr}$. We present results with and without short-run dynamics. When dynamics is allowed, an AR(1) specification is used. The time span is from January 1969 to December 2007 ($T = 468$). First, the augmented Dickey-Fuller type test (ADF) cannot reject the null of a unit root against the alternative of trend stationarity for all G7 countries. On the other hand, the $\mathcal{SW}$ test of Iacone et al. (2013) [37] detects a change in the slope of the trend. Allowing for a structural change in trend, the fractional unit root tests $\mathcal{LM}_{T,\hat{\lambda}_{tr}}$ and $\mathcal{LM}^*_{T,\hat{\lambda}_{tr}}$ lead to a rejection of the unit root in favor of fractional integration. Specifically, the test results state that the order of fractional integration is greater than unity for all G7 countries. We apply the two-step feasible exact local Whittle estimator $\hat{d}_{ELW}$ of Shimotsu (2010) [40] to the residuals from the fitted trend equipped with the estimate of the break date $\hat{T}_b$. This result is compatible with that in Gil-Alana (2008) [41], where he estimated the order of fractional integration for the U.S. CPI and found that the confidence intervals were located above unity. Hassler and Wolters (1995) [42] considered the inflation rates for various countries, and found that the order of fractional integration was located in an interval $(0, 0.5)$; that is, the inflation rate is a long-memory process.

Table 9. Empirical results for the logarithmic price indices of the G7 countries.

	ADF	$\mathcal{SW}$	Break Date	$\hat{d}_{ELW}$	$\mathcal{LM}_{T,\hat{\lambda}_{tr}}$	$\mathcal{LM}^*_{T,\hat{\lambda}_{tr}}$
Canada	−0.16 (4)	19.40 ***	1986 May [0.45]	1.30	9.44 ***	9.37 *** ⟨0.13⟩
France	−1.47 (6)	28.19 ***	1985 Nov [0.43]	1.69	34.65 ***	7.54 *** ⟨0.62⟩
Germany	−1.59 (1)	10.78 **	1982 Oct [0.35]	1.32	18.98 ***	8.01 *** ⟨0.41⟩
Italy	−0.61 (7)	16.37 ***	1986 Jul [0.45]	1.54	29.55 ***	11.64 *** ⟨0.52⟩
Japan	−2.50 (11)	18.86 ***	1980 Nov [0.31]	1.65	18.93 ***	8.73 *** ⟨0.42⟩
U.K.	−1.47 (7)	16.50 ***	1983 Nov [0.38]	1.51	9.46 ***	4.39 *** ⟨0.5⟩
U.S.A.	−0.44 (2)	15.75 **	1984 Jun [0.40]	1.29	12.71***	3.48 *** ⟨0.38⟩

Note: (1) The numbers in parentheses are the values of the autoregressive order selected by the Bayesian information criterion when constructing the ADF test; (2) the numbers in brackets $[\cdot]$ denote the estimated break fractions; (3) the numbers in $\langle\cdot\rangle$ are the estimates of the AR coefficient in the noise component. *, **, and *** denote a statistic significant at the 10%, 5%, and 1% level, respectively.

7. Conclusions

We established testing procedures for a fractional unit root, allowing for a structural change under both the null and alternative hypotheses. Following Robinson (1994) [13], Tanaka (1999) [14] derived a Lagrange multiplier test in the time domain, and Dolado et al. (2002, 2008) [15,19] and Lobato and Velasco (2007) [16] considered Wald-type tests for a unit root null hypothesis against fractional integration. Although Dolado et al. (2008) [19] introduced deterministic components, the case with a structural break in trend has not been considered in the literature. In contrast to the large amount of work related to testing the null hypothesis of long-memory against the alternative of stationarity with level shifts, and vice versa, work related to a fractional unit root test allowing for a structural break in trend is more scarce. To the best of our knowledge, this paper is the first that addresses testing for a fractional process allowing a structural break under both the null and alternative hypotheses.

Fractional unit root tests allowing for a structural break under both the null and alternative hypotheses have some desirable features: (i) given that economic variables are often subject to structural changes, our approach imposes a symmetric treatment of the change under both the null and alternative hypotheses; (ii) it is not required to distinguish long memory from structural change; (iii) the power of fractional unit root tests can be substantially improved when a break is actually present. Under some conditions, the proposed LM test statistics have the standard normal limit under the null hypothesis. Simulation experiments confirmed that the tests have good size and power. Hence, we believe that our procedures offer useful complements to existing tests and should be used in practical applications.

An extension of practical interest is to allow $I(d_0)$ processes under the null hypothesis, where $I(1)$ processes are included as a special case. The sufficient condition for the LM test statistic to have the standard normal limit may be different from that in Proposition 1. Recently, Chang and Perron

(2016) [33] extended PZ's analysis to cover the more general case of fractionally integrated errors for values of d_0 in the interval $(-0.5, 1.5)$ excluding the boundary case 0.5. In particular, they established the rate of the convergence of $\hat{\lambda}_s$ from the static regression [33] (Theorem 2). It is also important to examine the performance of $\hat{\lambda}_d$ and $\hat{\lambda}_{tr}$ under the null of $I(d_0)$ processes. Such investigations, and others, are the object of the ongoing subject.

Acknowledgments: We are grateful to academic editor Steve Cook, two anonymous referees, Tomoyoshi Yabu and participants at the 11th International Symposium on Econometric Theory and Applications (SETA 2015) for constructive comments, and Fabrizio Iacone, Dukpa Kim, and Katsumi Shimotsu for sharing their GAUSS and MATLAB codes. Chang's research was partly supported by the National Natural Science Foundation of China Grants No. 71131008 (Key Project).

Conflicts of Interest: The authors declare no conflict of interest.

Appendix A

Proof of Theorem A1. The DGP is specified by (4), that is, for $t = 1, \ldots, T$,

$$y_t = \mu_1 + \mu_b C_t + u_t, \quad \mu_b \neq 0.$$

Under H_0, take first differences of y_t and define $D(T_b)_t = 1$ if $t = T_b + 1$ and 0 otherwise. Then,

$$\begin{aligned} T^{-1}\textstyle\sum_{t=1}^{T}(\Delta y_t)^2 &= T^{-1}\textstyle\sum_{t=1}^{T}(\mu_b D(T_b)_t + \eta_t)^2 \\ &= T^{-1}\left(\textstyle\sum_{t=1}^{T}\eta_t^2 + 2\textstyle\sum_{t=1}^{T}\mu_b D(T_b)_t\eta_t + \textstyle\sum_{t=1}^{T}\mu_b^2 D(T_b)_t^2\right) \\ &= T^{-1}\left(\textstyle\sum_{t=1}^{T}\eta_t^2 + 2\mu_b\eta_{T_b+1} + \mu_b^2\right) \\ &= T^{-1}\textstyle\sum_{t=1}^{T}\eta_t^2 + o_p(1) \end{aligned}$$

and

$$\begin{aligned} T^{-1}\sum_{j=2}^{T}(-\log\Delta\Delta y_j)\,\Delta y_j &= T^{-1}\sum_{j=2}^{T}\left(\sum_{k=1}^{j-1}\frac{1}{k}(\mu_b D(T_b)_{j-k} + \eta_{j-k})\right)(\mu_b D(T_b)_j + \eta_j) \\ &= T^{-1}\sum_{j=2}^{T}\left(\sum_{k=1}^{j-1}\frac{1}{k}\mu_b D(T_b)_{j-k} + \sum_{k=1}^{j-1}\frac{1}{k}\eta_{j-k}\right)(\mu_b D(T_b)_j + \eta_j) \\ &= T^{-1}\sum_{j=2}^{T}\left(\sum_{k=1}^{j-1}\frac{1}{k}\mu_b^2 D(T_b)_{j-k}\right)D(T_b)_j + T^{-1}\sum_{j=2}^{T}\left(\sum_{k=1}^{j-1}\frac{1}{k}\mu_b D(T_b)_{j-k}\right)\eta_j \\ &\quad + T^{-1}\sum_{j=2}^{T}\left(\sum_{k=1}^{j-1}\frac{1}{k}\eta_{j-k}\right)\mu_b D(T_b)_j + T^{-1}\sum_{j=2}^{T}\left(\sum_{k=1}^{j-1}\frac{1}{k}\eta_{j-k}\right)\eta_j \\ &\equiv A_1 + A_2 + A_3 + A_4. \end{aligned}$$

It is easy to show that $A_1 = 0$. For A_2, we have

$$\begin{aligned} (A_2)^2 &= \mu_b^2\frac{1}{T^2}\left(\sum_{k=1}^{T-(T_b+1)}\frac{1}{k}\eta_{T_1+1+k}\right)^2 \leq \mu_b^2\frac{1}{T^2}\left(\sum_{k=1}^{T-(T_b+1)}\frac{1}{k^2}\right)\left(\sum_{k=1}^{T-(T_b+1)}\eta_{T_1+1+k}^2\right) \\ &\leq \mu_b^2\frac{\pi^2}{6}\frac{1}{T^2}\left(\sum_{k=1}^{T-(T_b+1)}\eta_{T_1+1+k}^2\right) = \mu_b^2\frac{\pi^2}{6}\left(\frac{1}{T}\sum_{k=1}^{T-(T_b+1)}\eta_{T_1+1+k}^2\right)\frac{1}{T} = O_p(T^{-1}) = o_p(1), \end{aligned}$$

where the first inequality follows from the Cauchy-Schwarz inequality, and the second inequality holds because $\sum_{k=1}^{\infty}k^{-2} = \pi^2/6$ (see Tanaka (1999) [14]). Because η_t is a short-memory zero-mean covariance stationary process, it is straightforward to show that $T^{-1}\sum_{k=1}^{T-(T_b+1)}\eta_{T_1+1+k}^2 = O_p(1)$. By the continuous mapping theorem, $|A_2| = o_p(1)$, which implies that $A_2 = o_p(1)$. Similarly,

$$(A_3)^2 = \mu_b^2\frac{1}{T^2}\left(\sum_{k=1}^{T_b}\frac{1}{k}\eta_{T_b+1-k}\right)^2 \le \mu_b^2\frac{1}{T^2}\left(\sum_{k=1}^{T_b}\frac{1}{k^2}\right)\left(\sum_{k=1}^{T_b}\eta_{T_b+1-k}^2\right)$$
$$\le \mu_b^2\frac{\pi^2}{6}\left(\frac{1}{T}\sum_{k=1}^{T_b}\eta_{T_b+1-k}^2\right)\frac{1}{T} = o_p(1).$$

Given the results previously,

$$\mathcal{LM}_M = \sqrt{T}\sqrt{\frac{6}{\pi^2}}\frac{T^{-1}\sum_{j=2}^{T}\left(\sum_{k=1}^{j-1}\frac{1}{k}\eta_{j-k}\right)\eta_j + o_p(1)}{T^{-1}\sum_{j=2}^{T}\eta_j^2 + o_p(1)} = \sqrt{T}\sqrt{\frac{6}{\pi^2}}\sum_{k=1}^{T}\frac{1}{k}\rho_k + o_p(1),$$

hence following Lemma A1 and Slutsky's theorem, we have $\mathcal{LM}_M \xrightarrow{d} \mathcal{N}(0,1)$. □

Proof of Theorem A2. Under $H_0 : d_0 = 1$, $\Delta y_t = \beta_1 + \Delta u_t = \beta_1 + \eta_t \mathbf{1}_{t\ge 1}$. Define $\widetilde{\Delta y_t} = \Delta y_t - \hat{\beta}_1$. First, consider the denominator of $\mathcal{LM}_T$. Under H_0, conditioning on $y_0 = 0$,

$$T^{-1}\sum_{t=1}^{T}\left(\widetilde{\Delta y_t}\right)^2 = T^{-1}\sum_{t=1}^{T}\left(\Delta y_t - \hat{\beta}_1\right)^2 = T^{-1}\sum_{t=1}^{T}\left(\beta_1 - \hat{\beta}_1 + \eta_t\right)^2$$
$$= (\beta_1 - \hat{\beta}_1)^2 + 2(\beta_1 - \hat{\beta}_1)T^{-1}\sum_{t=1}^{T}\eta_t + T^{-1}\sum_{t=1}^{T}\eta_t^2$$
$$= O_p(T^{-1}) + o_p(1) + T^{-1}\sum_{t=1}^{T}\eta_t^2 = T^{-1}\sum_{t=1}^{T}\eta_t^2 + o_p(1),$$

where we use the fact that $\hat{\beta}_1 - \beta_1 = O_p(T^{-1/2})$, and $T^{-1}\sum_{t=1}^{T}\eta_t \xrightarrow{p} 0$ by the weak law of large numbers. Second, the numerator of $\mathcal{LM}_T$ is given by

$$T^{-1}\sum_{j=2}^{T}\left(-\log\Delta\widetilde{\Delta y_j}\right)\widetilde{\Delta y_j} = T^{-1}\sum_{j=2}^{T}\left(\sum_{k=1}^{j-1}\frac{1}{k}\widetilde{\Delta y_{j-k}}\right)\widetilde{\Delta y_j}$$
$$= T^{-1}\sum_{j=2}^{T}\left(\sum_{k=1}^{j-1}\frac{1}{k}\left(\Delta y_{j-k} - \hat{\beta}_1\right)\right)\left(\Delta y_j - \hat{\beta}_1\right)$$
$$= T^{-1}\sum_{j=2}^{T}\left(\sum_{k=1}^{j-1}\frac{1}{k}\left(\beta_1 - \hat{\beta}_1 + \eta_{j-k}\right)\right)\left(\beta_1 - \hat{\beta}_1 + \eta_j\right)$$
$$= \left(\beta_1 - \hat{\beta}_1\right)^2 T^{-1}\sum_{j=2}^{T}\sum_{k=1}^{j-1}\frac{1}{k} + \left(\beta_1 - \hat{\beta}_1\right)T^{-1}\sum_{j=2}^{T}\left(\sum_{k=1}^{j-1}\frac{1}{k}\right)\eta_j$$
$$+ \left(\beta_1 - \hat{\beta}_1\right)T^{-1}\sum_{j=2}^{T}\left(\sum_{k=1}^{j-1}\frac{1}{k}\eta_{j-k}\right) + T^{-1}\sum_{j=2}^{T}\left(\sum_{k=1}^{j-1}\frac{1}{k}\eta_{j-k}\right)\eta_j$$
$$= B_1 + B_2 + B_3 + T^{-1}\sum_{j=2}^{T}\left(\sum_{k=1}^{j-1}\frac{1}{k}\eta_{j-k}\right)\eta_j,$$

where we use the expansion $-\log\Delta = L + \frac{1}{2}L^2 + \frac{1}{3}L^3 + \cdots$. We show that $B_i = o_p(1)$ for $i = 1, 2, 3$.

$$B_1 \leq \left(\beta_1 - \hat{\beta}_1\right)^2 T^{-1} T\left(\log T + \gamma + \zeta_T\right) = O_p(T^{-1})\left(\log T + \gamma + \zeta_T\right) = o_p(1),$$
$$B_2 = \left(\beta_1 - \hat{\beta}_1\right) T^{-1} \sum_{k=1}^{T-1}\left(\frac{1}{k}\sum_{j=k+1}^{T}\eta_j\right) = O_p(T^{-1/2})o_p(1) = o_p(1),$$
$$B_3 = \left(\beta_1 - \hat{\beta}_1\right) T^{-1} \sum_{k=1}^{T-1}\left(\frac{1}{k}\sum_{j=1}^{T-k}\eta_j\right) = O_p(T^{-1/2})o_p(1) = o_p(1),$$

where γ is the Euler-Mascheroni constant and $\zeta_T \sim 1/(2T)$ which approaches 0 as $T \to \infty$. The results for B_2 and B_3 follow from the arguments used in the proof of Theorem 1 for the terms A_2 and A_3. Hence,

$$T^{-1}\sum_{j=2}^{T}\left(-\log \Delta\widetilde{\Delta y_j}\right)\widetilde{\Delta y_j} = T^{-1}\sum_{j=2}^{T}\left(\sum_{k=1}^{j-1}\frac{1}{k}\eta_{j-k}\right)\eta_j + o_p(1).$$

Then, under H_0,

$$\begin{aligned}\mathcal{LM}_T &= \frac{T^{-1}\sum_{j=2}^{T}\left(\sum_{k=1}^{j-1}\frac{1}{k}\eta_{j-k}\right)\eta_j + o_p(1)}{T^{-1}\sum_{t=1}^{T}\eta_t^2 + o_p(1)} \\ &= \frac{T^{-1}\sum_{j=2}^{T}\left(\sum_{k=1}^{j-1}\frac{1}{k}\eta_{j-k}\right)\eta_j}{T^{-1}\sum_{t=1}^{T}\eta_t^2} + o_p(1).\end{aligned}$$

This completes the proof. □

Proof of Propositions A1 and A3. When the estimate of the break date is consistent, the proof is trivial and omitted. We here focus on having a consistent estimate of the break fraction at some rate $T^{\varkappa}$ for $0 < \varkappa \leq 1$. Specifically, suppose that the estimate of the break fraction $\hat{\lambda}$ satisfies that $\hat{\lambda} - \lambda_b = o_p(T^{-\varkappa})$ for $0 < \varkappa \leq 1$. For all models A1–A3, we have a detrended sequence $\{\tilde{y}_t\}$ based on the OLS method in PZ. The Lagrange Multiplier test statistic is given by:

$$\mathcal{LM}_{T,\hat{\lambda}} = \sqrt{T}\sqrt{\frac{6}{\pi^2}}\frac{\sum_{t=2}^{T}\left(-\log\Delta\Delta\tilde{y}_t\right)\Delta\tilde{y}_t}{\sum_{t=1}^{T}\left(\Delta\tilde{y}_t\right)^2} = \sqrt{T}\sqrt{\frac{6}{\pi^2}}\frac{\sum_{t=2}^{T}\left(\sum_{k=1}^{t-1}\frac{1}{k}\Delta\tilde{y}_{t-k}\right)\Delta\tilde{y}_t}{\sum_{t=1}^{T}\left(\Delta\tilde{y}_t\right)^2}.$$

We show that the stochastic orders of terms associated with the deterministic time trend are smaller than those of terms associated with the error process. We can write (9) as:

$$\tilde{Y} = \hat{M}_z Z(T_b)\phi + \hat{M}_z U = \hat{M}_z Z(T_b)_2\phi_2 + \hat{M}_z U = \tilde{M} + \tilde{U},$$

and $\Delta\tilde{Y} = \Delta\tilde{M} + \Delta\tilde{U}$. Since $\mathcal{LM}_{T,\hat{\lambda}}$ is a functional of $\Delta\tilde{Y}$ and subvectors of $\Delta\tilde{Y}$, it suffices to consider the inner product of $\Delta\tilde{Y}'\Delta\tilde{Y}$, that is,

$$\Delta\tilde{Y}'\Delta\tilde{Y} = \Delta\tilde{M}'\Delta\tilde{M} + 2\Delta\tilde{M}'\Delta\tilde{U} + \Delta\tilde{U}'\Delta\tilde{U}.$$

Note that we only need to check the stochastic order of $\Delta\tilde{Y}'\Delta\tilde{Y}$ because the lag of order k is controlled to be small relative to the sample size T. We want to show that the term $\Delta\tilde{U}'\Delta\tilde{U}$ dominates the others. It is straightforward to show that $\Delta\tilde{U}'\Delta\tilde{U} = O_p(T)$ uniformly over all admissible break dates $T_b \in \{\pi T, (1-\pi)T\}$ for some $\pi \in (0, 1/2)$ in all models. When $\Delta\tilde{M}'\Delta\tilde{M}$ has a smaller order of magnitude compared to that of $\Delta\tilde{U}'\Delta\tilde{U}$, so does $\Delta\tilde{M}\Delta\tilde{U}$ by the Cauchy-Schwartz inequality. Further, the order of magnitude of $\Delta\tilde{M}'\Delta\tilde{M}$ cannot be greater than that of $\tilde{M}'\Delta\tilde{M}$. The order of magnitude of $\tilde{M}'\Delta\tilde{M}$ is $O_p(T^{2-2\varkappa})$ for Models A2 and A3, which implies that the break fraction should be estimated consistently at some rate greater than $T^{1/2}$. On the other hand, for Model A1b, the stochastic order of $\tilde{M}'\Delta\tilde{M}$ is $O_p(T^{1+2\alpha})$. Hence, the orders of magnitude of terms associated with the deterministic trend are greater than those of the terms associated with the error process, thereby the LM statistic diverges as $T \to \infty$. □

References

1. Perron, P. The great crash, the oil price shock and the unit root hypothesis. *Econometrica* **1989**, *57*, 1361–1401.
2. Dickey, D.A.; Fuller, W.A. Distribution of the estimators for autoregressive time series with a unit root. *J. Am. Stat. Assoc.* **1979**, *74*, 427–431.
3. Perron, P. Testing for a unit root in a time series with a changing mean. *J. Bus. Econ. Stat.* **1990**, *8*, 153–162.
4. Christiano, L.J. Searching for a break in GNP. *J. Bus. Econ. Stat.* **1992**, *10*, 237–250.
5. Zivot, E.; Andrews, D.W.K. Further evidence on the great crash, the oil price shock and the unit root hypothesis. *J. Bus. Econ. Stat.* **1992**, *10*, 251–270.
6. Perron, P. Further evidence on breaking trend functions in macroeconomic variables. *J. Econom.* **1997**, *80*, 355–385.
7. Vogelsang, T.J.; Perron, P. Additional tests for a unit root allowing for a break in the trend function at an unknown time. *Int. Econ. Rev.* **1998**, *39*, 1073–1100.
8. Perron, P.; Zhu, X. Structural breaks with deterministic and stochastic trends. *J. Econom.* **2005**, *129*, 65–119.
9. Perron, P.; Yabu, T. Testing for shifts in trend with an integrated or stationary noise component. *J. Bus. Econ. Stat.* **2009**, *27*, 369–396.
10. Kim, D.; Perron, P. Unit root tests allowing for a break in the trend function at an unknown time under both the null and alternative hypotheses. *J. Econom.* **2009**, *148*, 1–13.
11. Carrion-i-Silvestre, J.L.; Kim, D.; Perron, P. GLS-based unit root tests with multiple structural breaks under both the null and the alternative hypotheses. *Econom. Theory* **2009**, *25*, 1754–1792.
12. Robinson, P.M. Testing for strong serial correlation and dynamic conditional heteroskedasticity in multiple regression. *J. Econom.* **1991**, *47*, 67–84.
13. Robinson, P.M. Efficient tests of nonstationary hypothesis. *J. Am. Stat. Assoc.* **1994**, *89*, 1420–1437.
14. Tanaka, K. The nonstationary fractional unit root. *Econom. Theory* **1999**, *15*, 549–582.
15. Dolado, J.J; Gonzalo, J.; Mayoral, L. A fractional Dickey-Fuller test for unit roots. *Econometrica* **2002**, *70*, 1963–2006.
16. Lobato, I.N.; Velasco, C. Efficient Wald tests for fractional unit roots. *Econometrica* **2007**, *75*, 575–589.
17. Cho, C-K.; Amsler, C.; Schmidt, P. A test of the null of integer integration against the alternative of fractional integration. *J. Econom.* **2015**, *187*, 217–237.
18. Kwiatkowski, D.; Phillips, P.C.B.; Schmidt, P.; Shin, Y. Testing the null hypothesis of stationarity against the alternative of a unit root: How sure are we that economic time series have a unit root. *J. Econom.* **1992**, *54*, 154–178.
19. Dolado, J.J; Gonzalo, J.; Mayoral, L. Wald tests of I(1) against I(d) alternatives: Some new properties and an extension to processes with trending components. *Stud. Nonlinear Dyn. E.* **2008**, *12*, 1–33.
20. Diebold, F.X.; Inoue, A. Long memory and regime switching. *J. Econom.* **2001**, *105*, 131–159.
21. Granger, C.W.J.; Hyung, N. Occasional structural breaks and long memory with an application to the S&P 500 absolute stock returns. *J. Empir. Finance* **2004**, *11*, 399–421.
22. Lu, Y.K.; Perron, P. Modeling and forecasting stock return volatility using a random level shift model. *J. Empir. Finance* **2010**, *17*, 138–156.
23. Perron, P; Qu, Z. Long-memory and level shifts in the volatility of stock market return indices. *J. Bus. Econ. Stat.* **2010**, *28*, 275–290.
24. Qu, Z; Perron, P. A stochastic volatility model with random level shifts and its application to S&P 500 and NASDAQ return indices. *Econom. J.* **2013**, *16*, 309–339.
25. Xu, J.; Perron, P. Forecasting return volatility: Level shifts with varying jump probability and mean reversion. *Int. J. Forecast.* **2014**, *30*, 449–463.
26. Varneskov, R.T.; Perron, P. *Combining Long Memory and Level Shifts in Modeling and Forecasting the Volatility of Asset Returns*; Department of Economics, Boston University, Boston, MA, USA; Unpublished manuscript, 2016.
27. Wright, J.H. Testing for a structural break at unknown date with long-memory disturbances. *J. Time Ser. Anal.* **1998**, *19*, 369–376.
28. Krämer, W.; Sibbertsen, P. Testing for structural changes in the presence of long memory. *Int. J. Bus. Econ.* **2002**, *1*, 235–242.

29. Robinson, P.M. The distance between rival nonstationary fractional processes. *J. Econom.* **2005**, *128*, 283–300.
30. Marinucci, D.; Robinson, P.M. Alternative forms of fractional Brownian motion. *J. Stat. Plan. Inference* **1999**, *80*, 111–122.
31. Davidson, J.; Hashimzade, N. Type I and type II Brownian motions: A reconsideration. *Comput. Stat. Data Anal.* **2009**, *53*, 2089–2106.
32. Hosking, J.R.M. Asymptotic distributions of the sample mean, autocovariances, and autocorrelations of long-memory time series. *J. Econom.* **1996**, *73*, 261–284.
33. Chang, S.Y.; Perron, P. Inference on a structural change in trend with fractionally integrated errors. *J. Time Ser. Anal.* **2016**, *37*, 555–574.
34. Hatanaka, M.; Yamada, K. A unit root test in the presence of structural changes in I(1) and I(0) models. In *Cointegration, Causality, and Forecasting: A Festschrift in Honour of Clive W.J. Granger*; Engle, R.F., White, H., Eds.; Oxford University Press: Oxford, UK, 1999; pp. 256–282.
35. Harvey, D.I.; Leybourne, S.J.; Newbold, P. Innovational outlier unit root tests with an endogenously determined break in level. *Oxf. B. Econ. Stat.* **2001**, *63*, 559–575.
36. Nunes, L.C.; Kuan, C-M.; Newbold, P. Spurious break. *Econom. Theory* **1995**, *11*, 736–749.
37. Iacone, F.; Leybourne, S.J.; Taylor, A.M.R. Testing for a break in trend when the order of integration is unknown. *J. Econom.* **2013**, *176*, 30–45.
38. Abadir, K.M.; Distaso, W.; Giratis, L. Nonstationarity-extended local Whittle estimation. *J. Econom.* **2007**, *141*, 1353–1384.
39. Andrews, D.W.K. Tests for parameter instability and structural change with unknown change point. *Econometrica* **1993**, *61*, 821–856.
40. Shimotsu, K. Exact local Whittle estimation of fractional integration with unknown mean and time trend. *Econom. Theory* **2010**, *26*, 501–540.
41. Gil-Alana, L.A. Fractional integration and structural breaks at unknown periods of time. *J. Time Ser. Anal.* **2008**, *29*, 163–185.
42. Hassler, U.; Wolters, J. Long memory in inflation rates: International evidence. *J. Bus. Econ. Stat.* **1995**, *13*, 37–45.

econometrics

MDPI

Article

Testing for the Equality of Integration Orders of Multiple Series

Man Wang [1] **and Ngai Hang Chan** [2,*]

[1] Department of Finance, Donghua University, Shanghai 200051, China; wangman@dhu.edu.cn
[2] Department of Statistics, The Chinese University of Hong Kong, Shatin, NT, Hong Kong
* Correspondence: nhchan@sta.cuhk.edu.hk; Tel.: +852-3943-8519

Academic Editor: Pierre Perron
Received: 15 July 2016; Accepted: 25 November 2016; Published: 15 December 2016

Abstract: Testing for the equality of integration orders is an important topic in time series analysis because it constitutes an essential step in testing for (fractional) cointegration in the bivariate case. For the multivariate case, there are several versions of cointegration, and the version given in Robinson and Yajima (2002) has received much attention. In this definition, a time series vector is partitioned into several sub-vectors, and the elements in each sub-vector have the same integration order. Furthermore, this time series vector is said to be cointegrated if there exists a cointegration in any of the sub-vectors. Under such a circumstance, testing for the equality of integration orders constitutes an important problem. However, for multivariate fractionally integrated series, most tests focus on stationary and invertible series and become invalid under the presence of cointegration. Hualde (2013) overcomes these difficulties with a residual-based test for a bivariate time series. For the multivariate case, one possible extension of this test involves testing for an array of bivariate series, which becomes computationally challenging as the dimension of the time series increases. In this paper, a one-step residual-based test is proposed to deal with the multivariate case that overcomes the computational issue. Under certain regularity conditions, the test statistic has an asymptotic standard normal distribution under the null hypothesis of equal integration orders and diverges to infinity under the alternative. As reported in a Monte Carlo experiment, the proposed test possesses satisfactory sizes and powers.

Keywords: asymptotic normal; fractional cointegration; Monte Carlo experiment; residual-based test

JEL Classification: C12; C32

1. Introduction

By allowing the equilibrium error to follow a fractionally integrated process, fractional cointegration constitutes a useful extension of classical cointegration. It has received considerable attention in the statistics, finance and econometric literature. There are several notions of (fractional) cointegration for a p-dimensional time series X_t (see Engle and Granger (1987) [1], Johansen (1996) [2], Flôres and Szafarz (1996) [3] and Robinson and Yajima (2002) [4] among others). In the definition studied in Robinson and Yajima (2002) [4], a p-vector X_t is partitioned into several sub-vectors such that elements in each sub-vector have the same integration order. Furthermore, X_t is said to be (fractionally) cointegrated if a cointegration exists in any of the sub-vectors. Under this setting, partitioning X_t requires testing for the homogeneity of integration orders of multiple time series, which has attracted much interest. Current procedures usually assume stationarity and invertibility. For example, Heyde and Gay (1993) [5] and Hosoya (1997) [6] investigate this problem based on a parametric setting, and Robinson (1995) [7] and Lobato (1996 and 1999) [8,9] study the problem using the semiparametric framework. When cointegration exists or the time series becomes nonstationary, some of these tests become invalid.

Robinson and Yajima (2002) [4] construct a single-test statistic that is valid in the presence of cointegration for testing the homogeneity of the fractional integration orders of multiple (asymptotically) stationary and invertible time series. They propose estimating the fractional integration order using the local Whittle likelihood method and introduce a user-chosen number to deal with the inversion of an asymptotically singular matrix. Nielsen and Shimotsu (2007) [10] extend this test statistic to accommodate both (asymptotically) stationary and nonstationary time series by applying the exact local Whittle likelihood method of Shimotsu and Phillips (2005) [11]. The simulation results in Nielsen and Shimotsu (2007) [10] show that the test statistic is sensitive to the choice of the user chosen number, which is assumed to satisfy certain conditions. Hualde (2013) [12] proposes a residual-based test, which covers the nonstationary and noninvertible series, and is valid irrespective of whether cointegration exists. Although this test is developed for a bivariate series, extending it to the multivariate case is non-trivial because multiple comparisons are needed when high-dimensional series are involved. There are two ways to extend the Hualde (2013) [12] result. The first involves testing the equality of each pair of integration orders, which requires $p(p-1)/2$ simple tests for a p-dimensional series. When p is large, this test procedure becomes computationally intensive. The second extension is to explore the possibility of a one-step single test, which is pursued here.

In this paper, a residual-based testing procedure for the equality of integration orders of a multiple fractionally integrated process is proposed. The test encompasses both the stationary/nonstationary and invertible/noninvertible situations, and is valid even when the time series is cointegrated. The procedure is computationally feasible because it is a one-step test without inverting ill-conditioned matrices under cointegration. The test can be computed very fast even when dealing with a large p. The test statistic converges to a standard normal distribution under the null hypothesis that all integration orders are equal, and diverges when there are different integration orders.

This paper is organized as follows. In Section 2, the testing procedure and asymptotic theory are presented. Empirical sizes and powers of the proposed test are given via a Monte Carlo study in Section 3. Section 4 concludes the paper.

2. Integration Orders

Consider the following p-dimensional time series $(x_{1,t}, x_{2,t}, \ldots, x_{p,t})'$, with prime denoting transposition and $t \in \{0, \pm 1, \pm 2, \ldots\}$,

$$\begin{aligned} x_{1,t} &= \Delta^{-\delta_1}\{v_{1,t}\mathbf{1}(t > 0)\}, \quad x_{1,t} = 0, t \leq 0, \\ &\vdots \\ x_{p,t} &= \Delta^{-\delta_p}\{v_{p,t}\mathbf{1}(t > 0)\}, \quad x_{p,t} = 0, t \leq 0, \end{aligned} \tag{1}$$

where $\mathbf{1}(\cdot)$ is the indicator function, $\Delta = 1 - L$, L is the lag operator, and $v_t = (v_{1,t}, \ldots, v_{p,t})'$ is a vector of zero mean covariance stationary processes. Note that the series $\{x_{i,t}\}$ is nonstationary for $\delta_i > 1/2$ and "asymptotically stationary" for $\delta_i < 1/2, i = 1, \ldots, p$. By Taylor's expansion, $\Delta^{\alpha} = \sum_{j=0}^{\infty} \pi_j(-\alpha)L^j, \pi_j(\alpha) = \frac{(\alpha)_j}{j!}$, where $(\alpha)_j = (\alpha)(\alpha+1)\ldots(\alpha+j-1)$. If α is not a negative integer, then $\pi_j(\alpha) = \frac{\Gamma(j+\alpha)}{\Gamma(\alpha)\Gamma(j+1)}$. When α is a negative integer, then $\pi_j(\alpha) = 0$ for $j > -\alpha$ and $\Delta^{-\alpha}$ becomes the usual formula of differencing with integer orders. The symbol $||\cdot||$ is used to represent the Euclidean norm and $A \sim B$ means that A/B converge to a constant or converge in distribution to a random variable as n goes to ∞.

Assumption 1. *Consider the process $v_t = A(L)\epsilon_t, t \in Z$ with $A(L) = \sum_{j=0}^{\infty} A_j L^j$. Assume that*

1.1. $\sum_{j=1}^{\infty} j||A_j||^2 < \infty$;

1.2. ϵ_t *are i.i.d vectors with mean zero, positive definite covariance matrix* Ω *and* $E||\epsilon_t||^q < \infty$ *for some* $q > max\{2, 1/(\bar{\delta} + 1/2)\}$, *where* $\bar{\delta} = min\{\delta_i\}_{i=1}^p$.
1.3. $f_{ii}(0) > 0, i = 1, 2$, *where* $f(\lambda)$ *is the spectral density matrix of* v_t *and* $f_{ij}(0)$ *is the* $(i, j) - th$ *element of* $f(0)$.

Assumption 1 is mild because it is satisfied by the usual stationary and invertible autoregressive moving average (ARMA) processes. This is a common assumption for applying the functional limit theorem of Marinucci and Robinson (2000) [13], and it has appeared in a similar form as Assumptions A–C of Marmol and Velasco (2004) [14], Assumption A of Hualde (2013) [12] and Assumption 1 of Wang, Wang and Chan (2015) [15]. In Particular, the moment condition in Assumption 1.2 is discussed by Johansen and Nielsen (2012) [16]. As pointed out in Wang, Wang and Chan (2015) [15], Assumption 1.1 ensures that the limiting process of the partial sum of v_t has nondegenerated finite-dimensional distributions. Assumption 1.1 implies that $f(\lambda)$ is $Lip(\gamma), \gamma > 0$.

Under Assumption 1, model (1) means that all $x_{i,t}, i = 1, \ldots, p$ are type-II fractionally integrated processes. Furthermore, based on the fractional cointegration definition given in Robinson and Yajima (2002) [4], if the integration orders of $x_{it}, i = 1, \ldots, p$ are the same and there exists a non-zero linear combination $\beta' x_t$ that is $I(b)(b < \delta_i)$, then the p-dimensional time series x_t is said to be cointegrated. Furthermore, any multiple time series containing x_t as a sub-vector is also said to be cointegrated.

To test whether all of the $\delta_i, i = 1, \ldots, p$ are the same, we need to estimate δ_i precisely. Thus, the following assumptions are introduced.

Assumption 2. *Under both the null and alternative hypotheses,*

2.1. *there exists a positive constant* $K < \infty$ *and estimates* $\hat{\delta}_i$ *of* δ_i, $i = 1, \ldots, p$, *respectively, such that*

$$\sum_{i=1}^{p} |\hat{\delta}_i| \leq K, \tag{2}$$

and there exists $\kappa > 0$,

$$\hat{\delta}_i - \delta_i \sim n^{-\kappa}; \tag{3}$$

2.2. *Letting* $\hat{f}(0)$ *be an estimate of* $f(0)$, *then* $\hat{f}(0) \xrightarrow{p} f(0)$, *where* $\xrightarrow{p}$ *stands for the convergence in probability.*

Assumption 2 is very mild, as condition (2) is satisfied if $\hat{\delta}_i, i = 1, \ldots, p$ are optimizers of the corresponding functions over compact sets. $\delta_i, i = 1, \cdots, p$ can be estimated by semiparametric methods (see, for example, the log periodogram estimate of Geweke and Porter-Hudak (1983) [17] studied by Hurvich et al. (1998) [18] or the narrow-band Gaussian or Whittle estimate introduced by Künsch (1987) [19] and studied in Robinson (1995) [7] and Lobato (1999) [9]. Equation (3) is satisfied by many estimation methods, such as that used in Beran (1995) [20] and Tanaka (1999) [21]. As pointed out by Hualde and Velasco (2008) [22], Equation (3) is satisfied if δ_i is estimated from $x_{i,t}$ using the usual parametric or semiparametric methods. For example, the Whittle pseudo-maximum likelihood estimation proposed by Velasco and Robinson (2000) [23] satisfies (3). In particular, if a parametric structure is imposed on v_t, then a $\sqrt{n}$-consistent estimator results by means of a multivariate extension of Robinson (2005) [24]. Assumption 2.2 is quite common and is satisfied by many classic semiparametric or nonparametric estimates. Actually, a stricter condition on the convergence rate of $\hat{f}(0)$ ($\hat{f}(0) - f(0) = O_p(n^{-\chi})$, with χ being a positive constant) is used in many articles, such as Hualde and Robinson (2006) [25], Hualde and Robinson (2010) [26], Hualde and Velasco (2008) [22] and Wang (2008) [27], among others. In particular, Hualde and Robinson (2006) [25] discuss the convergence rate of some estimates of f, including a weighted periodogram estimate that satisfies Assumption 2.2. Hualde and Velasco (2008) [22] point out that the nonparametric estimate of $f(0)$ introduced in their paper satisfies Assumption 2.2. Once $\hat{\delta}_i$ is estimated, the nonparametric estimator of $f(0)$ can be based on the weighted averages of the periodogram of the proxy $\hat{v}_t = (x_{1,t}(\hat{\delta}_1), \ldots, x_{p,t}(\hat{\delta}_p))'$, where $x_{i,t}(\hat{\delta}_i) = \Delta^{\hat{\delta}_i}\{x_{i,t}\mathbf{1}(t > 0)\}$.

Let $h_n > 0$ be a sequence such that

$$h_n^{-1} + n^{-\kappa} h_n \to 0 \text{ as } n \to \infty. \tag{4}$$

Let $d = \sum_{i=1}^{p} \delta_i$, $\hat{d} = \sum_{i=1}^{p} \hat{\delta}_i$ and

$$\hat{a} = (I_1, I_2, \ldots, I_p)', \tag{5}$$

where $I_i = \mathbf{1}\{A_i \cap B_i\}$, $A_i = \{n^{\kappa}(\hat{\delta}_i - \max_{j=1,\ldots,p, j\neq i}\{\hat{\delta}_j\}) \geq -h_n\}$ and $B_i = \{n^{\kappa}(\hat{\delta}_i - \max_{j=1,\ldots,i-1}\{\hat{\delta}_j\}) > h_n\}$. Furthermore, for $i = 1$, let $\max_{j=1,\ldots,i-1}\{\hat{\delta}_j\} = -\infty$. Clearly, B_1 is the entire sample space with $P(B_1) = 1$.

Defining $\delta_i^* = \frac{d-\delta_i}{p-1}$ and $\hat{\delta}_i^* = \frac{\hat{d}-\hat{\delta}_i}{p-1}$, we denote:

$$\hat{F} = F(\hat{\delta}, \hat{f}(0)) = \frac{\hat{a}' \sum_t x_t(\hat{\delta}_1^*, \ldots, \hat{\delta}_p^*)}{(2n\pi)^{1/2}\hat{a}'\hat{f}(0)\hat{a}},$$

as the test for $H_0 : \delta_1 = \cdots = \delta_p$ against the alternative H_1: there exists at least a pair of (i, j) such that $\delta_i \neq \delta_j$.

Theorem 1. *Letting Assumptions 1 and 2 hold, x_t is defined in (1), and then $\hat{F} \xrightarrow{d} N(0,1)$ under H_0 and $\hat{F} = O_p(n^{\frac{p*\max\{\delta_i\}-d}{p-1}})$ under H_1, where $\xrightarrow{d}$ stands for convergence in distribution as $n \to \infty$.*

Remark 1. *Denote the set of indices of the maxima of δ_i as $S = \{j, \delta_j = \max\{\delta_i\}_{i=1}^{p}\}$, and let m_0 be the smallest index of the maxima, that is, $m_0 = \min\{S\}$. Furthermore, let $a = \mathbf{e}_{m_0}$, where $\mathbf{e}_{m_0}$ is the unit vector that equals one at the m_0-th coordinate and zero otherwise. Then, it is shown in the proof of Theorem 1 that $\hat{a} \xrightarrow{p} a$.*

Remark 2. *The vector $\hat{a}$ can also be set as a vector of constants: $a = (a_1, \cdots, a_p)'$, which satisfies $a'f(0)a \neq 0$. As $\hat{f}(0) \to f(0)$ in probability, $a'\hat{f}(0)a > 0$ with probability 1. However, with $\{\delta_i\}_{i=1}^{p}$ unknown, it is not guaranteed that $\hat{F}$ diverges under H_1 at a rate as fast as that specified in Theorem 1. Wang (2008) [27] shows that different pre-determined $\hat{a}$ may lead to different divergence rates.*

Remark 3. *As pointed out in Remark 2, the choice of $\hat{a}$ has an influence on the diverging speed of $\hat{F}$. From the proof of Theorem 1, to get the theoretical diverging speed of $\hat{F}$ as in Theorem 1, define $\hat{a}$ by Equations (4) and (5). Then, $\hat{a} \xrightarrow{p} \mathbf{e}_{m_0}$ when $n \to \infty$, with m_0 being the smallest index of the maxima of $\{\delta_i\}_{i=1}^{p}$. Consequently, the denominator of $\hat{F}$ converges to $(2n\pi)^{1/2} f_{m_0,m_0}(0) > 0$. Similar to the analysis in Hualde (2013) [12] and Wang, Wang and Chan (2015) [15], it is natural to replace condition (4) by setting $h_n = 0$, in which case $\hat{a}$ converges to a random limit under H_0. Furthermore, the limits of the numerator and denominator of $\hat{F}$ are dependent, which complicates analysis of the asymptotic distribution of $\hat{F}$. From the definition of $\hat{a}$, it is obvious that the power of the proposed test with $h_n = 0$ is superior to that of tests with other choices of h_n. However, when the sample size $n \to \infty$, the powers of different cases will become the same. In practice, $h_n = \log n^{\kappa}$ or $h_n = n^{\kappa/2}$ are two possible choices. In particular, if the parametric method in Hualde and Robinson (2011) [28] is used, $\kappa = 1/2$, then we can set $h_n = n^{1/4}$.*

Remark 4. *If $(x_{1,t}, x_{2,t}, \ldots, x_{p,t})$ is cointegrated with $\beta' x_t = \Delta^b u_t$, $\beta \neq 0$, $b < \delta_1 = \delta_2 = \cdots = \delta_p$, then $f(0)$ would be singular. In this situation, most of the tests in the literature involve the inverse of $f(0)$ and become invalid under H_0. However, the proposed test still works in the presence of cointegration. As $f_{m_0,m_0}(0) > 0$ by Assumption 1, and $\hat{a} \xrightarrow{p} a = \mathbf{e}_{m_0}$ as mentioned in Remark 1, we have $a'f(0)a > 0$. Furthermore, as shown in*

Theorem 1, $\hat{a}' f(0)\hat{a}$ converges to $a' f(0)a > 0$ in probability. Then, $\hat{a}' \hat{f}(0)\hat{a}$ is positive with probability 1, and $\hat{F}$ remains valid under cointegration.

3. Simulation

To assess the performance of our testing procedure, we conduct two Monte Carlo experiments. For both experiments, we generate $(x_{1,t}, x_{2,t}, x_{3,t})'$ as in (1) with v_t being a three-dimensional white noise with $\mathrm{E}(v_t) = 0$, $\mathrm{Var}(v_{i,t}) = 1$ for $i = 1, 2, 3$, $\mathrm{Cov}(v_{i,t}, v_{j,t})$ =0.5. We compute $\hat{F}$ parametrically, which means $\hat{\delta}_i, i = 1, 2, 3$ are estimated as in Hualde and Robinson (2011) [28] and $f(0)$ is estimated by $\hat{f}(0) = (2\pi n)^{-1/2} \sum_{t=1}^{n} \hat{v}_t \hat{v}_t'$.

For the first experiment, using 10,000 replications and 3 different sample sizes $n = 100, 250$ and 500, we compute the proportion of rejecting $\hat{F}$ for nominal size $\alpha = 0.01$, 0.05, and 0.1 with different combinations of $(\delta_1, \delta_2, \delta_3)$. Letting $\phi = \frac{p * \max_{i=1,\dots,p} \{\delta_i\} - d}{p-1}$, we consider $\phi = 0, 0.3, 0.6, 0.8$ and 1.0. To investigate the sensitivity of the choice of h_n, we present the result for $h_{1n} = 0, h_{2n} = \log(n^{\kappa}), h_{3n} = n^{\kappa/2}$ with $\kappa = 1/2$ in Table 1.

Table 1. Empirical sizes and powers based on different δ and α.

	n	100			250			500		
h_n	α	0.01	0.05	0.1	0.01	0.05	0.1	0.01	0.05	0.1
	$\phi = 0$	0.0603	0.1572	0.2874	0.0453	0.1356	0.2317	0.0415	0.1228	0.1969
	$\phi = 0.3$	0.5687	0.6726	0.7508	0.6615	0.7473	0.7881	0.7357	0.8113	0.8522
h_{1n}	$\phi = 0.6$	0.8730	0.9116	0.9288	0.9334	0.9598	0.9657	0.9767	0.9814	0.9892
	$\phi = 0.8$	0.9427	0.9562	0.9653	0.9693	0.9805	0.9833	0.9861	0.9896	0.9932
	$\phi = 1.0$	0.9733	0.9750	0.9820	0.9922	0.9951	0.9964	0.9972	0.9985	0.9987
	$\phi = 0$	0.0134	0.056	0.1127	0.0060	0.0533	0.105	0.0057	0.0523	0.1024
	$\phi = 0.3$	0.4724	0.5803	0.6437	0.5360	0.6875	0.7480	0.7371	0.8158	0.8463
h_{2n}	$\phi = 0.6$	0.8651	0.9082	0.9224	0.9392	0.9537	0.9556	0.9675	0.9804	0.9893
	$\phi = 0.8$	0.9427	0.9562	0.9653	0.9693	0.9805	0.9833	0.9861	0.9896	0.9932
	$\phi = 1.0$	0.9733	0.9750	0.9820	0.9922	0.9951	0.9964	0.9972	0.9985	0.9987
	$\phi = 0$	0.0047	0.0507	0.1068	0.0046	0.0482	0.1035	0.0049	0.0484	0.1033
	$\phi = 0.3$	0.4230	0.5399	0.6045	0.5168	0.6404	0.7006	0.6385	0.7334	0.7842
h_{3n}	$\phi = 0.6$	0.8457	0.8873	0.9162	0.9384	0.9625	0.9706	0.9727	0.9748	0.9881
	$\phi = 0.8$	0.9427	0.9562	0.9653	0.9693	0.9805	0.9833	0.9861	0.9896	0.9932
	$\phi = 1.0$	0.9733	0.9750	0.9820	0.9922	0.9951	0.9964	0.9972	0.9985	0.9987

First, consider the sizes, that is, $\phi = 0$. We observe that for h_{1n}, $\hat{F}$ is oversized and the empirical sizes of case h_{2n} and h_{3n} are very close to the nominal sizes. As n increases, the empirical sizes under all scenarios approach the nominal sizes as expected. We also examine the power for $\phi = 0.3, 0.6, 0.8$ and 1.0. It can be seen that the empirical power increases as n and ϕ increase, and that $\hat{F}$ performs very well for all choices of $h_{in}, i = 1, 2, 3$. As expected, a smaller h_n leads to better power, so h_{1n} has the best power and h_{2n} has better power than h_{3n}. As ϕ increases, the difference decreases substantially, and it is clear that for $\phi \geq 0.6$, the powers of all $h_{in}, i = 1, 2, 3$ are almost the same. One explanation is that when ϕ is large enough, $n^{-\kappa} h_{in}, i = 1, 2, 3$ become relatively small compared with ϕ, leading to the same $\hat{a}$. As ARMA models are common in modeling stationary time series, autoregressive fractionally integrated moving averaging (ARFIMA) models constitute a reasonable approximation to x_t when the parametric method in Hualde and Robinson (2011) [28] is considered. In practice, if there is insufficient information about the true model, a general ARFIMA(p_1, δ_0, p_2) model is entertained first and a model selection procedure based on some information criteria is conducted to choose p_1 and p_2.

For the second experiment, we conduct a simulation to compare the proposed test $\hat{F}$ with the test in Nielsen and Shimotsu (2007) [10]:

$$\hat{T}_0 = m(S\hat{\delta})' \left(S\frac{1}{4}\hat{D}^{-1}\left(\hat{G}o\hat{G}\right)\hat{D}^{-1}S' + k_n^2 I_{p-1} \right)^{-1} (S\hat{d}),$$

where m is the bandwidth parameter; $\delta = (\delta_1, \delta_2, \cdots, \delta_p)'$ is the vector of integration orders of $(x_{1,t}, x_{2,t}, \ldots, x_{p,t})'$; o is the Hadamard product; I_{p-1} is the $(p-1)$-dimensional identity matrix; $S = [I_{p-1}, -\iota]$, with ι being the $(p-1)$-vector of ones; k_n is a positive sequence satisfying certain assumptions; G is the spectral density matrix of the δ'th differenced process around the origin; and D is the diagonal matrix of G. Using 5,000 replications and 3 different sample sizes n = 128, 256 and 512, we report the rejection frequencies of $\hat{F}$ with $h_{3n} = n^{\kappa}, \kappa = 1/2$, as well as $\hat{T}_0$ with bandwidth parameter $m = [n^{0.6}]$ and two choices of k_n, that is $k_{1n} = 1/\log(n)$ and $k_{2n} = 1/(\log(n))^{1/2}$ in Table 2. Here, $[z]$ denotes the largest integer smaller than or equal to z. The fractional integration order δ is estimated by the exact local Whittle likelihood for $\hat{T}_0$.

Table 2. Empirical sizes and powers of $\hat{F}$ and $\hat{T}_0$.

	n		128			256			512	
	α	0.01	0.05	0.1	0.01	0.05	0.1	0.01	0.05	0.1
$\hat{F}$ with h_{3n}	$\phi = 0$	0.02	0.0566	0.1148	0.016	0.0514	0.1118	0.0138	0.0514	0.1106
	$\phi = 0.3$	0.5172	0.6224	0.6842	0.5718	0.6698	0.7120	0.6398	0.7342	0.7842
	$\phi = 0.6$	0.8622	0.8976	0.9134	0.9328	0.9572	0.9680	0.9712	0.9758	0.9854
	$\phi = 0.8$	0.9592	0.9682	0.9742	0.9800	0.9850	0.9874	0.9902	0.9926	0.9938
	$\phi = 1.0$	0.9694	0.9758	0.9802	0.9858	0.9884	0.9902	0.9968	0.9976	0.9984
$\hat{T}_0$ with k_{1n}	$\phi = 0$	0.1310	0.2438	0.3278	0.1280	0.2438	0.3278	0.1010	0.2008	0.3076
	$\phi = 0.3$	0.5584	0.7144	0.7860	0.5584	0.7184	0.7860	0.5684	0.7184	0.7968
	$\phi = 0.6$	0.9722	0.9890	0.9944	0.9722	0.9890	0.9944	0.9742	0.9890	0.9974
	$\phi = 0.8$	0.9964	0.9994	0.9994	0.9968	0.9994	0.9994	0.9972	0.9996	0.9996
	$\phi = 1.0$	0.9988	0.9998	1	1	1	1	1	1	1
$\hat{T}_0$ with k_{2n}	$\phi = 0$	0.0490	0.1154	0.1808	0.0490	0.1154	0.1808	0.0498	0.1156	0.1810
	$\phi = 0.3$	0.3680	0.5662	0.6658	0.3680	0.5662	0.6658	0.3780	0.5682	0.6678
	$\phi = 0.6$	0.9352	0.9772	0.9868	0.9552	0.9782	0.9868	0.9552	0.9782	0.9868
	$\phi = 0.8$	0.9872	0.9962	0.9980	0.9892	0.9964	0.9980	0.9892	0.9964	0.9980
	$\phi = 1.0$	0.9950	0.9986	0.9994	1	1	1	1	1	1

We find that all of the three tests are oversized, and that their empirical powers increase when ϕ increases. However, the empirical powers and empirical sizes of $\hat{T}_0$ do not change much when the sample size changes from 128 to 512, while those of $\hat{F}$ improve significantly when n increases.

We first compare the simulation results of $\hat{T}_0$ with k_{1n} and k_{2n}. It is obvious that $\hat{T}_0$ is sensitive to the choice of k_n: $\hat{T}_0$ works reasonably well for $k_{2n} = 1/(\log n)^{1/2}$ and $\hat{T}_0$ over-rejects substantially for $k_{1n} = 1/\log n$. The test $\hat{T}_0$ is oversized for both k_{1n} and k_{2n}, and k_{2n} has a better empirical size and k_{1n} better empirical power. This phenomenon is also reported in Nielsen and Shimotsu (2007) [10].

We then compare $\hat{F}$ with $\hat{T}_0$ and find that, for all sample sizes n, $\hat{F}$ has much better empirical sizes than $\hat{T}_0$ for both k_{1n} and k_{2n}. The empirical power of $\hat{F}$ is not as good as that of $\hat{T}_0$ when the sample size is relatively small (128 and 256). However, as the sample size increases to 512, the empirical power of $\hat{F}$ becomes superior to that of $\hat{T}_0$.

4. Conclusions

A residual-based test for testing the equality of the integration orders of multiple fractionally integrated processes is proposed in this paper. The test is valid under cointegration and is computationally feasible. One needs only to estimate the integration order and the spectral density function of the process that generates the fractionally integrated processes. The proposed test enjoys standard asymptotics and possesses satisfactory finite sample behavior.

Acknowledgments: We thank the editor and three anonymous referees for their helpful comments and useful references, which led to an improved version of this paper. This research was supported in part by General Research Fund of HKSAR-RGC-GRF grant No. 400313, 14300514 and 14325216; HKSAR-RGCCRF:CityU8/CRG/12G; the Theme-based Research Scheme of HKSAR-RGC-TBS T32-101/15-R (Chan) and Fundamental Research Funds for the Central Universities 16D110810; and Donghua University Special Research Funds for Social Science 108-10-0108135 (Wang).

Author Contributions: Both authors contributed equally to the paper.

Conflicts of Interest: The authors declare no conflict of interest.

Appendix A

Lemma A1. *Let δ_i, δ_i^* and $\hat{\delta}_i^*$ be defined as in Section 2. Then* $n^{-1/2}\sum_{t=1}^n \Delta^{\hat{\delta}_i^*} x_{i,t} - n^{-1/2}\sum_{t=1}^n \Delta^{\delta_i^*} x_{i,t} = \begin{cases} o_p(1), & \text{under } H_0, \\ o_p(n^{\delta_i - \delta_i^*}), & \text{under } H_1. \end{cases}$

Proof. Let $g(\lambda, z_t) = \Delta^\lambda z_t$. Then $g(\lambda, z_t) = \sum_{i=0}^{t-1} \pi_i(\lambda) z_{t-i}$ if $z_t = 0$ for $t \leq 0$, where $\pi_i(\cdot)$, $i = 1, \ldots, t-1$ are as defined in Section 2 and the derivatives $g^{(r)}(\lambda, z_t) = \sum_{i=1}^{t-1} \pi_i^{(r)}(\lambda) z_{t-i}$, where $\pi_i^{(r)}(\lambda) = d^r \pi_i(\lambda)/d\lambda^r$. Based on Taylor's expansion around δ_i, for a certain constant R to be defined subsequently, we can show that

$$\begin{aligned}
& n^{-1/2}\sum_{t=1}^n \Delta^{\hat{\delta}_i^*} x_{i,t} - n^{-1/2}\sum_{t=1}^n \Delta^{\delta_i^*} x_{i,t} \\
=& n^{-1/2}\sum_{t=1}^n (g(\delta_i - \hat{\delta}_i^*; v_{i,t}) - g(\delta_i - \delta_i^*; v_{i,t})) \\
=& \frac{1}{\sqrt{n}} \sum_{r=1}^{R-1} \frac{(\delta_i^* - \hat{\delta}_i^*)^r}{r!} \sum_{t=1}^n g^{(r)}(\delta_i - \delta_i^*; v_{i,t}) + \frac{(\delta_i^* - \hat{\delta}_i^*)^R}{R!\sqrt{n}} \sum_{t=1}^n g^{(R)}(\delta_i - \tilde{\delta}; v_{i,t}) \quad \text{(A1)} \\
=& \begin{cases} o_p(1), & \text{under } H_0, \\ o_p(T^{\delta_i - \delta_i^*}), & \text{under } H_1, \end{cases} \quad \text{(A2)}
\end{aligned}$$

where $\tilde{\delta} \in (\min(\delta_i^*, \hat{\delta}_i^*), \max(\delta_i^*, \hat{\delta}_i^*))$.

(A1) and (A2) can be derived based on reasoning similar to that of Theorem 1 of Wang, Wang and Chan (2015) [15] or Theorem 1 of Hualde (2013) [12], under Assumptions 1 and 2. In particular, to verify (A2), we apply the functional central limit theorem as in Marinucci and Robinson (2000) [13], which is guaranteed by Assumption 1. □

Proof of Theorem 1. First, we show that $\hat{a} \xrightarrow{p} a$, where $\hat{a} = (I_1, I_2, \ldots, I_p)$, with $I_i = \mathbf{1}\{A_i \cap B_i\}$, $A_i := \{n^\kappa(\hat{\delta}_i - \max_{j=1,\ldots,p, j\neq i}\{\hat{\delta}_j\}) \geq -h_n\}$, $B_i = \{n^\kappa(\hat{\delta}_i - \max_{j=1,\ldots,i-1}\{\hat{\delta}_j\}) > h_n\}$, and B_1 is as defined in Section 2.

Note that $\forall i \in \{1, \ldots, p\}$,

$$1\{A_i \cap B_i\} + 1\{A_i^c \cup B_i^c\} = 1,$$

and $\hat{a} \xrightarrow{p} a$ is immediately obtained if we show that

$$1\{n^{\kappa}(\hat{\delta}_i - \max_{j=1,\ldots,p,j\neq i}\{\hat{\delta}_j\}) \geq -h_n\} = o_p(1), \quad \text{if } \delta_i < \max_{j=1,\ldots,p}\{\delta_j\}, \tag{A3}$$

$$1\{n^{\kappa}(\hat{\delta}_i - \max_{j=1,\ldots,p,j\neq i}\{\hat{\delta}_j\}) < -h_n\} = o_p(1), \quad \text{if } \delta_i = \max_{j=1,\ldots,p}\{\delta_j\}, \tag{A4}$$

$$1\{n^{\kappa}(\hat{\delta}_i - \max_{j=1,\ldots,i-1}\{\hat{\delta}_j\}) > h_n\} = o_p(1), \quad \text{if } \delta_i \leq \max_{j=1,\ldots,i-1}\{\delta_j\}, \tag{A5}$$

$$1\{n^{\kappa}(\hat{\delta}_i - \max_{j=1,\ldots,i-1}\{\hat{\delta}_j\}) \leq h_n\} = o_p(1), \quad \text{if } \delta_i > \max_{j=1,\ldots,i-1}\{\delta_j\}. \tag{A6}$$

The reason is that, if $i = m_0$, with m_0 as defined in Remark 1, $\delta_i = \max_{j=1,\ldots,p}\{\delta_i\}$ and $\delta_i > \max_{j=1,\ldots,i-1}\{\delta_i\}$, then $1\{A_i^c \cup B_i^c\} \leq 1\{A_i^c\} + 1\{B_i^c\} = o_p(1) + o_p(1) = o_p(1)$ and $1\{A_i \cap B_i\} \xrightarrow{p} 1$.

Otherwise, if $i \neq m_0$, which means $\delta_i < \max_{j=1,\ldots,p}\{\delta_i\}$ or $\delta_i \leq \max_{j=1,\ldots,i-1}\{\delta_i\}$, then $1\{A_i \cap B_i\} \leq 1/2(1\{A_i\} + 1\{B_i\}) = o_p(1) + o_p(1) = o_p(1)$.

Therefore, $I_i \xrightarrow{p} \mathbf{1}\{i = m_0\}$, and furthermore $\hat{a} \xrightarrow{p} a$.

Then, we prove (A3)–(A6). As the definition of $1\{B_i\}$ is similar to the terms that appear in Hualde (2013) [12] and Wang, Wang and Chan (2015) [15], (A5) and (A6) can be proved with similar reasoning. We prove (A3), which means that δ_i is smaller than $\max_{k=1,\ldots,p}\{\delta_k\} = \delta_j$. Denote $Q_n = n^{\kappa}(\hat{\delta}_i - \hat{\delta}_j - (\delta_i - \delta_j))$, then $|Q_n| = O_p(1)$ based on Assumption 2. First, we show that

$$\begin{aligned} 1\{A_i\} &= 1\{n^{\kappa}(\hat{\delta}_i - \max_{k=1,\ldots,p,k\neq i}\{\hat{\delta}_k\}) \geq -h_n\} \\ &= 1\{n^{\kappa}(\hat{\delta}_i - \hat{\delta}_j) \geq -h_n\} \\ &= 1\{Q_n + n^{\kappa}(\delta_i - \delta_j) \geq -h_n\} \\ &\leq \tfrac{|Q_n|}{-h_n + n^{\kappa}(\delta_j - \delta_i)} = o_p(1), \end{aligned} \tag{A7}$$

by (4).

Similarly, for (A4), when $\delta_i = \max_{k=1,\ldots,p}\{\delta_k\} \geq \max_{k=1,\ldots,p,k\neq i}\{\delta_k\}$,

$$\begin{aligned} 1\{A_i^c\} &= 1\{n^{\kappa}(\hat{\delta}_i - \max_{k=1,\ldots,p,k\neq i}\{\hat{\delta}_k\}) < -h_n\} \\ &\leq \textstyle\sum_{k=1,k\neq i}^{p} 1\{n^{\kappa}(\hat{\delta}_i - \hat{\delta}_k) < -h_n\} \\ &= \textstyle\sum_{k=1,k\neq i}^{p} 1\{Q_n + n^{\kappa}(\delta_i - \delta_k) < -h_n\} \\ &= o_p(1), \end{aligned} \tag{A8}$$

since

$$\begin{aligned} &1\{Q_n + n^{\kappa}(\delta_i - \delta_k) < -h_n\}, \\ = &\begin{cases} 1\{-Q_n > h_n\} \leq \frac{|Q_n|}{h_n} = o_p(1), & \text{if } \delta_i = \delta_k, \\ 1\{n^{\kappa}(\delta_i - \delta_k) < -h_n - Q_n\} \leq \frac{|Q_n| + h_n}{n^{\kappa}(\delta_i - \delta_k)} = o_p(1), & \text{if } \delta_i > \delta_k. \end{cases} \end{aligned}$$

Next, we prove that

$$\begin{aligned} &F(\delta, f(0)) = \frac{\sum_{t=1}^{n} a' x_t(\delta_1^*, \ldots, \delta_p^*)}{(2n\pi)^{1/2} a' f(0) a}, \\ &\begin{cases} \xrightarrow{d} N(0,1), & \text{under } H_0, \\ = O_p(n^{(p*\max\{\delta_i\} - d)/(p-1)}), & \text{under } H_1. \end{cases} \end{aligned} \tag{A9}$$

Under H_0, $\delta_i^* = \delta_i$, $\frac{n^{-1/2}a' \sum_t x_t(\delta_1,\ldots,\delta_p)}{(2\pi)^{1/2}a' f(0)a}$ converges in distribution to $N(0,1)$ in view of the functional limit theorem of the $I(0)$ process. Under H_1, $\delta_i - \delta_i^* = \frac{p*\delta_i - d}{p-1}$, $\frac{a' \sum_t v_t(-(\delta_1-\delta_1^*),\ldots,-(\delta_p-\delta_p^*))}{(2n\pi)^{1/2}a' f(0)a} = O_p(n^{\frac{p*\max\{\delta_i\}-d}{p-1}})$, based on the properties of the integrated process.

Finally, we show that

$$\begin{aligned} & n^{-1/2}\sum_{t=1}^{n}(\hat{a}' x_t(\hat{\delta}_1^*,\ldots,\hat{\delta}_p^*) - a' x_t(\delta_1^*,\ldots,\delta_p^*)) \\ = & \frac{(\hat{a}-a)'}{\sqrt{n}}\sum_{t=1}^{n} x_t(\delta_1^*,\ldots,\delta_p^*)) + \frac{\hat{a}'}{\sqrt{n}}\sum_{t=1}^{n}(x_t(\hat{\delta}_1^*,\ldots,\hat{\delta}_p^*) - x_t(\delta_1^*,\ldots,\delta_p^*)) \\ = & \begin{cases} o_p(1) & \text{under } H_0, \\ o_p(n^{(p*\max\{\delta_i\}-d)/(p-1)}), & \text{under } H_1. \end{cases} \end{aligned} \quad \text{(A10)}$$

By Lemma A1, $||\frac{1}{\sqrt{n}}\sum_{t=1}^{n}(x_t(\hat{\delta}_1^*,\ldots,\hat{\delta}_p^*) - x_t(\delta_1^*,\ldots,\delta_p^*))||$ is $o_p(n^{\max\{\delta_i-\delta_i^*\}})$; additionally, $p*\max\{\delta_i\} - d = 0$ under H_0. Thus, it is $o_p(n^{(p*\max\{\delta_i\}-d)/(p-1)})$ under H_1, and is $o_p(1)$ under H_0.

$||\frac{1}{\sqrt{n}}\sum_{t=1}^{n} x_t(\delta_1^*,\ldots,\delta_p^*))||$ is $O_p(n^{(p*\max\{\delta_i\}-d)/(p-1)})$ and $||(\hat{a}-a)||$ is $o_p(1)$, so $\frac{(\hat{a}-a)'}{\sqrt{n}}\sum_{t=1}^{n} x_t(\delta_1^*,\ldots,\delta_p^*))$ is $o_p(n^{(p*\max\{\delta_i\}-d)/(p-1)})$.

Furthermore, based on (A9) and (A10) and given that $\hat{a}'\hat{f}(0)\hat{a} \xrightarrow{p} a' f(0)a > 0$, the proof of Theorem 1 is complete. □

References

1. Engle, R.F.; Granger, C.W.J. Cointegration and error correction: Representation, estimation and testing. *Econometrica* **1987**, *55*, 251–276.
2. Johansen, S. *Likelihood-based inference in cointegrated vector autoregressive models*, 2nd ed.; Oxford University Press: Oxford, UK, 1996.
3. Flôres, R.G., Jr.; Szafarz, A. An enlarged definition of cointegration. *Econ. Lett.* **1996**, *50*, 193–195.
4. Robinson, P.M.; Yajima, Y. Determination of cointegrating rank in fractional systems. *J. Econom.* **2002**, *106*, 217–247.
5. Heyde, C.C.; Gay, R. Smoothed periodogram asymptotics and estimation for processes and fields with possible long-range dependence. *Stoch. Proc. Appl.* **1993**, *45*, 169–182.
6. Hosoya, Y. A limit theory for long-range dependence and statistical inference on related models. *Ann. Stat.* **1997**, *25*, 105–137.
7. Robinson, P.M. Gaussian semiparametric estimation of long-range dependence. *Ann. Stat.* **1995**, *23*, 1630–1661.
8. Labato, I.G. Multivariate Analysis of Long Memory Series in the Frequency Domain. Ph.D. Thesis, University of London, London, UK, 1996.
9. Lobato, I.G. A semiparametric two-step estimation on a multivariate long-memory model. *J. Econom.* **1999**, *90*, 129–153.
10. Nielsen, M.; Shimotsu, K. Determine the cointegration rank in nonstationary fractional systems by the exact local Whittle approach. *J. Econom.* **2007**, *141*, 574–596.
11. Shimotsu, K.; Phillips, P.C.B. Exact local Whittle estimation of fractional integration. *Ann. Stat.* **2005**, *33*, 1890–1933.
12. Hualde, J. A simple test for the equality of integration orders. *Econ. Lett.* **2013**, *119*, 233–237.
13. Marinucci, D.; Robinson, P.M. Weak convergence of multivariate fractional processes. *Stoch. Proc. Appl.* **2000**, *86*, 103–120.
14. Marmol, F.; Velasco, C. Consistent testing of cointegrating relationships. *Econometrica* **2004**, *72*, 1809–1844.
15. Wang, B.; Wang, M.; Chan, N.H. Residual-based tests for fractional cointegrations. *Econ. Lett.* **2015**, *126*, 43–46.

16. Johansen, S.; Nielsen, M. A necessary moment condition for the fractional functional central limit theorem. *Econom. Theory* **2012**, *28*, 671–679.
17. Geweke, J.; Porter-Hudak, S. The estimation and application of long memory time series models. *J. Time Ser. Anal.* **1983**, *4*, 221–238.
18. Hurvich, C.M.; Deo, R.; Brodsky, J. The mean squared error of Geweke and Porter-Hudak's estimates of the memory parameter of a long memory time series. *J. Time Ser. Anal.* **1998**, *19*, 19–46.
19. Künsch, H.R. Statistical aspects of self-similar processes. In *Proceedings of the First World Congress of the Bernoulli Society*; Prokhorov, Y., Sazonov, V.V., Eds.; VNU Science Press: Utrecht, The Netherlands, 1987; Volume 1, pp. 67–74.
20. Beran, J. Maximum likelihood estimation of the differencing parameter for invertible short and long memory autoregressive integrated moving average models. *J. R. Stat. Soc. Ser. B* **1995**, *57*, 659–672.
21. Tanaka, K. The nonstationary fractional unit root. *Econom. Theory* **1999**, *15*, 549–582.
22. Hualde, J.; Velasco, C. Distribution-free tests of fractional cointegration. *Econom. Theory* **2008**, *24*, 216–255.
23. Velasco, C.; Robinson, P.M. Whittle pseudo-maximum likelihood estimation for nonstationary time series. *J. Am. Stat. Assoc.* **2000**, *95*, 1229–1243.
24. Robinson, P.M. The distance between rival nonstationary fractionary fractional processes. *J. Econom.* **2005**, *128*, 283–300.
25. Hualde, J.; Robinson, P.M. Semiparametric Estimation of Fractional Cointegration. STICERD-Econometircs Paper Series No. EM/2006/502. 2006. Available online: http://sticerd.lse.ac.uk/dps/em/em502.pdf (accessed on 1 July 2016).
26. Hualde, J.; Robinson, P.M. Semiparametric inference in multivariate fractionally cointegrated systems. *J. Econom.* **2010**, *157*, 492–511.
27. Wang, B. Residual-based tests for fractional cointegrations. Ph.D. Thesis, The Chinese University of Hong Kong, Shatin, Hong Kong, 2008.
28. Hualde, J.; Robinson, P.M. Gaussian pseudo-maximum likelihood estimation of fractional time series models. *Ann. Stat.* **2011**, *39*, 3152–3181.

econometrics

MDPI

Article

Oil Price and Economic Growth: A Long Story?

María Dolores Gadea [1,*], Ana Gómez-Loscos [2] and Antonio Montañés [3]

1 Department of Applied Economics, University of Zaragoza, Zaragoza 50006, Spain
2 Directorate General Economics, Statistics and Research, Bank of Spain, Madrid 28045, Spain; agomezloscos@bde.es
3 Department of Economic Analysis, University of Zaragoza, Zaragoza 50006, Spain; amontane@unizar.es
* Correspondence: lgadea@unizar.es; Tel.: +34-976-76-1842

Academic Editor: Pierre Perron
Received: 30 August 2016; Accepted: 7 October 2016; Published: 28 October 2016

Abstract: This study investigates changes in the relationship between oil prices and the US economy from a long-term perspective. Although neither of the two series (oil price and GDP growth rates) presents structural breaks in mean, we identify different volatility periods in both of them, separately. From a multivariate perspective, we do not observe a significant effect between changes in oil prices and GDP growth when considering the full period. However, we find a significant relationship in some subperiods by carrying out a rolling analysis and by investigating the presence of structural breaks in the multivariate framework. Finally, we obtain evidence, by means of a time-varying VAR, that the impact of the oil price shock on GDP growth has declined over time. We also observe that the negative effect is greater at the time of large oil price increases, supporting previous evidence of nonlinearity in the relationship.

Keywords: oil price; business cycle; structural breaks

JEL Classification: C22; C32; E32; Q43

1. Introduction

The literature on oil and macroeconomic variables is very extensive (see [1,2]). There is an ongoing debate on the interaction between oil price and macroeconomic performance. However, analyses of the link between oil price shocks and the business cycle have concentrated almost completely on relatively short horizons, from the early 1970s on. In particular, two specific periods have received a great deal of attention: the 1970s in particular and, to a lesser extent, the years since the beginning of the 21st century. It is well recognized that this interest dates back to the 1970s because the 1970s (and also the early 1980s) were characterized by serious oil price fluctuations together with unfavorable oil supply shocks, considered as the reasons behind worldwide macroeconomic volatility and stagflation. The interest has been rekindled in more recent times, given the possibility of a recurrence of this scenario. Indeed, some authors have investigated the different effects between these two periods on the macroeconomic variables see [3,4].[1] Two notable exceptions to this relatively short-term perspective are [7], who investigate the volatility and persistence patterns of oil price shocks based on annual

[1] Since the seminal work of [5] for the US economy, a growing number of articles have analyzed the economic consequences of oil price shocks in industrialized countries. Most of the literature shows that the effect of oil price on the economy was very important during the 1970s, but has gradually disappeared since then (many studies support this view; the work in [2] provides a comprehensive review of the literature). The papers [4,6] show that this influence has revived, but with less intensity, since 2000 and, most important, is manifested on inflation.

data for 1861–2008,[2] and, more recently [8], who analyze the effects of oil prices on output and real dividends using a quarterly sample beginning in 1946.

The fact that the literature has focused on correctly identifying the source of shocks on oil prices, almost exclusively during the post-1970s period, is related to the frequent and tumultuous events in oil price markets at that time. It is also due to the absence of high-frequency data from earlier periods. However, much can be learned about the relationship between oil prices and macroeconomic conditions from the less-recent past. We expect that over such a long period there have been important changes in the demand and supply for oil that could lead to identify some structural breaks. For instance, prior to the mass production of automobiles, demand for oil focused on kerosene lamps. Regarding oil supply, the relative importance of Texas Railroad Commission and OPEC in setting world oil prices changed over this period. In this study, we aim to investigate changes in the behavior of oil prices and their influence on the US economy, using the longest available oil price series (January 1861–February 2016), which allows us to offer an alternative view to the literature of the historical role of the macroeconomic effects of oil.

The contributions of this study, which has some advantages over the previous literature, are twofold. First, we use data with a broader coverage in the time dimension than the previous studies (January 1861–February 2016 for oil prices and January 1875–February 2016 for GDP). In particular, our study is the first one, as far as we know, that captures the relationship between oil price shocks and the US GDP growth with such a long-term perspective. Second, we provide a comprehensive methodological framework to analyze the relationship between the two variables. We investigate the univariate properties of the series, focusing on the presence of structural breaks and volatility. Then, we adopt a multivariate perspective to delve into the relationship between oil price shocks and GDP performance in order to identify structural breaks in the multivariate regressions by employing three complementary tools: a VAR method, a rolling estimation of causality and long-term impacts, and the Qu and Perron (QP, henceforth) methodology [9]. Once the presence of instabilities in the series has been established, we propose a time-varying GDP-oil price model to capture the relationship between the two variables over time, detailing impulse responses during periods of intense shocks in the oil price markets.

The main findings of the study are as follows. First, although neither of the two series presents structural breaks in the mean, we identify in both of them, separately, different volatility periods associated with major events either in the economic performance of the US economy or in the oil markets. Second, delving deep into the relationship between the two variables through the full period, we observe that changes in oil prices have no significant effect on GDP growth. Nevertheless, it is reasonable to think that, with so many significant events in such a long period, both in business cycle dynamics and in the demand and supply factors of oil prices, the relationship between the two variables may have not been so stable. This is clear when we carry out a rolling analysis and investigate the presence of structural breaks in the multivariate framework. In particular, we clearly identify four different periods: February 1875–April 1912, January 1913–January 1941, February 1941–March 1970, and April 1970–February 2016. Third, we obtain evidence of a changing relationship over time regarding the time-varying VAR: the impact of an oil price shock on GDP growth has declined over time. We also observe that the negative effect is greater at the time of large oil price increases, supporting previous evidence of nonlinearity in the relationship.

The remainder of the paper is organized as follows. Section 2 describes the dataset used in the analysis. Section 3 investigates the univariate evolution of the series, focusing on the presence of structural breaks in mean and volatility. Section 4 analyzes the transmission of the effects between oil price shocks and GDP growth, adopting a multivariate perspective. Section 5 proposes a time-varying

---

[2] The authors find that the real price of oil has historically tended to be both more persistent and more volatile whenever rapid industrialization in the world economy coincided with uncertainty regarding access to supply.

VAR model to capture different behaviors in the relationship over time. Finally, Section 6 concludes the study.

2. Data

We use series beginning in the nineteenth century and running until the present for our analysis of oil prices and US GDP. Regarding the US GDP, we use real quarterly data from the Bureau of Economic Analysis (BEA) and the National Bureau of Economic Research (NBER), covering the period January 1875 to February 2016. In particular, the BEA GDP series from 1947 onward is linked to a historical dataset beginning in 1875, which is available at the NBER until 1983.[3]

The long crude oil price series in real terms is taken from the British Petroleum's Statistical Review of World Energy [11]. This series has an annual frequency and links three different price series: US average price (1861–1944), Arabian Light (1945–1983), and Brent (1984–2015). Since our aim is to analyze the relationship between oil price shocks and GDP, we adopt two strategies to be able to work with higher-frequency data, which would allow us to better capture the effects of oil prices on economic growth. First, we use the Chow-Lin interpolation technique [12] to convert the annual series of oil prices into a quarterly series dataset, using an intercept as high frequency indicator.[4] Figure 1 displays both historical series. Second, in the last part of our sample, we work with real quarterly Brent data from Datastream.[5] We have considered three options to link this quarterly series with the transformed annual data: (i) begin using the quarterly series in 1957, the first year for which Brent data are available; (ii) delay the use of the quarterly series until the 1970s, when data variability clearly increases; (iii) maintain the first two consecutive series of the British Petroleum database and link with the quarterly series in 1984. Figure 2 illustrates the different options, and we observe hardly any difference among the three (called oilp1, oilp2, and oilp3, respectively). To obtain more reliable quarterly data, we chose the Brent quarterly series beginning in 1957 (oilp3).[6] This series is more accurate due to its higher frequency and is directly obtained from Datastream. Thus, our final crude oil price time series consists of the quarterly interpolated British Petroleum historical dataset until 1956, linked to the quarterly Brent data from 1957 onward, and ranges from January 1861 to February 2016. Figure 3 displays the growth rates of oil prices and GDP, calculated as the first logarithmic differences, which we denote as $\Delta OILP_t$ and ΔGDP_t, respectively.

---

3 The first series is in real 2009 dollars, while the long historical series is in real 1972 dollars, but has been transformed to link both. The historical series is taken from Appendix B of [10].

4 Chow-Lin interpolation is a regression-based technique to transform low-frequency (annual, in our case) data into higher-frequency (quarterly, in our case) data. In particular, we apply the average version, which disaggregates the annual data into the means of four quarters and is the most suitable approach for price data, and select the maximum likelihood method. We use the Matlab toolbox of [13,14]. This approach gives us the best fit when compared to the available quarterly data. However, we have tested the accuracy of other disaggregation methods and the results remain broadly unchanged.

5 Prices are in 2009 US dollars per barrel, and the US GDP deflator data are from the IMF.

6 We have also considered other alternatives: (1) use the British Petroleum dataset, updating the last years with the annual Brent series and transforming the whole sample into quarterly data through the Chow-Lin procedure; (2) use the historical British Petroleum series linked to the West Texas Intermediate data or the Producer Price Index for crude petroleum (since they are available or from 1984 onward) instead of Brent prices. We have decided to disregard these options to obtain a more homogeneous dataset by using Brent prices. However, comparing the path of the alternative series to the one we use, we do not observe much difference. Furthermore, we repeated some calculations, obtaining quite similar results.

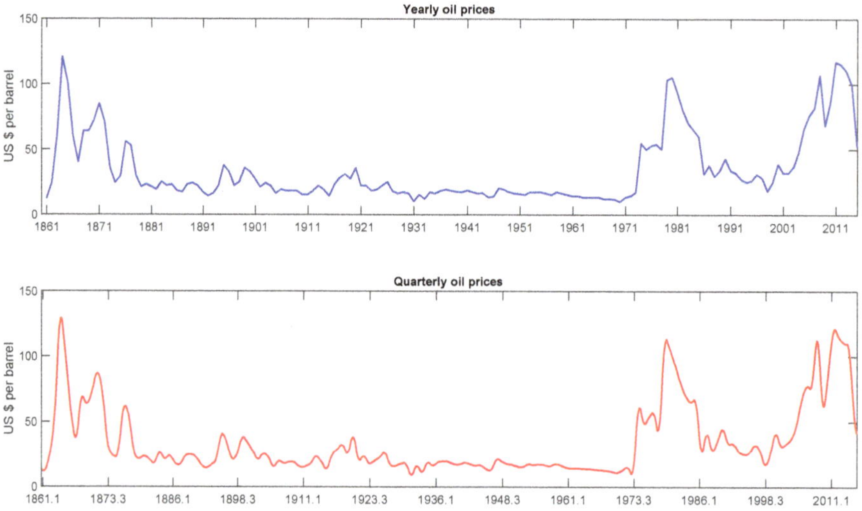

Figure 1. Historical oil prices. *Notes*: The top figure represents the annual BP oil price series, which are made of three different series: US average price (1861–1944), Arabian Light (1945–1983), and Brent (1984–2015). The bottom figure displays the same series converted to a quarterly frequency through the Chow-Lin interpolation technique. Dates are in year.month format.

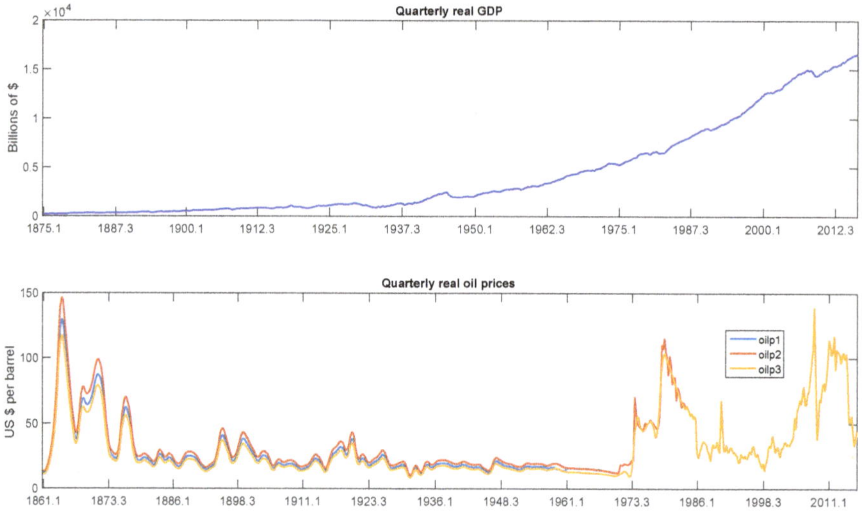

Figure 2. Oil prices and GDP. *Notes*: The top figure represents the US real quarterly GDP obtained from the BEA and the NBER (January 1875–February 2016). The bottom figure shows three different real quarterly oil price series: "oilp1" links the BP real quarterly series (transformed using the Chow-Lin technique) with Brent quarterly data from 1957 on; "oilp2" is composed of the BP real quarterly series (transformed using the Chow-Lin technique) and Brent quarterly data from 1970 on; "oilp3" puts together the BP real quarterly series (transformed using the Chow-Lin technique) and Brent quarterly series from 1984 on. Dates are in year.month format.

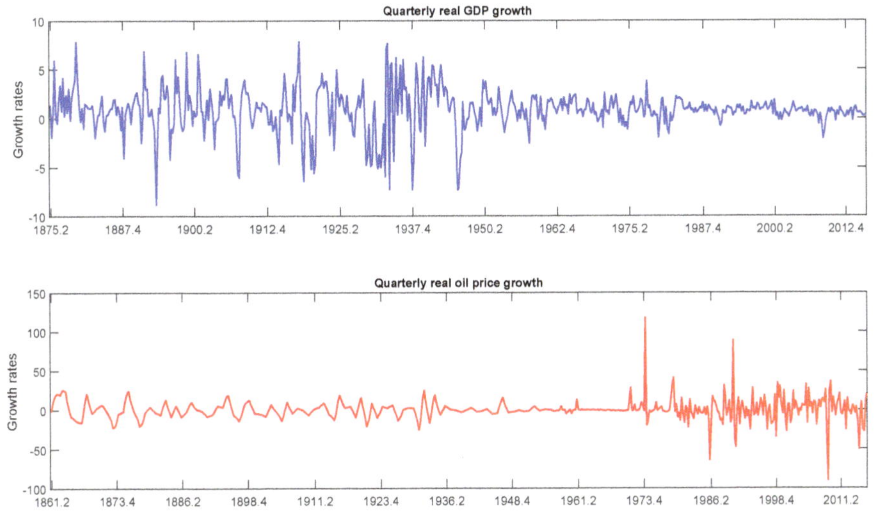

Figure 3. Oil prices and GDP growth rates. *Notes*: The top figure represents the growth rate of the US real quarterly GDP obtained from the BEA and the NBER (January 1875–February 2016). The bottom figure displays the growth rate of "oilp3", which consists of the quarterly interpolated BP historical dataset until 1956 linked to the quarterly Brent data from 1957 onward and ranges from January 1861 to February 2016. Dates are in year.month format.

3. Univariate Analysis of the Series

In this section, as a first data exploratory analysis, we examine the univariate evolution of each of the two series, oil prices and GDP growth rates. In particular, we explore the possible existence of structural changes in both mean and variance of the series.

3.1. Changes in Mean

In this subsection, we test for the presence of structural breaks in the mean of ΔGDP and $\Delta OILP$. To this end, we apply the methodology of Bai and Perron [15–17] (BP, henceforth).[7] The BP methodology looks for multiple structural breaks, consistently determining the number of break points over all possible partitions, as well as their location, and it is based on the principle of global minimizers of the sum of squared residuals. The methodology considers m possible breaks ($m + 1$ regimes) in a general linear model of the type:

$$y_t = x_t'\beta + z_t'\delta_j + u_t \tag{1}$$

where the explanatory variables β and δ_j ($j = 1, ..., m + 1$) are the corresponding vectors of the coefficients and $T_i, ..., T_m$ are the break points, which are treated endogenously in the model.

Using this method, [15] proposes three types of tests. The first one, called the $supF(k)$ test, considers the null hypothesis of no breaks against the alternative of k breaks. The second test, $supF(l + 1/l)$, considers the existence of l breaks, with $l = 0, 1, ...,$ as H_0, against the alternative of $l + 1$ changes. Finally, the so-called double maximum tests $UDmax$ and $WDmax$ (the third type) test the null of the absence of structural breaks against the existence of an unknown number of breaks. The strategy

[7] We have tested, but not rejected, the hypothesis that both series are I(0), using a battery of standard unit root tests. The stationarity of the series is a pre-condition for applying the BP method. Detailed results are available upon request.

suggested by Bai and Perron [16] consists of first beginning with the sequential test $supF(l+1/l)$. In case no break is detected, they recommend checking this result with the $UDmax$ and $WDmax$ tests to determine whether at least one break exists. When this is the case, they recommend continuing with the sequential application of the $supF(l+1/l)$ test, with $l = 1, \ldots$ In addition, information criteria such as the traditional Schwarz Bayesian information criterion (SBIC) and the modified Liu Wu Zidek criterion (LWZ)[8] are used to select the number of changing points.

This strategy has been followed to explore the existence of structural breaks in a model representing the mean of the variables, that is, a model with just a constant: $z_t' = 1$ and $x_t' = 0$. The disturbance term is allowed to present both autocorrelation and heteroskedasticity. A maximum number of five breaks has been considered in accordance with a sample size of $T = 565$ for GDP growth and 621 for oil price growth. Then, according to the length of the series, the selected trimming is $\epsilon = 0.15$. A non-parametric correction has been employed to consider these effects. Table 1 shows the results. According to the different tests, we cannot reject the hypothesis that neither ΔGDP nor $\Delta OILP$ presents structural changes in the mean.[9] For the whole period, the mean GDP growth is 0.80% and the mean oil price growth, 0.19%.

Table 1. Multiple structural breaks in mean (Bai-Perron methodology).

	ΔGDP	$\Delta POIL$
supF(k)		
$k = 1$	1.80	0.38
$k = 2$	1.70	0.94
$k = 3$	2.20	1.71
$k = 4$	2.08	1.32
$k = 5$	1.43	0.70
supF(l + 1/l)		
$l = 0$	1.80	0.38
$l = 1$	2.44	1.54
$l = 2$	2.77	0.58
$l = 3$	1.58	0.82
$l = 4$	–	–
UDmax	2.20	1.71
WDmax	3.56	2.46
T(SBIC)	0	0
T(LWZ)	0	0
T(sequential)	0	0

Notes: Changes are tested by selecting a trimming of $\epsilon = 0.15$ and a maximum number of five breaks. Serial correlation and heterogeneity in the errors are allowed. The consistent covariance matrix is constructed using the Andrews method [20]. Critical values in [15].

3.2. *Changes in Volatility*

To test for the possibility of structural breaks in the variance of the process, we consider the Inclán and Tiao (IT) test [21]. This test, which has been extensively used, allows for the detection of changes in the unconditional variance of a series and belongs to the CUSUM-type family of tests. The test is defined as follows:

8 See [18].

9 Alternatively, we tried a standard autoregressive model of order 1, with $z_t' = 1$ and $x_t' = (y_{t-1})$, finding similar conclusions. The results are also robust to considering a higher number of maximum breaks. A paper by [19] also confirms the absence of structural breaks in the mean of US GDP series.

$$\begin{array}{l} IT = \sup_k \left|\sqrt{T/2}D_k\right| \text{ where} \\ D_k = \frac{C_k}{C_t} - \frac{k}{t} \text{ with } D_o = D_T = 0 \\ C_k = \sum_{t=1}^{k} u_t^2 \end{array} \tag{2}$$

This test assumes that the disturbance u_t in equation $y_t = \mu + u_t$, being $y_t = \Delta OILP_t$ or ΔGDP_t, is a zero-mean, normally i.i.d. random variable and uses an iterated cumulative sum of squares ($ICSS$) procedure to detect the number of breaks. However, [22] shows that the asymptotic distribution of the IT test is critically dependent on normality. Indeed, the IT test has large size distortions when the Gaussian innovation assumption is not met in the fourth-order moment, or for heteroskedastic conditional variance processes, and consequently tends to overestimate the number of breaks.[10] To overcome this drawback, they propose a correction that explicitly takes into account both the fourth-order moment properties of the disturbances and the conditional heteroskedasticity (κ_1 and κ_2, respectively).

$$\begin{array}{l} IT(\kappa_1) = \sup_k \left|\sqrt{T/}B_k\right| \text{ where} \\ B_k = \frac{Ck - \frac{k}{T}C_T}{\sqrt{\widehat{\eta}_4 - \widehat{\sigma}^4}} \\ \widehat{\eta}_4 = T^{-1}\sum_{t=1}^{T} y_t^4, \widehat{\sigma}^4 = T^{-1}C_T \end{array} \tag{3}$$

$$\begin{array}{l} IT(\kappa_2) = \sup_k \left|\sqrt{T/}G_k\right| \text{ where} \\ G_k = \widehat{\omega}_4^{-1/2}(C_k - \frac{k}{T}C_T) \end{array} \tag{4}$$

where $\widehat{\omega}_4$ is a consistent estimator of $\omega_4 = \lim_{T\to\infty} E(T^{-1}(\sum_{t=1}^{k}(u_t^2 - \sigma^2))^2)$.

The US GDP growth series is not mesokurtic (in fact, its excess kurtosis series is 3.15) and has a fat right tail. Moreover, the conditional variance of the innovations is not constant over time.[11] These properties are even more accentuated for oil price growth series, in which excess kurtosis reaches 20.10 and shows very long tails. Consequently, we use the previous corrections in addition to the original ICSS algorithm.

Table 2 shows the results of the $ICSS(IT)$, $ICSS(\kappa_1)$, and $ICSS(\kappa_2)$ tests applied to the US GDP and oil price growth rates. We observe overestimation of break dates when using the original IT test (and even in the $ICSS(\kappa_1)$ test), which is especially dramatic for oil price growth, considering the properties of this series. Therefore, we focus on the results of the $ICSS(\kappa_2)$ test, which includes all corrections. We find three breaks in the variance of GDP growth, chronologically located in April 1917, February 1946, and January 1984, confirming the findings of [19].[12] These break dates approximately match the end of each of the world wars and the beginning of the Great Moderation. Thus, a secular reduction in volatility is observed in US GDP growth.

The results of the variance tests applied to the oil price growth rate show only two changes in variance, in April 1878 and April 1973. Indeed, oil prices are more volatile in the beginning and ending periods (the last period being significantly more volatile), while a much less volatile period is observed from 1878 to 1973 (see Figure 3). These break points to are related to a combination of technological

---

10 The IT approach is extended to more general processes by [23], showing that the correction for non-normality proposed by [22] is suitable when the test is applied to the unconditional variance of raw data. Furthermore, [24] carry out a Monte Carlo experiment that highlights the adequacy of this procedure when the mean or other coefficients in the regression do not change; otherwise, the test has important size distortions, which increase with the magnitude of change in the mean.

11 The US GDP growth rates can be approximated by leptokurtic densities as shown by [25]. This indicates that output growth changes tend to be quite uneven in the sense that large positive or negative changes seem to be more frequent than a Gaussian model would predict.

12 The authors offer a thorough analysis of the sources and features of these different volatility periods.

and geographic factors affecting the oil market by [7],[13] along with a booming demand for oil, driven by the large-scale industrialization of the US and East Asia.[14]

Table 2. Multiple structural breaks in variance (ICSS methodology).

	ΔGDP	$\Delta OILP$
ICSS(IT)		
	April 1917	April 1878
	February 1946	February 1914
	February 1984	March 1921
	April 2007	March 1930
	February 2009	February 1934
		March 1936
		April 1944
		March 1947
		April 1960
		April 1970
ICSS(κ_1)		
	March 1929	January 1862
	March 1934	January 1963
	February 1946	April 1878
	January 1984	March 1930
		February 1934
		April 1973
ICSS(κ_2)		
	April 1917	April 1878
	February 1946	April 1973
	January 1984	

Note: Dates of the detected changes in variance. $ICSS(i), i = \{IT, \kappa_1, \kappa_2\}$.

To provide robustness to the previous results, we use an additional test within the parametric framework, which consists in applying the BP test to the mean of the absolute value of the estimated residuals $\sqrt{\frac{\pi}{2}}\,|\epsilon_t|$ from one of the following specifications:[15]

$$\begin{aligned}
&\text{Model 1: } y_t = \mu + \epsilon_t \\
&\text{Model 2: } y_t = \mu + \rho y_{t-1} + \epsilon_t \\
&\epsilon_t = z_t'\delta_j + u_t \\
&z_t' = 1
\end{aligned} \tag{5}$$

where y_t represents $\Delta OILP_t$ or ΔGDP_t.

Table 3 roughly confirms the $ICSS(\kappa_2)$ test results. We focus on the results of Model 1. Regarding the identification of structural breaks in the GDP growth rate, we identify three break points as in the previous exercise. However, the dates differ, as a structural break in March 1929 coincides with the 1929 Crash as against the one related to the end of the first world war.[16] Concerning the oil prices,

[13] Construction of the first long-distance pipeline began in 1878, allowing the railroad monopoly over oil transportation to end. However, US control over excess exploitable reserves ended and OPEC dominance increased in 1969.

[14] See also [26] for a historical survey of the oil industry with particular focus on the events related to significant oil price changes.

[15] A paper by [24] shows that, in case changes in the mean of the series are not taken into account, the test suffers from severe size distortions. However, we have shown that our series do not have structural breaks in the mean. This method has been used in several studies: [27–29], among others.

[16] Notice that these break points are the least significant ones with both approaches. Indeed, the break of March 1929 is not even identified with Model 2 of the BP methodology.

we find three break points instead of two. The new break point is located in February 1935, while the other two are the same previously identified. This methodology to the annual series of oil prices by [7], finding roughly the same three break points. They link the new break to both a major oil discovery a few years earlier (the East Texas oil Field) and a worldwide recession.

Table 3. Multiple structural breaks in variance (Bai-Perron methodology).

ΔGDP	$\Delta OILP$
Model 1	
March 1929	April 1878
January 1947	February 1935
February 1984	April 1973
Model 2	
March 1946	March 1973
April 1983	

Notes: The BP method is applied on the corrected square residuals of $y_t = \mu + \epsilon_t$, Model 1 or $y_t = \mu + \rho y_{t-1} + \epsilon_t$, Model 2. Changes in the mean are tested selecting a trimming of $\epsilon = 0.15$. and a maximum number of 10 breaks. Serial correlation and heterogeneity in the errors are allowed. The consistent covariance matrix is constructed using the Andrews method [20]. Critical values in [15].

4. Multivariate Analysis of the Series

After studying the univariate evolution of both oil price and GDP growth rates, this section analyzes the transmission of the effects between them and their direction. To this end, we first use a standard VAR methodology and, subsequently, consider different methodologies to take into account the possible instability of the VAR parameters. In particular, we compute a rolling causality test and cumulative impulse response functions. In addition, we analyze the presence of structural breaks in our VAR equation.

4.1. VAR Estimation

A simple way to analyze the dynamic relationship between oil price variations and GDP growth is the use of a standard VAR(*p*) model. Following [30,31], among many others, we define this model as follows:

$$Y_t = \mu + \sum_{i=1}^{p} \Psi_i Y_{t-1} + \varepsilon_t, t = 1, 2, ..., T \tag{6}$$

where $Y_t = (\Delta GDP_t, \Delta OILP_t)'$ is a 2×1 vector composed of observations of the variables, Ψ_i $(i = 1, ..., p)$ are 2×2 coefficient matrices, $\varepsilon_t = (\varepsilon_{1t}, \varepsilon_{2t})'$ with $\varepsilon_{it}, (i = 1, 2)$ is an unobservable zero mean white noise vector of dimension T, and p is the parameter that determines the VAR dimension, chosen according to the SBIC criterion.[17] The model is specified as follows:

$$\begin{bmatrix} \Delta OILP_t \\ \Delta GDP_t \end{bmatrix} = \begin{bmatrix} \psi_{11} & \psi_{12} \\ \psi_{21} & \psi_{22} \end{bmatrix} \begin{bmatrix} \Delta OILP_{t-1} \\ \Delta GDP_{t-1} \end{bmatrix} + \begin{bmatrix} \varepsilon_{1t} \\ \varepsilon_{2t} \end{bmatrix} \tag{7}$$

The VAR estimation is reported in Table 4. The results show no significant effect of oil price growth on GDP growth, which means $\Delta OILP$ does not influence—that is, does not Granger-cause—GDP

17 The SBIC criterion selects one lag. Nevertheless, other information criteria, such as the Akaike information criterion (AIC) and the Hannan-Quinn (HQ) criterion select five lags. Therefore, we use a VAR(1) as the preferred model and estimate, additionally, a VAR(5) to check the robustness of our results. For simplicity, and to save space, we only present the results for the VAR(1) and discuss whether some interesting results or significant differences appear with respect to the VAR(5).

growth. We obtain a similar result in the opposite direction, as the effect of GDP growth on oil price growth is not significant.

Table 4. Estimation of the VAR system.

	Coeff.	***p*-Value**
Dependent variable: ΔGDP		
Intercept	0.486	0.000
ΔGDP	0.392	0.000
$\Delta OILP$	−0.003	0.649
Dependent variable: $\Delta OILP$		
Intercept	−0.049	0.932
ΔGDP	0.175	0.478
$\Delta OILP$	0.132	0.002
Granger causality		
$\Delta OILP \rightarrow \Delta GDP$	0.207	0.649
$\Delta GDP \rightarrow \Delta POIL$	0.504	0.478

Note: The null hypothesis for the Granger causality test is that $\Delta OILP$ does not cause ΔGDP or vice versa.

Furthermore, the parameter ψ_{12} is negative and ψ_{21} is positive. This means that the effect of oil price growth on output growth is negative, while the effect of GDP growth on oil price is positive. Although these findings are quite suggestive and support our intuition about the causal effects between GDP and oil prices, we test them more formally.

The previous framework allows us to test for causality direction. Following [32], a variable (or group of variables), z_1, is found to help predict another variable (or group of variables), z_2. Then, z_1 is said to Granger-cause z_2. We can test this hypothesis by simply studying whether the Ψ matrices are triangular, which is a remarkably visual test for a VAR(1). Additionally, a more formal Wald test is computed, where the null hypothesis is that z_1 does not cause z_2. More specifically, z_1 does not lead to z_2 if $E(z_{2t}|z_{2t-1}, z_{2t-2}, ...; z_{1t-1}, z_{1t-2}, ...) = E(z_{2t}|z_{2t-1}, z_{2t-2}, ...)$.[18] The results of the Granger causality analysis are presented in the last rows of Table 4, confirming the previous findings.[19]

We also employ impulse-response functions (IRFs) to capture the dynamics of the shocks. To obtain IRFs, we use a moving average representation of the VAR system, which is defined in the following expression:

$$Y_t = \begin{bmatrix} \mu_1 \\ \mu_2 \end{bmatrix} + \sum_{s=0}^{\infty} \begin{bmatrix} \psi_{11} & \psi_{12} \\ \psi_{21} & \psi_{22} \end{bmatrix}^s \begin{bmatrix} \varepsilon_{1t-s} \\ \varepsilon_{2t-s} \end{bmatrix} \tag{8}$$

or in matrix notation and in terms of the innovations of the structural model: $Y_t = \mu + \sum_{s=0}^{\infty} \Phi_(s)\varepsilon_{t-s}$.

The coefficients of the succession of matrices $\Phi_(s)$ represent the impact that a shock in the structural innovation has on the variables of the VAR system over time. Results of IRF computations with a horizon of 5 years (20 quarters) are displayed in Figure 4, where confidence intervals at 90% are computed according to bootstrap-after-bootstrap method of [33]. We conclude that the effects, which are negative for the response of ΔGDP to an impulse of $\Delta OILP$ and positive for the response of $\Delta OILP$ to an impulse of ΔGDP, last between 7 and 8 quarters and are not significant at any length. We also observe a high degree of uncertainty during the time of non-zero IRFs.[20]

18 We have repeated the analysis with annual data as a robustness check, finding qualitatively the same results.
19 An estimation of a VAR system with five lags does not change this conclusion.
20 As is well-known, the order of variables is relevant for IRF computation, as the Cholesky decomposition requires triangulation. To test the robustness of the results, we have redone all calculations with the system in the inverse order:

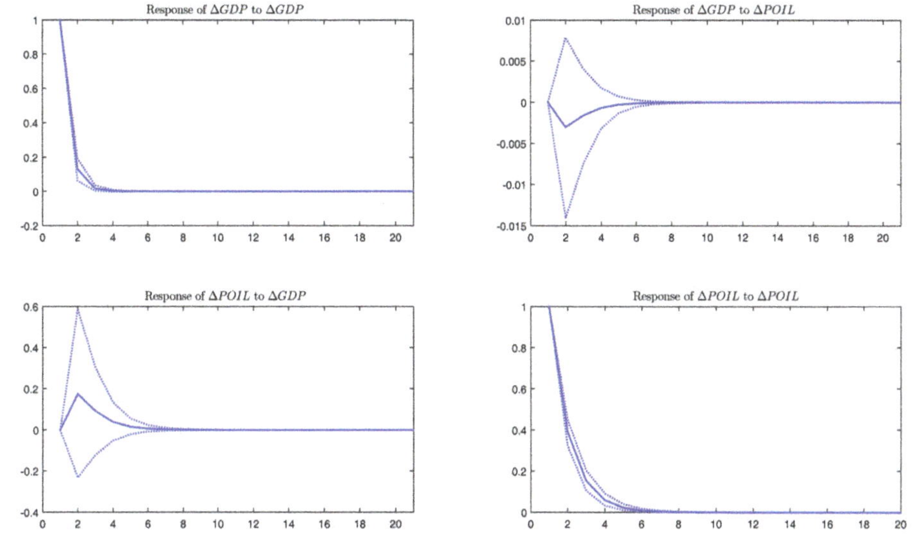

Figure 4. Impulse-response functions (IRFs) of a VAR(1) for GDP and oil price growth rates. *Note*: Confidence intervals at 90% of confidence level have been computed according to [33].

In addition, we compute cumulative impulse-response functions (CIR), defined as $CIR = \sum_{h=0}^{\infty} IRF(h)$, which allow us to identify the same effects in the long run. Thus, considering the full period (February 1875–February 2016), $\Delta OILP$ has a negative effect (-0.0057) on ΔGDP, while ΔGDP has a positive effect (0.3306) on $\Delta OILP$, although neither is significant.[21]

Summing up, we do not observe any significant effect between changes in oil prices and GDP growth when considering the full period. Nevertheless, it is reasonable to think that in such a long period in which significant events have occurred, both in the business cycle dynamics and in the demand and supply factors of oil prices, the relationship between the two variables may have not been so stable. In fact, our findings in the previous section already show several structural breaks in volatility that correspond to important changes in the characteristics of the business cycle and different periods in the evolution of oil prices. The hypothesis of a changing relationship is explored in the following subsections.

$Y_t = (\Delta OILP_t, \Delta GDP_t)'$ and have also calculated the generalized IRF. The findings are the same, which is not surprising, given the results of casualty.

21 The confidence intervals are (-0.0269, 0.0151) and 0.3306 (-0.4279, 1.1086), respectively. They were computed with the same bootstrap methodology as for the IRFs.

4.2. Rolling Sample Analysis

The previous section provides some insights about the direction of the relationship between oil inflation and the US GDP growth. However, it is possible that this relationship has been modified across time, as suggested by [4]. Thus, it is advisable to estimate the model for different subsamples in order to verify whether the parameters change. In this regard, we adopt two alternative strategies: (i) compute causality test and (ii) calculate CIRs, as a measure of long-run impacts, instead of using short-run parameters. We consider a rolling estimation with a window of 40 quarters in both cases.

Regarding the causality test, results are displayed in Figure 5, which plots a heat map of p-values of the Granger causality test. Different colors represent the different significance levels at which we can reject or accept the Granger causality test. Values in yellow and dark blue mean that we can reject the null hypothesis of non-causality, whereas values in no colour indicate no causality between the variables. In general, we scarcely observe periods of significant causality, given the overwhelming presence of no color in the figure. Focusing on causality from $\Delta OILP$ to ΔGDP (left-hand side of the figure) and with a liberal threshold of the 0.10 significance level, we identify two stable and long periods where oil prices clearly influence GDP growth: January 1879–April 1894 and January 1981–February 1999. In the rest of the period, we only find isolated dates during mid-20th century (the 1950s) and at the beginning of the period, before April 1879. Results basically hold when considering a tighter significance level of 5%, although the instability during the 1980s and 1990s increases. To sum up, the influence of oil price growth on GDP growth is significant only for 14% of the sample at the 10% significance level.

As for the opposite direction of causality, from ΔGDP to $\Delta OILP$ (right-hand side of the figure), the proportion of the sample where the influence is significant is similar at 10% level but reduces to 9% at the 5% significance level. Periods of causality from GDP growth to oil price variations are found in February 1911–April 1923, February 1953–February 1971, and February 1988–February 2000.[22] We conclude that the relationship between the two variables is relatively weak in the long run. However, at shorter horizons, the major intensity in the bidirectional relationship is located in the 1980s and 1990s.

With respect to CIRs, Figure 6 displays the results of impulses from ΔGDP to $\Delta OILP$ (upper panel) and from $\Delta OILP$ to ΔGDP (lower panel). Focusing on the rolling estimation of CIRs between the two variables, we observe that the estimated response to an impulse from ΔGDP to $\Delta OILP$ remains close to zero, and non-significant, over the whole sample, except for the estimated impulse response over the periods 1961–1971[23] and 1937–1946.[24] The estimated impulse from $\Delta OILP$ to ΔGDP presents higher variability. Indeed, from the mid-1960s to the end of the century, it is positive most of the time. The effect turns negative during the noughties of the 21st century. Nonetheless, the confidence intervals show no significant effect in the short periods, also identified in the upper panel of the figure.[25]

---

[22] Since 2005, the causality test is near the 10% threshold limit of significance. This result agrees with that of [34], who document a positive and significant effect of GDP growth on oil prices since the 2000s.

[23] This was an extraordinary growth period in the US economy. The increasing demand for oil caused oil price increases.

[24] During this period, the US economy had to face World War II with devastating economic consequences (the first postwar US recession began at the end of 1948). The demand for petroleum products caused a sharp increase in the price of oil and although the US increased oil production enormously during World War II, there were shortages in several plants.

[25] We have repeated the analysis using annual data, reaching the same conclusions.

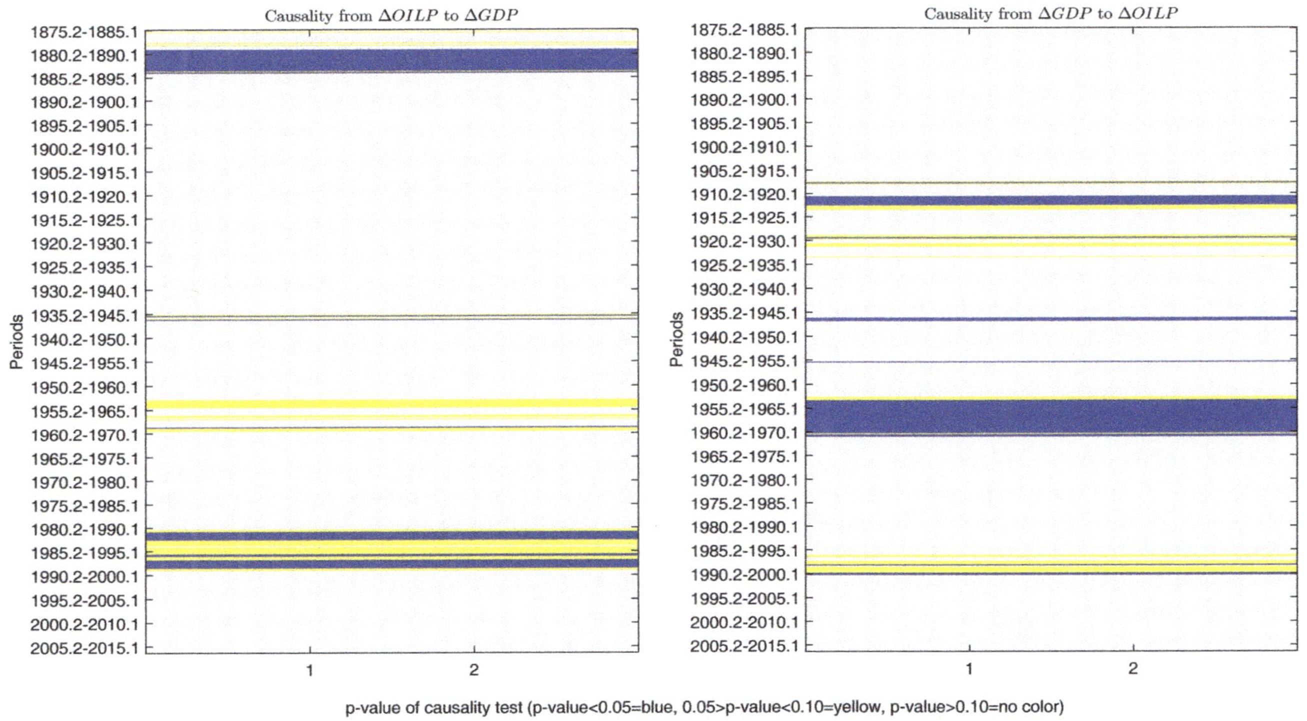

Figure 5. Rolling estimation of causality test. *Notes*: We estimate the causality test with a rolling window of 40 quarters. The left-hand side of the figure presents results of Granger causality from $\Delta OILP$ to ΔGDP; the right-hand side shows the results of Granger causality from ΔGDP to $\Delta OILP$. Values in dark blue mean that we can reject the hypothesis of non-causality at 5% significance level and values in yellow mean that we can reject it at 10% significance level, whereas no color indicates no causality between the variables. Dates are in year.month format.

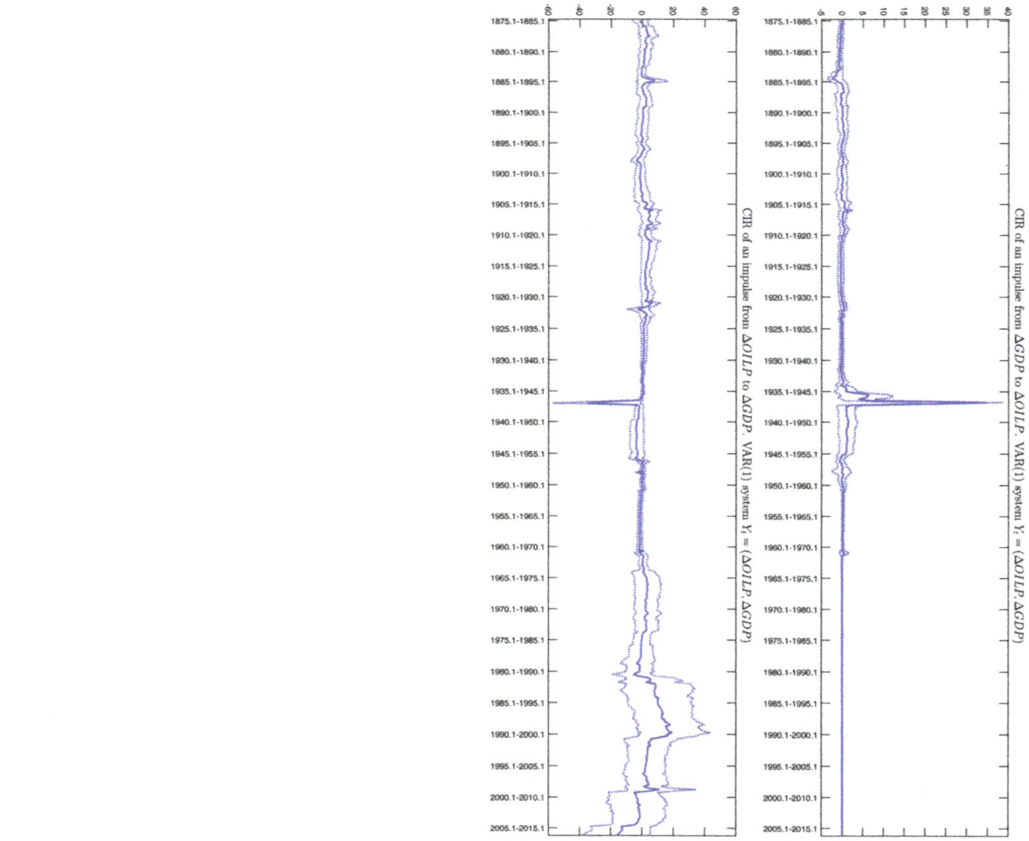

Figure 6. Rolling estimation of CIR. *Notes*: We estimate the CIRs with a rolling window of 40 quarters. Confidence intervals at 90% of confidence level. CIR: Cumulative Impulse Response Function. Dates are in year.month format.

4.3. Structural Breaks in the Relationship between Oil Prices and GDP

The univariate analysis of the series offers some evidence of structural breaks in the volatility of the two series. Additionally, the rolling results of the previous subsection are not conclusive about the hypothesis of parameter stability. Thus, it seems to be appropriate to consider the existence of structural breaks in our multivariate specification. To that end, the Qu and Perron (QP) [9] approach provides a valid technique to find structural breaks,[26] as it allows for multiple structural changes that occur at unknown dates in a general system of equations, which indeed include the one defined in (10).

Following these authors, we assume that we have n equations and T observations, the vector Y_t includes our two endogenous variables (ΔGDP and $\Delta OILP$), the parameter q is the number of regressors, and z_t is a set that includes the regressors from all the equations. The selection matrix S is of dimension $np \times q$ with full column rank, where q is the total number of parameters. It involves elements that take the values 0 and 1, indicating which regressors appear in each equation. The total number of structural changes in the system is m, and the break dates are denoted by the m vector $T = (T_1; ...; T_m)$, considering that $T_0 = 1$ and $T_{m+1} = T$, with j indexing the regime ($j = 1, ..., m+1$). Then, the model proposed takes the following form:

$$Y_t = \left(I \otimes z_t'\right) S\beta_j + u_t \tag{9}$$

with u_t having mean 0 and covariance matrix $\sum_j$ for $T_{j-1+1} \leq t \leq T_j$. In our present case, we should note that $z_t = (1, \Delta GDP_{t-1}, ..., \Delta GDP_{t-p}, \Delta OILP_{t-1}, ..., \Delta OILP_{t-p})$, and $S = I_{2q}$, where $q = 2 + p(2+1)$ and p is the selected number of lags. Again, the number of lags has been chosen by taking into account the SBIC.

To determine the number of breaks in the system, we first use the $UD_{max}LRT(M)$ statistics to test whether at least one break is present. When the tests reject it, the test $Seq_t(l+1|l)$ is sequentially applied for $l = 1, 2 \ldots m$ until it fails to reject the null hypothesis of no additional structural break. Additionally, we compute the $SupLR)$ to test $l = 1, 2 \ldots, m$ versus $l = 0$.

According to the critical values derived from the response surface regressions, the tests offer evidence of three breaks ($m = 3$) in the system of equations, which satisfies the minimal length requirement, notice that because of our sample size ($T = 562$), we have carried out the procedure with a trimming parameter of 0.2. Results of the application of this procedure are reported in Table 5. The three break dates are located in April 1912, January 1941, and March 1970. Notice that the first two breaks are quite close to those identified in the univariate analysis of structural breaks in volatility of the GDP growth, while the third break is near the last structural volatility break in oil prices. Hence, we identify four different periods in the relationship between oil price shocks and the US GDP growth.[27] For each of the four periods, we repeat the analysis presented in Section 4.1. The number of lags for each period has been selected according to different information criteria (they appear in brackets in Table 5).

The first interval covers the period between January 1875 and April 1912. Thus, the imminent beginning of World War I (WWI, henceforth) marks the end of this period. The sample begins just after the panic of 1873, when the US was still facing its economic consequences. A few years later, the US economy had to cope with the aftermath of the 1893 panic, while already in the 20th century, the US economy faced WWI (1914–1918). Regarding oil prices, this period is characterized by the evolution of the oil industry along with the exhaustion in production of key oil fields, at a time in which the demand was strong.

---

26 This methodology has been used to test the effects of oil price shocks on GDP growth and CPI inflation for the G7 countries in [4] and for the Spanish economy in [6].

27 For a detailed analysis of the dynamics of US GDP growth over these periods, see [19]. For the case of oil price evolution, see [7,26].

Table 5. Structural breaks in the VAR system (Qu and Perron methodology).

WD_{max}	*SupLR*			*Seq(l + 1/l)*		TB_i
	0 vs. 1	0 vs. 2	0 vs. 3	$l = 1$	$l = 2$	
979.130 [a]	979.130 [a]	1104.231 [a]	1159.779 [a]	156.685 [a]	64.157 [a]	April 1912, January 1941, March 1970
			Granger-Wald causality test			
			February 1875–April 1912 (6)	January 1913.1–January 1941 (6)	February 1941–March 1970 (5)	April 1970–February 2016 (5)
$\Delta OILP \nrightarrow \Delta GDP$			0.481	0.339	0.400	0.100
$\Delta GDP \nrightarrow \Delta OILP$			0.251	0.272	0.000	0.497

Notes: [a] means values significant at 1% level. TB_i denotes the date of a structural break. The null hypothesis for the Granger causality test is that $\Delta OILP$ does not cause ΔGDP or vice versa. We show *p*-values for the Granger causality test. For each subperiod, we present in brackets the number of lags selected according to several information criteria.

The second period starts in January 1913 and ends in the early 1940s. During that time, the US economy was affected by some of the most influential economic events of the 20th century, such as the Crash of 1929, with devastating economic effects during the next decade, and WWII (1939–1945). Concerning the historical oil price shocks, this period was much influenced by the Great Depression, with an associated decline in oil demand, and the introduction of state regulation of industry and restrictions on competition. No Granger causality is identified from any of the two variables to the other in either of the first two subperiods.

The third period runs from February 1941 to March 1970. In terms of the US economy dynamics, this period is characterized by a post-war economic boom that lasted until the 1970s. Indeed, during the 1950s, and especially the 1960s, the US experienced its longest, almost uninterrupted period of economic expansion in history. Oil prices were quite stable during this period. OPEC was established in 1960 with five founding members. Throughout the post-WWII period, exporting countries experienced an increasing demand for oil, and the volume of oil that Texas producers could produce was no longer limited, but the power to control crude oil prices shifted from the US to OPEC. During this period of economic boom, ΔGDP has a significant effect on $\Delta OILP$.

Finally, the last period begins in the early 1970s and ends in February 2016. The 1970s were characterized by the end of the Bretton Woods system and substantial oil price shocks, economic growth became stagnant, and inflation grew. In the 1980s, these disequilibria were reversed, and the US economy witnessed a reduction in the volatility of the business cycle. The last period of the sample (from 1984 on) is called the Great Moderation. During this period, the US enjoyed long economic expansions, interrupted only by three recessions, the last one being the Great Recession (2007–2009), which was followed by a weak recovery. The evolution of oil prices during this period and its effect on macroeconomic performance have been extensively studied in the literature. The US, as did most industrialized economies, became heavily dependent on imported crude oil from the Middle East, and the 1970s were a tumultuous decade in terms of oil market events.[28] Other political events that influenced oil prices took place during the rest of the period.[29] During this final period, the effect of $\Delta OILP$ on ΔGDP is significant at 10%.

To sum up, the Granger causality between the two variables is significant only in two periods. ΔGDP has a significant effect on $\Delta OILP$, on the one hand, in the February 1941–March 1970 sample, when the US economy experienced a huge economic boom, and, on the other, in the March 1970–February 2016 sample (in the opposite causality direction), when oil price shocks exerted a significant influence on economic performance.

Figures 7–10 display IRFs in different regimes delimited by structural breaks. We observe that $\Delta OILP$ has a negative effect on ΔGDP in all periods except February 1941–March 1970. Regarding the effect of the ΔGDP shock on $\Delta OILP$, the sign changes, highlighting the positive influence in the last period. Nevertheless, these effect are non significant for the most part of all sub-periods.

---

[28] The Arab-Israel war in 1973, which followed the long-lasting Arab-Israeli conflict, and the Iranian revolution in 1978–1979 are a few examples.

[29] Such as the Iran-Iraq war of 1980–1988, the Persian Gulf War of 1990–1991, the Venezuelan crisis of 2002, the Iraq War of 2003, or the Libyan uprising of 2011.

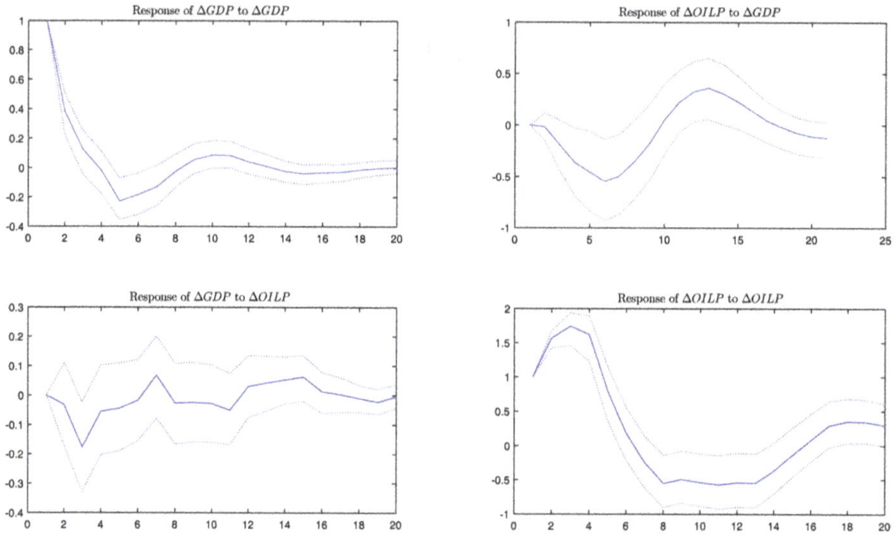

Figure 7. IRF of February 1875–April 1912. *Note*: Confidence intervals at 90% of confidence level.

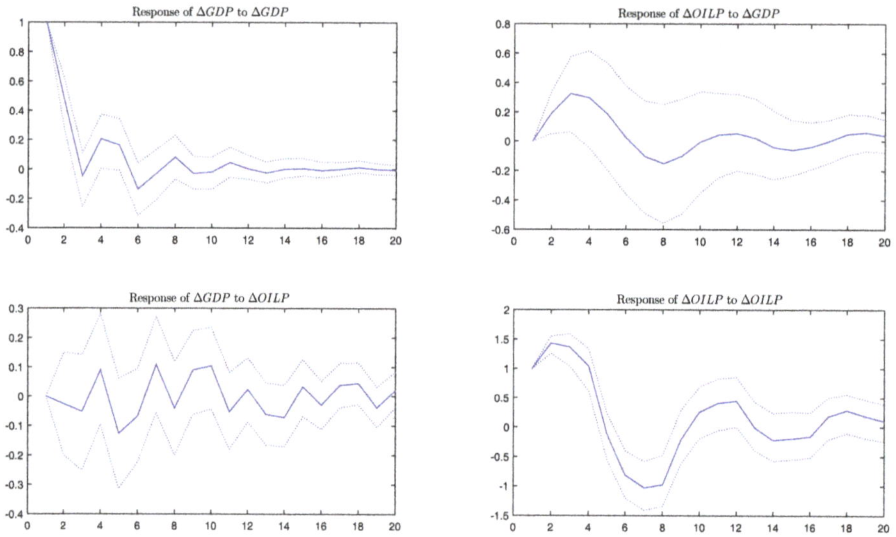

Figure 8. IRF of January 1913–January 1941. *Note*: Confidence intervals at 90% of confidence level.

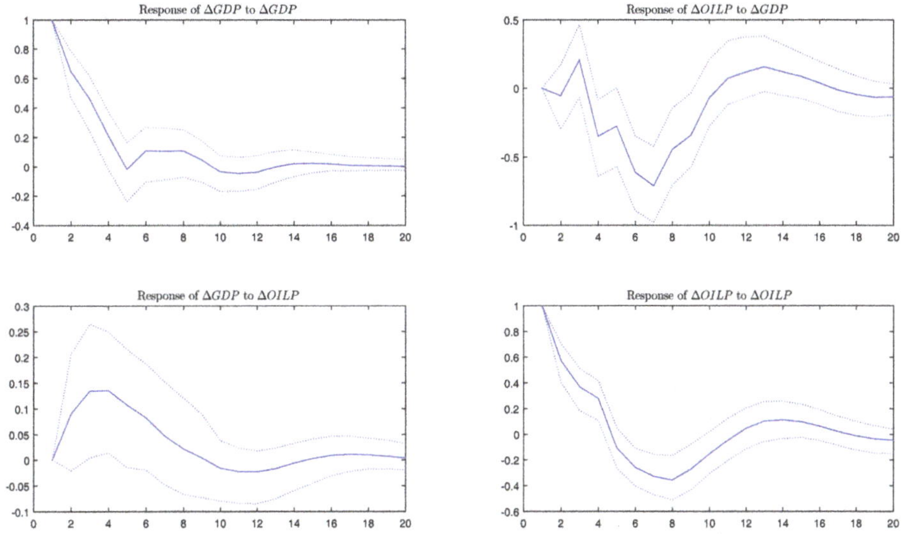

Figure 9. IRF of February 1941–March 1970. *Note*: Confidence intervals at 90% of confidence level.

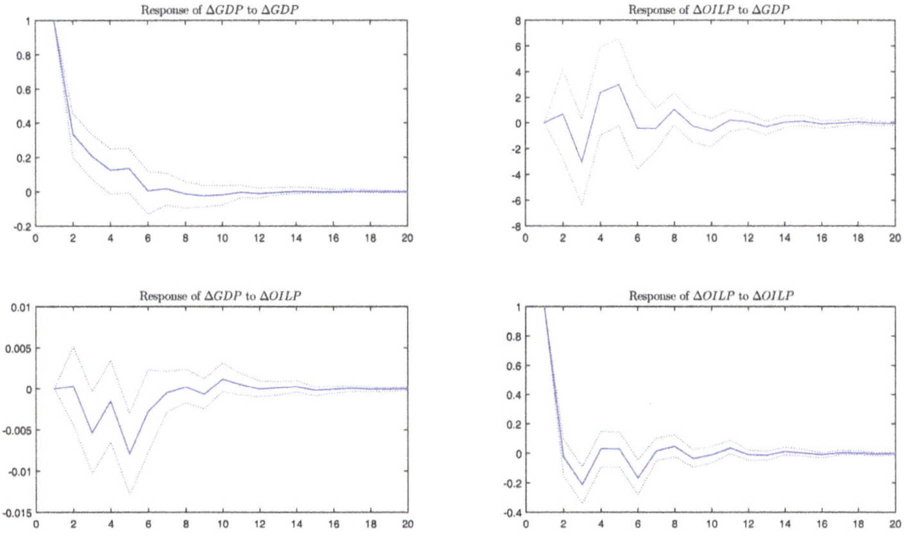

Figure 10. IRF of April 1970–February 2016. *Note*: Confidence intervals at 90% of confidence level.

5. A Time-Varying GDP-Oil Price Model

In previous sections, we find ample evidence of instability and non-linearities in the relationship between real GDP growth and oil price shocks. In this section, we use a more subtle and sophisticated econometric tool, a time-varying structural VAR model, to further explore the relationship between the two variables. Following [35], we consider the model

$$Y_t = \mu_t + \sum_{i=1}^{p} \Upsilon_{i,t} Y_{t-1} + \varepsilon_t, t = 1, 2, ..., T \tag{10}$$

where μ_t is a 2×1 vector of time-varying coefficients for the constant term; $\Psi_{i,t}$ is a 2×2 matrix of time-varying coefficients, and ε_t contains heteroskedastic unobservable shocks with the variance-covariance matrix Σ_t. After a triangular reduction of Σ_t, we obtain the following model:

$$\begin{aligned} y_t &= I_n \otimes [1, y'_{t-1}, ..., y'_{t-p}]\Psi_t + \Phi_t^{-1}\Sigma_t u_t \\ \Phi_t \Omega_t \Phi'_t &= \Sigma_t \Sigma'_t \end{aligned} \tag{11}$$

where Φ_t is a lower triangular matrix and Σ_t is a diagonal matrix.

The time-variant nature of the VAR model derives both from the coefficients and the variance-covariance matrix of the innovations. Its estimation is based on a Markov chain Monte Carlo algorithm with a Bayesian approach.[30]

The identification conditions of the model allow us to capture oil price shocks affecting GDP growth, but these shocks are exogenous to GDP growth, as well as the reaction of oil prices to GDP growth evolution. Thus, we focus on exogenous oil price shocks, which can be isolated in the time-varying system and are more relevant considering the previous analysis. Figure 11 presents the posterior mean of the time-varying standard deviation of oil price shocks. The post-1970s period exhibits a substantially higher variance of oil price shocks than other periods. Although not our primary concern, the time-varying standard deviation of GDP growth, too, reveals interesting results. We can observe a secular decline in volatility and identify several periods delimited by WWII and the Great Moderation.[31]

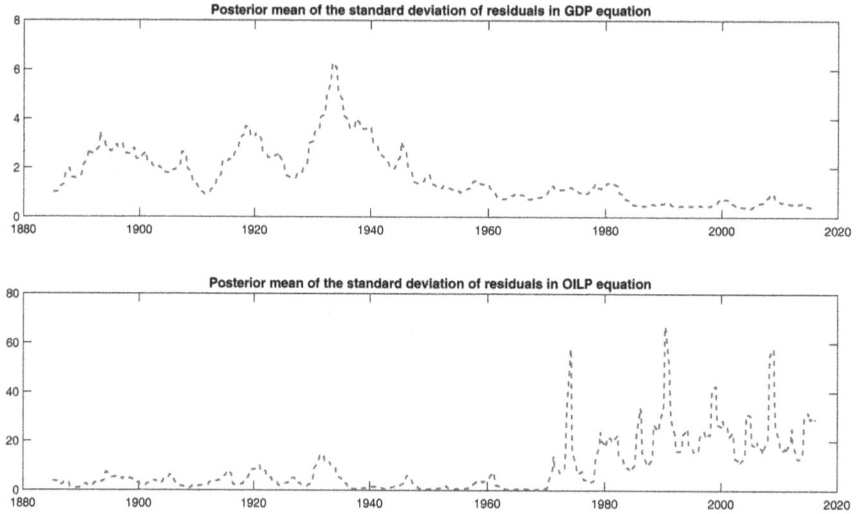

Figure 11. Posterior means of the standard deviation of residuals.

More interestingly, the time-varying VAR approach allows us to calculate IRFs at different points of time and assess different responses. The dates are not arbitrary, but capture major shocks behind the largest movements in oil price markets, which could have exerted an influence on the economic conditions regarding the relationship between oil prices and GDP growth in those dates. In particular, we select the oil price downturns of April 2014, April 2008, January 1986, January 1991, and March 2008, ordered from the highest to the lowest decline (−91.1%, −65.1%, −51.4%, −48.0%, and −39.6%,

[30] For technical details, see [35]. An adaptation of its Matlab code has been used to compute the estimates.
[31] These results confirm those obtained by [19].

respectively), and the increases that took place in January 1974, March 1990, February 1979, February 2009, and January 1999, from the highest to the lowest value (118.2%, 89.5%, 41.5%, 36.6%, and 35.1%, respectively). They are displayed in Figure 12. In the following paragraphs, we describe the events affecting world oil markets during these dates in chronological order.

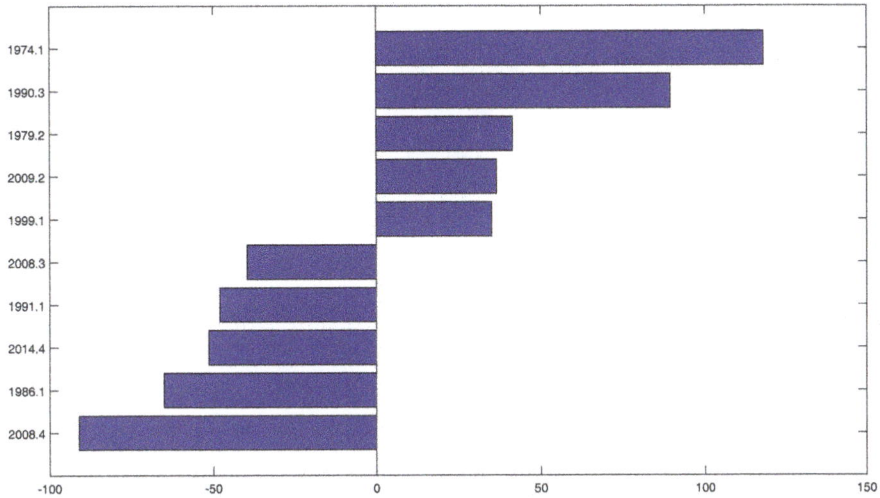

Figure 12. The five largest downturns and increases of real quarterly oil price.

The Arab oil-exporting nations' embargo of 1973 against countries (in particular, the US and many other developed countries) supporting Israel in the Yom Kippur War, at a time of rising demand and decreasing OPEC production, caused oil prices to abruptly increase. Specifically, by the first quarter of 1974, the increase reached 118.2%.

From 1974 to 1978, crude oil prices were relatively flat, but the crises in Iran and Iraq in 1979 and 1980 led to a new round of increases. Indeed, the Iranian revolution was the cause of one of the highest oil price rises, in spite of its relatively short duration. In the second quarter of 1979, the oil price jump was 41.5%.

In 1986, there was a collapse in crude oil prices, which was due to the fact that the OPEC cut output significantly to defend its official price in response to declining world oil demand and increasing production in non-OPEC countries. In the first quarter of the year, the decrease in oil prices reached 65.1%.

The Persian Gulf War also affected world oil markets. The Iraqi invasion of Kuwait in 1990 caused a rapid oil price escalation. Indeed, in the third quarter of 1990, oil prices rose by 89.5%. However, after two months of oil price increases, the United Nations approved the use of force against Iraq and oil prices began falling. In the first quarter of 1991, oil prices diminished by 48%.

In early 1999, oil prices began to grow, after the downward trend during the previous year, caused by a decline in consumption in Asian economies and higher OPEC production. This rise in oil prices was due to the reduction of OPEC production. This organization decided to cut production by about three million barrels per day, and the increase in oil prices in the first quarter of 1999 was 35.1%.

In 2008, after the Great Recession began,[32] falling petroleum demand, at a time when speculation in the crude oil futures market was exceptionally strong, decreased oil prices. In the third quarter of 2008, this decrease was 39.6%, while in the fourth quarter, the decline deepened to 91.1%. Nevertheless, an OPEC production cut in early 2009, some tensions in the Gaza Strip, and a rising demand from Asian countries increased oil prices steadily. In the second quarter of 2009, oil prices peaked at 36.6%.

The oil price decline in 2014 came after a period of stability. This drop was due to several factors. There was a slowdown in global economic activity. Indeed, the same countries that pushed up the price of oil in 2008 helped bring oil prices down in 2014. The US and Canada increased their production of oil, cutting their oil imports sharply, which put further downward pressure on world prices. Furthermore, Saudi Arabia decided to keep its production stable in order not to sacrifice their market share and restore the price. The oil price decline in the fourth quarter of 2014 was −91.1%.[33]

Results of impulse-response analysis over time are displayed in Figures 13 and 14. It should be noted that at selected dates (either increases or decreases), we introduce a normalized shock in the model (always positive) to see to what extent the conditions of the economy could have changed over time. Oil price growth shocks have temporary effects on GDP growth. At the time of large oil price increases, we observe a GDP decline over the first three quarters, while at the time of large oil price decreases, the effect on GDP is not so clear. However, confidence intervals are quite large during the first two years and a half. Figures 15 and 16 compare the magnitude of GDP growth changes in different periods. We observe that all the oil price increase dates considered have a similar negative effect on GDP growth, except the one in February 2009. We find the same pattern for the effect of oil price decreases. The impact of an oil price shock on GDP growth has declined over time, although there is more dispersion among different episodes in this case. Overall, oil price elasticity with respect to GDP has declined.[34] Finally, Figure 17 compares the average effects at the time of large oil price increases and decreases. We observe that the negative effect of oil price shocks on GDP growth is greater at the time of large oil price increases, which confirms previous evidence of nonlinearity in the relationship [37].

---

[32] The Great Recession has been the worst recession in the US economy since the Great Moderation. For an analysis of the Great Moderation in the face of the Great Recession, see [29].

[33] See [36] for a thorough analysis of this episode.

[34] These results would be in line with [3], who find a changing relationship over time, such that the economy is more resilient to an oil price shock today than in the past.

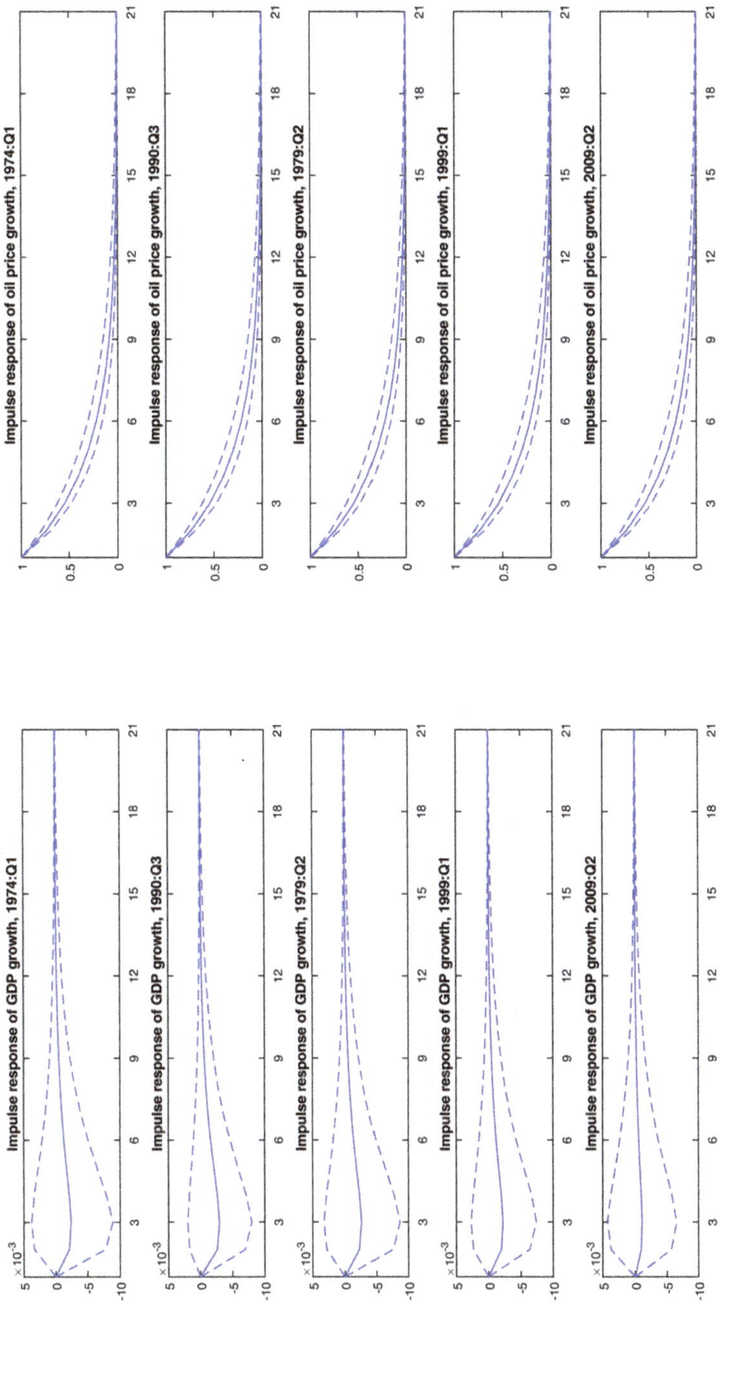

Figure 13. IRFs to oil price shocks at the time of the five largest increases of oil prices. *Note:* Confidence intervals at 90% of confidence level.

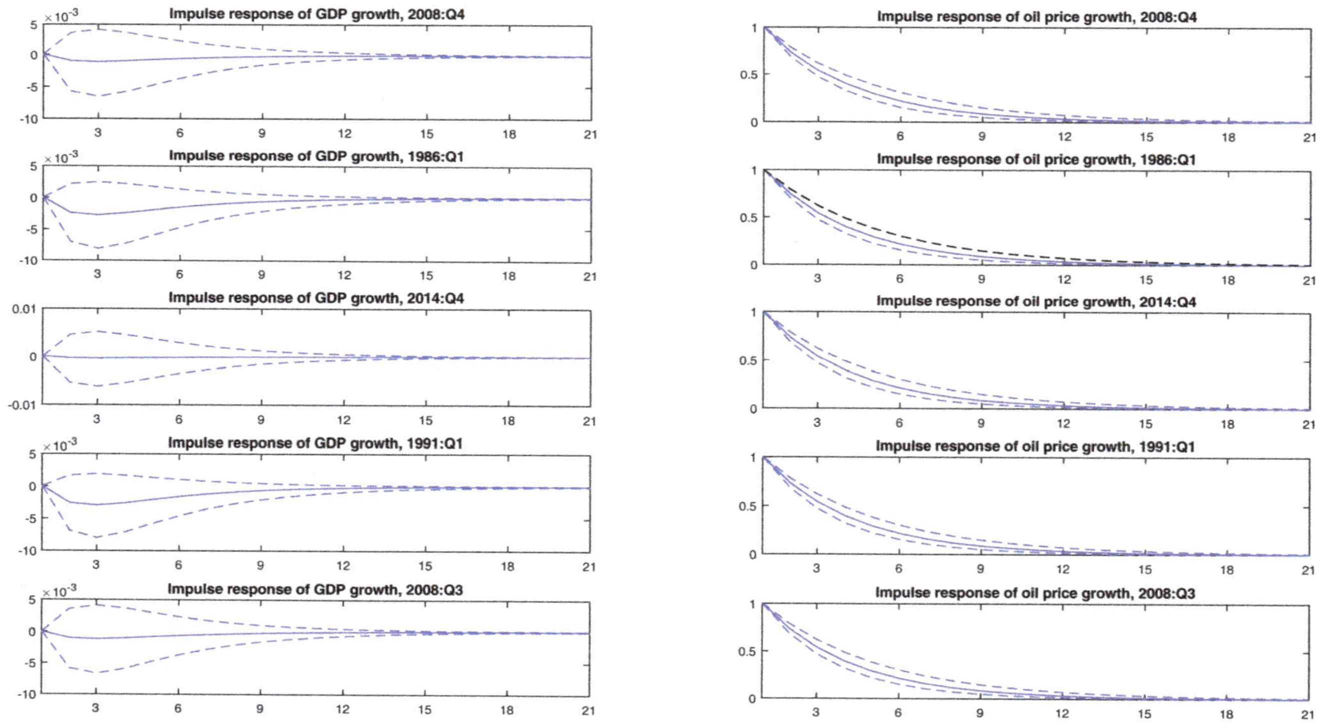

Figure 14. IRFs to oil price shocks at the time of the five largest decreases of oil prices. *Note*: Confidence intervals at 90% of confidence level.

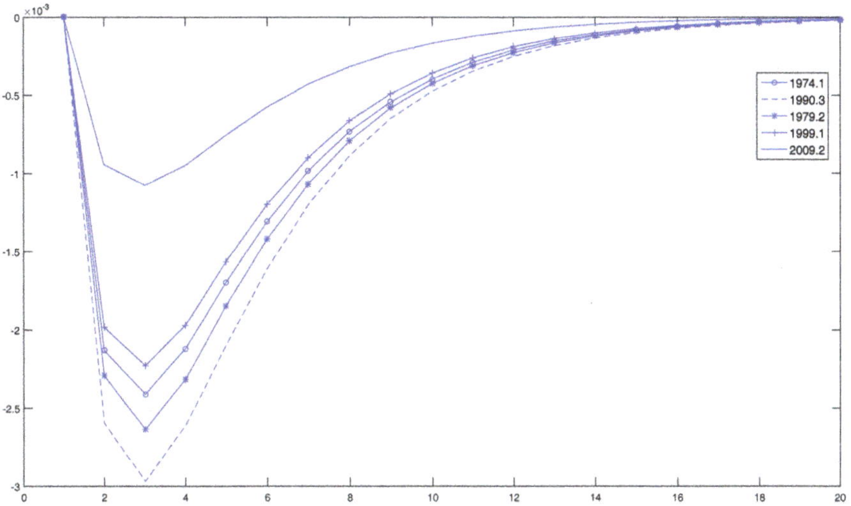

Figure 15. IRFs of ΔGDP to $\Delta OILP$ shocks at the time of the five largest increases of oil prices. *Note*: Confidence intervals at 90% of confidence level.

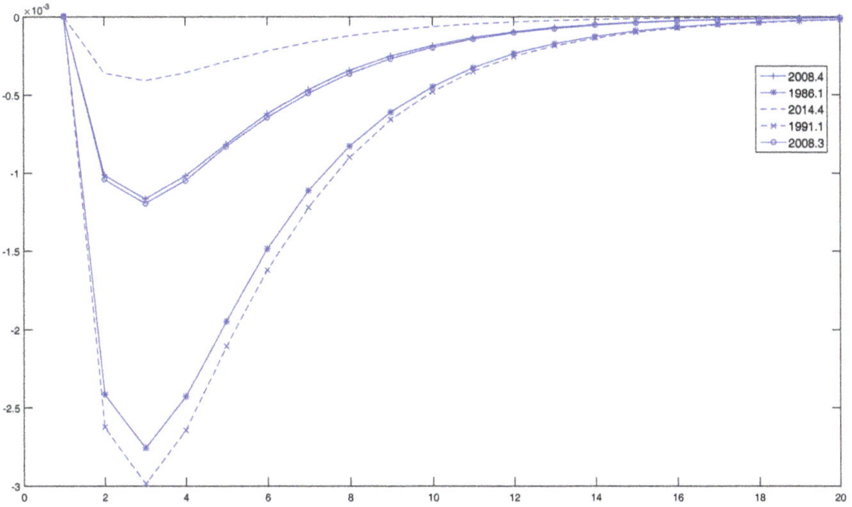

Figure 16. IRFs of ΔGDP to $\Delta OILP$ shocks at the time of the five largest decreases of oil prices. *Note*: Confidence intervals at 90% of confidence level.

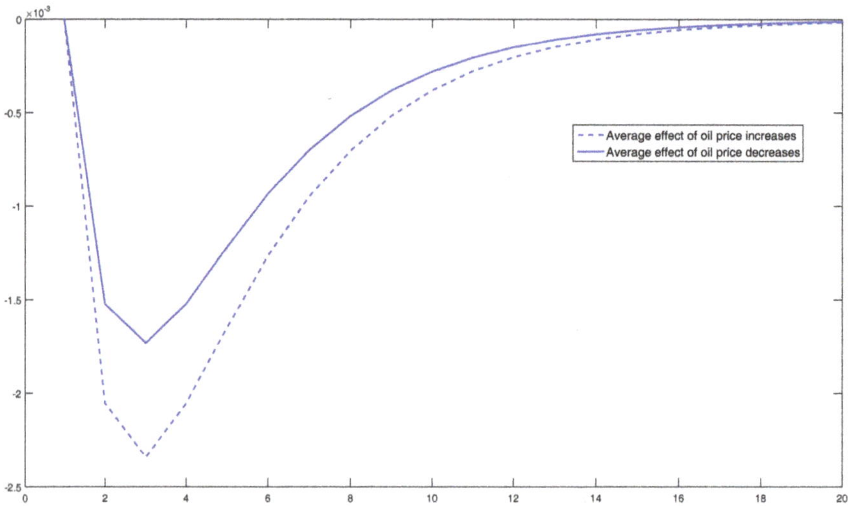

Figure 17. Comparison of the effects of ΔGDP to $\Delta OILP$ shocks at the time of the five largest increases and decreases of oil prices.

6. Conclusions

This study analyzes the relationship between oil prices and GDP from a long-term perspective, from the last third of the 19th century, when crude oil started to be commercially produced in Pennsylvania, to the present. Using different econometric tools, we analyze the individual dynamics of the series, as well as their interaction. The univariate study of the series shows that none of them presents structural breaks in mean. However, this apparent tranquility hides a considerable, and divergent, volatility. While real GDP growth has evolved into a secular volatility reduction, the variability of oil prices has substantially changed over the sample period.

Considering the whole sample, the evidence of the influence between GDP and oil prices is extremely weak, and not statistically significant, which could be due to the fact that there are instabilities in the relationship masking it. Indeed, over such a long period there have been important changes in the demand and supply for oil that could lead to identify some structural breaks. Therefore, we use several econometric techniques to detect and isolate different episodes, finding three break dates which are located in 1912, 1941, and 1970. Only this last period has been thoroughly studied in the literature.

We find that the period of the strongest relationship, characterized by a negative effect of oil price increases on GDP growth, occurs after the 1970s. However, in this last period, a time-varying model shows a decline in the impact of oil price shocks on GDP growth since then. Furthermore, we identify an asymmetric effect between large oil price increases and decreases. We notice that the negative effect of oil price shocks on GDP growth is greater at the time of large oil price increases. We also observe that the response of GDP to oil is significant over the periods 1961–1971 and 1937–1946.

Overall, the story of the relationship between GDP and oil prices is relatively turbulent. Although our findings point to a negative influence from oil price increases on economic growth, this phenomenon is far from being stable and has gone through different phases over time. Further research is necessary to fathom this complex relationship.

Acknowledgments: The authors acknowledge financial support of the Ministerio de Ciencia y Tecnología under grants ECO2014-58991-C3-1-R and ECO2014-58991-C3-2-R (M. Dolores Gadea) and ECO2015-65967-R (A. Montañés). The views expressed in this paper are the responsibility of the authors and do not necessarily represent those of the Banco de España or the Eurosystem.

Author Contributions: The authors contributed equally to this work.

Conflicts of Interest: The authors declare no conflict of interest.

References

1. Hamilton, J.D. Oil and the macroeconomy. In *The New Palgrave Dictionary of Economics*; Durlauf, S.N., Blume, L.E., Eds.; Palgrave Macmillan: London, UK, 2008.
2. Kilian, L. The Economic Effects of Energy Price Shocks. *J. Econ. Lit.* **2008**, *46*, 871–909.
3. Blanchard, O.J.; Galí, J. The Macroeconomic Effects of Oil Price Shocks: Why are the 2000s so different from the 1970s? In *International Dimensions of Monetary Policy*; NBER Chapters; National Bureau of Economic Research, Inc.: Cambridge, MA, USA, 2007; pp. 373–421.
4. Gomez-Loscos, A.; Gadea, M.D.; Montañés, A. Economic growth, inflation and oil shocks: Are the 1970s coming back? *Appl. Econ.* **2012**, *44*, 4575–4589.
5. Hamilton, J.D. Oil and the Macroeconomy since World War II. *J. Political Econ.* **1983**, *91*, 228–248.
6. Gómez-Loscos, A.; Montañés, A.; Gadea, M.D. The impact of oil shocks on the Spanish economy. *Energy Econ.* **2011**, *33*, 1070–1081.
7. Dvir, E.; Rogoff, K.S. *Three Epochs of Oil*; NBER Working Paper; National Bureau of Economic Research, Inc.: Cambridge, MA, USA, 2009.
8. Mohaddes, K.; Pesaran, M.H. Oil prices and the global economy: Is it different this time around? USC-INET Reseach Paper, No. 16-21. 2016, Available online: https://papers.ssrn.com/sol3/papers.cfm?abstract_id=2808084 (accessed on 6 June 2016).
9. Qu, Z.; Perron, P. Estimating and testing structural changes in multivariate regressions. *Econometrica* **2007**, *75*, 459–502.
10. Gordon, R.J. *The American Business Cycle: Continuity and Change*; NBER Book Series Studies in Business Cycles; National Bureau of Economic Research: Cambridge, MA, USA, 1986.
11. British Petroleum. *BP Statististical Review of World Energy*; Technical report; British Petroleum: London, UK, 2016.
12. Chow, C.; Lin, A.L. Best linear unbiased interpolation, distribution, and extrapolation of time series by related series. *Rev. Econ. Stat.* **1971**, *53*, 372–375.
13. LeSage, J. Applied Econometrics Using MATLAB. 1999. Available online: http://www.spatial-econometrics.com/html/mbook.pdf (accessed on 9 July 2016).
14. Quilis, E.M. A Matlab library of temporal disaggregation methods. *Instituto Nacional de Estadística, Internal Document*, Madrid, Spain, 2004.
15. Bai, J.; Perron, P. Estimating and Testing Linear Models with Multiple Structural Changes. *Econometrica* **1998**, *66*, 47–78.
16. Bai, J.; Perron, P. Computation and analysis of multiple structural change models. *J. Appl. Econom.* **2003**, *18*, 1–22.
17. Bai, J.; Perron, P. Critical values for multiple structural change tests. *Econom. J.* **2003**, *6*, 72–78.
18. Liu, J.; Wu, S.; Zidek, J. V. On Segmented Multivariate Regressions. *Statistica Sinica* **1997**, *7*, 497–525.
19. Gadea-Rivas, M.D.; Gómez-Loscos, A.; Pérez-Quirós, G. *The Great Moderation in Historical Perspective. Is It That Great?* CEPR Discussion Paper No. 10825; Center for Economic Policy Research: London, UK, 2014.
20. Andrews, D.W.K. Heteroskedasticity and Autocorrelation Consistent Covariance Matrix Estimation. *Econometrica* **1991**, *59*, 817–858.
21. Inclán, C.; Tiao, G.C. Use of Cumulative Sums of Squares for Retrospective Detection of Changes of Variance. *J. Am. Stat. Assoc.* **1994**, *89*, 913–923, doi:10.1080/01621459.1994.10476824.
22. Sanso, A.; Arago, V.; Carrion-i Silvestre, J.L. Testing for changes in the unconditional variance of financial time series. *Revista de Economia Financiera* **2004**, *4*, 32–53.
23. Deng, A.; Perron, P. The Limit Distribution of the Cusum of Squares Test Under General Mixing Conditions. *Econom. Theory* **2008**, *24*, 809–822.
24. Zhou, J.; Perron, P. *Testing for Breaks in Coefficients and Error Variance: Simulations and Applications*; Working Papers Series No. wp2008-010; Department of Economics, Boston University: Boston, MA, USA, 2008.

25. Fagiolo, G.; Napoletano, M.; Roventini, A. Are output growth-rate distributions fat-tailed? some evidence from OECD countries. *J. Appl. Econom.* **2008**, *23*, 639–669.
26. Hamilton, J.D. *Historical Oil Shocks*; NBER Working Paper No. 16790; National Bureau of Economic Research, Inc.: Cambridge, MA, USA, 2011.
27. Herrera, A.M.; Pesavento, E. The Decline in U.S. Output Volatility: Structural Changes and Inventory Investment. *J. Bus. Econ. Stat.* **2005**, *23*, 462–472.
28. Stock, J.H.; Watson, M.W. *Has the Business Cycle Changed and Why?* NBER Working Paper No. 9127; National Bureau of Economic Research, Inc.: Cambridge, MA, USA, 2002.
29. Gadea, M.D.; Gomez-Loscos, A.; Perez-Quiros, G. *The Two Greatest. Great Recession vs. Great Moderation*; CEPR Discussion Paper Series No. 10092; Center for Economic Policy Research: London, UK, 2014.
30. Sims, C. Macroeconomics and Reality. *Econometrica* **1980**, *48*, 1–48.
31. Lütkepohl, H. *Introduction to Multiple Time Series Analysis*; Springer: Berlin, Germany, 2005.
32. Granger, C. Investigating Causal Relations by Econometric Models and Cross Spectral Methods. *Econometrica* **1969**, *37*, 424–438.
33. Kilian, L. Small-Sample Confidence Intervals For Impulse Response Functions. *Rev. Econ. Stat.* **1998**, *80*, 218–230.
34. Gadea, M.D.; Gomez-Loscos, A. Oil price shocks and the US economy: What makes the latest oil price episode different. *Int. Econ. Lett.* **2014**, *3*, 36–44.
35. Primiceri, G.E. Time Varying Structural Vector Autoregressions and Monetary Policy. *Rev. Econ. Stud.* **2005**, *72*, 821–852.
36. Baumeister, C.; Kilian, L. Understanding the Decline in the Price of Oil since June 2014. *J. Assoc. Environ. Resour. Econ.* **2016**, *3*, 131–158.
37. Hamilton, J.D. What is an oil shock? *J. Econom.* **2003**, *113*, 363–398.

econometrics

MDPI

Article

Structural Breaks, Inflation and Interest Rates: Evidence from the G7 Countries

Jesús Clemente [1], María Dolores Gadea [2], Antonio Montañés [1,*] and Marcelo Reyes [1,†]

1 Department of Economic Analysis, University of Zaragoza, Gran Vía 2, 50006 Zaragoza, Spain; clemente@unizar.es

2 Department of Applied Economics, University of Zaragoza, Gran Vía 2, 50006 Zaragoza, Spain; lgadea@unizar.es

* Correspondence: amontane@unizar.es; Tel.: +34-976-76-2221

† Our beloved Marcelo Reyes passed away on 27 July 2015. We will always miss you.

Academic Editor: Pierre Perron

Received: 24 August 2016; Accepted: 25 January 2017; Published: 17 February 2017

Abstract: This study reconsiders the common unit root/co-integration approach to test for the Fisher effect for the economies of the G7 countries. We first show that nominal interest and inflation rates are better represented as I(0) variables. Later, we use the Bai–Perron procedure to show the existence of structural changes in the Fisher equation. After considering these breaks, we find very limited evidence of a total Fisher effect as the transmission coefficient of the expected inflation rates to nominal interest rates is very different than one.

Keywords: unit roots; structural breaks; interest rates; inflation; Fisher effect

JEL Classification: C22; E43

1. Introduction

One of the most important results from classical economic theory is that the movements of nominal variables have no impact on real economic variables. This result, which can be verified by testing the long-run neutrality proposition, implies that a permanent movement in the inflation rate has no effect on the equilibrium real interest rate. The traditional way to represent this phenomenon is to decompose nominal interest rates into two separate components that reflect expected inflation and the "real" interest rate. Following Fisher's (1930) study [1], which is very influential, this relationship can be stated through the well-known Fisher equation:

$$R_t = \pi_t^e + r_t \quad (1)$$

where R represents the nominal interest rate, π^e is the expected rate of inflation and r is the (ex-ante) real interest rate. In simple economic models, this last variable is determined by deep structural parameters, such as investor preferences or the marginal efficiency of capital, and is often assumed to be constant over long horizons. According to (1), moneylenders need a nominal interest rate that compensates them for the purchasing power lost over the duration of the loan, which is proxied by the expected inflation. Thus, if there is no money illusion, then a change in the expected inflation rate should be fully transmitted to the nominal interest rate to maintain a constant real interest rate.

Equation (1) provides useful information, both for theoretical research and for those making economic policy decisions. For example, if the Fisher effect holds, then the expected inflation is a good predictor of the nominal interest rate. Further, there is evidence of the superneutrality of money hypothesis. Consequently, it comes as no surprise that a significant body of literature analyzes the relationship between nominal interest rates and inflation or, more exactly, whether the so-called Fisher effect holds. The most common approach starts by estimating the following equation:

$$R_t = \alpha + \beta \pi_{t+1} + e_t \tag{2}$$

which implicitly assumes the presence of perfect rational expectations ($\pi_{t+1} = \pi_t^e$) and that α reflects the (ex-ante) real interest rate. It is clear that, whenever the value of the parameter β, often referred to as the Fisher coefficient, is equal to one, this equation is equal to (1), and therefore, we should conclude that the Fisher effect holds. At first sight, the analysis of this effect appears to be quite straightforward, in the sense that it only requires an estimation of (2) and a subsequent test of the null hypothesis H_0: $\beta = 1$. However, the literature confirms that there are several points that should be considered to accurately estimate this parameter and to test this hypothesis. Our study proposes a different statistical methodology to test the relationship between inflation and the nominal interest rate, adding to the controversy over which technique is the most suitable for testing the Fisher effect. [1] Here, we consider the appropriate treatment of the time series properties of the variables, as well as the possible presence of changes in the values of the parameters α and β. In this study, we consider the importance of these two points.

With respect to the first, there seems to be an almost unanimous opinion in the literature about the existence of unit roots in both the nominal interest rate and the inflation rate. Therefore,"standard" econometric models are no longer valid; rather, the co-integration approach should be employed. There are several examples of the use of this unit root/co-integration approach, beginning with the seminal studies of Rose (1988) [4] and Mishkin (1992) [5], whose methodology was subsequently applied in the more recent studies of Crowder and Wohar (1999) [6], Koustas and Serletis (1999) [7], Rapach (2002) [8], Laatsch and Klein (2003) [9] and Rapach and Weber (2005) [10], amongst many others. Some recent studies opted to use the panel data unit root/co-integration approach, as is the case of Westerlund (2008) [11] and Ozcan and Ari (2015) [12].

Nevertheless, some authors, such as Cox et al. (1985) [13], Malliaropoulos (2000) [14], Lanne (2001) [15], Olekalns (2001) [16], Gil-Alaña (2002) [17] and Atkins and Coe (2002) [18], questioned the presence of a unit root in the evolution of both the nominal interest rate and the inflation rate. Similarly, some other authors suggest the possibility that these variables may follow a long-memory process. We can cite the papers of Baum et al. (1999) [19], Phillips and Perron (1998) [20], Tsay (2000) [21], Sun and Phillips (2004) [22], Gil-Alaña (2004) [23] and Gil-Alaña and Moreno (2012) [24], in the case of the nominal interest rate, and Hassler and Wolters (1995) [25] and Bos et al. (1999) [26] with respect to the inflation rate. In light of this, the use of the unit root/co-integration approach is now open to debate.

In addition to the doubts raised by the authors above, we tentatively offer a new source of criticism in this study based on the potential non-constancy of the parameters included in the Fisher equation in the spirit of Lucas's critique (Lucas (1976) [27]). Our argument is based on the fact that most of the studies analyzing the Fisher effect use sample sizes covering the period from the 1970s to the present day. However, none of these appear to account for the different monetary policies in effect during this very lengthy period of time, making the constant parameter hypothesis doubtful. Instead, we argue that it is more appropriate to consider the hypothesis that some structural breaks affect the Fisher relationship. They may arise, if we consider that the presence of which can be understood if we consider, for example, that the real interest rate is the consequence of the interaction between savings and investment, and it may change when savings owners modify their behavior.

In this regard, and as Chadha and Dimsdale (1999) [28] point out, demographic change, technological progress, fiscal incentives, changes in the taxation of profits, the size of the public

[1] Recently, Caporale and Pittis (2004) [2], and Panopoulou (2005) [3] emphasized that this is a key issue in the empirical evidence supporting the Fisher relationship.

debt, investors' perception of risk and the degree of regulation or deregulation of capital markets could alter the constant and inflation parameters. Another source of possible variation in the parameters of (2) comes from the fact that the influence of inflation on the nominal interest rate can also vary. More robust inflation targeting and a more active monetary policy, as indicated by Söderlind (2001) [29] and Olekalns (2001) [16], or constraints on capital markets could be important determinants of the final value of these parameters.

Against this background, this study aims to analyze the Fisher effect for the G7 group of countries by explicitly accounting for the both variables and, more importantly, that the presence of structural breaks can affect the parameters of the Fisher equation. In order to illustrate this starting hypothesis, we begin by testing the time series properties of nominal interest and inflation rates. If we can find evidence that leads us to better characterize these variables as being I(0), then we should not use the co-integration approach because applying, similar arguments as Malliaropoulos (2000) [14] does, this may lead to spurious evidence of the Fisher effect. Furthermore, and in order to reflect the possible non-constancy of the Fisher equation, we allow for the presence of some breaks in the relationship between the nominal interest rate and the inflation rate. In a stationary scenario, we can apply Bai and Perron's (1998, 2003) [30,31] proposed procedure to test for the stability of the Fisher effect equation. This method also has the advantage of providing consistent estimations of both the number of breaks and the periods when these occur. Finally, we can use the results obtained by applying these techniques to estimate the Fisher relationship when we incorporate the structural breaks and the dynamic effects.

The rest of the paper is organized as follows. In Section 2, we describe the tests we employ to test for the time series properties of the variables. When these are applied to the nominal interest and inflation rates of the economies of the G7 countries, we find that they allow us to reject the unit root null hypothesis, a result that suggests that it is more advisable to analyze the Fisher effect in a stationary framework, rather than in a non-stationary one. In light of this result, in Section 3, we first propose the use of the Bai–Perron procedure to determine the presence of structural breaks in the Fisher equation. We then apply this procedure to analyze the Fisher effect for the economies of the G7 countries. Section 4 closes the paper with a review of the most important conclusions.

2. Fisher Effect with Non-Integrated Variables

Following Nelson and Plosser's (1982) seminal study [32], most empirical analyses based on the use of variables measured as time series begin by studying the time properties of the variables. If these are better characterized as being integrated, then researchers use co-integration techniques. If, by contrast, they are stationary, then we can use standard econometric techniques. The study of the Fisher effect is a scenario in which we can clearly appreciate the application of this strategy and, since Mishkin's (1992) [5] classic study, most of the literature devoted to this issue has followed such an approach.

However, some studies appear to have raised some questions about the appropriateness of the unit root model when seeking to accurately describe the evolution of both inflation rates and nominal interest rates. Malliaropoulos (2000) [14] and Baum et al. (1999) [19] showed that USA nominal interest and inflation rates can be better represented using broken trend stationary models. This finding is very important in the sense that, at least for the USA data, it casts doubts on the adequacy of the co-integration approach to test for the Fisher effect. A common method under this approach is to test whether the real interest rate is integrated. If we can conclude that the real interest rate is not integrated, this will be interpreted as evidence of the Fisher effect. However, this method is only valid when the nominal interest rate and the expected inflation rate are integrated. To better appreciate this, let us consider an expected inflation (π) and a nominal interest rate (R) represented as I(0) variables. Any combination of these variables, say $R - \beta\,\pi$, will also be an I(0) variable. However, this does not imply that the Fisher effect holds, because it only does so when the parameter β is one. Thus, in the presence of I(0) variables, admitting that the real interest rate is not integrated, does not necessarily imply that the Fisher effect holds.

This finding requires a careful analysis of the time properties of the nominal interest rates and inflation rates, which is precisely the aim of the next subsection.

2.1. Analysis of the Time Properties of the Nominal Interest Rates and Inflation Rates

We have already made the point that an analysis of the time properties of the nominal interest rates and inflation rates should be carried out carefully, and should certainly not be regarded as just a prior step in using co-integration techniques. There is a great range of statistics devoted to this issue. For example, most of the studies related to this area base their analysis on augmented Dickey–Fuller (ADF) tests (Dickey and Fuller (1979) [33]; Said and Dickey (1984) [34]), the methods presented in Phillips and Perron (1988) [20] or subsequent modifications of these types of statistics proposed by Ng and Perron (2001) [35], which compare the performance of a wide range of unit root statistics. For example, these authors consider the ADF^{GLS}, which is based on the very popular ADF test. Following Elliot et al. (1996) [36], this can be obtained by estimating the following model:

$$y_t = \delta_t + \rho\, y_{t-1} + \sum_{i=1}^{\ell} \phi_i \Delta y_{t-i} + \varepsilon_t \tag{3}$$

where δ_t reflects the deterministic elements, [2] and subsequently calculating the pseudo t-ratio to test whether the parameter ρ is one. The differences between this and the simple ADF test lie in the fact that ADF^{GLS} is based on the use of GLS (Generalized Least Squares) estimation methods instead of OLS (Ordinary Least Squares) estimators and on determining the value of the lag truncation parameter (ℓ) by using an information criterion, called MIC (Modified Information Criteria), also proposed in Ng and Perron (2001) [35]. This type of statistics is not useful to reject the presence of a unit root in nominal interest rates and inflation. This is why some authors have recently employed different statistics to analyze the time series properties of the variables to take advantage of the cross-sectional information of a database. Thus, it seems suitable to use a panel data approach to test for the presence of a unit root in the variables in the Fisher equation. In order to select the most appropriate type of panel data unit root test, we should first know the characteristics of the database, because of the possible presence of a cross-sectional correlation between the variables.

It is common to begin by testing for the null hypothesis of cross-sectional independence using Pesaran's (2004) CD (Cross Dependence) statistic [37], which has the following definition:

$$CD = \sqrt{\frac{2T}{N} \sum_{j=1}^{N} \hat{\rho}_j^2} \sim N(0,1) \tag{4}$$

where T is the sample size, N the cross-sectional dimension and $\hat{\rho}$ is the pair-wise Pearson's correlation coefficients $\hat{\rho}_j$, $j = 1, ..., n$, $n = N(N-1)/2$ of the residuals obtained from augmented Dickey–Fuller type regression equations. If we cannot reject this null hypothesis, then we should use the CIPS statistics because they correct the distortion caused by the cross-sectional correlation. Following Pesaran (2007) [38], the CIPS (cross-sectionally augmented panel unit root test) statistic is defined as follows:

$$CIPS = N^{-1} \sum_{i=1}^{N} \bar{t}_i \tag{5}$$

---

[2] In our present case, we only include an intercept in the model specification.

with $\bar{t}_i$ being the OLS t-ratio to test the $H_o : \alpha_i = 0$ in the following cross-sectional ADF regressions:

$$\Delta y_{it} = \delta_{it} + \alpha_i \, y_{it-1} + \gamma_i \, \bar{y}_{t-1} + \sum_{j=1}^{p} \phi_{ij} \, \Delta y_{i,t-j} + \sum_{j=0}^{p} \varphi_{ij} \, \Delta \bar{y}_{t-1} + \varepsilon_{it} \tag{6}$$

where $\bar{y}_{t-1}$ denotes the cross-sectional mean of y_{it}. Tables II(a)–(c) in Pesaran (2007) [38] provide the critical values for the CIPS tests, in addition to a proposed truncated version of this statistic, commonly referred to as CIPS*, which will be used in the following section.

2.2. Empirical Evidence from the G7 Countries

As we mentioned earlier, the methodology to employ to analyze the Fisher effect depends on the time properties of the variables that are necessary to study it, namely the nominal interest rates and inflation rates. Thus, we should be careful when determining the integration order of these variables. To that end, we apply the statistics presented in the previous section to the nominal interest rates and inflation rates of the G7 countries. We take two different measures of the nominal interest rates. First, we select a short-run variable, measured through the three-month treasury bill rate (or equivalent) for each sample country. Second, we take the 10-year government bond (or equivalent) for each sample country as a measure of the long-run behavior of nominal interest rates. We obtain the annualized inflation rates from the Consumer Price Index (CPI). We obtain all data from the OECD Main Economic Indicators. Finally, the quarterly data, where possible, cover the sample period 1970:Q1–2015:Q4. [3] Figures 1–3 illustrate these variables, whilst Tables 1 and 2 report the results of applying the previously-mentioned statistics to our database.

Table 1 reflects the results of the CD statistic to test the null hypothesis of no cross-sectional dependence. We can easily reject this null hypothesis, and consequently, we should employ panel data unit root tests that account for its presence. The CIPS* statistic, whose results are presented in Table 2, takes into account the cross-sectional dependence. As we can see, there is only very robust evidence against the unit root null hypothesis. However, some countries may exhibit the presence of the unit root in any of the analyzed variables. [4] In order to explore this possibility, we have considered several subgroups of countries. We have taken all of the possible combinations of five and six countries, and the values of the CIPS* statistic always allows the rejection of the null hypothesis, the average p-value being lower than 0.01 Thus, this lack of evidence against the null hypothesis matches the results of Constantini and Lupi (2007) [40] and Lee and Chang (2007, 2008) [41,42], who reject the presence of a unit root in the inflation rate for different sample sizes of OECD countries using the LM (Lagrange Multiplier) tests proposed in Lee and Strazicich (2003, 2013) [43,44], which consider the presence of broken trends in the evolution of these variables. These statistics can also provide evidence against the unit root null hypothesis for the nominal interest rates, as is reflected in Gadea et al. (2009) [45]. Thus, the global consideration of all of this evidence leads us to an analysis of the Fisher effect using I(0) variables instead of the much more common approach of using I(1) variables.

---

3 The Italian short-term interest rates for 1970:Q1–1970:Q4 were estimated using the evolution of Italy's long-term interest rates.

4 See Pesaran (2012) [39] in this regard.

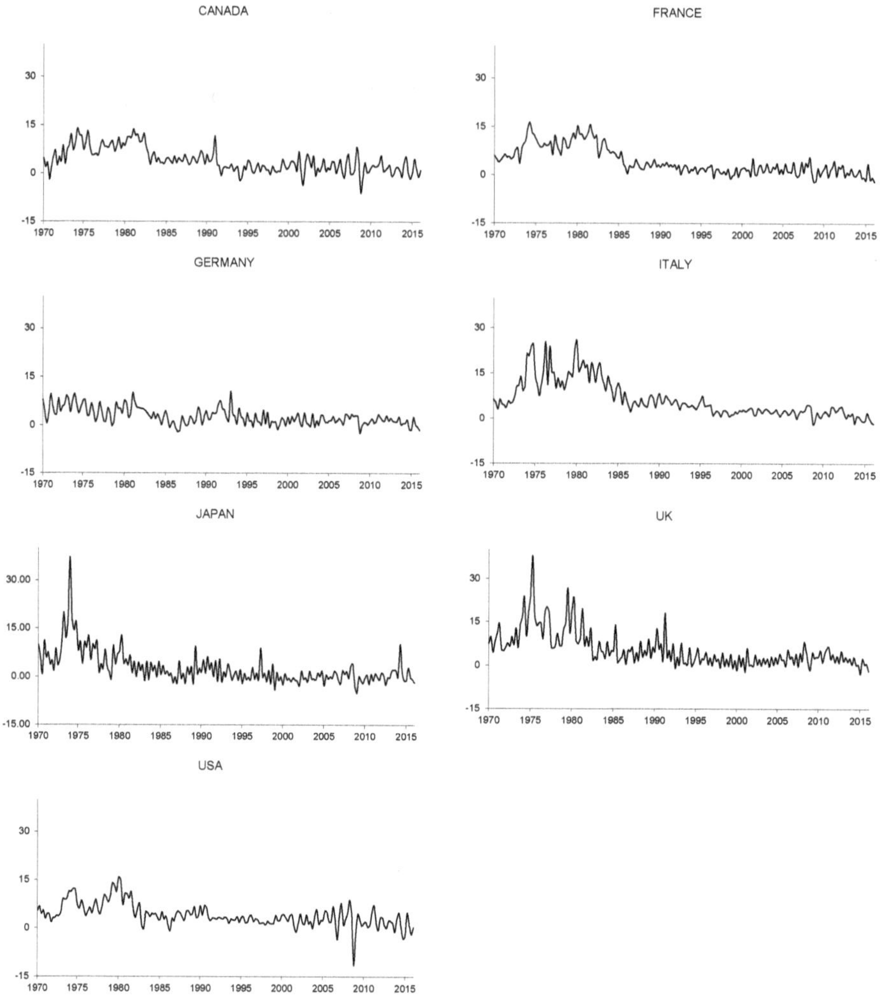

(a)

Figure 1. *Cont.*

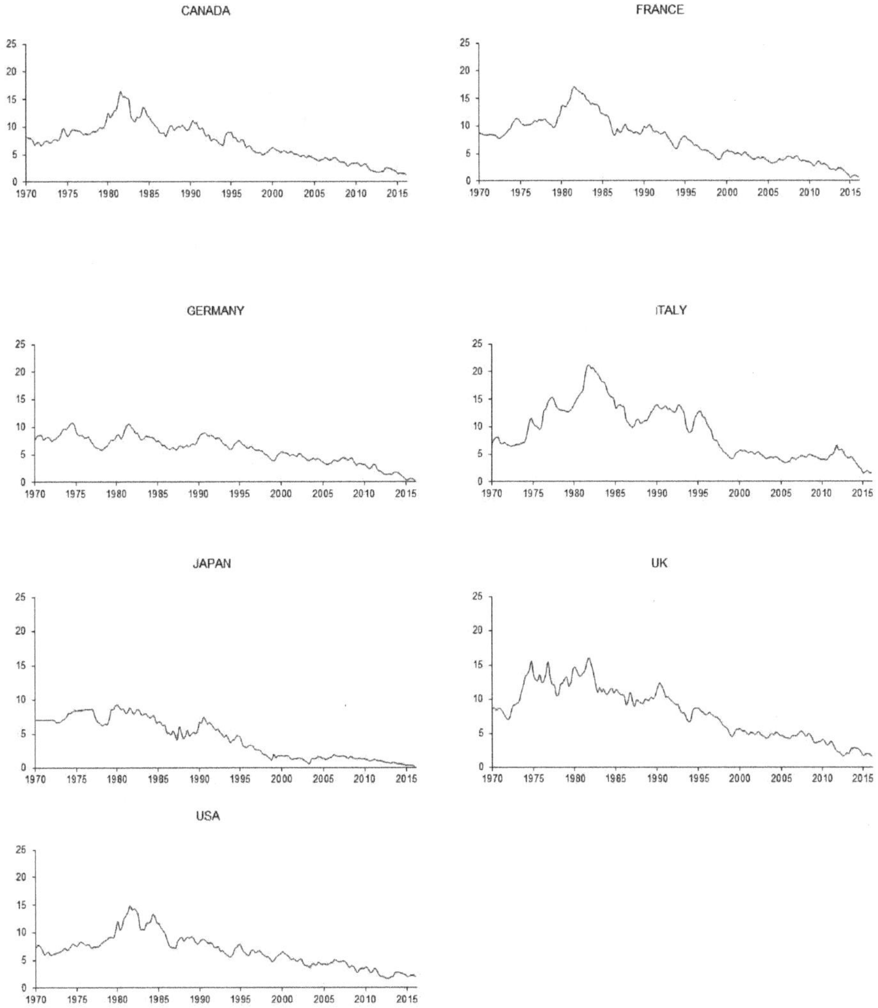

(b)

Figure 1. *Cont.*

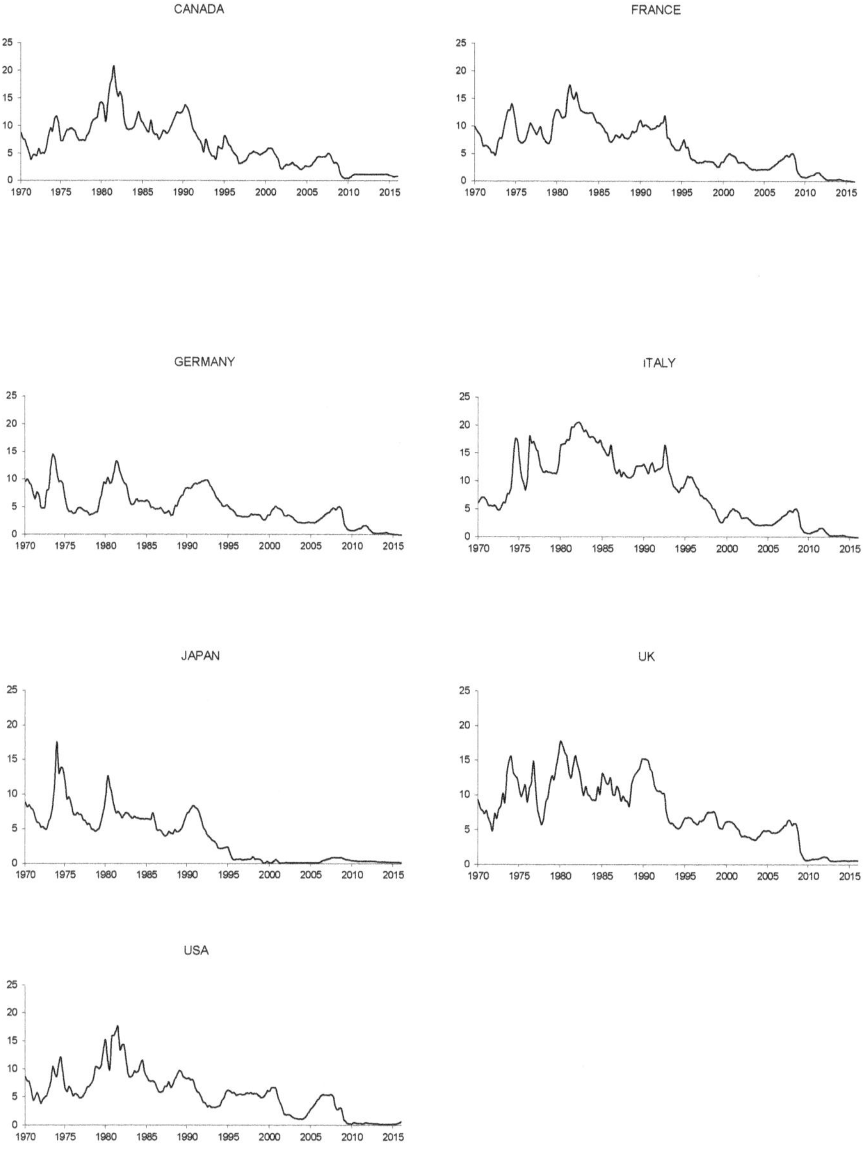

(c)

Figure 1. (**a**) Expected Inflation rates; (**b**) Long-run nominal interest rates; (**c**) Short-run nominal interest rates.

Table 1. Testing for cross-sectional dependence.

	Long-Run Nominal Interest	Short-Run Nominal Interest	Inflation
p = 0	29.25 *	19.13 *	20.06 *
p = 1	26.33 *	15.39 *	20.32 *
p = 2	25.85 *	15.52 *	19.27 *
p = 3	25.16 *	15.32 *	19.83 *
p = 4	24.76 *	15.28 *	18.78 *

This table reports the values of the CD (Cross Dependence) statistic proposed in Pesaran (2004) [37] to test the non-cross-sectional dependence null hypothesis. The values were obtained by estimating a Dickey–Fuller-type equation without trend, with fixed effects and for different lag values (p = 1,..,4). *: rejection of the null hypothesis even for a demanding 1%.

Table 2. CIPS* panel data unit root tests.

	Long-Run Nominal Interest	Short-Run Nominal Interest	Inflation
p = 0	−2.89 **	−6.73**	−12.94 **
p = 1	−3.08 **	−7.19**	−12.46 **
p = 2	−2.27 *	−6.14**	−10.79 **
p = 3	−2.38 **	−5.67**	−7.52 **
p = 4	−2.36 **	−5.87**	−7.50 **

This table reports the values of the CIPS* (cross-sectionally augmented panel unit root test, truncated version) statistic proposed in Pesaran (2007) [38] to test the unit root null hypothesis. The values were obtained by estimating (6), where the specification includes only an intercept. ** and *: rejection of the null hypothesis at the 5% and the 1% significance level, respectively.

3. Structural Breaks and the Fisher Effect

As we have seen, the presence of a unit root in the variables under examination is not supported by our data. Consequently, we argue that we should test for the Fisher effect by considering that nominal interest rates and inflation rates are not integrated. Malliaropoulos (2000) [14] and Atkins and Chan (2004) [46] tried to provide an appropriate reply to studies of the Fisher effect with stationary variables. These authors first filter the broken trend component for both the nominal interest rate and the inflation rate and then study the relationship between the cyclical components of these two variables. However, we should note that this method does not account for the fact that the presence of breaks may affect the relationship between these variables. To explore this possibility, we can use Bai and Perron's (1998, 2003) procedure [30,31]. [5] This method allows us to detect the presence of an unknown number of breaks, as well as to estimate the relationship of the Fisher effect. We estimate the following expression, in which up to m breaks may appear:

$$R_t = \alpha_j + \beta_j \pi_{t+1} + u_t, \; t = TB_{j-1}, ..., TB_j \; j = 1, 2, ...m+1 \tag{7}$$

with TB_j representing the period in which the break appears, m representing the number of breaks and $TB_0 = 1$ and $TB_{m+1} = T$. The Bai–Perron procedure estimates the above equation by considering that the break may appear in any period of the sample. We then define a Chow-type test in order to determine the existence of a first break, which coincides with the period in which this Chow-type statistic attains its maximum value. We subsequently analyze the existence of multiple breaks by applying this procedure sequentially, combining it with the repartition method described in Bai (1997) [51]. To determine the existence of breaks, we can use the UD_{max} and WD_{max} statistics, which test the null hypothesis of no structural breaks versus the presence of an unknown number of breaks. Note that we consider a maximum of five breaks and that we use the quadratic spectral kernel to account for the presence of possible autocorrelation and heteroskedasticity in the residuals

[5] We should note that Garcia and Perron (1996) [47], Bierens (2000) [48], Lanne (2006) [49] and Panopoulou and Pantelidis (2016) [50] have also considered the presence of non-linearities in the Fisher equation.

and the Andrews (1991) [52] automatic bandwidth selection. This method should help us account for the possible dynamic components of the relationship, and consequently, Equation (7) also offers an appropriate scenario in which to test for the Fisher effect from a long-run perspective. The results of this analysis appear in Table 3. These results clearly confirm our suspicion of the presence of breaks in the structural relationship between the interest rates and inflation rates. We can verify this by observing the values of WD_{max}, which clearly reject the null hypothesis of no breaks for almost any level of significance. Thus, it is necessary to consider the presence of these breaks in order to reflect this relationship appropriately.

The findings of this study contribute to different debates with respect to the relationship between nominal rates and expected inflation. First, previous research highlighted the importance of the term structure of interest rates because it contains some information to forecast inflation (Fama (1990) [53]). Furthermore, by using short-run interest rates, we only observe a liquidity effect instead of the Fisher relationship. Fahmy and Kandil (2003) [54] conclude that the ability of nominal interest rates to capture inflationary expectations increases with maturity, attaining a one-to-one relationship for assets of five-year maturity. On the other hand, numerous studies, including that of Fisher himself, test the Fisher effect using short-run interest rates (e.g., Mishkin (1992) [5] and Evans and Lewis (1995) [55]).

In this framework, we find some significant differences in the results using short- and long-term interest rates. First, we can see that the number of breaks is greater when using the long-run rather than the short-run nominal interest rate. This can be interpreted by considering that the short-run interest rates react more quickly than the long-run interest rates to the changes in the inflation. We can also observe that there is some coincidence with respect to the estimation of the periods in which the breaks appear and, of special interest, the break related to the Great Recession.

Table 3. Estimation of the Fisher coefficient.

	$WD^{0.05}_{max}$	ψ_1	$TB1$	ψ_2	$TB2$	ψ_3	$TB3$	ψ_4	$TB4$	ψ_5	$TB5$	ψ_6
Panel A: long-run nominal interest rates												
Canada	616	0.53	79:2	0.61	86:1	0.42	96:3	0.63	07:4	0.18	-	-
France	258	0.61	79:4	1.37	86:3	1.11 $	96:3	0.68	09:1	1.02	-	-
Germany	178	0.40	96:3	0.73	08:4	1.50	-	-	-	-	-	-
Italy	218	0.95	76:3	1.27 $	84:2	1.52	97:2	1.15	-	-	-	-
Japan	1337	0.20	85:2	0.47	95:1	0.07	01:4	0.71	-	-	-	-
UK	495	0.67	76:3	0.13	83:2	0.24	91:3	0.86	98:2	0.07	08:4	0.50
USA	254	0.52	78:4	2.63 $	85:4	0.62	92:2	0.99	00:4	0.12	08:3	0.38
Panel B: short-run nominal interest rates												
Canada	642	0.86	79:1	0.89	92:1	0.15	08:4	0.08	-	-	-	-
France	375	0.86 $	81:1	0.68	95:3	0.03	08:4	0.31	-	-	-	-
Germany	185	0.70	95:3	0.92	09:1	0.40	-	-	-	-	-	-
Italy	586	0.80	79:4	0.79	86:3	1.75	98:3	1.71	-	-	-	-
Japan	266	0.55	92:4	0.13	-	-	-	-	-	-	-	-
UK	526	0.08	79:2	0.53	92:3	0.10	08:4	0.03	-	-	-	-
USA	500	0.71	79:2	0.92	86:1	1.43	01:3	−0.70	08:4	−0.01	-	-

This table presents the results of the Bai–Perron procedure and the estimation of the Fisher coefficient for the different estimated regimes. $WD^{0.05}_{max}$ (WD_{max} at 5% significance level) tests for the null hypothesis of no structural breaks, rejecting this hypothesis for any significance level considered. These statistics have been obtained by correcting the possible autocorrelation/heteroscedasticity by way of the quadratic spectral kernel with the bandwidth being selected according to Andrews (1991) [52]. $TB1, \ldots, TB5$ are the estimated break periods according to the LWZ (modified Schwarz criterion) statistic. $\psi_1, \ldots, \psi_6$ are the estimations of the Fisher coefficients defined in (8) and (9) for each estimated regime. $ means that a second order ARDL (Autoregressive Distributed Lag) model was estimated.

We can now analyze the estimation results for the β parameter, which determines whether the Fisher effect holds. To that end, instead of using the estimated Equation (7), it seems to be much more appropriate to split the sample by using the estimated breaks and, then, to include some lags in the specification to better capture the dynamics of the relationship by way of an ARDL (Autoregressive Distributed Lag) of order one.

$$R_t = \alpha_j + \beta_j \pi_{t+1} + \gamma_j R_{t-1} + \phi_j \pi_t + u_t, \ t = TB_{j-1} + 2, \ldots, TB_j \ j = 1, \ldots m+1 \tag{8}$$

and, subsequently, obtain the long-run multiplier for the Fisher coefficient defined as:

$$\psi_j = \frac{\beta_j + \phi_j}{1 - \gamma_j} \tag{9}$$

We should note that the effective sample removes the initial observations of each segment in order to assure that all of the information belongs to the same estimated period. Later, we use bootstrap methods based on 1000 replications to obtain the confidence intervals of the estimated ψ. Figures 2 and 3 present the results for the long- and short-run nominal interest rates, respectively.

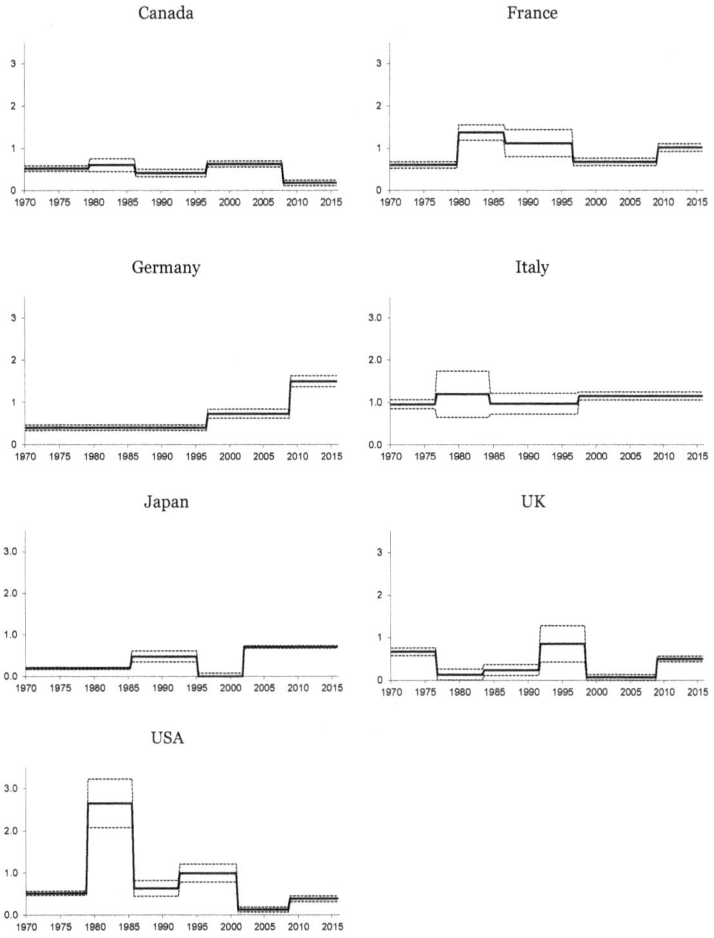

Figure 2. Estimated Fisher Coefficient. Long-run nominal interest rate. The solid line represents the estimated Fisher coefficient defined by (9), whilst the dotted line reflects twice the standard deviation, obtained by way of bootstrapping techniques.

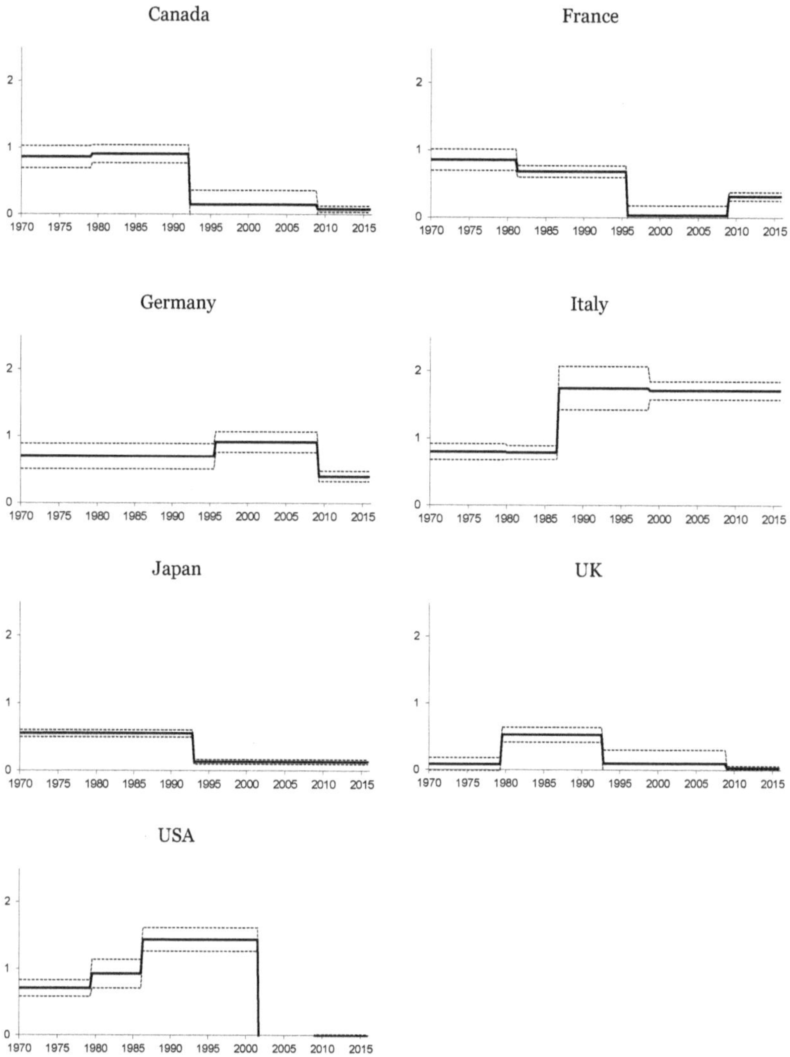

Figure 3. Estimated Fisher Coefficient. Short-run nominal interest rate. The solid line represents the estimated Fisher coefficient defined by (9), whilst the dotted line reflects twice the standard deviation, obtained by way of the bootstrapping techniques.

We can first observe that there is a clear relationship between interest rates and expected inflation, although the estimated coefficients are some distance from unity, and therefore, the transmission of the effect from expected inflation rates to interest rates is not exactly the one predicted by the Fisher effect. Moreover, we can frequently reject the null hypothesis that the ψ_j coefficients are equal to one, thus failing to provide evidence of the Fisher effect for most periods of the sample. Therefore, we can broadly conclude that there is a weak Fisher effect or, in other words, that the nominal interest rate "under-adjusts" to a change in inflation evolution, and consequently, a transmission to real rates exists.

This is a crucial issue in macroeconomics and monetary economics because it implies rejecting superneutrality. This hypothesis holds if changes in the money supply affect inflationary expectations and, in turn, real rates. In the absence of a full Fisher effect, shocks to inflation would translate into disturbances in real rates, which is a controversial result in the context of standard models of inter-temporal asset pricing and would break monetary neutrality. However, our estimation results show a link between nominal rates and expected inflation, but not the required full one-to-one adjustment of the former to the latter. Rapach and Wohar (2005) [56] obtain similar results.

Many studies propose explanations of the lack of empirical evidence of the Fisher hypothesis. Together with the inability to measure inflationary expectations directly, the Mundell–Tobin effect emerges as the most likely theoretical explanation for a β coefficient less than one, in accordance with the results in Table 2. Following the Tobin (1965) [57] formulation, agents replace nominal assets for real money balances in response to increases in expected inflation. This reallocation process increases capital stock and lowers the long-run real return to capital. In Mundell's (1963) model [58], an increase in inflation raises savings if they depend on a real money balance, via the wealth effect, and thus, the real interest rate falls. Accordingly, the Mundell–Tobin effect predicts a negative long-run real interest rate response to an increase in inflation, and thus, the nominal interest rate would rise by less than unity. [6]

By assuming some degree of inflationary monetary transmission to real interest rates, it is interesting to study the influence of changes in monetary policy on the Fisher effect. Using a dynamic expectations model with staggered price-setting, Söderling (2001) [29] claims that a more active monetary policy decreases the Fisher effect. This finding has been supported in the well-documented case of the USA. Numerous studies (e.g., Miskhin (1992) [5] and Lanne (2001) [15]) find strong evidence supporting the Fisher hypothesis for the period between the early 1950s to 1979, characterized by interest rate targeting while the Federal Reserve was especially concerned with growth and the employment level. On the other hand, the effect is absent in the post-1970 sub-sample periods when monetary policy emphasized inflation targeting.

The analysis of the periods in which the breaks appear provides some rich insights. We can see that the most common breaks appear in four fairly well-defined periods: in the late 1970s, in the mid-1980s, in the mid-1990s and, finally, in the second part of the 2000s, clearly related to the Great Recession. [7] The periods in which the breaks appear can be easily interpreted from an economic point of view. The first and second breaks are connected with the general tightening of monetary policy applied with different rhythms in each country. The case of the USA, where the Federal Reserve introduced new operational procedures in 1979 and the inflation target gained weight in its reaction function, is a good example. [8] The third break is not connected with a single cause; rather, its origin may be related to multiple causes because it coincides with a somewhat convulsive period as far as monetary policy is concerned. For instance, we should consider that the crisis of the European Monetary System occurred during that period. Therefore, it comes as no surprise that the estimation of this break is less accurate than the estimation of the other breaks. However, and despite some occasional episodes, monetary policy in the 1990s tended towards more stability and greater credibility of central banks that maintained their inflation targets. Finally, the recent international crisis is clearly behind the last period.

---

6 This hypothesis has recently been re-examined with optimizing agents in an overlapping generations context. See Rapach (2003) [59] for a comprehensive survey.

7 In order to analyze the robustness of the estimated periods, we have obtained the Bai–Perron statistics for the 1980:Q1–2015:Q4 and for the 1970:Q1–2007:Q4 samples. In this latter case, the estimated periods of breaks almost coincide with those of the full sample. In the former, the variations are a bit larger, especially for the short-run case. The total number of estimated breaks is 19, 15 being coincident with the full sample analysis. For the long-run model, the new total of estimated breaks is 23, 20 being coincident. In summary, given this high degree of coincidence in the results and taking into account that these new estimated breaks are a consequence of the decrease in the size of the lowest segment, we can conclude that the Bai–Perron procedure offers very robust results in this scenario.

8 See Clarida et al. (2000) [60]. The consequences have been exhaustively studied in different contexts, such as the analysis of the evolution of the real exchange rates. See Gadea et al. (2004) [45], amongst others.

If we analyze the estimations of the β coefficients from a historical perspective, some further insights emerge. We begin with the long-run equation in which we can see that the estimated values of the β coefficients for the first regime are lower than one. Italy exhibits the highest value (0.95) and Japan the lowest value (0.20). The rest of the estimated coefficients are around 0.5, clearly rejecting the Fisher hypothesis.

Interestingly, we can also appreciate that the first oil crisis does not seem to affect the Fisher equation, despite the fact that this phenomenon clearly affected inflation in all of the countries included in our study. Moreover, some previous studies, such as that of Rapach and Wohar (2005) [56], detect a break for the real interest rate in industrialized countries in 1973. Therefore, according to our results, the increase in the inflation rate during that period was absorbed by the movements in the nominal interest rates and, consequently, the Fisher relationship remained unaltered.

The second period covers the years running from the late 1970s to the mid-1980s. The most noteworthy economic event of this time was the change in monetary policy, which became more restrictive. The main finding associated with this period is the increase in the estimated value of the coefficients, especially remarkable for France and the USA and much more moderate for Canada and Italy. The evolution of the Fisher coefficient during the 1990s and 2000s shows a downward path for France, the USA and, to a lesser extent, the UK, whilst Germany, Japan and Italy show slight increases. In any event, except for the case of Italy, the value of this coefficient is well below one. Finally, the effect of the Great Recession implies a clear increase in this parameter for France and Germany, in excess of one. These increases are much more moderate for the UK, Japan and the USA.

Let us now consider the short-run model. The estimated values of the Fisher parameter are not globally distant from those of the long-run model, being quite similar to or slightly higher than those up to the 2000s, but showing a clear decline in the final part of the sample. We can thus conclude that the values of the expected inflation rates are again transmitted to short-run nominal interest rates for the sample countries. Note, however, that the amount transmitted is below the value predicted by the Fisher hypothesis and is slightly slower than that transmitted to the long-run nominal interest rates, especially after the Great Recession. The exception to this behavior is Italy, which exhibits a somewhat stable value of more than one for this coefficient.

We can also see that the estimated values of the β coefficients show an upward trend from the beginning of the sample to the mid-1990s. Finally, we can observe that the estimated value of the β coefficient exhibits a clear reduction from the mid-1990s onwards, especially noticeable after the Great Recession. Thus, the expected inflation rate does not act as a good predictor of the short-run nominal interest rates during this period. This situation is quite understandable for the EU countries, which lost their independence in terms of monetary policy following the introduction of the euro and the fixing of nominal interest rates by the European Central Bank. The Japanese results can be explained by the substantial reduction in the nominal interest rates that aimed to re-activate the economy. This makes it easy to explain why the estimated values of both the intercept and the β coefficient decreased since the 1990s. By contrast, the transmission of the expected inflation to nominal interest rates remained virtually unaltered in the USA. In short, the Fisher effect seems to decrease, and nearly disappear, in the 1990s, coinciding with more stable inflation expectations because central banks halted price pressures in the economy to meet their inflation targets. As a result, the nominal and real interest rates move in parallel.

4. Conclusions

In this study, we offer evidence of the fact that the nominal interest rates and inflation rates of the G7 group of countries are better characterized as I(0) variables than as first order integrated variables. We obtain this conclusion by using recently developed panel data unit root tests. Consequently, we should note that using techniques based on unit root/co-integration tests should be carefully reconsidered when analyzing the relationship between nominal interest rates and inflation rates, which are commonly studied by estimating the Fisher equation.

We also considered the presence of some breaks in the Fisher equation in order to capture the different monetary regimes that co-exist across the sample. Using a procedure recently proposed in Bai and Perron (1998, 2003) [30,31] confirms our hypothesis, offering robust evidence of the existence of different regimes in the relationship between nominal interest rates and inflation rates.

This procedure also offers an excellent scenario for testing for the Fisher effect, considering the presence of breaks in the relationship that affects both parameters. The results based on this method show that there is a clear connection between nominal interest rates and expected inflation rates. However, there is no evidence of a total Fisher effect for the G7 countries. Inflation is not always transmitted to nominal interest rates. In fact, we should note that the Fisher coefficient estimates have very high variations. The changes in the monetary policy produced an adjustment in the transmission of the effect of inflation to nominal interest rates.

We also observed the existence of four different regimes in the relationship between nominal interest rates and expected inflation rates in the estimated periods, in which the regimes changed during the late 1970s, mid-1980s, mid-1990s and the late 2000s. It is remarkable to notice that there is no break associated with the first oil crisis (around 1973), despite the fact that previous studies analyzing real interest rates offered evidence of a break at that time. We should nevertheless note that these studies consider that the β coefficient of the Fisher equation is equal to one, a value that is consistently rejected for most of the cases analyzed in the present study.

Finally, we observed that the transmission of the expected inflation to nominal interest rates was greater in Italy than in the other countries and was very low in Japan, the UK and Canada. France, the USA and Germany also showed periods with a significant transmission of the inflation rates to nominal interest rates, even exceeding the value of one.

To sum up, our findings show that regime changes govern the Fisher equation. The estimations show a link between nominal interest rates and expected inflation, but a weak Fisher effect, which does not support the monetary neutrality hypothesis. The values obtained for the Fisher coefficients lead us to conclude that there is "under-adjustment" of nominal rates to inflationary expectations and, consequently, of their transmission to real rates. Furthermore, as stated above, the weakness of the Fisher effect increases with the credibility of monetary policy.

Acknowledgments: The authors benefited from the helpful comments made by the Editor and four anonymous referees; this version owes much to them. Financial support from the Ministerio de Ciencia y Tecnología under Grants ECO2014-58991-C3-1-R, ECO2014-58991-C3-2-R and ECO2015-65967-R is gratefully acknowledged. They also acknowledge support from the CASSETEM consolidated research group. The usual disclaimer applies.

Author Contributions: The authors contributed equally to this work.

Conflicts of Interest: The authors declare no conflict of interest.

References

1. Fisher, I. *The Theory of Interest*; MacMillan: New York, NY, USA, 1930.
2. Caporale, G.M.; Pittis, N. Estimator Choice and Fisher's Paradox: A Monte Carlo Study. *Econom. Rev.* **2004**, *23*, 25–52.
3. Panopoulou, E. A Resolution of the Fisher Effect Puzzle: A Comparison of Estimators. IIIS Discussion Paper, 67, 2005. Available online: https://ssrn.com/abstract=680401 (accessed on 15 July 2016).
4. Rose, A.K. Is the Real Interest Rate Stable? *J. Financ.* **1988**, *43*, 1095–1112.
5. Mishkin, F. Is the Fisher effect for real: A Reexamination of the Relationship between Inflation and Interest Rates. *J. Monetary Econ.* **1992**, *30*, 195–215.
6. Crowder, W.J.; Wohar, M.E. Are Tax Effects Important in the Long-Run Fisher Relationship? Evidence from the Municipal Bond Market. *J. Financ.* **1992**, *54*, 307–317.
7. Koustas, Z.; Serletis, A. On the Fisher Effect. *J. Monetary Econ.* **1999**, *44*, 105–130.
8. Rapach, D.E. The Log-run Relationship between Inflation and Real Stock Price. *J. Macroecon.* **2004**, *24*, 331–351.

9. Laatsch, F.; Klein, D.P. Nominal Interest Rate and Expected Inflation: Results from a Study of US Treasury Inflation-Protected Securities. *Q. Rev. Econ. Financ.* **2003**, *43*, 3405–3417.
10. Rapach, D.E.; Weber, C. Are Real Interest Rates Really Nonstationary? New Evidence from Tests with Good Size and Power. *J. Macroecon.* **2005**, *26*, 409–430.
11. Westerlund, J. Panel cointegration tests of the Fisher effect. *J. Appl. Econom.* **2008**, *23*, 193–233.
12. Ozcan, B.; Ari, A. Does the Fisher hypothesis hold for the G7? Evidence from the panel cointegration test. *Econ. Res.-Ekon. Istraz.* **2015**, *28*, 271–283.
13. Cox, J.C.; Ingersoll, J.E.; Ross, S.A. A theory of the term structure of interest rates. *Econometrica* **1985**, *53*, 385–407.
14. Malliaropulos, D. A Note on Nonstationarity, Structural Breaks and the Fisher Effect. *J. Bank. Financ.* **2000**, *24*, 695–707.
15. Lanne, M. Near Unit Root and the Relationship between Inflation and Interest Rate: A Reexamination of the Fisher Effect. *Empir. Econ.* **2001**, *26*, 357–366.
16. Olekalns, N. An Empirical Investigation of the Structural Breaks in the Ex Ante Fisher Effect. Research Paper Number 786; Department of Economics, University of Melbourne, Melbourne, Australia, 2001.
17. Gil-Alaña, L.A. A Mean Shift Break in the US Interest Rate. *Econ. Lett.* **2002**, *77*, 357–363.
18. Atkins, F.J.; Coe, P.J. An ARDL Bounds Test of the Long-term Fisher Effect in the United States and Canada. *J. Macroecon.* **2002**, *24*, 255–266.
19. Baum, C.F.; Barkoulas, J.T.; Caglayan, M. Persistence in International Inflation Rates. *South Econ. J.* **1999**, *65*, 900–913.
20. Phillips, P.; Perron, P. Testing for a Unit Root in Time Series Regression. *Biometrika* **1988**, *75*, 335–346.
21. Tsay, W.J. The long memory story of the real interest rate. *Econ. Lett.* **2000**, *67*, 325–330.
22. Sun, X.; Phillips, P.C.B. Understanding the Fisher Equation. *J. Appl. Econom.* **2004**, *19*, 869–896.
23. Gil- Alaña, L.A. Estimation of the order of integration in the UK and the US interest rates using fractionally integrated semiparametric techniques. *Eur. Res. Stud.* **2004**, *7*, 29–40.
24. Gil-Alaña, L.A.; Moreno, A. Fractional integration and structural breaks in U.S. macro dynamics. *Empir. Econ.* **2012**, *43*, 427–446.
25. Hassler, U.; Wolters, J. Long Memory in Inflation Rates: International Evidence. *J. Bus. Econ. Stat.* **1995**, *13*, 37–45.
26. Bos, C.S.; Franses, P.H.; Ooms, M. Long Memory and Level Shifts: Reanalysing Inflation Rates. *Empir. Econ.* **1999**, *24*, 427–449.
27. Lucas, R.E., Jr. Econometric Policy Evaluation: A Critique. *Carnegie-Rochester Conf. Ser. Public Policy* **1976**, *2*, 19–46.
28. Chadha, J.S.; Dimsdale, N.H. A Long Review of Real Rates. *Oxf. Rev. Econ. Policy* **1999**, *15*, 17–45.
29. Söderlind, P. Monetary Policy and the Fisher Effect. *J. Policy Model.* **2001**, *23*, 491–495.
30. Bai, J.; Perron, P. Estimating and Testing Linear Models with Multiple Structural Changes. *Econometrica* **1998**, *66*, 47–78.
31. Bai, J.; Perron, P. Computation and analysis of multiple structural-change models. *J. Appl. Econom.* **2003**, *18*, 1–22.
32. Nelson, C.R.; Plosser, C.I. Trends and Random Walks in Macroeconomic Time Series: Some Evidence and Implications. *J. Monetary Econ.* **1982**, *10*, 139–162.
33. Dickey, D.; Fuller, W. Distribution of the Estimators for Autoregressive Time Series with a Unit Root. *J. Am. Stat. Assoc.* **1979**, *74*, 427–431.
34. Said, S.E.; Dickey, D. Testing for Unit Roots in Autoregressive-Moving Average Models of Unknown Order. *Biometrika* **1984**, *71*, 599–607.
35. Ng, S.; Perron, P. Lag Length Selection and the Construction of Unit Root Tests With Good Size and Power. *Econometrica* **2001**, *69*, 1519–1554.
36. Elliot, G.; Rothenbert, T.J.; Stock, J.H. Efficient tests for an autoregressive unit root. *Econometrica* **1996**, *64*, 813–836.
37. Pesaran, M.H. General Diagnostic Tests for Cross Section Dependence in Panels. IZA Discussion Paper 1240, 2004. Available online: http://www.econ.cam.ac.uk/research/repec/cam/pdf/cwpe0435.pdf (accessed on 1 August 2016).

38. Pesaran, M.H. A simple panel unit root test in the presence of cross-section dependence. *J. Appl. Econom.* **2007**, *22*, 265–312.
39. Pesaran, M.H. Testing Weak Cross-Sectional Dependence in Large Panels. IZA Discussion Paper 6432, 2012. Available online: http://ftp.iza.org/dp6432.pdf (accessed on 1 August 2016).
40. Costantini, M.; Lupi, C. An analysis of inflation and interest rates. New panel unit root results in the presence of structural breaks. *Econ. Lett.* **2007**, *95*, 408–414.
41. Lee, C.C.; Chang, C.P. Mean reversion of inflation rates in 19 OECD countries: Evidence from panel Lm unit root tests with structural breaks. *Econ. Bull.* **2007**, *3*, 1–15.
42. Lee, C.C.; Chang, C. P. Trend stationary of inflation rates: Evidence from LM unit root testing with a long span of historical data. *Appl. Econ.* **2008**, *40*, 2523–2536.
43. Lee, J.; Strazicich, M. Minimum LM Unit Root Tests with Two Structural Breaks. *Rev. Econ. Stat.* **2003**, *40*, 1082–1089.
44. Lee, J.; Strazicich, M. Minimum LM Unit Root Test. *Econ. Bull.* **2013**, *33*, 2483–2492.
45. Gadea, M.D.; Montañés, A; Reyes, M. The European Union Currencies and the US Dollar: From post-Bretton-Woods to the Euro. *J. Int. Money Financ.* **2004**, *23*, 1109–1136.
46. Atkins, F.J.; Chan, M. Trend breaks and the Fisher Hypothesis in Canada and the United States. *Appl. Econ.* **2004**, *36*, 1907–1913.
47. Garcia, R.; Perron, P. An Analysis of the Real Interest Rate under Regime Shifts. *Rev. Econ. Stat.* **1996**, *78*, 111–125.
48. Bierens, H.J. Nonparametric Nonlinear Co-Trending Analysis, with an Application to Inflation and Interest in the U.S. *J. Bus. Econ. Stat.* **2000**, *18*, 323–337.
49. Lanne, M. Nonlinear dynamics of interest and inflation. *J. Appl. Econom.* **2006**, *21*, 1157–1168.
50. Panopoulou, E.; Pantelidis, T. The Fisher effect in the presence of time-varying coefficients. *Comp. Stat. Data Anal.* **2016**, *100*, 495–511.
51. Bai, J. Estimation of a Change Point in Multiple Regression Models. *Rev. Econ. Stat.* **1997**, *79*, 551–563.
52. Andrews, D.W.K. Heteroskedasticity and Autocorrelation Consistent Covariance Matrix Estimation. *Econometrica* **1991**, *59*, 817–858.
53. Fama, E.F. Term structure forecast of interest rates, inflation and real returns. *J. Monetary Econ.* **1990**, *25*, 59–76.
54. Fahmy, Y.A.F.; Kandil, M. The Fisher effect: New evidence and implications. *Int. Rev. Econ. Financ.* **2003**, *12*, 451–465.
55. Evans, M.; Lewis, K. Do expected shifts in inflation affect estimates of the long-run Fisher relation? *J. Financ.* **1995**, *50*, 225–253.
56. Rapach, D.E.; Wohar, M.E. Regime Changes in International Real Interest Rates: Are They a Monetary Phenomenon? *J. Money Credit Bank.* **2005**, *37*, 887–906.
57. Tobin, J. The interest-elasticity of transactions demand for cash. *Rev. Econ. Stat.* **1956**, *38*, 241–247.
58. Mundell, R. Inflation and Real Interest. *J. Polit. Econ.* **1963**, *71*, 280–183.
59. Rapach, D.E. International Evidence on the Long-run Impact of Inflation. *J. Money Credit Bank.* **2003**, *33*, 23–48.
60. Clarida, R.; Galí, J.; Gertler M. Monetary policy rules and macroeconomic stability evidence and some theory. *Q. J. Econ.* **2000**, *115*, 147–180.

MDPI
St. Alban-Anlage 66
4052 Basel, Switzerland
Tel. +41 61 683 77 34
Fax +41 61 302 89 18
http://www.mdpi.com

Econometrics Editorial Office
E-mail: econometrics@mdpi.com
http://www.mdpi.com/journal/econometrics

www.ingramcontent.com/pod-product-compliance
Lightning Source LLC
Chambersburg PA
CBHW041218220326
41597CB00033BA/6007
* 9 7 8 3 0 3 8 4 2 8 1 1 4 *